LOS ANGELES

With Contributions by Mark Ehrman, Barak Zimmerman, and Bob Howells

Making the Dream Work" by Robert J. Kelly

Windsor Publications, Inc.
Chatsworth, California

LOS ANGELES

Realm Of Possibility

A CONTEMPORARY PORTRAIT BY A. DONALD ANDERSON,

CHARLES F. QUEENAN, ELLEN HOFFS, AND SUSAN VAUGHN

**Windsor Publications, Inc.—
Book Division**
Managing Editor: Karen Story
Design Director: Alexander D'Anca
Photo Director: Susan L. Wells
Executive Editor: Pamela Schroeder

Staff for *Los Angeles: Realm of
Possibility*
Senior Manuscript Editor: P. Schroeder
Manuscript Editor: Kate Coombs
Photo Editor: Larry Molmud
Developmental Editor:
Teri Davis Greenberg
Senior Editor, Corporate Profiles:
Jeffrey Reeves
Production Editor, Corporate Profiles:
Lisa Woo
Proofreader: Annette Nibblett Arrieta
Customer Service Manager:
Phyllis Feldman-Schroeder
Editorial Assistants: Elizabeth Anderson,
Alex Arredondo, Michael Nugwynne,
Lori Erbaugh, Wilma Huckabey
Publisher's Representatives, Corporate
Profiles: Allison Alan-Lee,
June Knight, Jeff Larsen
Layout, Corporate Biographies:
C.L. Murray
Designer: Ellen Ifrah

Windsor Publications, Inc.
Elliot Martin, Chairman of the Board
James L. Fish III, Chief Operating Officer
Mac Buhler, Vice President/Acquisitions

Library of Congress Cataloging-in-Publication
Data

Los Angeles : realm of possibility : a contemporary portrait / by A. Donald Anderson . . .
[et al.] ; contributions by Mark Ehrman, Barak
Zimmerman, and Bob Howells : "Making the
dream work" by Robert J. Kelly. — 1st ed.
p. 448 cm. 23 x 31
Includes index.
ISBN 0-89781-399-5
1. Los Angeles (Calif.)—Civilization. 2. Los
Angeles (Calif.)—Description. 3. Los Angeles
(Calif.)—Economic Conditions. 4. Los Angeles
(Calif.)—Industries. I. Anderson, A. Donald,
1930-
F869.L85L67 1991
979.4'94—dc20   91-17322
                                 CIP

Right: Photo by Amy Seidman-Tighe

Following page: Photo by Bob
Rowan/Progressive Image

Pages 12/13 and 250/251: Photo by
Joseph Sohm/Chromosohm

CONTENTS

MAYOR'S MESSAGE

Los Angeles is truly a city where all things are possible. It is a city emulated by the world, where new ideas, wealth, and novelty are generated. It is a city with a strong economic climate fueled by a remarkably diverse economy. Where abundant business and employment opportunities keep pace with an increasing population. It is a city for all seasons and all cultures.

Looking at Los Angeles today, it is hard to imagine the city as it was in 1781, a tiny pueblo established by 11 multiracial families (black, white, and Indian) on behalf of the King of Spain. Just like today, the city was diverse from its beginnings.

Under Mexican control, the city's vast acreage was parceled into 500 land grants by 1822. A steady stream of migrants poured into Los Angeles since its founding. There were particular surges during the gold rush era, oil boom, and dust bowl years. The advent of rail and highway transportation gave way to further development by farmers and land developers. The pursuit of jobs and a better life also attracted a large migration of blacks from the south and refugees from Asia.

The resilience and growth of the city today may be due in part to its almost recession-proof mix of industries. Business, financial and creative services, tourism, aerospace and high-tech industries, together with a can-do spirit, continue to drive the economy. Overseas economic development on the Pacific Rim over the past decade has also given enormous impetus to business in the Los Angeles area.

The city's face has changed many times over the past two hundred years. We are a proud inter-national community with a blend of more than 8.5 million people from all over the U.S.A., and from 140 countries around the world speaking 85 different languages. More ethnic groups are represented in Los Angeles than anywhere else in the world. They have brought with them unique art, architecture, and cultural styles. It is projected that by the year 2010, the population of the metropolitan area will increase from 14.5 million people to 18 million.

Since the time I became mayor of this great city 20 years ago, I have continued to build on the framework established by the dynamic, visionary, and dedicated leadership of people who have great talent. With the support of our city's leaders, citizens, and business community, I look forward to meeting the challenges of the next century and ensuring that Los Angeles will indeed be the "City of the Century."

This book is a celebration of the strength and vitality of Los Angeles.

Tom Bradley

Mayor Tom Bradley

Top: Mayor Tom Bradley, in shamrock-colored tie, shares in Saint Patrick's Day festivities. Photo by Joseph Sohm/Chromosohm

Right: Downtown Los Angeles presents its majestic cityscape. Photo by Joseph Sohm/Chromosohm

Part One

CITY OF DREAMS

These opening chapters describe the incredible diversity that makes up Los Angeles. People, businesses, arts, and ideas from all over the world have come together here on the Southern California coast to create a vibrant metropolis.

THE CITY OF ANGELS

Everything Under the Sun

E*ven in its lustiest boomtown days, Los Angeles was never a typical frontier town. Few desperadoes shot it out on Main Street. Saloons were always outnumbered by banks and real estate brokers. A good zoning fight was sure to get bigger media play than a stagecoach robbery. It is true that Wyatt Earp, the hero of the gunfight at the OK Corral, met his end in Los Angeles, but it came peacefully, in bed, when he was 80 years old. His six-guns had long since been retired.*

"THE TOWERS OF THE NEW DOWNTOWN LOS ANGELES SKYLINE CAST LONG SHADOWS ACROSS A BUSTLING PLAIN WHERE AN INDIAN VILLAGE, A SPANISH COLONIAL SETTLEMENT, A MEXICAN PROVINCIAL CAPITAL, AND A YANKEE BOOMTOWN LIE BURIED BENEATH THE SAME ASPHALT BLANKET."

—JOHN D. WEAVER, *EL PUEBLO GRANDE*, 1973

But during the last half of the twentieth century Los Angeles—officially El Pueblo de Nuestra Señora la Reina de los Angeles *(the Town of Our Lady the Queen of the Angels)—has managed to overcome its quotidian origins. Today it is the social and economic flywheel of a metropolitan complex stretching 200 miles from the Mexican border to Santa Barbara, a cultural mosaic that is home to more than 14 million people.*

In a sense, Los Angeles was founded on possibility rather than content. Early settlers here had little enough to encourage them: a semiarid plain dotted with clumps of scrubby trees, a problematic

The Academy Award ceremonies attracts thousands of stargazers to Shriners Auditorium in downtown L.A. Photo by Joseph Sohm/Chromosohm

B y   A .   D o n a l d   A n d e r s o n

Right: Two mystical "witches" prepare to divine the future at the annual Renaissance Pleasure Faire. The carnival features knights, jesters, damsels, minstrels, and tasty fare from centuries ago. Photo by Larry Molmud

streambed that some optimist called the Los Angeles "River," and soil that would have daunted a modern agronomist, let alone eighteenth-century pioneers.

But what a climate! Despite occasional barbs from songwriters (" . . . hate California, it's cold and it's damp . . .") and stand-up comics ("I love to wake up to the coughing of the birds . . ."), the weather of Los Angeles has unquestionably been its greatest draw over the years. It was enough to make one overlook a lot.

The first to come were the land developers, followed in short order by wildcat oilmen and madcap moviemakers. As Hollywood's movies started to fan out across the world, the glamour and excitement they projected attracted thousands more. And as each new wave of immigrants arrived, they saw new possibilities—in agriculture, manufacturing, services of all kinds. The region became a spawning ground for ideas and new products—a process that has only accelerated with the passage of time.

Today Los Angeles is on the cutting edge of social and economic change in America,

Two new homeowners luxuriate in their room with a view. Photo by Shelley Gazin.

and therefore the world. Once the mecca of motion pictures, the city now attracts leading scientists, philosophers, and trendsetters who recognize there are few limits in this "realm of possibility."

With 3.5 million residents living within the city itself and with a gross annual product approaching $100 billion, Los Angeles exceeds most states and all but a handful of nations in its economic vigor. For example:

- The city produced more goods and services in 1990 than all but 10 states, including California.

- As the 1990s began, per capita income in Los Angeles reached around $22,000 a year, higher than that of any state in the Union, more than double that of Sweden or West Germany, and nearly three times that of Great Britain.

- Annual retail sales in the Los Angeles metropolitan area will exceed $70 billion by the mid-1990s, about 25 percent ahead of New York City.

- Employment in Los Angeles will pass the 2 million mark in the early 1990s, making this the second largest job market in America—and one of the most skilled,

More than three million people reside within the city itself. Photo by Joseph Sohm/Chromosohm

ANOTHER DAY IN PARADISE

A Statistical Day in the Life of Los Angeles

As any Angeleno knows, there really is no such thing as a "typical" or "average" day in Los Angeles—not in a statistical sense, anyway. Certainly, the temperature rarely registers exactly 65.3 degrees (L.A. County's average temperature), nor do the rain gauges regularly measure .039 inches of rainfall (L.A. County's average daily rainfall) for any given day. That's not to say these statistics don't have their uses. Breaking the numbers down into daily totals and calling the result a "typical" day serves to paint an impressive picture of the sheer volume of activity that goes on in every strata of the city every day, and offers another vantage point from which to appreciate L.A.'s urban might.

With a population of around 8.8 million people in Los Angeles County alone (14.5 million in the five-county area that includes Los Angeles, Orange, Riverside, San Bernardino, and Ventura counties), the various municipal service agencies and utilities have their work cut out for them. A typical day at the Metropolitan Water District means they'll be sending 2 billion gallons of water to L.A. County homes and businesses, while over at the Southern California Gas Company, their job consists of supplying the 2.8 billion cubic feet of natural gas that the county consumes daily. The Department of Water and Power oversees the distribution of the roughly 60 million kilowatt-hours of power that go to its Los Angeles city customers each day, while the rest of the county—another 1,815,936 customers—are served by Southern California Edison, which handles another 91 million kilowatt-hours, bringing the county's total daily electrical consumption to 151 million kilowatt-hours.

Phone service is handled by two phone companies, Pacific Bell and GTE, who, combined, work to connect the 68.5 million calls a day that are dialed from L.A. County telephones. Those deciding to write instead of call will contribute to the 35 million pieces of mail that the three local postal districts—which cover an area bounded by San Luis Obispo, Lancaster, Ontario, and San Clemente—handle on a daily basis.

Finally, the less desirable but equally vital task of picking up what Angelenos throw out goes to L.A. County sanitation workers, whose job it is to clear away the nearly 60,000 tons of garbage created here. Ten to twenty percent of this is currently being recycled, leaving roughly 50,000 tons earmarked for landfills. County officials expect recycling to account for a larger percentage of total volume in the future.

Sadly, 180 deaths will be recorded on this typical day, but this is more than offset by the 490 babies being born. Similarly, while 166 disgruntled couples will file for divorce, the county will issue 306 marriage licenses to happier pairs. Factoring in the births, deaths, immigrants, and emigrants, the population of the county will grow by 342 people today. To help house these new arrivals, 107 new homes will be built.

The 511 miles of L.A.'s freeways will see 9.4 million vehicle trips made today. While the average speed on the freeway is calculated to be only 43 miles per hour, many people will go considerably

Thousands of robust competitors vie for position in the Los Angeles Marathon. Photo by Joseph Sohm/Chromosohm

faster than that. These speeders will account for most of the 2,100 citations the California Highway Patrol will issue.

The old cliche, "nobody rides the bus in L.A.," hardly holds true. The fact is that the Rapid Transit District (RTD), with a fleet of 2,632 buses, will carry 1.3 million passengers on its 213 routes today. Add in the Long Beach, Santa Monica, Orange County, and other smaller bus lines, and the number of bus riders swells to well over 1.5 million in the greater metropolitan area. The Blue Line, Metrorail's first operating route, will handle another 24,000 passengers, and more mass transit riders are expected when the entire Metrorail project is completed.

Los Angeles International Airport (LAX) will handle 1,800 flights carrying around 125,000 passengers and 3,562 tons of cargo in the next 24 hours. Long Beach, Burbank, and John Wayne (Orange County) airports will handle another 900 flights and 70,334 more passengers. This brings the total daily air traffic—minus flights to and from Ontario, Van Nuys, and L.A.'s many small municipal airports—in the skies over L.A. to 2,700. Because of this volume, Los Angeles is the only city to have unique flight rules written for it by the FAA. And L.A.'s traffic volume extends to its waters, as well. At sea, 25 ships a day will sail in and out of the ports of Los Angeles and Long Beach. They will carry 391,000 tons of cargo valued at $300 million from cities all over the world.

Consumer spending is still strong, and $152.8 million will be spent on taxable retail goods—$10.3 million of which will be sent to the state treasury as sales tax. L.A.'s consumer icon—the new car—is the largest single retail sales category. It alone accounts for $23 million in sales per day. An additional $11.6 million a day—the third largest retail category—is spent at service stations filling up and maintaining L.A. County's 5.6 million cars, trucks, RVs, and motorcycles.

Possibly, this rush to spend is due to the fact that the Consumer Price Index for the five-county area will rise .0019% before tomorrow. L.A. does not spend all the money it makes, however. At the end of the day, there will still be $193.7 billion in deposits left in Los Angeles County banks and other savings institutions.

The Pacific Stock Exchange will see 11,000 transactions on this typical day, with 6.4 million shares with a value somewhere around $163 million changing hands. Hollywood—the business, not the city—has an average total of 40 feature films, TV shows, and commercials being shot in and around L.A. on any given day. This is in addition to the game shows and sitcoms regularly taped here at permanent studio locations before live audiences. The nearly 100,000 apparel industry workers here will help bolster L.A.'s reputation as a burgeoning fashion capital by producing $17.2 million worth of clothing. Another income source in L.A. comes from underfoot—119,574 barrels of oil will be pumped out of the ground and offshore wells. The oil's value comes out to roughly $18 to $24 per barrel per day on the wildly fluctuating market.

Altogether, 4.5 million adults will be working on this typical day. Meanwhile, the Los Angeles Unified School District will be educating 1,102,027 children in classes K through 12. Thousands more will attend L.A.'s many private and parochial schools. Educating and caring for its children is probably Los Angeles' most critical task—for as this typical day comes to an end, many people will have to stand ready to fill the needs of the typical day of tomorrow.
—*Mark Ehrman*

Statistics compiled in March 1991. Unless otherwise noted, statistics refer to Los Angeles County.

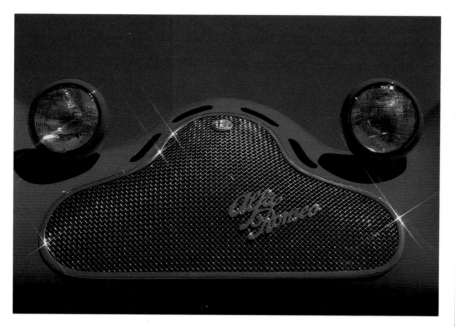

Luxury cars—Ferraris, Rolls Royces, Alfa Romeos, and even vintage Duesenbergs—are a common sight on L.A.'s roadways. Photo by Joseph Sohm/Chromosohm

with 25 percent more high-tech jobs than Silicon Valley.

• International trade through the Los Angeles Customs District, valued at more than $120 billion a year, has surpassed that of every other U.S. city, including New York.

Above all, Los Angeles is probably the world's most imitated city. From freeways to dress styles, from cuisine to automobile design, from hot tubs to tanning salons, the city pours forth a veritable cornucopia of new concepts that spread quickly across the country and around the world.

Teenagers visiting here from Singapore, Stockholm, or Capetown, for example, know more about Melrose Avenue—the center of pop culture in Los Angeles—than many Angelenos do. Their designer jeans, leather jackets, and spiked hairstyles reflect the enormous social impact and global reach of the Los Angeles culture.

Affluent shoppers from around the world flock to Rodeo Drive in Beverly Hills, perhaps the most opulent marketplace in the world, where commercial rents are around $15 a square foot per month and where $3,000 men's suits vie with $125,000 watches and $1,700 crocodile shoes for the consumer's attention.

Behind the remarkable statistics and trendsetting life-style of Los Angeles is an urban infrastructure that includes 175 miles

of freeways, more than 7,000 miles of underground water lines, 30,000 miles of electric distribution lines, 15 million miles of telephone lines, and 6,800 miles of surface streets. Los Angeles also has more single-family residences—around 400,000 in 1990—than any other city in America.

In fact, real estate and the dream of owning a home have driven the growth of Los Angeles from the start. "Waves of immigrants made the area over to suit themselves," states the L.A. 2000 futures study issued in 1990. "Neighborhoods and locales became powerfully linked to self-expression. Hillsiders, flatlanders, valleyites, beach people, west-siders, canyon dwellers all have a distinctive mind set—what we are is where we live."

Except for a mini gold rush in the 1850s and a small oil boom bubble that burst in 1895, the lure was always land, not riches. Or rather, land and riches. The *Los Angeles Times*, one of the most successful newspa-

Left: A leprechaun-green '59 Cadillac motors past well-wishers during Hollywood's St. Patrick's Day parade. Photo by Joseph Sohm/Chromosohm

Below: City dwellers feared the worst traffic snarls in history during the 1984 Olympics in Los Angeles. But top-notch urban planning and community cooperation actually reduced highway traffic flow during the historic event. Photo by Joseph Sohm/Chromosohm

COMING TO TERMS WITH L.A.

A Guide to the Greater Los Angeles Area

Tourists and newcomers trying to get oriented in Los Angeles are often stymied by the region's daunting multiplicity of place names, cities, neighborhoods, and areas. "Los Angeles," for instance, refers to a city—a loose, open patchwork of a city at that—a county, which contains the city of Los Angeles, 87 other cities, and 120 more unincorporated areas; and a vague, loosely defined "greater metropolitan area." Names like "L.A.," "the Basin," "Southern California," and "the Southland" seem to be used interchangeably, while sections of the megalopolis are referred to as the Westside, East Side, South Bay, and Valley, with few clues for the uninitiated to sort out the boundaries.

Although definitions of geographical terms can be as hazy as the August sky, it is possible to achieve a working grasp of the many monikers people use to describe the unwieldy, sprawling urban mass most of the world thinks of as simply "Los Angeles."

Starting with the big picture, Southern California, (synonymous with the Southland) refers pretty much to everything between the Santa Barbara area to the north, Arizona to the east, and the Mexican border to the south, while that fuzzy term, "Greater L.A. Area," at its grandest usually refers to the area enclosed by Ventura/Oxnard, Lancaster, San Bernardino, Riverside, and Costa Mesa. The five-county area (Los Angeles, Orange, San Bernardino, Riverside, and Ventura counties), while having the advantage of being precisely defined, contains regions to the north and east that are considered outside the orbit of Los Angeles.

The tall mountain ranges that ring Los Angeles on all but its ocean side, while creating the inversion layer responsible for smog, also give the city some clear-cut topographical dividers. This enclosed area—bordered by the Pacific Ocean to the west, the Santa

Monica and San Gabriel mountains to the north, and the San Bernardino and San Jacinto mountains to the east—forms a land and air mass which has come to be called by smog-watchers "the South Coast Air Basin."

Another "basin" term, the "L.A. Basin," is usually used to refer to the

At no time is the term "Greater L.A." more evident than when one gets the high view of the patchwork of cities and communities that comprise the Southland. Here, the South San Fernando Valley is seen from Mulholland Drive as it snakes through the Santa Monica Mountains. Photo by Mark E. Gibson

areas of Los Angeles open to the ocean—as opposed to the landlocked valleys (San Gabriel, San Fernando, Simi, Antelope, and Santa Clarita) to the east and north.

And speaking of valleys, when used generically "the Valley" almost always refers to the San Fernando Valley, an area bordered by the Hollywood Hills to the south, the Santa Susana Mountains to the west and north, and the San Gabriels to the north and east. Cross Mulholland Drive at the crest of the Hollywood Hills and technically you've entered the Valley, although many residents of the luxury homes and estates that dot the north-facing hillsides prefer to say they live in the Hollywood Hills. Pasadena is generally recognized as the Valley's easternmost edge, while San Fernando and Chatsworth form its northern corners, and Woodland Hills/ Calabasas defines its western limit.

Boundaries can become even more amorphous in explanations of the often-used but seldom-defined term, "Westside," which usually refers to Los Angeles' affluent and trendy western half. While the *Los Angeles Times* distributes its Westside section as far east as Hollywood, most Angelenos would say the Westside extends no further than West Hollywood, with even more conservative definitions cropping it as far west as Westwood or even the 405 freeway. When used in a demographic sense, the Westside usually refers to all the upmarket communities from Beverly Hills to Malibu and down the beaches to Marina and Playa del Rey.

Moving roughly counterclockwise, "the South Bay" loosely describes the area formed by a line drawn from LAX across to the Harbor Freeway and down to San Pedro. While the inclusion of Inglewood in the South Bay is an iffy proposition, it is generally agreed that the communities of Torrance and El Segundo—where much of Southern California's aerospace and defense industry is concentrated—Palos Verdes, and the charming ocean-cooled towns of Manhattan Beach, Hermosa Beach, and Redondo Beach form the South Bay's core. Together they give the South Bay its identity as an area that, while perhaps affluent, is generally distinct from the glitz and trendiness that characterizes the Westside.

Not quite so affluent is South-Central Los Angeles, an area that begins south of downtown at the University of Southern California and Exposition Park and stops short of the Pacific Ocean between San Pedro and Long Beach. The area now boasts L.A.'s first rail mass transit line, the Blue Line, which whizzes right past South-Central L.A.'s most popular attraction, the 107-foot-tall Watts Towers.

Although imprecise, "the Westside" is still an often-used term, but "the East Side" is so poorly defined that it is almost never used except in contrast to the Westside. It has been invoked to refer to neighborhoods as far away from each other as Hollywood and Pomona. "East L.A.," however, while an actual neighborhood, has also come to include the area east of downtown from the Los Angeles River out as far as Alhambra and Montebello. While East L.A. is known primarily for its Latino flavor—indeed on Brooklyn Avenue or Soto Street you'll find murals, fine Mexican shops and restaurants, as well as a strolling mariachi band or two—nearby communities like Monterey Park are becoming quite a draw for Asians, who more and more define that area's multicultural look.

Having made something of a full circle, the center—which some would argue is not central to anything at all—is downtown Los Angeles, which

after decades of neglect is finally coming into its own. While it has begun creeping westward of late, downtown is usually defined as the area between the 110 (Harbor) Freeway or Beaudry Avenue to the west, Temple Street or the 101 Freeway to the north, the L.A. River to the east, and the 10 (Santa Monica) Freeway to the south.

Is this a harbinger of the transportation of the future, or just another motivated Angeleno at a southland beach? Photo by Joseph Sohm/Chromosohm

Downtown's western half has seen an explosion of skyscrapers and shopping centers which have completely transformed the Los Angeles skyline. Taking advantage of the many loft spaces in downtown's low-rise eastern end, a Soho-like artistic community has sprung up. Because of this, after-hours downtown, far from the ghost town it was once thought to be, now boasts a dynamic and thriving nightlife.

Los Angeles is a complicated place and even native Angelenos keep a detailed map book in their cars to help them navigate. To get to know Los Angeles, there's really no substitute for getting behind the wheel and driving its streets and freeways. It's a slow process; but in a city as multifaceted as Los Angeles, ultimately a rewarding one. —*Mark Ehrman*

pers in America, prospered largely on classified ads, most of which (in the early days, at least) promoted real estate.

"People came to Los Angeles in the first place because they saw it as a fine place to live," says the L.A. 2000 study. "Attracted by its natural setting and its congenial climate, they found opportunity, mobility, elbow room, affordable houses, and a variety of ways to enjoy themselves."

Because of the automobile and the availability of land, Los Angeles' development defied the precedents of New York, Chicago, and other cities that grew up around dense urban cores. Instead, Los Angeles developed a system of satellite communities tied loosely to a low-rise downtown section.

After World War II, the satellite communities—the San Fernando Valley, the beach cities, Hollywood, Beverly Hills, Westwood—began to take on a life of their own. They soon developed their own high-rise cores, surrounded by hotels, car lots, trendy shopping centers, and upscale restaurants.

Critics called Los Angeles "faceless" and bemoaned the absence of an identifiable center, ignoring the fact that most people—starting with the first great wave of newcomers in the 1880s—came here to escape precisely the urban model these critics extolled.

The city's growth over the last century

demonstrates the durability of that vision. During the land boom of the 1880s, the city's population increased fivefold, from 10,000 to more than 50,000. It doubled again in the next decade, tripled in the next, and by 1920 stood at nearly 600,000. (Some growth came through annexation of surrounding unincorporated areas, but the vast majority came through migration from other states.)

Though by then ranked among the nation's top ten cities, Los Angeles in the 1920s remained California's "second city," far less known outside the state than its sophisticated rival, San Francisco. Los Angeles' greatest growth came, however, during the Roaring Twenties, when the population more than doubled again, topping 1.2 million in 1930. The Depression and World War II slowed the influx to a comparative trickle, but after the war the population rush resumed, and by 1980 there were 3 million people living in Los Angeles.

In the meantime, the city's multipolar growth pattern had begun to spawn clusters of high-rise development in Century City, along the Wilshire Corridor, in Pasadena, in Universal City, and in Encino.

The downtown core was also expanding. Confined until the 1960s with height limitations restricting buildings to 13 stories, the downtown exploded with high-rise development during the 1970s and 1980s, giving the city an identifiable silhouette for the first time. That silhouette was topped off in 1989 by the city's tallest structure, McGuire-Thomas Partners' 70-story postmodern Library Tower, designed by I.M. Pei.

As the value of the U.S. dollar plunged over the five years from 1985 to 1990, dozens of major properties were snapped up by foreign bargain hunters—the largest was Shuwa Corporation's purchase of the ARCO-Bank of America twin towers in 1987 for $650 million. In all, Japanese companies now own about 30 percent of downtown Los Angeles real estate.

If land was the magnet that lured millions to Los Angeles, the automobile was the totem they adopted once they arrived. The city of Los Angeles, with more than 2.5 million registered vehicles, has more cars per capita than any other city in the world, and (despite a reputation for having the poorest transit system of any major metropolis) more than 4,236 miles of bus routes plied by more than 2,500 buses.

Not surprisingly, cars are big business in Los Angeles, with its more than 250 new and used car dealerships, 2,000-plus auto repair shops, 108 car washes, more than 200 auto rental outlets, and several thousand acres of parking lots and garages. New car sales here are approaching $2 billion a year, and drivers in Los Angeles consume a veritable lake of gasoline, more than 1.5 billion gallons annually, or enough to overflow the capacious Hollywood Reservoir.

There is only one auto assembly plant here—a General Motors facility in Van Nuys that turns out Chevrolet Camaros and Pontiac Firebirds—but eight of the nine top Japanese car companies, plus Hyundai of Korea, have their U.S. headquarters in the area. In addition, auto stylists watch the Los Angeles market closely to spot new trends (such as the return of the convertible in the mid-1980s) that often end up sweeping the country.

The freeway system that serves Los Angeles and the surrounding counties is an engineering marvel that is rapidly becoming overwhelmed by the increase in traffic volume in recent years. Built to accommodate

around 1,200,000 vehicles per day, the system is now handling more than 1,500,000 cars and trucks every 24-hour period.

Recognizing the limits to freeway expansion, planners now look to car pooling, public transportation, and decentralization as long-term solutions. The city's first subway system, Metrorail, will open its initial 4.4-mile section from downtown to Hollywood in 1993, at a cost of more than $1.45 billion. A 22-mile light rail line from downtown to Long Beach started operation in 1990, the first link in a proposed area-wide system that will put Los Angeles back where it was, transitwise, in the 1920s.

As it has throughout the postwar era, the Los Angeles business community continues to benefit in the nineties from a diversity of economic activity that makes it highly recession-proof. Even the city's $5-billion-a-year defense sector—dominated by aerospace giants like Lockheed, McDonnell Douglas, and Hughes Aircraft, and buffeted by fallout from the easing of Cold War tensions—is buttressed by healthy backlogs in contracts for civilian aircraft, space vehicles, and consumer products.

The Los Angeles Area Chamber of Commerce identifies seven basic industries that drive the economy here. These are business and professional services, tourism, aerospace/high tech, wholesale trade and distribution, health services, direct international trade, and the creative industries.

Additionally, the city is headquarters to three of the nation's leading petroleum companies, ARCO, UNOCAL, and Occidental Petroleum. The Los Angeles Basin has itself been a major producer of oil and gas since

the first discoveries here in the 1870s. Over the intervening 120 years, the vast hydrocarbon formations here (from Signal Hill in the south to the Newhall fields in the north) have yielded more than 10 billion barrels of crude oil—as much as the famed Prudhoe Bay field in Northern Alaska.

Economic development of the Pacific Rim over the last two decades has also given enormous impetus to business in the Los Angeles area. "Aggressive development programs at the two major harbors serving the

region, Long Beach and Los Angeles, and at Los Angeles International Airport, plus the size of the local market have been the catalysts of the rapid growth of foreign trade," according to the Los Angeles Area Chamber of Commerce. In all, the chamber estimates that more than 250,000 jobs here are the result of trade flow.

Tourism, always a Southern California staple, continued to flourish as the nineties began. The value of tourist spending in Los Angeles—for attractions like the Universal Studios Tour, local theme parks, major science and art museums, and the area's natural splendors—exceeded $10 billion in 1990, more than one fourth of all tourist spending in the state. In all, more than 300 million vis-

A Long Beach pilot boards his jet at sunset,. Photo by Joseph Sohm/ Chromosohm

itors are expected to come through the city during the next ten years.

Several economic studies in recent years predict that Los Angeles will become an increasingly service-oriented economy in the twenty-first century. Banking and financial services will be a major engine of this growth, with several of the nation's eastern banking giants (Citibank, Chase Manhattan, Manufacturers Hanover) as well as some 130 foreign banks scrambling for larger shares of the exploding California market. Bank deposits here more than doubled in the 1980s, compared with a 20 percent growth in New York.

A recent 20-year projection by Wells Fargo Bank said overall growth here will be around three percent a year, with services gaining by over four percent annually. Construction will be the next most robust sector, with projected growth of about three percent a year. Manufacturing will also grow during this period, but at a slower pace—averaging about one percent annually through the year 2010.

Three world-class institutions of higher education—the University of California at Los

Above and left: The University of California at Los Angeles is considered one of America's finest public four-year colleges. Each year, 8,500 well-prepared graduates leave its Romanesque environs to start challenging new careers. Photos by Joseph Sohm/Chromosohm

Angeles (UCLA), the University of Southern California (USC), and the California Institute of Technology (Caltech)—plus four California State University campuses and several well-regarded independent schools make up a kind of eighth basic industry for Los Angeles.

These institutions, with combined enrollments of more than 140,000, provide the region with a steady feedstock of talent for all the other industries.

In addition, the vital research these universities conduct—in fields as diverse as microbiology and business management—makes the area a global center for new ideas. The UCLA Medical Center, for example, made the first important breakthroughs in AIDS research, and a leading member of the center's faculty, Dr. Robert Gale, was flown to the Soviet Union in 1986 by industrialist Armand Hammer to head the medical team treating victims of the Chernobyl nuclear accident.

Dr. William Ouchi of UCLA's Graduate School of Management has written pioneering studies of business structures (*Theory Z, The M-Form Society*) that are now standard texts for management analysts. In addition,

he is a much sought after consultant for several major U.S. and Japanese companies.

At USC's School of Cinema and Television, students work with such industry giants as producer-director (and former USC student) George Lucas (*Star Wars, Raiders of the Lost Ark*). In the sciences, USC's Loker Hydrocarbons Research Institute, under the direction of Dr. George Olah, is conducting breakthrough studies into the nature of petroleum molecules that could vastly expand the world's supplies of liquid fuels. In all, USC researchers received $161 million in study grants during 1989, in fields ranging from biology to political science. Also in 1989, USC completed the most successful fund drive in the history of U.S. higher education, raising more than $504 million.

Caltech, which celebrated its centennial in 1991, is a focal point for advanced research in mathematics, chemistry, and

physics. The famous Richter Scale for earthquake measurement was developed at Caltech, and the institution has continued to be a center for seismological study. The university's contributions to the nation's atomic energy program and, through its nearby Jet Propulsion Laboratory, to the nation's space program have also been pivotal. Caltech scientists are recognized worldwide as leaders in a number of research fields, with 21 Nobel Prizes awarded to its faculty and graduates—including scientific giants like Robert Millikan and Linus Pauling—since 1923.

Los Angeles boasts several important institutions specializing in the arts. Art Center College, for example, has been a wellspring of automotive design talent for three generations, with graduates serving in key design posts at many major auto makers in the U.S., Europe, and Japan. California Institute of the Arts and the Otis-Parsons Art Institute also graduate many leading figures in fine arts, graphic design, film animation, and photography.

The 1960s saw the growth of large non-profit think tanks in a number of regions, and one of the earliest and most distinguished was the Rand Corporation, with headquarters in Santa Monica. Its studies of national defense, education, municipal government, and other public issues have had a significant impact on government policy over the last three decades.

In noneconomic areas, Los Angeles also points the way to the future. During the 1970s and 1980s a wave of immigration turned the city into a truly international community, and more ethnic groups are represented here today than anywhere else in the world. By the turn of the century, demographers estimate, minority children will make up 70 percent of

The Tournament of Roses Parade in Pasadena is viewed on all continents by a TV audience of more than 100 million. Photo by Joseph Sohm/ Chromosohm

Right: A family enjoys the Los Angeles Street Scene Festival Jubilee, a multicultural, multiethnic celebration featuring mimes, marching bands, samba dancers, parades, and clowns . . . and of course exotic and savory ethnic foods. Photo by Shelley Gazin

Facing page, top: On the streets of Chinatown traditional Asian culture mingles with Western commerce and architecture. Photo by Joseph Sohm/Chromosohm

Facing page, bottom: Many practitioners of alternative lifestyles make a habit of participating in West L.A.'s Gay and Lesbian Parade every year. Photo by Larry Molmud

the public school population.

The city's cultural and ethnic evolution has stimulated positive changes in the arts, education, and business. The cultural agenda now includes arts and entertainment from every corner of the globe, performed in centers as diverse as the city's population. Two major arts facilities built in the last decade are the new multiuse Japanese Cultural Center in the downtown area and Plaza de la Raza in East Los Angeles, home to many Latino cultural events.

Ethnic enrollment, spurred by bold affirmative action programs, has soared at all major institutions of higher learning in Los Angeles, enriching the curricula and stimulating long-sought changes in the way these schools are administered.

Ethnic participation has also reshaped the fabric of the business community here. Already America's most entrepreneurial city, with nearly 10 percent of its work force self-employed (the national average is 6.8 percent), Los Angeles pulses with exotic new enterprises. In ethnic enclaves like Koreatown, the East Side barrio, South Broadway, and Little Tokyo, new arrivals compete head-to-head with more established firms for their share of the economic pie.

"Growth in percentage terms could be most rapid among Asian-owned businesses, because of the high rate of Asian 'entrepreneurship,'" according to the Wells Fargo study. "Los Angeles' emergence as the principal gateway for Pacific Basin trade is creating a range of opportunities in legal, financial, and other trade-related services."

In response, many large firms here have moved aggressively to attract ethnic buyers with new product lines, advertising approaches, and even entire new marketing concepts. Many supermarkets are stocking products aimed at Asian, Latino, and other ethnic buyers. For example, the Vons supermarket chain has opened several Tianguis supermarkets that cater exclusively to Latino shoppers. Spanish-language billboards dominate the cityscape in several neighborhoods.

In publishing, the *Los Angeles Times* has begun printing a Spanish-language supplement called *Nuestro Tiempo* ("Our Time"), and following the massacre at Beijing's Tienanmen Square in 1989 the *Times* published a special Chinese-language section devoted to that tragic confrontation.

The eighties saw Los Angeles emerge as a capital of international culture. Its renowned Philharmonic began its 1991 season under the baton of Finnish-born conductor Esa-Pekka Salonen, one of the foremost musical directors in the world today. Salonen follows such distinguished past L.A. Philharmonic conductors as Zubin Mehta, Carlo Maria Giulini, and Andre Previn. The highly regarded Los Angeles Chamber Orchestra also came into its own during the eighties under the baton of British violinist-conductor Iona Brown.

In addition, Los Angeles abounds with

The Dorothy Chandler Pavilion is dedicated to the wife of *Los Angeles Times* publisher Herman Chandler. Dorothy Chandler led efforts to create the Los Angeles Music Center in the 1960s. Photo by Shelley Gazin

performing arts organizations of all stripes, from a score of little theater groups to major arts companies like the Center Theatre Group at the downtown Music Center, the Los Angeles Master Chorale, the Joffrey Ballet (which moved here from New York in 1984), and the Bella Lewitzky Dance Company, a cultural landmark in Los Angeles for decades.

The eighties also saw the opening of the exciting new Museum of Contemporary Art (MOCA) in downtown Los Angeles. Housed in a striking postmodern building designed by architect Arata Isozaki, MOCA was financed entirely through private contributions and has been endowed with many works from important private collections, including those of Barry Lowen, Leo Castelli, Douglas Cramer, and Frederick and Marcia Weisman. Along with its adjunct facility, the Temporary Contemporary Gallery in Little Tokyo, MOCA provides a modernist counterpoint to the more traditional offerings of the older Los Angeles County Museum of Art (LACMA) in Hancock Park.

LACMA also underwent major expansions in the last decade, with the addition of the $30-million, 115,000-square-foot Robert O. Anderson wing, which houses the museum's collection of twentieth-century works, and the new Pavilion for Japanese Art, which opened in 1988. These additions make LACMA the largest facility of its kind in the Western United States, and one of the region's leading cultural attractions, with attendance of more than a million in 1990.

As a mecca of popular entertainment for nearly a century, the mythic realm of Hollywood continues to spin out a prodigious volume of films, television programming, recordings, and live entertainment for the world market. While out-of-town or "run-

away" film and television production has sapped some of Hollywood's vigor in recent years (around a third of all U.S. theatrical films are produced elsewhere), it remains the fount of most of the industry's creative and economic energies. Measured by box office revenues, the U.S. film industry achieved a major milestone in 1990, when it passed the $5 billion mark in gross ticket sales.

Hollywood has long outgrown its origins in the musty barns at the end of the trolley line from downtown Los Angeles, where early filmmakers like Cecil B. DeMille established their dream factories. Today, some would say, Hollywood's boundaries extend from the corporate boardrooms of Sony Corporation in Tokyo (which acquired Columbia Pictures in 1989 for more than $3.5 billion) to London's West End, where more than one property destined for the screen had its birth.

While the major film lots—Warner's,

Columbia, Paramount, and 20th Century Fox, for example—still exist, the dynamics of the industry have changed radically in recent years. Most of today's motion pictures are produced by smaller companies that hire the production facilities and marketing services of the big studios, but retain creative control and a lion's share of the profits. Deals are highly complex, with few stars under contract for more than one or two pictures at a time.

Most of the industry's clout has shifted from studio heads to the big talent agencies, to entertainment lawyers and individual stars, writers, and producers. This trend has spawned a new breed of Hollywood entrepreneur, the so-called "packager," who assembles the raw elements of a film project and sells it to a studio or production company.

As production budgets climb (the average cost of a film produced in 1990 was more

Composer/conductor John Williams works with members of the Young Musicians Foundation Debut Orchestra. Young musicians from ages 13 to 23 are chosen from Los Angeles' multi-ethnic neighborhoods and communities to join the orchestra and gain experience in professional performing. Photo by Shelley Gazin

than $10 million, versus an industry average of $3 million in 1980), companies are looking increasingly for blockbuster movies—those that gross $100 million or more at the box office. In 1989 seven films exceeded that figure, versus only one, *Superman,* a decade earlier. Warner's *Batman* was the decade's champion, with domestic ticket sales of more than $300 million in its first year. With foreign grosses and ancillary sales such as tee shirts and posters, *Batman* could become Hollywood's first billion-dollar property.

Though headquartered in New York, the three principal television networks, ABC, CBS, and NBC, maintain major facilities in the Los Angeles area and produce most of their programming here. Such long-running series as "Roseanne," "L.A. Law," and "Cheers," as well as leading game shows like "Jeopardy!" and "Wheel of Fortune" and the late-night entries of "The Tonight Show" and "The Arsenio Hall Show" are produced at local studios.

In addition, the Fox Television Network and several cable television companies are headquartered in the Los Angeles area. Univision, a major producer and worldwide distributor of programming for Latino audiences, also operates from facilities here. In all, the Los Angeles area probably accounts for fully 30 percent of the film, television, and recording production worldwide.

One of the prime attractions of Los Angeles since its beginning has been a salubrious Mediterranean climate matched by a wide variety of recreational options. In an era of increasing regional competition for talent and resources, such assets can play a decisive role in luring visitors, employees, and new businesses to the area.

The choice of activities here is almost limitless. Within the city are many miles of hiking and riding trails, a score of inviting beaches (the beach season is almost year-round, with hearty souls braving the local surf in almost any weather), championship golf courses, and countless tennis complexes. Only a few miles away from urban areas, the mountains abound in wildlife and provide excellent skiing opportunities in winter.

Los Angeles also boasts the world's largest man-made recreational boat marina at Marina Del Rey, with moorings for 10,000 vessels, along with a wide range of associated services. On a busy summer weekend, more than 35,000 to 40,000 visitors pass in and out of the marina each day. Facilities for thousands of other sail- and motorboats are available in nearby San Pedro, Redondo Beach, and Long Beach harbors.

With the growth of public interest in personal health, gyms and spas have proliferated here, creating an entire new industry that has spread across the nation. Jane Fonda Workouts, Pritikin Longevity Centers, and Herbalife International are but three nation-

Every major professional sport is represented by a Los Angeles franchise, and some by two. Nearly all are stunningly successful, with several clubs consistently leading their leagues in annual attendance (the Los Angeles Dodgers have had several seasons with attendance of three million).

Unlike most cities, where major-league teams have had to start as new franchises, the crop here is made up largely of franchises transplanted from other sites—which has

meant that pennants and championships have been faster in coming for local fans.

The Los Angeles Dodgers, for example, won their first pennant and world championship only a year after arriving here from Brooklyn in 1958. Since then they have been crowned National League champs eight times and World Champions four times. Gene Autry's California Angels, on the other hand, are pennant-less, but still manage to perform as contenders in their division of the American League nearly every year.

The city's two pro football teams, the Rams and the Raiders, came from Cleveland (1946) and Oakland (1982), respectively, and won world championships within their first few years here.

The Los Angeles Lakers, which didn't win a National Basketball Association title until 1972, 12 years after arriving from Minneapolis, made up for lost time in the 1980s by winning nine divisional and five playoff

Above: A gaggle of celebrities, including Mick Fleetwood, Bonnie Raitt, Olivia Newton-John, Belinda Carlisle, and Rita Coolidge perform "Spirit of the Forest," a song written and produced by British rock group Gentlemen Without Weapons to raise funds for rain forest preservation. Photo by Shelley Gazin

al companies spawned by the robust health and fitness boom in this area. Ancillary businesses like designer sportswear (Catalina and Guess) and footwear (L.A. Gear) are also major beneficiaries of the fitness revolution.

In terms of spectator sports, the city is also unrivaled. Local teams like the UCLA Bruins and USC Trojans are almost always among the top-ranked men's and women's teams in football, basketball, baseball, and track and field. In recent years several local Cal State University teams and teams from independent schools like Pepperdine and Loyola have also begun to gain national attention and rankings.

Award-winning Hollywood makeup artist Michael Westmore poses with a likeness of "Star Trek: The Next Generation" character "Data," played by Brent Spiner in the series. The work of Westmore and others contributes to the mystique of movie-making, which has drawn tourists and would-be stars to L.A. for decades. Photo by Shelley Gazin

championships. As a result, tickets for Lakers games are among the most expensive ($200 for a courtside seat) and hardest to get in town. The city's other NBA franchise, the Clippers, came here from San Diego in 1984. They are still title-less but showed vast improvement in the late 1980s.

In addition, in 1967 the city gained a National Hockey League entry, the Los Angeles Kings, which struggled near the bottom of the standings until it became a contender by

the PGA's annual tour since 1926, and the Ladies' Professional Golf circuit usually includes at least one tournament each year in the Los Angeles area.

Despite all it has to offer in terms of sports, recreation, and business, no American city spends more time in self-examination than Los Angeles. Every year, it seems, someone like Rand Corporation or a local financial institution commissions another "futures study" to try and peek behind the

A Hollywood director and cinematographer plan their next shot of a Los Angeles panorama. Photo by Joseph Sohm/ Chromosohm

acquiring Wayne Gretzky ("The Great One") from Edmonton in 1988.

Two of the nation's leading racehorse tracks, Santa Anita and Hollywood Park, also enrich the sporting environment of the region. Santa Anita, founded in 1934, handles the largest amount of betting of any track in America, with more than $650 million wagered at the track in 1989-1990.

On the city's golf scene, the million-dollar Los Angeles Open has been a major stop on

curtain of tomorrow. These reports bulge with auguries both ominous and rosy for the community's future.

The condition must be infectious, for no city is so relentlessly probed and prodded by outsiders as well. At least one major national or international publication *(Newsweek, Atlantic Monthly, New York Times Sunday Magazine,* the *Economist)* devotes a lead article, or an entire issue, to Los Angeles each year. And no self-respecting New York pub-

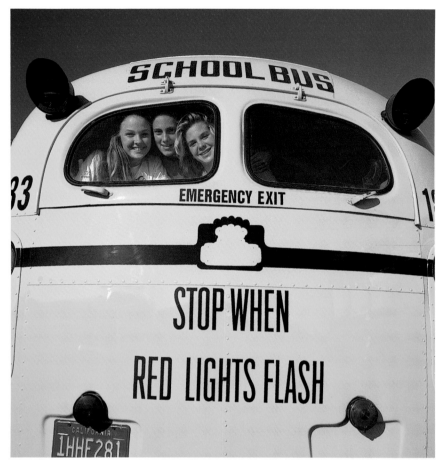

Above: High school co-eds "ride-share" in a yellow school bus. Photo by Joseph Sohm/Chromosohm

Right: A record 101,273 people watched Washington trounce Iowa 46-34 at the 77th Rose Bowl in Pasadena. Photo by Joseph Sohm/Chromosohm

lishing house would be caught without a Los Angeles novel or nonfiction entry on its annual list.

Conclusions about Los Angeles in these studies are generally mixed, but increasingly favorable. The city has risen from its status as "Kooksville" in the 1940s and 1950s to its current eminence as a major trendsetter and its probable role as dominant American city in the twenty-first century. "Los Angeles rivals New York in attracting ambitious people who want to make it, in almost every professional endeavor and field of business," commented *Atlantic Magazine* in 1988. "If present trends continue . . . Los Angeles might even emerge as the Western Hemisphere's leading city in the early twenty-first century."

As long as the city continues to generate ideas, wealth, and novelty—and there is no sign of letup in this "realm of possibility" —*Atlantic*'s prognosis looks pretty safe. Indeed, as Los Angeles approaches the year 2000, it is clearly the front-runner for the title of "City of the Century."

FROM PUEBLO TO SUPERCITY

Los Angeles Grows Up

*L*os Angeles is an international city—a potpourri of ethnic heritages and architectural styles, a blending of suburban hamlets and urban villages nestled in an amphitheater of mountains. It is a colossal city-state, where 14.5 million people speak 85 languages and drive nearly 100 million miles each day in 8 million cars. It is

"OVER A PERIOD OF SEVERAL DECADES, LOS ANGELES HAS PROBABLY BEEN THE MOST RAPIDLY CHANGING URBAN CENTER IN THE WESTERN HEMISPHERE."

—EARL HANSON AND PAUL BECKETT,

LOS ANGELES: ITS PEOPLE AND ITS HOMES, 1944

also a great beauty. Los Angeles boasts green foothills, rugged mountains, endless valleys, white sand beaches, and postcard-perfect sunshine. As one real estate salesman boasted in 1880, "We sold them the climate and threw the land in." Los Angeles' unique allure has attracted the largest migration of people in United States history.

Los Angeles is also a dreamscape of past, present, and future, where exotic and natural worlds collide and mingle. Spanish adobes, Swiss chalets, French chateaux, sleek Modernes, ornate Victorians, Arabian castles, and Mexican ranches are owned by African Americans, Latinos, Anglos, Vietnamese, Chinese, Filipinos, Cambodians, Soviets, Japanese, Indians, Iranians, Koreans,

A Century City skyscraper rises rakishly into the clouds. Photo by Joseph Sohm/Chromosohm

Britons, and Australians.

How did a small Indian village called Yang-na become a world-famous metropolis called Los Angeles? It is a story of explorers, waterways, oil booms, missionaries, Hollywood starlets, Big Red trolley cars, and freeways. It stars millionaires, Dust Bowl immigrants, South American refugees, Japanese executives, and World War II veterans. The story is set in a sprawling 465-mile galaxy dotted with cliffs, beaches, grasslands, woodlands, oceans, and towering 50-story skyscrapers. The building of Los Angeles is a saga, exciting and huge. And it is unique, just like Los Angeles.

Century City's twin towers are proud landmarks of this growing business district. Photo by Joseph Sohm/Chromosohm

In 1542 Los Angeles (Yang-na) was untamed wilderness inhabited by Gabrielino, Chumash, and Shoshone Indians. They lived in mud and adobe huts and grew corn, beans, olives, and citrus fruits beside a blue-watered river. Spanish explorers, led by Father Juan Crespi, christened the river *El Río de Nuestra Señora la Reina de los Angeles de Porciúncula* in 1769. Twelve years later, 11 families from Mexico built a pueblo on its banks. From the pueblo eventually stretched Los Angeles' first road, El Camino Real, a Spanish military road, which led to the La Brea Tar Pits (tracing today's Wilshire Boulevard), then veered off toward the distant presidios of Monterey and San Francisco.

By 1822 Los Angeles was under Mexican control. Its 8 million acres were parceled into 500 land grants. Mexican families proudly erected a church in the pueblo's fast-growing central plaza. Nearly 1,000 settlers arrived, establishing huge missions and ranchos. But in 1848 they were displaced by American treasure-hunters when California—and Los Angeles—became United States territory. A gold rush in Northern California attracted gamblers, bandits, drifters,

rustlers, and hustlers. They migrated to Los Angeles. Saloons, gambling parlors, and prostitution houses sprang up. Bedlam ruled. Prim Easterners referred to young Los Angeles as "Los Diablos" and "City of the Fallen Angels." One embittered inhabitant described the place as "a town of crooked, ungraded, unpaved streets; low, lean, rickety adobe houses, with asphaltum roofs, and here and there an indolent native, hugging the inside of a blanket." Another lamented, "I've never seen her looking so bad."

But by the end of the Civil War, western migrations of farmers, merchants, bankers, and land developers poured into Los Angeles. The new arrivals retamed the town, even raising $602,000 to subsidize a Southern Pacific Railroad route through Los Angeles to San Francisco and points east. Its construction led to a huge land boom in the 1870s. Land near the rails was subdivided and sold. Los Angeles' population doubled in four years, from 5,500 to 11,000. Streets were paved and gas lamps added at every corner.

A city hall, hospital, public school, college, theater, and even an opera house were constructed. Their designs imitated East Coast styles—Queen Anne, Italianate, Romanesque, and Eastlake architecture. Two-story homes were built "Monterey-style," blending adobe and New England construction with Greek Revival and Federal detailing. By the end of the 1870s, "Monterey" had become the dominant architectural style of Los Angeles.

By 1874 horse-drawn streetcar lines con-

Many a wild Melrose store is crammed with blow-up toys, plastic ducks, gaudy cards, and other consumable Los Angeles diversions. Photo by Bob Rowan/ Progressive Image

During the boom, not all immigrants came by train. Historian Carey McWilliams describes the Europeans who arrived via steamer and sailing ship: ". . . exotic Polish intellectuals, British remittance men, Chinese immigrants, Basque sheepherders, French and German peasants, and German Jewish merchants and financiers . . ." The immigrants built Spanish haciendas with pantiled roofs, adobe walls, and arcaded courtyards. Indiana farmers formed an agri-

Left: A multicolored tower graces the Los Angeles Coliseum, site of the 1984 Olympics. Photo by Joseph Sohm/Chromosohm

nected Los Angeles' business district at Spring and Sixth streets with the fashionable residential zone growing near Hill Street. Over the next 15 years, new lines opened up in Pasadena, Pomona, San Bernardino, and Ontario. Pacific Electric's Big Red Cars would eventually operate over 1,164 miles of track in the 50-odd communities which today define Greater Los Angeles—from Balboa to the mouth of the Santa Monica Canyon, up into the San Fernando Valley, to Riverside, Corona, and San Bernardino, then into La Habra and Anaheim and on to Orange. Los Angeles' marvelous interurban line allowed Angelenos to work in the city but live in the country. Today freeways duplicate the old railway lines.

The Great Rate Wars of 1887 between the Santa Fe and Southern Pacific railroads lured a huge influx of Midwestern immigrants to Los Angeles. Passenger fares from Kansas City to Los Angeles plummeted from $125 to $12, and then, on March 6, 1887, to $1. An estimated 120,000 people rushed west on the Southern Pacific alone. Railroad promoters and subdividers created townsites along the tracks. Real estate agents—2,000 strong—peddled 500,000 building lots at $100 to $300 each in hundreds of makeshift "towns" across Los Angeles.

cultural collective in Pasadena; Mormon settlers colonized San Bernardino; German vintners founded Anaheim; English immigrants settled in El Toro. Townships formed apart from downtown, resulting in a land boom that would last until 1900. Los Angeles' population exploded to 50,000.

By the early 1900s Los Angeles' large farming communities were harvesting pomegranates, potatoes, bananas, tomatoes, oranges, limes, apricots, peaches, pears, apples, olives, and squash from Los Angeles' lush soils. But soon Los Angeles' local water supply was exhausted. Los Angeles annexed the San Fernando Valley in 1902, and diverted water from the Owens Valley 250 miles north. Neighboring communities, similarly water-starved, joined the growing city of Los Angeles.

Oil strikes in Glendale, in the Fairfax District, and near the La Brea Tar Pits lured even more people to Los Angeles. By 1900

Above: Few cities can rival L.A. for colorful, stylized architecture. Photo by Bob Rowan/Progressive Image

Facing page: A popular, though controversial Venice landmark, *Ballerina Clown*, by Jonathan Borofsky, attracts continual attention—and comments—from passersby. Photo by Shelley Gazin

HIDDEN TREASURES
Touring Historic Downtown

Easterners claim Los Angeles has no past. But hidden among the monoliths of Los Angeles' downtown district are historic jewels. They reflect a 250-year saga of Indian villages, Mexican and Spanish occupation, Anglo influence, and twentieth-century industrialization. Some of these buildings are world famous. Others are legendary in their history and beauty. All are accessible to the public.

Avila Adobe (1818), 10 Olvera Street—The oldest existing house in Los Angeles, the adobe was built by wealthy cattle rancher Don Francisco Avila for his family. It was later used as military headquarters during the Mexican-American War, and as a boarding house, hotel, and restaurant over the next 100 years. Earth floors, thick walls, and cowhide furniture reflect the adobe's original style. Its porch is covered in grapevines, and its corridor faces a dusty Early California courtyard.

La Iglesia de Nuestra Señora la Reina de los Angeles (1822), 535 N. Main Street—The first major public building in Los Angeles, the church was the center of social, political, and religious life in the early 1800s. Franciscan fathers and local Indians built the original church. Today, after several restorations and additions, the building stands in its current form—two-story, adobe, with a Spanish-style facade, tiled roof, and bell tower. Spanish-speaking Catholics flock from near and far to the church, now known as Our Lady Queen of Angels, for services and sacraments.

Bradbury Building (1893), 304 S. Broadway—Inside this modest sand-

Depictions of fierce South American deities festoon the facade of the Mayan Theater in downtown Los Angeles. Photo by Larry Molmud

stone-and-brick building is a palatial expanse of light. Rising five stories, the Bradbury Building features a glass roof, Belgian marble staircases, a central court surrounded by Victorian cast-iron grillwork, open-cased elevators, and deeply polished wood. The Bradbury Building was built by Lewis Bradbury, a mining millionaire turned real estate developer, and architect George Wyman, who was inspired, legend has it, by the ghost of his recently departed brother.

Farmers and Merchants Bank (1904), 401 S. Main Street—Built by Los Angeles pioneer Isaias Hellman, the bank is an example of Los Angeles' early Beaux Arts-style "Temples of Finance." It is one of the oldest continually operating banks in Los Angeles.

Million Dollar Theater (1917), 307 S. Broadway—On opening night Mary Pickford, Lillian Gish, and Charlie Chaplin arrived at the Million Dollar Theater to see William S. Hart in *The Silent Man*. Countless vaudeville and movie greats including Judy Garland

and Rudolph Valentino appeared here. The Million Dollar Theater, built by entrepreneur Sid Grauman, is one of the earliest movie palaces in the United States. In its heyday it boasted 2,200 seats, coffered ceilings, Wild West icons (bisons, six-shooters, longhorn skulls), and fine art statues. Today it features Spanish-language films and live shows.

Barker Brothers Building (1925), 818 W. 7th Street—This Renaissance Revival building is the former headquarters of Barker Brothers furniture. It was inspired by the Strozzi Palace in Florence, and features a three-story arched entranceway and a 40-foot-high lobby court with beamed and vaulted ceilings. Shoppers once enjoyed pipe organs playing in the mezzanine galleries as they shopped. Barker Brothers held public forums on home economics and decorating in a 600-seat auditorium nearby. The building now houses retail shops and offices.

Mayan Theater (1926), 1044 S. Hill Street—Resembling the monumental pre-Columbian buildings of Uxmal and Chichen Itza in Yucatan, Mexico, the Mayan features cast-stone walls etched with entwined serpents, owl heads, and colossal warrior kings in ceremonial robes. The theater has a colorful past. Opening August 15, 1927 to a Gershwin musical, the Mayan later evolved into a movie theater, burlesque house, pornography theater (featuring *Stephanee's Lust Story* and *Ring of Desire*), and Spanish-language film house. It is currently a nightclub. Legend has it that in 1948 (according to Richard Lamparski's *Hidden Hollywood*) Marilyn Monroe appeared here as a stripper.

Oviatt Building (1928), 617 S. Olive Street—In the 1920s the Oviatt was the last word in men's furnishings stores. Completely embellished in glass and marble from France, the Oviatt Building was an emblem of pre-Depression opulence. It contained the largest collection of Lalique glass lamps, panels, and chandeliers ever assembled in the world. Its style was Art Deco, against a

The Coca Cola Building, built in 1936 on Central Boulevard, features sleek, nautical styling, and still functions as a production plant. The building was designed by noted Streamline Moderne architect Robert Derrah. Photo by Shelley Gazin

Romanesque facade. A crest of angels and chime bells framed its entranceway. The Oviatt was renovated in 1976 for $4.5 million. Today cast-iron nymph-topped gates and panels of brilliant Deco-esque designs greet visitors.

Eastern Columbia Building (1929), 849 S. Broadway—The last major building constructed in L.A.'s downtown between the Depression and the end of World War II, the Eastern Columbia Building was constructed by an optimist, Polish immigrant Adolph Sieroty, who believed in America's future. Sieroty's investment put people back to work. The Eastern Columbia Building is an Art Deco-style, bluish terra-cotta building pulsing with zigzags, plant motifs, and chevrons. A radiating sunburst explodes from its entranceway.

Los Angeles Theater (1931), 615 S. Broadway—The last great movie palace built in downtown Los Angeles, the Los Angeles Theater took only 90 days to construct, using prefabricated material. It opened featuring Charlie Chaplin's

City Light. Broadway had to be closed as teeming crowds and limousines surrounded the theater. Its exterior is an extravagant French Renaissance design. Its interior—considered the most lavish of all Los Angeles theaters—is a narrow, elaborate lobby awash in ornamented ivory and gold. The ladies room features mahogany vanities and 13 types of marble. Today the theater shows Spanish-language films.

Coca Cola Building (1936), 1334 S. Central Boulevard—Architect Robert Derrah unified four Spanish-style structures into one sleek nautical sailing ship, creating a Streamline Moderne masterpiece resembling an ocean liner. The building has long horizontal lines (typical of 1930s design), portholes, a promenade deck, flying bridges, catwalks, louvered round-headed doors, and an interior derived from an 1890s cruise ship. Inside, Coca Cola employees churn out 18,000 to 20,000 cases of Coke per eight-hour shift.

Union Station (1939), 800 N. Alameda Street—Union Station is the last major railroad terminal built in the United States; half a million people attended its opening ceremony in 1939. Famous transcontinental trains like Santa Fe's *El Capitan* and *Super Chief* and Union Pacific's *City of L.A.* arrived here. The first railroad ever built in Los Angeles traversed its grounds in 1869; its earliest trains carried Anglo settlers and Chinese laborers to adobe settlements and farmlands beyond. The building's exterior is Spanish style, with graceful Streamline Moderne touches. Inside are spacious halls, 50-foot ceilings, 3,000-pound chandeliers, an Art Deco cocktail lounge, tiled floors and roofs, and tall-arched windows. Famous Union Station patrons have included Jackie Gleason, Walter Winchell, director John Madden, and Ronald Reagan.

Formal tours of the historic downtown district and outlying areas are offered by the Los Angeles Conservancy, 727 7th Street, Los Angeles, on Saturdays at 10 a.m. —*Susan Vaughn*

The historic downtown neighborhood of Bunker Hill has been redeveloped, and the new high-rise complex in L.A.'s downtown features fountains, Parisian steps, and some of Los Angeles' toniest corporate residences. Above, this back alley offers two necessities for the busy Bunker Hill exec: a garage and a barber shop. Photo by Bob Rowan/Progressive Image

the northwest side of Los Angeles was a forest of derricks, and oilmen like Alphonzo Bell, who earned $100,000 a month in oil revenues, constructed spectacular mansions and buildings from their profits.

The downtown center reflected the design of civic centers across the country—decorative and classical. It boasted massive Neo-Romanesque and Beaux Arts-style commercial buildings. Structures were designed with terra-cotta exteriors, fluted Corinthian columns, ornate cornices, domed corner towers, and marble-and-stained glass lobbies. City Hall, the County Courthouse, and the Bradbury Building are extant examples of the glorious building boom of the era. Other noteworthy early twentieth-century buildings include the Los Angeles Public Library (a blend of Mediterranean, Roman, Islamic, Egyptian, and Byzantine styles topped by a tiled pyramid), the Farmers and Merchants Bank, a Beaux Arts building at Fourth Street and Main, the Tower Theater at South Broadway (which resembles the Paris opera house), and

the Los Angeles Theater nearby (modeled after the Versailles Hall of Mirrors).

Innovative designers like Irving Gill, Frank Lloyd Wright, and the firm of Greene & Greene developed new architectural styles in Los Angeles. Overwrought Victorian designs evolved into "California bungalows" —well-crafted homes modeled after the "bangala" dwellings of East India, costing less than $1,000 to construct. They were cool in summer and warm in winter. The Gamble House, built in 1908, and the Dodge House, built in 1916, are two existing examples of this style.

In the early 1900s Los Angeles' famous port became a reality, too. A breakwater was built to enclose the harbor at Wilmington/San Pedro, making the Port of Los Angeles the largest man-made harbor in the world. It allowed for expanded overseas trade, particularly after the Panama Canal opened, shortening coast-to-coast water travel. Today the Port of Los Angeles processes over $4 billion in cargo each year. Together with the Port of Long Beach, it handles more tonnage than the combined New York-New Jersey Port Authority.

The infant movie industry was born in 1907 when Selig Polyscope, an East Coast film concern, shot a one-reeler, *The Count of Monte Cristo,* in an abandoned Los Angeles barn. Nestor Film Company and the Jesse Lasky Feature Play Company followed, setting up shop in empty saloons and bars at Sunset and Gower, and shooting films in the San Fernando Valley, at the beaches of Santa Monica, and downtown. The burgeoning Los Angeles movie industry generated thousands of jobs and land opportunities. By 1915 movie industry payrolls in Los Angeles totaled $20 million. By 1920, 100,000 Angelenos were employed by the industry, which grossed one billion dollars, making it Los Angeles' biggest business concern. Lasky Studios bought 10 acres at Sunset and Vine, and a rambling ranch in the San Fernando Valley. Universal City, dedicated by Carl Laemmle in 1915, covered 230 acres five miles north of Hollywood, and eventually produced nearly a film a day.

Hollywood was still a lima bean field then. It had been abandoned by oil syndicates

Hundreds of Charlie Chaplins outside the Liberty Theater hope to win first prize as best look-alike tramp. Photo courtesy KFWB

which found it barren, and was purchased by two devout Methodists in 1887. They subdivided the territory and banned liquor, sanitariums, slaughterhouses, oil wells, and movie theaters. But when Hollywood ran out of water in 1910, it agreed to be annexed to Los Angeles to gain access to the Owens Valley Aqueduct. Prohibitions were removed. Movie companies streamed in, having been banished from cities like Glendale, South Pasadena, and Santa Monica for their noisy, space-consuming, disruptive activities. They erected offices resembling Southern plantations, English cottages, and Roman forums. They built theaters resembling Egyptian and Mayan temples, Moorish mosques, Chinese pagodas, Spanish baroque cathedrals, Renaissance palaces, and Roman palazzos.

Hollywood's stars became rich, left their boardinghouses, and built luxurious homes in Beverly Hills. The upper-class suburb was well planned, with lightly curving roads running northwest from Santa Monica Boulevard into the hills. Beverly Hills homes— Italian Renaissance, neo-Gothic, Moorish, Georgian, and neo-Spanish mansions—boasted manicured lawns, lush foliage, sweeping front drives, terraces, and tiled verandas. Douglas Fairbanks erected a Tudor-style mansion, hunting lodge, swimming pool, canoeing ponds, and six-stall stable on 14 acres. Harold Lloyd built a 36,000-square-foot, 40-room, 26-bath mansion on a hillside, with an 800-foot canoeing lake, 9-hole golf course, and handball and tennis courts. Twenty-three-year-old Gloria Swanson purchased a 22-room, 5-bath Italian Renaissance mansion. Tom Mix, Will Rogers, Charlie Chaplin, Rudolph Valentino, John Barrymore, and Buster Keaton also relocated to Beverly Hills.

Miles away, a swampland

called Venice where city folk shot ducks was being transformed into a beachside suburb. Cigarette salesman Abbot Kinney developed Venice into a popularized version of Italy's Venice in 1904. He designed Venetian canals and imported gondolas and gondoliers from Italy to navigate the waters. Vendors hawked taffy twists and ice cream on a colorful promenade. Visitors arrived via Pacific Electric's interurban railway, which by now carried 225,000 persons 73,000 miles a day in 600 cars.

The Big Red Cars also carried mail, sugar beets, oranges, tourists, vacationers, and commuters past the beaches, oil fields, sugar beet fields, and almond, lemon, and orange groves still abundant in Los Angeles. Groups chartered private trolleys for Sunday school picnics and moonlight excursions. By the 1920s Pacific Electric's railway was one of the largest interurban systems in the nation. Communities sprouted where the Big Red

Cars went; development followed their tracks.

During the twenties an additional 1.3 million people poured into Los Angeles, primarily from the Midwest. It was the largest internal migration in American history. Real estate salesmen were everywhere, offering free bus rides, lunches, and souvenirs, and hawking half-acre lots for $525 apiece. As rapid land subdivisions occurred farther from Pacific Electric's interurban system, residents became more dependent upon the automobile. The automobile, coupled with real estate sales, eventually undid Pacific Electric's marvelous urban transport system. More cars and more subdivision of lots caused the creation of more intersections, grade crossings, and traffic snarls. Trains were held up and schedules disrupted. Service deteriorated and streetcar accidents increased.

Los Angeles' motor age dawned in the late 1920s, when automobile registration climbed from 55,217 to 441,000. Los Ange-

The California bungalow, a popular architectural design for Southern California homes, is a frequent sight in most L.A. neighborhoods. Photo by Joseph Sohm/Chromosohm

At the Beverly Hills Car Show, Kenny Kragen's '57 Chevy is a standout. Photo by Joseph Sohm/Chromosohm

les had more cars per citizen—and still does—than any other city in the United States. By the late 1930s Los Angeles' streets were upgraded to boulevards, and traffic lights were installed and synchronized at every major intersection. The Pasadena Freeway, first of the freeway systems built, was completed in 1939. It ran from downtown Los Angeles to Pasadena—six miles in all—and caused even more Angelenos to reject the growingly impractical interurban railway system. The Hollywood, San Bernardino, and Santa Ana freeways were started one year later and finished after World War II. Their completion coincided with the demise of the Big Red Cars.

Even the Depression did not stop the flow of immigrants into Los Angeles. By 1930 Los Angeles' population stood at 2 million, having doubled in 10 years. Its seemingly Depression-proof industries—movies, oil, and tourism—and its amicable climate lured optimistic citizens west. As one Depression-era settler wrote, "You might starve, but you won't freeze here."

The Depression and a burgeoning International Movement (led by designers Le Corbusier, Walter Gropius, and Mies van der Rohe) brought an end to the Art Deco renaissance that flourished briefly in Los Angeles. Colorful, playful designs of the 1920s, like the Fox-Wilshire Theater, were

replaced by stark hospital-like buildings. International Moderne's brooding, intellectual form also rendered the city's imitation Spanish haciendas obsolete. Moderne was practical, more subtle, and less expensive. One Los Angeles-based Modernist, Richard Neutra, designed cube-like apartments with open private gardens to accommodate Depression-struck budgets. Then Moderne style evolved into Streamline Moderne—with horizontal lines, rounded corners, and sleek machine-like exteriors. The Shangri-La Hotel in Santa Monica, the downtown Central Post Office, City Hall, and Robert

Derrah's downtown Coca Cola bottling plant (which resembles an ocean liner, with ship bridge, promenade deck, portholes, and nautical detailing) are still-standing examples of Streamline Moderne.

Wilshire Boulevard's "Miracle Mile" (a broad strip of avenue running west from Beverly Hills and east to downtown), named after a Marxist oil millionaire, featured fine shops and theaters like Art Deco-style Bullocks (1928), the Zigzag Moderne Wiltern Theater (1930), and Moderne-style May Company. The new stores rivaled the upscale establishments downtown, enabling shoppers from affluent suburbs like Beverly Hills, Hollywood, and Wolfskill Ranch (later Westwood and Holmby Hills) to patronize locally. Westwood Village, only miles away, eventually grew into a younger, more fashionable rival of the Miracle Mile.

From the 1930s onward, Los Angeles merchants oriented their stores toward parking lots instead of streetcar tracks. The shops were brightly decorated to catch motorists' eyes. Restaurants were shaped like oranges, derbies, hotdogs, owls, milk cans, dogs, igloos, shoes, and donuts. Logos were emblazoned in luminous reds, greens, blues,

Influences of Hollywood's past can still be seen throughout the area. Photo by Joseph Sohm/Chromosohm

THE WRIGHT STUFF

The Master's Legacy to Los Angeles

Frank Lloyd Wright, America's pre-eminent master builder, arrived in Southern California in 1919. He surveyed the landscape around him—miles and miles of imitation Spanish missions—and decided that Southern California needed something new . . . something breathtaking . . . something *organic* that would blend in with the area's climate, flora, and cultural heritage.

Wright's Pacific ruminations resulted in nine starkly original buildings that still can be seen today. The most famous of these is **Hollyhock House**. It has been designated by the American Institute of Architects as one of 17 buildings in the United States most reflective of Wright's architectural contribution to American culture.

Oil heiress Aline Barnsdall loved Southern California's sunny climate, oceanfront vistas, and semitropical foliage. She dreamed of owning a home in the Los Angeles hills, and in 1918 she contacted Frank Lloyd Wright to fulfill her vision. Money, it seemed, was no object. "She wanted no ordinary house," wrote Wright in his autobiography, "for she was no ordinary woman."

Aline Barnsdall asked Wright to build a lavish 36-acre retreat at Olive Hill (now Hollywood Boulevard). The proposed retreat would celebrate the fine arts in Los Angeles. It would feature a main residence (Hollyhock House), two guest residences, a theater and a house for Barnsdall's theater director, a movie theater, an apartment building for actors, craftsmen's shops and living quarters, and a children's art center.

Barnsdall envisioned her property as a mecca for Southern California's burgeoning community of artists. Frank Lloyd Wright saw it as a potential *romanza*—"beautiful the way that California herself is beautiful." He set to work drawing plans for Hollyhock House, a startlingly innovative monument which would be composed of exotic woods,

flowing water, nile-green and bronze interiors, and cement. "We would take that despised outcast of the building industry—the concrete block—out from underfoot or from the gutter . . . and make it live as a thing of beauty—textural like the trees . . ."

By 1919 Hollyhock House was under way. It was a study in space and strength—an impregnable retreat from a hostile world amid pools of water and gray-green olive trees. But by 1920 Barnsdall and Wright were suffering serious "creative differences."

Barnsdall criticized Wright's drawings and requested changes. "She would drop suggestions as a war plane drops bombs and sails away into the blue," lamented Wright in his autobiography. The embittered Wright was forced to modify many of his designs.

In 1921 Hollyhock House was finished. It stood like a Mayan temple atop Olive Hill, surrounded by pine groves, eucalyptus trees, and great carpets of flowers planted by Aline Barnsdall. French doors swept out to secluded green courtyards. Rooftop terraces overlooked the cityscapes of Hollywood and Los Angeles. A babbling stream flowed under the house and through the living room, encircling the fireplace. And Hollyhock's perforated concrete blocks stood as beacons of light and shadow, lending intricacy, stateliness, and power to the house's overall design.

Hollyhock House seemed a paean to nature and to mankind itself. But just

two years later, in 1923, Aline Barnsdall moved out. She claimed she did not like living in the house—it was too cold and dark; the doors were too heavy. Her plans for an arts community mecca were scrapped. Instead, Barnsdall bequeathed Hollyhock House to the City of Los Angeles in 1927, stipulating that it be used as a club for local artists. At first the new California Arts Club was popular, and musicians like Xavier Cugat (then a classical violinist) staged recitals in the house's central patio-theater. Later, however, the house was abandoned and fell into severe disrepair.

In 1974 Mayor Tom Bradley and the City of Los Angeles allocated $500,000 for Hollyhock's restoration. Wright's son, Lloyd Wright, was chosen as head

Above and facing page: Built in 1921, Frank Lloyd Wright's Hollyhock House is a secluded palace of art deco interiors and monumental splendor. Photos by Joseph Sohm/Chromosohm

architect of the project. Wright and a team of expert restorers worked diligently to match Frank Lloyd Wright's paints, carpeting, furniture, and wood trim. Due to lack of funds, Hollyhock House is still under renovation today, but it has been opened to the public three or four days a week for tours.

"A very proud house is the Hollyhock House," Frank Lloyd Wright wrote years after the house's infamous completion. Perhaps soon Hollyhock House will be restored to its previously denied glory.

Other Buildings by Frank Lloyd Wright:

Millard House ("La Miniatura"), 645 Prospect Court (1923). This is the first of Wright's "textile block" construction houses, built for Midwestern heiress Alice Miller. Set against a wooded expanse, the Millard House resembles a Mayan ruin in a jungle ravine. When cost exceeded the agreed $10,000 remodelling budget, Wright put in $6,000 of his own money to complete the project.

Storer House, 8161 Hollywood Boulevard (1923). A romantic creation of decorated concrete block nestled on a hillside, the house features an expansive two-story living room which opens to terraces in front and rear. The house is currently being restored by motion picture producer Joel Silver, aided by Eric Lloyd Wright (Frank Lloyd Wright's grandson).

Ennis House, 2607 Glendower Avenue (1924). Called by various critics a mausoleum, fortress, Mayan temple, and palace, the Ennis House rests on a steep hillside, held in place by great double-concrete retaining walls. The house's exterior is broad and commanding, overlooking a breathtaking vista.

Sturges House, 449 Skyway Road, Brentwood (1939). This rakishly designed building appears windowless from the street side, but its cantilevered terrace offers a spectacular vista; its bedrooms open onto wide, glass-encased balconies.

Oboler House, 32436 Mulholland Drive, Malibu (1940, 1941, 1944, 1946). Frank Lloyd Wright was hired by 3D and horror filmmaker Arch Oboler to create a soaring, dramatic mountaintop aerie called Eaglefeather. Alas, due to Oboler's financial difficulties, Eaglefeather was never built. Instead, Oboler commissioned Wright to build a gatehouse and modest studio on the cliffside of Malibu. Both the gatehouse and studio were done in stonework, and feature lapped board walls and parapets, borrowed from Oboler's original Eaglefeather design.

Anderton Court Building, 32B Rodeo Drive, Beverly Hills (1953-1954). Considered one of Wright's more zany productions, the Anderton Court Building features a zigzagging ramp flanked by expensive shops. Legend says the building was not built to Wright's specifications.

Freeman House, 1962 Glencoe Way (1924). The Freeman House was built for Samuel Freeman, and its living room commands a sweeping view of Los Angeles. The interior is lofty and cool; light enters through lattice-like perforated concrete blocks. Former owner Freeman once remarked to interviewers, "I have been living in this house for 50 years, half a century, and still to this day . . . I see something that I did not see before."

—Susan Vaughn

yellows, and oranges.

World War II brought another tide of immigrants to Los Angeles: blacks from the
Deep South, industrial workers from the
Midwest and East, sharecroppers from Oklahoma, and farmhands from Texas. Air travel,
a growingly popular mode of transportation,
brought more immigrants from overseas to
Los Angeles, too. During the 1940s, more
European, South American, and Asian travelers adopted Los Angeles as their first home
than any other city in the United States. Los
Angeles' population soared to 7 million.

Modern Los Angeles soon emerged as a
premier West Coast port for ships and

planes, and a world-class industrial power.
By 1950 Los Angeles was handling more sea-
port tonnage than San Francisco and landing
more fish than Boston. It was making more
planes than any city on earth, assembling
more cars than any city but Detroit, and
fashioning more clothing than any city except New York. Job opportunities lured even
more immigrants, and Los Angeles' boundaries strained to accommodate the incoming
hordes. Orange groves were cut down and
mountains shaved to make way for tract
homes—modest, affordable ($5,000 to
$6,000), but indistinguishable. Los Angeles'
sprawl expanded west across the San Fernando Valley, east into the San Gabriel Valley, and south to Orange County. Small
commercial and industrial centers arose
away from downtown, providing local jobs
and services for residents of the single-family homes and apartments. The downtown
area began to suffer as fewer businesses and
workers settled within its borders.

The recession of the 1950s slowed construction of single-family homes in Los Angeles, though defense industry workers and
military personnel still poured in from other
parts of the country. Builders shifted their
activities to multiple unit dwellings—two-
story stucco boxes with futuristic ornaments,
modish lettering, and foliage-surrounded
pools. They raised buildings one level to pro-

on April 8, 1961. The last trolley car stopped a few years later. Highways like the Harbor, Ventura, and San Diego freeways replaced trolley tracks. Between 1945 and 1960 Los Angeles' freeway system grew tenfold, to 250 miles. By 1953 the world-famous "Stack"—a downtown four-level interchange connecting the Harbor, Pasadena, Hollywood, and Santa Ana freeways—was completed. Its image, plastered across postcards and magazine covers, became Los Angeles' most famous symbol.

Post-recession Los Angeles continued to develop with optimism during the 1960s—

The Capitol Records Tower on Hollywood Boulevard was the first round office building erected in America. Photo by Joseph Sohm/ Chromosohm

vide subterranean parking for cars. Los Angeles' apartment boom reached its peak during the late 1950s, when onslaughts of middle-class immigrants poured into the city.

The city's architectural golden age dawned in the 1950s, too, when futuristic modernism prevailed: brightly lit and plastic-coated supermarkets, neon gas stations, highly polished offices, streamlined bowling alleys, and science-fiction car washes lined every street. The Capitol Records Building in Hollywood (resembling a stack of records) and the Watts Towers (Simon Rodia's glass-and-pottery obelisks) were constructed at this time. "Case study houses," like the Eames and Entenza residences in Pacific Palisades, were experimental designs for simple living, erected by Los Angeles' best architects: Richard Neutra, Eero Saarinen, Charles Eames, Raphael Sorieno, and Pierre Koenig. The modest California ranch-style house became popular, too. Architect Cliff May designed over 1,000 variations of the ranch house for Angelenos during the 1950s and 1960s.

Meanwhile, as Los Angeles suburbs blossomed, the Pacific Electric interurban system shriveled. The last Big Red Car stopped

more jobs, more people, more growth. A bright future for the burgeoning international city lay ahead. Downtown was being renovated: startling new edifices like the Bonaventure Hotel, the twin Arco Towers, and the red granite Crocker Center Complex arose, looking streamlined and futuristic, replaced their glass-box predecessors. The Dorothy Chandler Pavilion, a neo-classical music center, was completed in 1969 at Bunker Hill, a downtown area being fiercely redeveloped. Other monumental buildings were born: the J. Paul Getty Museum in Malibu, resembling the Villa del Papyri, a sprawling Roman villa buried in the Mount Vesuvius eruption of A.D. 79; and the Crystal Cathedral in Garden Grove, an awe-inspiring glass-and-cement vision by Philip Johnson and John Burges.

Century City, a cluster of office towers built between Beverly Hills and Westwood in 1965 to relieve freeway pressure, quickly

Above: Signs of the times, graffiti and traffic symbols merge. The task of getting around town is such an integral part of L.A. life that radio stations warn of traffic tie-ups, and best-selling books offer shortcuts. Photo by Joseph Sohm/ Chromosohm

Left: Even the apartment complexes on Sunset Boulevard reflect the area's flair for colorful geometry. Photo by Bob Rowan/Progressive Image

THE SINGULAR FRANK GEHRY
Building without Boundaries

"If you try to understand my work on the basis of . . . order, structural integrity, and formalized definitions of beauty, you are apt to be totally confused."
—*Frank Gehry*

The year was 1978. The place was a quiet corner lot at 22nd Street and Washington Avenue in Santa Monica. Someone had transformed a 1920s Dutch colonial house into a mishmash of chicken-wire, glass, aqua-painted concrete, chain-link fencing, and crooked windows. "A masterpiece," exclaimed the mayor of Santa Monica. "The most daring alteration of an ordinary suburban house any architect has yet attempted," said the *New York Times*. "A monstrosity," claimed a next-door neighbor.

The mastermind of this bizarre transformation was Frank Gehry, the most controversial, talked-about architect in the West. His works have been analyzed, criticized, and apotheosized throughout the world. His buildings have been copied, case-studied, and reviewed. He has received 65 merit awards, citations, design awards, fellowships, and honorary doctoral degrees since 1967. He has won the Pritzker Prize, architecture's most coveted award. And Frank Gehry continues to be one of America's most controversial and admired architects. Why?

In 1962 Frank Gehry set up office in Los Angeles. His first two projects, the Steeves House in Brentwood (a Frank Lloyd Wright-inspired ranch) and the Hillcrest Apartments in Santa Monica, were conventional—in Frank Gehry terms. But by 1964 Gehry's work showed signs of defiant originality. At a time when most Los Angeles architects were happy building reproduction-Spanish villas and mock-Art Deco apartments, Gehry was designing a bold geometric "fortress" on Melrose Avenue. The Danzinger Studio and Residence featured high ceilings, cleresto-ry windows, and spacious living areas behind a double-walled stucco enclosure. It was unlike any other building on the block.

In 1968 Gehry created the O'Neill Hay Barn in San Juan Capistrano. It was a rakish structure built from telephone poles and corrugated metal, inspired by Northwest Indian architecture.

Many of Gehry's earliest clients were artists and art patrons who, like Gehry, spurned conventional approaches to life—and to its buildings. The clients liked Gehry's creativity and his obliviousness to architectural tradition. They appreciated his use of cheap materials like cardboard, fiberglass, polyester, raw plywood, cement, and corrugated metal to create unique forms and keep costs low. "The whole idea of doing houses for rich people was just abhorrent to me," said Gehry.

In 1968 Gehry designed the Ron Davis House in Malibu for abstract painter Ron Davis. It was a unique work of art—a corrugated metal trapezoid Shangri-la, employing tricks of perspective taken from Davis' own abstract paintings. Construction elements were left exposed. "Buildings under construction look nicer than buildings finished," Gehry said.

In 1972 Gehry was hired by the Rouse Company, (developers of Boston's Faneuil Hall) to create a 9-acre, $50-million shopping mall in Santa Monica. Santa Monica Place became a three-tiered, 163-store quadrangle of light, ocean, and sky. To interact with the sea horizon four blocks away, Gehry kept building height low and colors muted.

Then in 1976 Gehry's style changed oh-so-slightly. While remodelling a Malibu beachside guest house and gallery for multimillionaire art collector and industrialist Norton Simon, Gehry introduced expensive materials (like rose-hued marble for the bathrooms and teak for the stairs) to his trademark cheap elements (like plywood and tree trunks). The results were casual yet impeccable living quarters and a display center for some of the world's most priceless objets d'art. A wall-length window of glass exposed a 180-degree view of the ocean. A trellis angled dangerously across the roof appears about to collapse. "The soft stuff, the pretty stuff . . . puts me off because it seems unreal," Gehry once said.

But of all Gehry's creations, the Dutch colonial on 22nd Street gained him most notoriety. "I tried to make it more important," Gehry later explained. Indeed, he made it legendary.

Before its conversion, the house was a salmon-pink gambrel-roofed bungalow, peacefully occupied by Gehry and his family. But by 1978 the architect had begun a sophisticated, shocking, and controversial transformation of the place he called home. He stripped interior walls, exposing lath and 2x4 framing; knocked out a ceiling over the master bedroom "for a treehouse effect"; and paved the kitchen floor with asphalt. He created chicken-wire cupboards. He placed a 42-foot corrugated metal wall along the house's 22nd Street exterior, and hung a chain link fence sculpture from the second-floor terrace. "The structure looks like no house ever seen before," babbled the *Los Angeles Times*. Neighbors, art afficionados, paparazzi, and political notables flocked to the house. Everyone had to see.

Few who were invited inside the unusual domicile came away unimpressed. Frank Gehry had managed to open up the house's 3,750-square-foot interior by eliminating walls and interweaving architectural elements. Suddenly the house seemed alive, larger, brighter, and definitely "more important."

In 1979 Gehry designed a museum *Art in America* called "an iconoclastic new design unlike other aquariums or natural history museums." The Cabrillo Marine Museum, a 20,000-square-foot compound near the San Pedro beach, was Gehry's salute to the ocean. He combined indoor and outdoor exhibit areas within a fence-linked marine village, and sheltered open air tidal pools beneath a spectacularly layered fan-shaped cage. And he did it cheap. While taking a tour of the newly opened facilities, an astonished Mayor Tom Bradley asked the curator, "You got all this for under $3 million?"

By the early 1980s Frank Gehry was receiving numerous, eclectic commissions. He approached each one with wit and innovation. When asked to build the Benson Home in 1981, Gehry consulted the client's children. From their design input, Gehry created two buildings—one tall and brown, the other small and blue. The buildings were crowned with a treetop fortress and encircled by a moat. Drawbridges connected one to the other.

The "Other Frank" (Frank Lloyd Wright) established himself as a brilliant architect through the use of repetitious forms and elaborated motifs. But Frank Gehry considers himself the "Anti-Wright." Gehry's best work—according to Gehry—is episodic and fragmented, a chaotic collision of materials.

The transformation of a Santa Monica Dutch colonial house into a Frank Gehry original has sparked mixed reviews. Photo by Larry Molmud

Whereas Frank Lloyd Wright's designs were predictable and stable, Frank Gehry's are dissonant and contradictory. That's how life is, Gehry explains. That's how people are.

In 1984 Gehry was asked to make a building fly. He was given an old armory building in a rundown part of town, and told to build the California Aerospace Museum. The result was a seven-sided polygon cantilevered rakishly over the street. Inside, like Saturnine rings, three spiralling platforms overlook an 80-foot high exhibition space. Outside, a curvy ramp sweeps from the sidewalk into the museum's flying-saucer entrance. A Lockheed F-104 *Starfighter* dangles precariously above the museum's exterior.

Gehry's most recent creations in-

clude Los Angeles' Temporary Contemporary Museum; a museum complex on Santa Monica's Main Street; and Rebecca's, a $1.5-million Mexican *nouvelle cuisine* restaurant in Venice featuring formica-chip alligator and octopus chandeliers. In 1988 Gehry was unanimously chosen by the 10-member Disney Hall Committee to create the $100-million Walt Disney Concert Hall on Bunker Hill, the future home of the Los Angeles Philharmonic.

After 40 years of practice, Gehry continues to shatter common perceptions and architectural myths. He is a major force in American architecture, and is inspiring new architects by his example to pursue impossible dreams. Gehry's proven they're not so impossible.
—*Susan Vaughn*

emerged as a powerful financial center. Burbank, Pasadena, Santa Monica, Brentwood, West Los Angeles, Sherman Oaks, and Long Beach also experienced unprecedented commercial building booms. Suburbia was becoming metropolitan.

Minimalism and whim, strained geometry and perverted materials became buzzwords for suburban commercial design during the 1970s. "The Blue Whale," the huge cobalt-blue Pacific Design Center in West Hollywood, was built to resemble a leviathan ship. Innovator Frank Gehry created the Loyola Law School Building as a galvanized steel-and-brick abstract art design. Gehry further shocked Angelenos in 1978 when he redesigned a Santa Monica house on Washington Street out of a mishmash of corrugated sheet metal, chain link fencing, asphalt, plywood, and studs. Then in 1983 he reconstructed Los Angeles' Temporary Contemporary Art Museum from a downtown municipal garage. "Unstructured structure construction"—the mingling of formal and informal space—overtook Los Angeles architecture.

The 1970s brought even more diversity and excitement to Los Angeles as the immigrant population increased 49 percent during the decade, compared with less than 10 percent in the 1960s. Eighty percent of the newcomers hailed from Asia and Latin America. The Latino population doubled and the Asian population tripled, while Los An-

LANDMARK ACHIEVEMENTS
Preserving the City's Past

Contrary to Los Angeles' image as a city indifferent to its past, Angelenos are serious about their cultural and historical landmarks. Consider that in 1962 Los Angeles pioneered one of the nation's first preservation ordinances and established a trendsetting Cultural Heritage Board that certified individual landmarks rather than entire neighborhoods. Thirty years ago the concept of protecting individual buildings was a new idea, says lawyer and architectural historian David Cameron.

Today the five-member Los Angeles Cultural Heritage Commission and the Los Angeles Conservancy, a private non-profit preservation group, work to keep a permanent record of the city's architectural and historic past. The Conservancy, founded in 1978, is the strongest citizens' preservation group in the Western United States. Among their more than 500 volunteers are architects, planners, and 120 docents who lead 10 regularly scheduled walking tours and a number of special architectural tours. Conservancy volunteers also man the popular film series, *Last Remaining Seats*, held each June in downtown Los Angeles at the world's largest assemblage of historic movie houses.

"When I talk with members of preservation organizations in other parts of the country, they're always impressed with the amount of involvement we have from volunteers," says Jay Rounds, executive director of the Conservancy.

"There are two strongly developed groups among our membership," Rounds explains. "One is native Angelenos whose involvement has to do with nostalgia and the memory of the way the city was in their youth. On the other hand, we have a strong group of membership among young people, many of whom are new in the city. For them, membership is a way of putting down roots and developing a sense of connection and participation in the community."

While Conservancy volunteers learn about and show off Los Angeles, the Conservancy's primary mission is to support neighborhood preservation groups and to preserve individual landmarks. As laws now stand, if a property owner is determined to tear down a monument, landmark status and environmental review only buy time for negotiation. Nevertheless, time may be all that is needed to save an important landmark.

Though Hangar 1 at Los Angeles International Airport was declared a cultural/historical monument in 1966, the hangar would have been demolished if preservationists had not had the means to delay demolition. The Spanish Colonial Revival-style building, constructed in 1929, is the city's only link with Mines Field, L.A.'s first airport. Mines Field, today Los Angeles International Airport (LAX), was a dusty landing strip in the midst of rows of beans and barley when Mary Pickford, America's sweetheart, dedicated the hangar.

Its history is woven into Los Angeles' past. Soon after Hangar 1 was dedicated, the German dirigible *Graf Zeppelin* anchored on the hangar's tarmac. Charles Lindbergh used the hangar during the National Air Races. And actor Jimmy Stewart kept his Stinson biplane in it from 1929 to 1935. Later the hangar was used by scores of tenants, including its first tenant, the Curtis-Wright Flying School, and Los Angeles Airways, a helicopter service.

Nevertheless, by the mid-1970s most thought the hangar's days of usefulness were gone forever. The two-story brick and concrete building was padlocked because it did not meet the city's earthquake specifications. By 1981 the Board

geles' total population grew by 1.8 million between 1960 and 1970. Almost 33 percent of Angelenos were immigrants.

The influx of foreign money, consumers, and workers enabled old-time shopping districts like Westwood Village and Main Street in Santa Monica to be transformed into trendy retail areas during the 1970s. Huge postmodern shopping centers like the Beverly Center at Beverly and La Cienega boulevards and the Westside Pavilion at Pico and Overland boulevards were completed. Minimalls sprouted at busy intersections.

During the 1980s more malls sprang up, requiring seas of parking space. Old mansions were demolished; homes by Greene & Greene, Irving Gill, R.M. Schindler, and

Richard Neutra were razed. Architectural landmarks like the Brown Derby and the Art Deco Richfield Office Tower were leveled so that condominiums and multi-unit apartment complexes could be built on the land. Los Angeles was "urbanizing." Its freeway system now spanned 700 miles, and 7 million cars vied in its lanes. Rush hour expanded, traffic spilled onto local streets. Roadways were widened, sidewalks were narrowed. Neighborhood ambience began to suffer. The city built by the automobile was being conquered by it.

But planning in the late 1980s stopped the cycle. Drastic action was taken. Industries relocated to Los Angeles' suburbs, closer to workers' homes, where taxes were lower

of Airport Commissioners had decided to bulldoze Hangar 1 to make room for a new cargo facility. Realizing that the landmark building was threatened, the Conservancy stepped in.

"It was a classic preservation case," says Ruthann Lehrer, then executive director of the Conservancy and now preservation officer for the City of Long Beach. "The Conservancy received a routine notice from the Department of Airports of an intent to demolish Hangar 1. The airport felt an environmental review was not warranted because demolition would not have a significant impact. They saw Hangar 1 as a cargo facility. We said, 'This action is illegal. You have to do an Environmental Impact Report and evaluate alternatives to demolition in the study.' They agreed. At that point we knew we had to find a user for the building."

The Conservancy launched a media and public relations campaign both to pressure the airport not to demolish the building and to find an alternate use for it. That's when Bryan Cochran, vice president and West Coast principal of Texas-based AVIA Development Group, saw an article about the hangar in the Conservancy newsletter.

The fit was perfect. Cochran was the developer who could put together the financing, design, approvals, construction,

and management. Moreover, his interest in preserving a piece of Los Angeles history welled from two sources—lifelong passions for preservation and for the aviation industry. Cochran's father had worked for Continental and Cochran had flown for Braniff.

After negotiations between airport management officials, city officials, and the Conservancy, Hangar 1's restoration was assured. The hangar cost about $120 a square foot to restore, but costs were balanced by two new adjacent cargo buildings built at $40 a square foot. Hanger 1's $2-million renovation preserves the integrity of the original building down to the paint color. The hangar, too small for modern planes, will be used for offices and as a warehouse for cargo.

During a tour of the building, Bryan Cochran looks at the airport from the tower in Hangar 1, and over the roar of jets remarks with satisfaction that the view of the airport beats an ocean view every time. Looking back, however, he says the job was a difficult one. "It's been an uphill battle for five years. During the early days of construction I hated to hear the phone ring. I knew it was going to be another problem."

Cochran did not expect the project to uncover Los Angeles' underground aviation history. But as construction pro-

gressed, he came upon seven underground storage tanks for fueling planes and a quarter-million rounds of expended 30-millimeter ammunition that had been fired from an airplane into a test cell and buried in an underground vault. These had to be removed, along with layers of asphalt, concrete paving, tons of asbestos, and about a thousand tons of contaminated soil.

"We hung in because we believe the Los Angeles market is phenomenally strong for air cargo requirements," Cochran remarks. "We knew we'd be rewarded long-term with pride in doing Hangar 1, and economically the project was cost-effective as a total package."

Hangar 1 is a perfect example of the goals set forth in a statement by the Los Angeles Cultural Heritage Commission. Preservation is "not for the purpose of living in the past, but for keeping a permanent record of historic, cultural, aesthetically beautiful, or architecturally important sites . . . The Cultural Heritage Commission endeavors to preserve certain structures and makes an effort to blend them with the modern environment. It is hoped that important works being created today may also be preserved for posterity, so that future generations will have a chronological 'living' record of the beauty and history of their surroundings." —*Ellen Hoffs*

and land was more available. Radical transportation alternatives, like corporate shuttles, park-n-ride stations, and city-sponsored van pools, were implemented.

Today Los Angeles County has four of North America's five busiest freeways. Eight million vehicles maneuver its roads each day. More Angelenos carpool, and downtown businesses shuttle their employees to work every day in comfortable vans. RTD and local bus lines have increased their routes and schedules. Beginning in 1993, a $3.5-billion Metrorail service will move commuters from downtown, through Hollywood, and to the San Fernando Valley—a 155-mile course—using streetcars and subways.

City planners are also considering multimodal transportation for the future—double-deck trains and monorails, powered by methanol, hydrogen, and electricity; deregulated taxi service; community van pools; and more. They will eventually serve all major business centers, campuses, airports, harbors, large shopping centers, and entertainment and sports complexes.

The 1990s will be the decade of historic preservation for Los Angeles. Organizations like the Los Angeles Conservancy, Hollywood Heritage, and Pasadena Heritage are saving many old favorites, including the Wiltern Theater, the Biltmore and Roosevelt hotels, and the modern Pan Pacific Auditorium, as well as scores of downtown neo-classical office buildings. Historic landmarks like Farmers Market (1934), an open-air multiethnic shopping center in Los Angeles' historic Fairfax district, are being salvaged, even as multiuse complexes and apartment buildings spring up at their perimeters.

Los Angeles' downtown is still a large urban village core, though it holds only 8 percent of the city's total office space and 3 percent of its jobs. Within its four square miles different worlds are forming: a Latino shopping district along Broadway—the busiest shopping district west of Chicago—Little Tokyo, a revitalized Skid Row, the Garment District, a wholesale flower mart, and a growing Soho-like artists' colony. Corporations are enhancing their images by erecting playful,

Night falls over the Harbor Freeway. Photo by Joseph Sohm/Chromosohm

uniquely designed buildings. Upscale shops, apartments, condos, and hotels are being built—an additional 10 to 25 million square feet of office space is being added by 1995. City planners envision the new downtown as a garden city with meandering bridges, walkways, and alleys connecting courtyards of southwestern design. Foreign investments are providing additional capital to make these new projects possible.

It is estimated that by the year 2010 Los Angeles will contain some 18 million people. What will the future hold for this supercity of the twenty-first century? Will it be a megalopolis of interconnected townships, gleaming clean-fueled buses and monorails, and grassy parks . . . or will it be an endless urban sprawl of gnarled highways and littered cement plains?

Architects and engineers, planners and visionaries see the future in bold new concepts. "There are positive possibilities and potential nightmare scenarios," says Kate Diamond, AIA, a partner at Siegel and Diamond Architects in West Los Angeles. Diamond envisions a network of "highly dense urban cores" connected by smoothly functioning mass transit systems. Citizens of twenty-first century L.A. would be able to shop, dine, attend recreational events, and work only blocks from their homes.

"One of the errors we made in the past was to create a linear city of low-density, one-story commercial buildings," says Dia-

"THE DIVINITY OF FAITH ITSELF"
CICERO

City Hall is flanked by the Southland's omnipresent palms on a clear and sunny day downtown. Photo by Joseph Sohm/Chromosohm

mond. "Commercial buildings thrive with high density. That's why the malls have killed many of our well-established streets. The streets of the future could be thinner. They could have offices on top of shops, and housing on top of offices. The density would make the streets into vibrant places."

Diamond mentions Playa Vista, a Los Angeles community currently under development, as a realization of this dream. Just miles from the Los Angeles International Airport, Playa Vista will be a mixed-use community of attractive buildings and storefronts, pedestrian walkways, and green public parks. It will be completed by the year 2000.

Others offer even more sweeping visions for the future. Rob Kennard, FAIA, president of the Kennard Design Group in Los Angeles, says that transportation will remain one of the city's most urgent problems. He believes that alternative modes of transportation should be implemented to replace the automobile in Los Angeles, and further suggests that L.A.'s world-famous freeways be converted into "green links" between urban centers. "I like the way L.A. is set up, but its connections are bad," says Kennard. "They could certainly be improved, and in such a way that people enjoy seeing and using them."

Landscaping will pose another hurdle for the ever-expanding megalopolis of Los Angeles. Will a cement ocean blanket its cityscape? Will grass, shrubs, and trees be visible only at suburban botanical gardens? Rob Kennard thinks the greening of Los Angeles should be a top priority as the twenty-first century nears. "People should be able to walk through the city, to enjoy themselves, and enjoy the greenery," says Kennard. "Look at Washington, D.C., the Champs Elysees. Their architecture is pretty nondescript, but their streetscape—the landscaping, the trees, the spaces between the buildings—is outstanding. I'd like to see a lot more greenery in Los Angeles."

The future of Los Angeles may be predicated on its resource management. Ronald Altoon, president of the American Institute of Architecture, Los Angeles chapter, and partner of Altoon & Porter in the Mid-Wilshire district, wonders aloud: Will the city be able to supply water to its exploding population? Offer fast and efficient public transportation? Absorb the immense cultural diversity which may one day transform Los Angeles into the most international city in the world?

"Here in Los Angeles, we have been able to free ourselves from the social restraints that pervade other cities, particularly in the East and Europe," says Altoon. "We can explore, and experience, and perceive in ways that are startling to our colleagues in other parts of the country. This is because we are so tolerant and progressive a city."

Michael Rotundi, AIA, partner at Morphosis and founder of the Southern California Institute of Architecture in Santa Monica, believes that the answer to Los Angeles' cultural integration problem is already visible in the streets of contemporary East Los Angeles. "Here, everyone of all cultures lives in one place. On the East Side, people coexist. They're tolerant of each other's differences. They're accepting. The East Side is an exciting place to be, and I think that as the city becomes denser, we'll see more cross-cultural integration like what's already happened here."

Rotundi further hopes that L.A.'s communities of the future retain their individuality. "They have to be developed by the people who live in them," explains Rotundi. "If this came to be, each community would be completely different from another, because each would developed by its own members, and not by some centralized group within the city."

By the year 2000 Los Angeles will be the most populous city in America. Its developed territory will expand southeast to Orange County and eastward to San Bernardino and Riverside counties. Real estate values will continue to rise; old townships and industrial complexes will be renovated. Historic buildings will be restored "as was." The city will remain the prime port of entry for new immigrants. No one group will dominate; no urban center will prevail. Instead, people and regions will blend. Los Angeles' future, like its past, will be shaped by innovation, partnership, diversity, and a blending of old and new.

"There is a potential for a fabulous city," says Kate Diamond. "We are still amazingly undeveloped. This is just our second growth. Cities in Europe and the East Coast have already gone through this round, where the small-scale is torn down, and the larger scale is put up. Bigger things are needed to suit the next generation's needs. It's not an easy task."

But Los Angeles' architects have already established themselves as the most innovative and iconoclastic in the United States. Theirs will be a most difficult job—creating breathtaking styles, manipulating space to solve social and cultural problems, while adding their own personal signatures to the collective consciousness of the Los Angeles cityscape. Currently Los Angeles architectural innovations are being scrutinized worldwide. By the year 2000, the city may very well be recognized as one of the world's great architectural design capitals. According to Ronald Altoon, its unusual character will make this come true.

"We are a creative city—the movie industry is here, the art community is here, aerospace and technology are here. We can do it better and we can do it different. And we can do it just to be brash. It's a fever that exists here. It's like no other city: Los Angeles is an environment that allows choices."

BEHIND THE SCENES

Services and Spirit

Los Angeles is a sprawling 465-square-mile kaleidoscope of unique neighborhoods. Amazingly, the city works as a whole. Streets are cleaned. Garbage is collected. Even the notorious traffic tie-ups are cleared. To keep the governmental machine running, Los Angeles employs some 40,000 city workers, from council members to traffic coordinators, who provide a host of interrelated services.

"For all its power and wealth and contrasting poverty and powerlessness, for all its size and complexity, Los Angeles is a strongly non-arrogant community, willing to shift and re-examine its problems, indeed its fundamental premises."

—Kevin Starr, Los Angeles 2000 report, 1988

Three times a week at 10 a.m., Mayor Tom Bradley and the 15-member City Council, elected every four years, meet in the council chamber in downtown City Hall. With an annual budget of close to $3.7 billion, they work to iron out the city's far-flung problems. However, Angelenos needn't travel all the way downtown to keep up-to-date on city government. Council meetings are accessible by way of cable television, and citizens can call the City Council Minute Clerk to find out when specific items are scheduled to be discussed by the council.

Since downtown City Hall may be far from the area represented by a council member, each council member has at least one field office to attend to the needs of constituents. Also, area coordinators

Each Christmas, nearly 5,000 free dinners are served to Los Angeles' homeless population by resident volunteers. Photo by Joseph Sohm/Chromosohm

B y   E l l e n   H o f f s

represent the mayor in six different parts of the city. One coordinator covers the West Los Angeles and Pacific Palisades area; a second is in South-Central Los Angeles; a third covers Hollywood to Venice, Mar Vista to Westchester, Playa del Rey to the Marina, and Hancock Park; a fourth represents San Pedro to Wilmington; a fifth, East Los Angeles to Los Feliz; and the sixth is in the San Fernando Valley.

The city supplies many services that most citizens are not aware of or may take for granted. The Los Angeles City Attorney Officer Hearing Program helps unclog the court system by handling disputes in a nonadversarial manner. Residents can pay traffic fines at three branch city halls located in West Los Angeles, Van Nuys, and San Pedro. Minor complaints such as those involving abandoned cars or potholes are handled quickly by state-of-the-art citizen hot lines. During flood emergencies, local fire departments provide residents with free sandbags.

The next layer of government is the region's five-member Los Angeles County Board of Supervisors. In 1990 Los Angeles County's budget exceeded $10.8 billion, and the county employed more than 75,000 people. For over 100 years Los Angeles County's vast 4,083 square miles has been divided into five supervisorial districts. Today each supervisor represents 1.5 million people, three times as many as served by a Southern California congressional representative.

In 1990, in response to a lawsuit, a judge ordered the county to redraw the supervisorial districts to better represent the Latinos who now make up one third of the county's population. In a special election held in February 1991, citizens elected the county's first Latina supervisor, Gloria Molina.

In addition to its vast constituency within the county, the Board of Supervisors governs about 1.5 million residents who live on unincorporated land. And it offers services, by contract, to the 88 independent cities located within the county. Los Angeles, which is largely self-sufficient, is the largest of those cities. Yet it contracts with the county for health services and enforcement of health ordinances such as restaurant codes. The county provides the city with lifeguard services and maintenance of traffic signals as well.

Proposition 13, the tax revolt initiative Californians overwhelmingly passed in 1978, profoundly affected county services. The county lost 60 percent of its chief source of revenue because of lower property taxes. State government replaced about 75 percent of the loss, and county government scrambled to find creative ways to save money. For example, duplicate departments were eliminated. The 53 departments operated by the county at the beginning of the decade have now been reduced to 39. Also, the county doubled court sessions, using existing courthouses at night to handle the increasing caseload.

One of the most successful cost-reduction programs was the privatization of some county services. The same year that citizens passed Proposition 13, Los Angeles County voters approved Proposition A, the county charter amendment which allowed the county to contract work out to nongovernment contractors who could do the work for a lower price. By June 1990 the county had about 428 active contracts. Analysts estimate that since the program began the county has saved $250 million.

In spite of Proposition 13, neither the city nor the county has scrimped on funds to improve traffic control. Before the 1984 Los Angeles Olympics, the Los Angeles Department of Transportation buried 400 special six-foot octagonal traffic sensors inches below the surface of the street at 118 traffic signals near the Los Angeles Memorial Coliseum. The sensors have helped gather a historical data base that forecasts what will happen to the volume and pattern of traffic before and after a big game, a rock concert, or the five o'clock rush hour. Traffic management becomes especially critical during major events such as the annual USC/UCLA football game, which draws close to 100,000 fans.

Los Angeles' state-of-the-art Automated Traffic Surveillance and Control (ATSAC) system is located five floors underground in the basement of City Hall East in downtown Los Angeles. The system has the potential to move traffic with 36 different traffic timing schedules. Since about 95 percent of the traffic signal possibilities are programmed into the system, it almost runs itself. Still, ATSAC's computer-filled room is surprisingly simple, considering the gargantuan task the system manages.

At the control center ATSAC experts observe 25-inch color monitors. Data is pulsed

when there are fewer than 200 cars per lane, green for 200 to 500 cars, and pink for 500 to 800. A red light flashes when more than 800 cars fill the road. Another computer records the second-by-second operation of selected signals. And a master computer logs everything that happens in the system.

The room is quiet except for an occasional subtle beeping sound. The beep occurs each time an important message is relayed to the system. ATSAC experts come

On Earth Day, Los Angeles Mayor Tom Bradley and hundreds of concerned citizens gathered to launch an impressive inner-city cleanup campaign. Photo by Joseph Sohm/Chromosohm

in from traffic sensors buried in the streets, as well as from three closed-circuit color television cameras located on the roof of City Hall South, on top of the Jewelry Center near Pershing Square, and at Patriotic Hall near Flower Street and Washington Boulevard.

Pictures from the television monitors and traffic data pulsed in from the traffic sensors are translated into brilliant color on graphic display screens. The graphics are easy to read and more lively than the map boards that traffic analysts used before the advent of computer-generated displays. One square-shaped graphic on the monitor represents the number of cars traveling hourly in each traffic lane. The square turns light blue

to the rescue if the beep signals a significant problem, such as a power failure or a green light signaling simultaneously in two directions instead of one. In any case, the system always records the problem and eventually solves it.

Currently, ATSAC guides traffic in about 18 percent of the city. Included are areas around the Coliseum, the downtown Civic Center, the Ventura Boulevard Corridor in the San Fernando Valley, Los Angeles International Airport, and Westwood. Engineers hope that by 1997 all 4,000 traffic signals in the city will be connected to the system.

The California Department of Transportation (Caltrans) takes over the responsibility

GETTING THERE
The Future of Transportation

F or a city already struggling with smog, traffic congestion, and a stubborn attachment to the automobile, transportation is one of the most critical issues facing Los Angeles today. Indeed, future mobility poses such an acute challenge that dozens of experts in urban transportation have been hard at work on plans to tame the monster.

The cumulative result of one organized effort—five years in preparation and based on information culled from 66 different studies—is the inch-thick Regional Mobility Plan of the Southern California Association of Governments (SCAG), which represents 175 municipal governments in six counties.

SCAG's findings and recommendations range over a 25-year period, from 1984, when the work began, to the projected transportation scene in the year 2010. SCAG predicts that for every 1,000 vehicles in use in 1984, there will be 1,420 on the road in 2010. If the crush is allowed to build unattended, daily personal trips will soar from 40.2 million to 57 million, and work commutes from 7.3 million to 10.3 million.

"The region's highways and streets—many of which have already reached saturation levels during peak commuting hours—will have to cope with the vehicles of new residents, as well as the increased freight traffic that serves consumer needs and the region's economy," the plan states. "If nothing is done to improve the transportation system, by 2010 these additional trips may bring traffic to a near halt on much of the system for much of the day."

The eventual success of the Regional Mobility Plan depends largely on public cooperation, and transportation officials have long been trying to pry commuters loose from their beloved cars. Ralph J. Cipriani, one of the main architects of the plan, doesn't feel local drivers are being selfish or uncooperative in clinging to their wheels. He compared trans-

Above and facing page: **New subway lines currently under construction in Los Angeles will soon carry 300,000 people daily at speeds of up to 70 m.p.h. Photos by Shelley Gazin**

Left: **Smog Alerts are rare in Los Angeles nowadays. EPA's stringent requirements for automobile emissions have assured better air and more efficient fuel conversion.**

portation in New York City and Los Angeles to illustrate his point:

"Everything in New York City is close and easily accessible by subway or bus, and parking is impossible, so you don't need a car, anyway. In Los Angeles, distances are great, there's been no subway, bus service is sketchy, freeways take you everywhere, and there's plenty of parking, much of it free. In New York, you just naturally take the subway; in L.A., you really do need a car. Under these circumstances, it isn't surprising that this is a car-oriented society."

However, Los Angeles eventually will have its own subway—and, in fact, construction is already under way on the first phases of what is by far the biggest, costliest, and most ambitious transit project in the city's history.

The new Metro Red Line subway is being built in three segments totaling 17.4 miles, with 16 stations as it links downtown Los Angeles with the San Fernando Valley. Work is currently in progress on the first section, a 4.4-mile route which will run from Union Station to Wilshire/Alvarado, and is scheduled to open in late 1993.

Another segment, covering 6.7 miles and due for completion in 1996, will extend from Wilshire/Alvarado to the legendary corner of Hollywood and Vine in Hollywood. The third segment, to be completed shortly after the year 2000, will carry the subway another 6.3 miles to Universal City and North Hollywood.

The Rail Construction Corporation, a subsidiary of the Los Angeles County Transportation Commission, estimates that the new subway line eventually will carry 300,000 passengers daily, and that one six-car train will eliminate the equivalent of 28 crowded buses or 500 cars from city streets. With an exclusive underground right-of-way free of traffic and pedestrians, Red Line trains will whisk passengers at speeds of up to 70 miles per hour from Union Station to the final stop in the Valley in a total running time of 28 minutes.

The surface phase of the overall regional transit program is built around a nucleus of five commuter light-rail lines linking South Orange County, Saugus, Ventura/Oxnard, and San Bernardino to Los Angeles, and San Bernardino/Riverside to Orange County. A feeder network of buses and vans serving regional park-n-ride facilities, and a local bus and paratransit network will complete the system.

The first segment of the surface rail system is already in operation, and it has been a rousing success. The 22-mile Los Angeles-Long Beach Blue Line opened in July 1990 with a projected daily ridership of 5,000. It was soon carrying 18,000 commuters a day. For older residents the Blue Line brought back fond memories of the wonderful Red Cars that stopped running in the 1950s. Most important, the rail system's success clearly indicates that commuters are eager for alternate transportation when it is available. Officials predict that this line alone will be carrying 54,000 riders per day by the year 2000.

Another light rail line is also under construction at this time. The 20-mile Green Line will intersect the Blue Line and run down the middle of the new I-105 (Glenn Anderson Freeway, formerly called the Century Freeway). It will extend from Norwalk to El Segundo and the Los Angeles International Airport, with opening scheduled for the fall of 1994. The County Transportation Commission projects total daily ridership on other rail transit systems to exceed 500,000 as early as 2010.

Even with wholesale acceptance of the rail transit system, an intensive, ongoing campaign to encourage car pooling will be needed to offset the increasing number of vehicles as the population grows by an estimated 5 million by 2010.

Already functioning to promote car pooling is the South Coast Air Quality District's Regulation XV, under which public and private employers with 100 or more employees offer incentives to encourage ride-sharing. The ultimate goal is to increase ride-sharing to 1.6 million daily trips.

One of the revolutionary benefits of the computer age is that many office jobs that once had to be performed in the workplace can now be done elsewhere. The SCAG plan estimates that three million daily work trips can be eliminated through work-at-home assignments and telecommunications.

Although clearly the most visible culprit in the traffic mess, the automobile shouldn't be given all the blame. The Regional Mobility Plan lists several improvements in road management that it claims would eliminate 800,000 hours of daily traffic delay. They include increased ramp metering, improved placement and coordination of traffic signals at key intersections, and more efficient response to traffic accidents.

Trucks have long contributed to both traffic congestion and pollution, and inevitably their numbers will increase with population growth. The plan recommends broader use of intermodal services, routes and schedules away from peak hours, and the coordination of various municipal regulations to improve movement and access, especially at main shipping centers where trucks must concentrate.

The SCAG plan also proposes that local governments review their zoning laws and work with developers to provide affordable housing near employment centers.

The unequivocal message in all this is that it will take an army numbering in the millions to battle the area's transportation problems. The rank and file of this volunteer force will be comprised largely of ordinary citizens willing to share rides, use transit facilities, and pay the gasoline and sales taxes needed to improve our transportation systems.

No other region offers its people such an abundance of attractions, pleasures, and opportunities. Ultimately, it will be up to the people who enjoy these riches to make sure they can still get to them. —*Charles F. Queenan*

for traffic when Angelenos drive onto highways and freeways. Closed-circuit television cameras at Caltrans Traffic Operations Center (TOC) monitor accidents in areas of heaviest traffic: a segment of the Santa Monica Freeway, the four-level interchange in downtown Los Angeles, the East Los Angeles interchange, and the portion of the Hollywood Freeway that feeds into downtown. Eventually Caltrans plans to install 400 closed-circuit cameras throughout California's freeway system.

For the first time since the 1984 Los Angeles Olympics, governmental agencies are working together on a state-of-the-art method of traffic management that promises to help ease L.A.'s traffic congestion in the future. The Smart Corridor Demonstration Project, devel-

oped by the Los Angeles County Transportation Commission, is scheduled to begin in the spring of 1993 and is estimated to cost about $50 million. New computer software will automatically consolidate information generated by six principal agencies. The central data base will be located at the main Smart Corridor station at Caltrans Traffic Operations Center in downtown Los Angeles.

To demonstrate the project's technology and team approach, the participating agencies have chosen a specific corridor of the Santa Monica Freeway (I-10). The heavily traveled corridor stretches from the East Los Angeles interchange to Centinela Boulevard, west of the San Diego Freeway (I-405), and includes five streets that parallel the freeway. A traffic control operator will analyze com-

puter suggestions and make choices about how to manage traffic best. Advice about which streets to take will be available on message signs located on the freeway and surface streets.

Los Angeles will need the help of the new system. Analysts predict that by the year 2000 the city's licensed drivers will increase by 32 percent, and there is likely to be a 41 percent increase in vehicle miles traveled. The South Coast Air Quality Management District (AQMD) estimates that the region's population will grow from 12 million to 18 million by the year 2010.

By then the region may be using some of the cleaner technologies being developed by the AQMD. State law requires the AQMD to design more vigorous air quality control plans in Southern California than in the rest of the state. As a result, the agency has become the clean air laboratory for the nation and, most likely, the world.

Not satisfied with simply controlling the region's air pollution, the agency spends more money to discover new and cleaner technologies than any state or local air pollution control agency in the nation. Funds add up to $6 million a year for research, development, and demonstration. With matching grants, funding climbs to more than $12 million a year.

Among the innovative technologies being developed are a fuel cell-powered bus, a new type of battery-operated electric vehicle that accelerates faster than standard gas-powered cars, and paints that don't pollute.

The AQMD, created by the state legislature in 1977, is made up of representatives from the counties of Los Angeles, Orange, Riverside, and San Bernardino. More than 1,000 people work at the El Monte headquarters and four satellite offices located in Anaheim, Colton, Long Beach, and Pasadena. Staff includes scientists, engineers, chemists, planners, attorneys, technicians, and inspectors who enforce AQMD rules and collect penalties for not following pollution standards.

Almost 88 percent of the agency's $101.4 million budget comes from fees and fines.

Engineers evaluate thousands of requests for permits to build, alter, and run equipment that either causes or controls air pollution. Even cars that are belching smoke do not escape the AQMD. The agency contracts for eight full-time California Highway Patrol officers who give citations to drivers whose cars are polluting the air.

AQMD's 12-member governing board has the power to adopt rules and regulations, such as those contained in the three-foot high, 45-volume Air Quality Management Plan. The 20-year plan, updated every three years, suggests changes such as the elimination of barbecue lighting fluid. Depending on the season, each day the region's air absorbs an average of two to four tons of hydrocarbons from the fluid.

The AQMD's work is paying off. In spite of an increasing population, the region is steadily progressing toward cleaner air. The greater Los Angeles area has not had a third-stage air pollution alert since the early 1970s, when every summer brought at least one third-stage alert and dozens of second-stage alerts.

Ozone, the region's most serious air pollutant, has decreased since 1955, when the air

Felicia Marcus, Los Angeles Board of Public Works commissioner, cofounder of Heal the Bay, and spirited environmental activist, poses in hard hat at the Hyperion Plant, Los Angeles' main sewage treatment facility. Photo by Shelley Gazin

contained .68 parts per million of ozone on peak days. In 1989 the ozone peak was .34 per million. Although L.A.'s ozone level is not yet at the federal standard of .12, levels have decreased significantly since 1955, when ozone levels were five times the federal standard.

Police and paramedic response times have also improved due to the area's 911 system. When a caller dials 911, the call is one of 5,000 to 6,000 received every day at the largest computer-aided dispatch system in the nation. Automatically, the caller's phone number and address appear on the 911 operator's computer screen located five floors

The City of Santa Monica has been widely praised for its progressive recycling program. Here, a city truck dumps recyclable metal cans into a Community Center collection bin. Photo by Joseph Sohm/Chromosohm

underground in City Hall East. The 911 operator knows after hearing a short explanation that an emergency is occurring. While the caller is put on hold, the operator dispatches a police car, then gets back to the caller with more questions.

Meanwhile, the police radio telephone operator, sitting in the same room, can hear the 911 operator through earphones and see the message on a computer screen. Any incidents involving police within 500 yards of the caller's house are also noted on the screen.

All 911 calls are divided into three categories: emergency dispatchable, non-emergency dispatchable, and non-dispatchable. If the caller's situation had not been an emer-

gency, the 911 operator would have switched the call to a 912 operator to leave the line open for emergencies. If the primary 911 operators had been busy when the call came in, the automatic call distribution system would have forwarded the call to secondary operators, and finally to two Spanish-speaking operators.

Los Angeles County's 911 system is not centrally dispatched. Instead, computers switch calls to answering stations throughout the county. One Christmas Day sheriff's deputies answered an especially poignant 911 call. A six-year-old boy called at 9:30 p.m. to report that Santa Claus had not yet arrived at his house. The sheriff's deputies made sure that Santa Claus promptly brought the child his toys.

Angelenos have never had to wait for a plentiful and clean supply of water. The plant that provides the citizens of Los Angeles with 75 percent of their water has one of the largest and most technically advanced water filtration systems in the nation. The Los Angeles Aqueduct Filtration Plant, opened in Sylmar in 1987, uses ozone as its special weapon. There are numerous advantages to using ozone as a primary disinfectant rather than chlorine, the conventional disinfectant.

Repeated use of chlorine may cause the production of trihalomethanes (THMs)—a family of chemical substances that are suspected of causing cancer in laboratory animals. The aqueduct uses chlorine only once during the final chlorinating process. This reduces the potential for THMs forming. Also, ozone improves the taste, odor, and color of water, and helps cluster the tiny particles that must be filtered out to make water drinkable.

Each day at the Los Angeles Aqueduct Filtration Plant, 600 million gallons of water go through more preparation than a runner training for the Olympics. First, screens filter out the twigs and pebbles that the water collects during its journey from the Sierra Nevada mountains. Then the water enters four large tanks, where it is injected with ozone. The unused ozone rises to the surface

Above: Four ecologically-minded high school students pitch in on Earth Day during Mayor Bradley's "Clean And Green" campaign. Photo by Joseph Sohm/Chromosohm

Left: A 1990 oil tanker spill in Huntington Beach summoned hundreds of Los Angeles volunteers to the beach. Photo by Joseph Sohm/Chromosohm

Santa Monica Bay is treasured by its residents. Heal the Bay, a nonprofit organization dedicated to raising funds for bay cleanup, educates the public about ocean pollution hazards, stages local demonstrations to protest unhealthy sewage dumping, and lobbies local politicians. Photo by Joseph Sohm/Chromosohm

of the tank and moves through a special unit, where it is converted into oxygen before it is released into Los Angeles' air.

Meanwhile, the water moves into mixers, where it is churned and chemicals are added to help remove cloudiness. The chemicals react with the fine particles suspended in the water to make them cluster together, so they can be removed during filtration. Next the system channels the water to large basins, where it slows down and is gently stirred by paddles. Here small particles form into larger particles, and fi-

nally the water is ready to be filtered. During the filtration process the water flows over 24 large concrete beds containing a six-foot layer of crushed anthracite coal, placed over a thin layer of gravel. As the water travels, the coal traps the large particles and leaves the water clean and clear. Chlorination is the final step before the water is piped to the people of Los Angeles.

To establish ways to manage the city's water supply during a drought, the Los Angeles Department of Water and Power (DWP), the largest municipally owned utility

project is a pilot program that uses oxygen rather than ozone to remove contaminants from well water without producing harmful by-products. Lastly, the plan suggests methods of protecting existing water supplies from contamination, and, if necessary, ways of cleaning up groundwater supplies.

The County Sanitation Districts (CSD) run a landfill that will not contaminate groundwater supplies. It is one of the largest and cleanest landfills in the world. Each day 2,000 trucks bring nearly 13,000 tons of trash to Puente Hills Landfill, a lush landscaped hill located across the Pomona Freeway from CSD's main office in Whittier. Seagulls that usually flock around landfills avoid Puente Hills because their landing patterns are disrupted by movable wires. Methane gas created by the rubbish is collected by state-of-the-art technology. The gas generates 50 megawatts of power, enough to supply power to 100,000 homes; and the CSD earns over $2 million a month from the sale of the power to Southern California Edison.

To cut down on the need for landfills, the City of Los Angeles has started the largest recycling program in the nation. Spurred by public pressure, the program is a response to a California law that went into effect in 1990 requiring all cities to eliminate 25 per-

An ocean of metal cans at the Santa Monica Recycling Center represents Angelenos' efforts to preserve the environment. Photo by Joseph Sohm/Chromosohm

in the nation, drafted the Urban Water Management Plan in March 1991. The plan includes 35 measures for pursuing economically efficient water conservation at the local and state levels. It suggests ways to develop reliable and cost-effective alternative sources of water supplies. For example, the DWP and seven other agencies are involved in a study to build a desalinization plant with the Bechtel Corporation in Baja California, Mexico. And the plan recommends ways to improve the quality and reliability of water supplied from the State Water Project. One

cent of their trash by 1995 and 50 percent by the year 2000. The city is encouraging large-scale participation by making the voluntary curbside recycling program easy. The program allows residents to place more than one type of recyclable material in the same container, and sanitation workers will separate the recyclables. By Jan-

grand prize for their water reclamation program, one of the largest and most advanced in the world.

The award-winning system is made up of nine water reclamation plants that treat 120 million gallons of wastewater a day. First the wastewater goes through primary treatment. Here chlorine is added, and dirt,

Two Department of Water and Power workers toil late into the evening. Photo by Shelley Gazin

uary 1993 city officials expect more than 720,000 residences to be participating in the $200-million program.

Like modern-day alchemists, workers at sanitation departments in the greater Los Angeles area are turning wastewater (sewage) into clean water and sludge into fertilizer and power. And they are winning prizes for their work. In 1990 the American Association of Environmental Engineering awarded the County Sanitation Districts a

heavy materials, floating solids, and oils and grease are removed. Then secondary treatment uses oxygen to remove both the tiny waste particles that are too light to settle and the dissolved organic matter. The process leaves the water 95 to 98 percent free of the original solids and organic matter. A third advanced treatment filters, chlorinates, and dechlorinates the water, leaving it 99.9 percent clean.

Currently 60 million of the 120 million

gallons of wastewater treated and reclaimed each day are sold to various industries and local water companies. The CSD uses about 40 million gallons to replenish the county's groundwater table, a boon during the area's recent drought. The rest goes to industry and to irrigate over 140 sites, including college campuses, parks, country clubs, and agricultural land. Many local water companies are scrambling to build distribution systems to use the remaining treated wastewater that now flows into the San Gabriel and Rio Hondo rivers.

Los Angeles is spending $3.4 billion for a program to improve the city's water reclamation and sanitation facilities. One billion dollars is going to update the Hyperion Sewage Treatment Plant in Playa del Rey, the largest sewage treatment plant in Los Angeles. During the 1980s, 75 percent of the 350 million gallons of wastewater that went through Hyperion received only primary sewage treatment before it was discharged into Santa Monica Bay.

In 1987 a U.S. Environmental Protection Agency (EPA) lawsuit forced Hyperion to use secondary treatment on all its wastewater. The extraordinary speed with which the city met the EPA's challenge is a model for the rest of the nation. Today Hyperion has reached the 50 percent level, and by 1998 all wastewater going through the plant will be given secondary treatment.

Also, the city is proud of its innovative sludge program. The program has received a special EPA award for its highly effective and rapid conversion from dumping to reuse. Before 1987 Hyperion dumped about 1,400 tons of wet sludge into Santa Monica Bay each day. Today a strong environmental ethic has taken over the city. Los Angeles has not only stopped dumping its sludge into Santa Monica Bay, but has found environmentally beneficial ways to use 100 percent of it. And the benefits go beyond cleaning up Santa Monica Bay. Reuse reduces the need for landfills and even produces fertilizer that is high in nitrogen and low in chemicals.

Los Angeles now uses its sludge in several ways. The city converts sludge to a soil sub-

stitute and uses it for land applications for non-foodstuff crops. Also, Hyperion makes the sludge into an excellent fertilizer, or mixes it with green waste and turns it into compost. And energy is recovered from sludge. Gas produced by wet sludge generates 80 percent of the plant's power. Dried sludge that is turned into powder supplies the plant's remaining energy needs. Moreover, the plant's gas turbines produce minimal air pollution and generate an average of 20 megawatts of electricity.

The idea that a big city has to be a polluter is wrong, says a spokesperson for the city's sludge management division. She points out that the city's strong pretreatment program helps Los Angeles produce some of the cleanest sludge in California and the nation.

However, sludge contaminated with industrial or hazardous wastes cannot be reused. Los Angeles has come down hard on toxic waste polluters. The Enforcement Division of Los Angeles' Bureau of Sanitation operates one of the toughest industrial and hazardous waste inspection and enforcement programs in the nation. When inspectors from one of the seven district offices become suspicious that a company or an individual is dumping waste illegally, they take a sample near the location where the suspect has dumped toxic material. Inspectors collect about 80,000 samples a year. If necessary, they take samples from sewer lines up- and downstream from the building they are inspecting.

The Enforcement Division has wide-ranging powers. In 1982 Los Angeles was the first city in the nation to issue search warrants for crimes involving hazardous waste dumping. Today the division can issue cease-and-desist orders in cases in which they decide that dumping is an imminent hazard to the community.

Angelenos have shown their support for responsible waste disposal by flocking to hazardous waste disposal roundup days. In April 1990 the Sanitation Districts of Los Angeles County and the Los Angeles County Department of Public Works set a national record for hazardous waste disposal when

PUTTING DOWN ROOTS:

L.A.'s TreePeople

Steven Brye, an urban planner with the Los Angeles County Transportation Commission, raised 3,000 redwood seedlings and enlisted volunteers to plant them in the Stanislaus National Forest. Architect Peter Lassen organized a planting of 100 trees on Los Angeles' Skid Row. Retired English professor Eudora Russell mobilized volunteers to plant 400 trees on Martin Luther King Boulevard in Los Angeles.

All three used the expertise provided by TreePeople, a 22,000-member Los Angeles environmental group committed to warding off the greenhouse effect by planting trees. TreePeople furnishes tree planting and organizational know-how along with the help of 250 active volunteers. Andy Lipkis, TreePeople founder, believes that community support is essential to maintaining trees and avoiding vandalism.

Eudora Russell already had her neighborhood's backing when she approached TreePeople about planting trees on Martin Luther King Boulevard. She and her neighbors had been waiting for the city to beautify the boulevard since 1982, when the seven-mile stretch that extends from Crenshaw Boulevard through the central city was renamed in Dr. King's honor. When a company offered TreePeople $5,000 to plant trees in Los Angeles, the group remembered Russell's suggestion and chose Martin Luther King Boulevard.

True to TreePeople's doctrine of promoting community involvement, Russell made sure that every possible group played a role in the King Boulevard Memorial Project. The project was launched with the help of the mayor and representatives from the Los Angeles City Council, the Board of Public Works, the traffic department, the Department of Transportation, and the police and fire departments. Following an initial planting of trees, serious planning for the event began in October 1989, and three and a half months later the project's organization was in place.

On Martin Luther King's birthday, January 13, 1990, the boulevard was closed to traffic and, in spite of rain, 3,000 volunteers turned out to plant 400 large Canary Island pine trees. Today Russell and about 40 volunteers meet each month to take care of the trees.

Andy Lipkis is the founder of Treepeople, and promotes community involvement in tree maintenance and replenishment. Photo by Shelley Gazin

They rebuild the water basins, pick up trash, and network with individuals along the boulevard who care for their adopted trees.

"Lots of trees have been adopted and have names," says Russell. "Quite a few are Rosa Parks and Coretta King. Others are Brotherhood and Peace. Some are named for people who have died, like Gilda Radner."

Russell attributes TreePeople's success to their "anything is possible" attitude. However, even the enthusiastic members of TreePeople were skeptical when they heard urban planner Steven Brye's proposal. Brye told them he wanted to build an addition to TreePeople's existing nursery cage (a greenhouse without glass) and raise 3,000 redwood seedlings. He said he would provide the seeds as well as pay for and build the addition.

Brye maintains, "TreePeople first got a sense that we were serious when our orders for lumber and cinder blocks for the foundation came in and the plastic pipe for the sprinkler system started arriving."

Brye had considered replanting trees in Sequoia National Forest since he was 10 years old, when a park ranger told him that a third of the trees had been cut down. After he finished college and paid off his student loan, he started thinking about how he should spend the extra money from his paycheck. He explains, "I saw ads encouraging me to buy a sports car or a stereo. That didn't interest me. I flashed back to what the ranger had said about the trees."

In 1987 Brye found his opportunity. He heard that a forest fire had wiped out 115,000 acres in the Stanislaus National Forest. He called the United States Forest Service to ask if redwood seedlings would grow in the burnt-out area. The ranger assured him they would grow. But where would he get thousands of seedlings?

Soon after, Brye met with TreePeople at their headquarters, a 45-acre city park they maintain at Mulholland Drive and Coldwater Canyon Boulevard. He recalls, "I told them, 'If you will give me a chance to raise the trees, I will pay for a 20x30-foot extension to your nursery cage and install an automatic sprinkler system for the addition. If you don't like it, I'll tear it down at no cost and bring it to the city dump.'"

Brye went home and began working on his design. Luckily, one of his roommates, Robert Schulte, was looking over his shoulder. Schulte, a bridge engineer for Caltrans, could see that Brye needed help. He offered to complete the design and pay for half of the addition. The cost, with seeds and fertilizer, would total close to $20,000.

Every weekend for four months Brye and Schulte, both 30, worked on the addition. They started early and finished after dark, using their automobile headlights for illumination. After the exterior was completed, they built shelves and installed the automatic sprinkler system. Finally they were ready to plant the *sequoiadendron giganteum* seeds in test tubes. It took two years to raise seedlings that were large enough to plant, and three days for 84 volunteers to plant all 3,000 in the forest soil. Awards and a dance topped off the planting.

Brye reports proudly, "We were hoping that 10 percent might make it, but actually 48 percent survived." He advises, "Whatever species of tree you're interested in, the first thing to do is contact the U.S. Forest Service and ask for help."

Architect Peter Lassen, former chief architect for a firm that builds low-income housing on Skid Row, considered the needs of urban people before deciding on what kinds of trees to plant there. He settled on trees that shed their leaves in the fall and flower in spring, because they signal the seasons and bring the passage of time to the concrete streets. Over three years, Lassen supervised TreePeople volunteers and locals who neatly planted 100 deciduous sycamores and flowering Bradford pear trees.

"When people volunteer to plant the trees they name them and take care of them," Lassen says. "I've got one that's named Sobriety put in by a group of ex-alcoholics, and another is called Serenity. The people in these developing communities are proud of their place and what they are doing."

Even when it comes to the environment, Steven Brye explains, Los Angeles is the land of opportunity for innovators or people with an entrepreneurial spirit. What makes the city unique, he says, is a can-do attitude, and an awareness that environmental problems have to be confronted. —*Ellen Hoffs*

more than 4,000 cars traveled to the Pasadena Rose Bowl to take part in their one-day hazardous waste roundup.

But the public's enthusiasm for safe disposal stops when government wants to build a hazardous waste site near home or work. "Not in my backyard" is the standard reply. Casmalia, about 200 miles from Los Angeles, is the only site where it is legal to dispose of the region's almost one million tons of hazardous waste produced every year.

In 1990 the Southern California Association of Governments (SCAG) designed a regional plan for hazardous waste disposal. Rather than go it alone, eight counties in the region worked together to develop a plan that meets new federal and state laws. Dumping untreated hazardous waste on land is now illegal. The plan stresses that everyone has to take a fair share of the responsibility for disposal and instructs governments on how to make toxic waste contamination proof. Also, the plan sets standards for building sites where waste residuals can be stored until the time when there is a safe method of treating them for disposal. The plan proposes three sites for the disposal of residuals from toxic wastes and four sites for treatment.

The City of Los Angeles has pioneered a model program for teaching the public, government, and industry how to minimize hazardous waste. In August 1988 the Los

Treepeople, a nonprofit ecological organization, conducts vigorous drives to educate Angelenos about native tree species and their importance to the community. Volunteers plant young saplings throughout Los Angeles. The young trees beautify the landscape and "clean the air" through photosynthesis. Photo by Joseph Sohm/ Chromosohm

Angeles Board of Public Works pioneered the Hazard and Toxic Materials Project (HTM). The project provides city agencies and businesses with case studies, literature, and free technical assistance on ways to reduce, recycle, and prevent toxic waste. The city rewards citizens' efforts with the Mayor's Award of Excellence for Outstanding Achievement in Pollution Prevention. Highland Plating, one of the 1990 winners, developed a substitute for the cyanide commonly used for copper plating. Cyanide is a toxic waste, and metal workers must use another hazardous material, chlorine compounds, to make the cyanide disposable. Highland Plating accomplishes the same job by substituting a noncyanide product. Workers can easily treat the new product, and it is safe for the environment.

Greater Los Angeles is a remarkable region both because of its natural attributes and its people, who turn ideas and ideals into action. Angelenos are increasingly aware that their environment can be destroyed and that they play an important role in preserving it for future generations. Thousands of energetic volunteers work for nonprofit organizations that make the region a better place to live.

Heal the Bay has had an extraordinary impact on the seawater of Southern California. Swimmers and lifeguards were aware of deteriorating water quality in Santa Monica Bay, but nothing was done about it until the mid-1980s, when activists from Heal the Bay began protesting to Los Angeles officials about the quality of the water. The 1987 EPA lawsuit, in which Heal the Bay acted as a friend of the court, forced Los Angeles to stop dumping sludge into the ocean and to provide full secondary wastewater treatment at its Hyperion plant by 1998.

Currently the organization is focused on two issues. The group's primary concern is cleaning the city's storm drains that empty into Santa Monica Bay. Heal the Bay is working to persuade cities to pass ordinances that will reduce the flow and toxicity of runoff flowing into storm drains from private and public property. Also, volunteers are conducting an educational campaign in schools and on television to teach people that what they throw into storm drains will end up in the ocean as untreated waste. A second issue involves the County Sanitation Districts. Heal the Bay is working with the EPA to force the County Sanitation Districts to give full secondary treatment to the 350 million gallons of wastewater it discharges into the ocean at Palos Verdes Peninsula. Those enjoying Los Angeles' scenic beaches can thank the volunteers of Heal the Bay for safeguarding precious ocean water.

The Mountains Restoration Trust gets much of the credit for preserving the city's open space. Los Angeles has an abundance of mansions and condos, but open space is more difficult to find and keep. The nonprofit Mountains Restoration Trust was created in 1981 to buy and accept donated land in the 55-mile Santa Monica mountain range and preserve it for public use. Starting with a 525-acre parcel now known as the Cold Creek Canyon Preserve, the trust has expanded and bought other acreage and sold or donated acreage to the National Park Service. Today the trust owns 1,200 acres of some of the most valuable real estate on the West Coast. To acquire the wilderness area, the trust appealed to the conservationist instincts of landowners and explained the tax benefits of donating land. Along with preserving open space, trust volunteers improve hiking trails, train docents to lead tours for schoolchildren, and renovate buildings on the land.

Los Angeles Beautiful is another nonprofit organization devoted to improving the area's environment. Since 1949 the city has benefited from the organization's work. Los Angeles Beautiful sponsors a program with the Los Angeles Unified School District which encourages citizens, from preschool children to adults in vocational schools, to work on environmental projects. In addition to conducting its educational programs, the organization's volunteers help develop parks, conserve open space, and plant trees in honor of individuals and groups who have contributed to bettering the local environment.

Green-shirted volunteers
prepare to wage a clean-
up war on the banks of
the Los Angeles River.
Photo by Joseph Sohm/
Chromosohm

TreePeople, another leader in the beautification of Los Angeles, gained recognition
before the 1984 Olympics. The seed of the
organization was planted twenty years ago
when Andy Lipkis saw trees dying from
smog pollution at the camp he attended in
the San Bernardino mountains. He persuaded camp counselors to allow him and his
friends to plant smog-resistant seedlings
near the camp. TreePeople began three
years later when Lipkis convinced the directors of almost two dozen summer camps
to join him in replanting 8,000 pine
seedlings. Before the 1984 Los Angeles
Olympics, TreePeople coordinated the
planting of one million trees in the Los Angeles basin.

The Coalition for Clean Air began in Los
Angeles in 1970. Today it is the only
statewide nonprofit citizens' action organization that works solely for the elimination of
air pollution in California. Two lawsuits in
which the coalition participated are partly
responsible for the tough 1989 Air Quality
Management Plan. The first, initiated against
the EPA by the coalition's program director,
proved that California's air pollution plan
was not in compliance with federal standards. The coalition intervened in a follow-
up lawsuit and showed that the EPA's plan
for the area would not help the region meet
air quality standards.

Besides working to improve their environment, L.A.'s volunteers also devote thousands of hours to working with people-
oriented groups. A *Los Angeles Times* article
published in 1979 inspired Tanya Tull to
found Para Los Niños (For the Children).
The article described the grim life of
children living in downtown Skid Row

hotels. Six weeks after reading the article, Tull raised $5,000 from the Atlantic Richfield Foundation and leased a Skid Row warehouse. Within a year the agency was serving 90 children. Since 1981 the agency has provided assistance to more than 5,000 families, including more than 15,000 children. Its budget has grown to $1.2 million, half of which is raised by the private sector.

Among the many services provided by Para Los Niños are emergency and crisis intervention, and after-school protection and care for homeless and transient children and victims of child abuse and neglect. The agency also provides full-day programs and educational and enrichment activities for at-risk elementary schoolchildren during school vacations. Intervention and prevention programs are also available for teenagers at risk of entering the juvenile justice system or first offenders referred by law enforcement agencies. Para Los Niños runs these programs from two renovated warehouses it owns on East Sixth Street in downtown Los Angeles.

Skid Row facilities served only men until Jill Halverson founded the Downtown Women's Center in 1978. Today a day-care center and a 48-room residential hotel serve the chronically ill, poor, and addicted women of downtown Los Angeles. Since both buildings are owned by the center, the privately funded organization is able to work efficiently on a small budget. Halverson runs the day-care center on $200,000 a year. The $165 monthly rent paid by the hotel patrons supports the hotel. Six paid staff members and 40 regular volunteers help operate both facilities. The hotel was given an Award for Excellence by the Urban Land Institute, a national organization of real estate developers.

A group rather than an individual is responsible for creating the Venice Family Clinic. Twenty years ago beachside residents of Venice were angry about the lack of affordable health care in the area. The Venice Family Clinic was founded as a temporary facility to give free medical care to the people living in the beach community. Unfortunately, the need for free services increased over the years. In 1990 the clinic tripled in size. The 11,000-square-foot expansion means that now it can handle about 45,000 patient visits a year.

Today the Venice Family Clinic is a required or elective rotation for nine physician-training residency programs in the Los Angeles area. And 300 of the clinic's 1,500 volunteers are physicians. Each year loyal volunteers help the Venice Family Clinic

Actor Dennis Weaver, along with Valerie Harper, is a founder of L.I.F.E. (Love Is Feeding Everyone), a nonprofit organization dedicated to improving the living conditions of Los Angeles' transient population. Photo by Shelley Gazin

FIFTYSOMETHING
And Planning for the Future

After a year of looking for full-time work, Skake Rose, 57, needed support and encouragement. She found both at Second Careers, a nonprofit employment agency in Los Angeles that specializes in finding jobs for people 50 and over.

Rose, whose applications were on file at many of the city's employment agencies, says with satisfaction, "Julie, who interviewed me, asked the right questions and really wanted to know what I had endured during my job hunting."

Within a month Second Careers made a match. Rose took a job as an assistant to a well-known literary agent, where she could use the skills she learned working in publishing and communications. Her employer, Shelly Wile, gained a loyal employee. Wile reflects, "There's an enormous turnover among young people. They want to be agents immediately, and don't want to pay their dues."

Salvador Pilar, 54, opened his own management training business after working for years as director of personnel at a number of local hospitals. When he decided to close the business and become an employee again, he was surprised to find that jobs for which he seemed qualified were going to younger candidates. "I suspected my age was the problem, because a number of times I'd meet the other finalist at an interview, and the other person was always younger."

Through Second Careers, Pilar found a job for which he was perfectly suited—employment manager with

Loyola Marymount University. The university had been looking for an individual to head their outreach program, which stresses the hiring of underserved minorities and older people.

"Generally speaking, older workers are more in demand than ever before," says Tod Lipka, director of Second Careers. "Many employers are looking for the old-fashioned qualities of reliability, common sense, and trustworthiness. Growing up 30, 40, or 50 years ago the whole notion of work was different, and these people still have the same work ethic." Lipka adds half-jokingly, "We talk about how our people are cursed with the work ethic."

Society's attitude toward seniors has come a long way since Second Careers, sponsored by the Volunteer Center of Los Angeles, opened its doors in 1976. At that time few companies had retirement training programs, and retired people wanting to work could only go to a conventional employment agency.

Second Careers' original purpose was twofold: to provide volunteer opportunities for retired workers, and to plan and develop preretirement programs for corporations. The agency was assisted by a $150,000 grant from the Edna McConnel Clark Foundation of New York. "The foundation was interested in older people, retirees, and the use of retirees as a resource," Lipka says. "You have to remember that a lot of the federal programs were just beginning to get started and the rocking chair notion was the predominant one."

But change was in the air. In the seventies California law prohibited mandatory retirement at a specific age. The notion that the retiree could go back to work was becoming acceptable because of increased longevity and changing notions of old age. And inflation was making it difficult for older workers to live on Social Security benefits. As the economy of the seventies declined, retirees were coming to Second Careers' counselors asking for paid employment rather than volunteer opportunities.

Earline Hughes, May Buzzell, and Lucille Helwig (in a tiara) are three royal members of the Queen for a Day Club. Composed of former "Queen for a Day" show winners, the club meets monthly in Bellflower and North Hollywood, and has raised money for Children's Hospital since 1962. The Queen for a Day Club is one of many groups of L.A. seniors active in community service. Photo by Shelley Gazin

Some were as young as 50.

Setting a trend, Second Careers changed its focus in 1980 and became a full-scale, fee-charging—albeit non-profit—employment agency for temporary and permanent job placement. Applicants pay no fees, and rates are lower than those of commercial agencies. Since 1980 more than 8,500 people have registered for work. Today 4,500 are actively registered. In 1990 Second Careers interviewed 750 people and filled 523 positions. "We don't turn anybody away," says Lipka. "We deal with older workers who have been file clerks and corporate presidents."

Always on the lookout for the changing needs of older workers, Second Careers opened a computer laboratory in September 1989. The staff realized that older job seekers needed computer training to get better jobs, but were not taking advantage of already existing programs. Older people were intimidated by community college classes in which they had to compete with mainly younger students. And private classes were prohibitively expensive. At Second Careers each 90-minute class costs a low $7.50 with a minimum of four classes. To date, 400 people have taken advantage of the program.

Most work orders coming through Second Careers are for skilled office workers. However, more and more of the positions filled are in higher level management. The highest paying position Second Careers has filled was for a Chief Financial Officer with a defense firm which paid more than $150,000 full-time. The job, now part-time, pays $75,000. Also, Second Careers has worked with large corporations such as Arco and the Times-Mirror Corporation to develop a pool of retired workers for temporary assignments.

Second Careers' success is partly due to the large pool of skilled workers located in Los Angeles. Some retirees are attracted by the region's climate, says Lipka. Others, who are considering going back to work, come to the city because of its economic diversity. Lipka explains, "I think the West Coast tends to be a little more liberal than the middle part of the country. I think there's a greater receptivity here to the role older workers can play in the work force." —*Ellen Hoffs*

reach its $2-million-a-year operating budget. Eighty percent comes from private contributions, including the Venice Art Walk, one of the city's most successful cultural events. In 1990 the Art Walk netted $600,000.

As this small sample of the city's volunteer organizations shows, Angelenos are quick to step in and deliver services that government does not provide. Most of the time Angelenos take the services offered by government for granted. However, when there is a threat to the community's people or environment, inevitably someone becomes alarmed and forms an organization to bring about change. The organization pressures politicians and regulatory agencies. And in time public opinion adds more pressure. Then, after what seems like endless hearings, newspaper editorials, and angry interchanges, government finds the funding to carry out needed changes.

The region works as a whole because of its people. Angelenos and their government working together provide a system of checks and balances that supplies the energy and motivation to meet the region's growing challenges.

Doris Bloch is the executive director of the Los Angeles Regional Foodbank, which distributes products donated by 490 local organizations to L.A.'s needy communities. Photo by Shelley Gazin

FOLLOWING THE DREAM

L.A.'s Cultural Kaleidoscope

It was altogether fitting that those 44 stalwart peasants who trudged hundreds of miles over rough, trackless terrain from Mexico to establish the tiny pueblo of Los Angeles in 1781 were an ethnically diverse party of Spaniards, Mexicans, blacks, Indians, and mixed-blood mestizos. In a seminal sense, they set a pattern, a harbinger of things to come.

Slightly over 200 years later, that dusty little hamlet has grown not only into one of the most famous and charismatic cities in the world, but also the greatest cultural kaleidoscope ever, with a regional population of 14.5 million from 140 countries. During the last few decades the classic misfortunes of mankind that have fueled mass migrations in the past have been at work—grinding poverty, bloody civil wars, genocide, and regressive, terroristic governments—or simply the unending human quest for a better life.

The immigrants have come in varying numbers from near and far, from all corners of the globe: Canada and Mexico, Central and South America, Asia and the Pacific Islands, Europe and the Middle

"WE ARE WITNESSING A TRANSFORMATION OF THE LOS ANGELES BASIN INTO THE FIRST CONTINENTAL, MULTIRACIAL AND MULTI-ETHNIC METROPOLIS IN THE U.S., THAT IS, WHERE WHITES ARE NO LONGER THE PREDOMINANT MAJORITY."

—KEVIN MCCARTHY, *WALL STREET JOURNAL*, 1985

Craig McEwen learns the fine art of chopstick coordination from his wife, Sally, at Thousand Cranes Restaurant, atop the New Otani Hotel. Photos by Shelley Gazin

B y   C h a r l e s   F. Q u e e n a n

East, and Africa. En masse, they have combined to inflate a fairly orderly flow of newcomers into a tidal wave of immigration that has had a profound impact on the local scene. They have brought to Los Angeles the greatest diversity of culture, food, entertainment, language, clothing, religion, and politics to be found anywhere. And they have altered the character and appearance of Los Angeles forever.

The floodgates were opened with major changes in U.S. immigration laws in the 1960s, together with the inability of the understaffed Immigration and Naturalization Service (INS) to control an increasing volume of undocumented immigrants across California's southern border. Then came the removal of barriers to Third World countries in 1965, and immigrants from Asia and Latin America flooded major population centers. In Zena Pearlstone's book, *Ethnic L.A.*, the author points out that during the 1970s Los Angeles' Hispanic population doubled, while its Asian population nearly tripled. The Master Plan of the Los Angeles Cultural Affairs Department states: "The significant and continued immigration from Latin America and

from Asia, along with several other factors, have completely reshaped and will continue to reshape the map of Los Angeles."

The foreign-born population in Los Angeles County soared by 49 percent in the 1970s, and the trend continued into the 1980s. "Between 1982 and 1985," writes Pearlstone, "the ten immigrant groups admitted/processed in the District of Los Angeles in descending order of frequency were Vietnam-

A wave of Southeast Asian immigrants have brought a great diversity of culture, food, entertainment, language, clothing, and religion to Los Angeles. Photo by Joeseph Sohm/Chromosohm

Facing page: Each Memorial Day, Scottish Americans gather at the Orange County Fairgrounds for the Highland Gathering and Festival, to compete in traditional games like tossing the caber (a heavy pole) and throwing the hammer. Photo by Joseph Sohm/ Chromosohm

Left: Lunch break for these high school boys in "Little Mexico," downtown L.A. Photo by Bob Rowan/Progressive Image

ese, Koreans, Chinese (from Taiwan, Hong Kong and People's Republic of China) Filipinos, Mexicans, Iranians, Cambodians, Salvadorans, Soviets and Indians."

By the 1990s Los Angeles had the unusual distinction of becoming the first large American city where Anglos were not the majority of the total population. Official 1990 census figures show Los Angeles County to be 40.8 percent Anglo, 37.8 percent Latino, 10.5 percent black, 10.2 percent Asian/Pacific, and 0.5 percent "other." Of the county's total population, nearly 3.5 million are Latino.

However, these figures do not include well over one million undocumented immigrants, and might represent only about half of the Asian-born population. Los Angeles officials have judged that Asians were undercounted by 7.3 percent in the 1980 census. In 1990 the State Department of Finance listed the Southeast Asian refugee population in Los Angeles County at 57,548, while

Asian-American community leaders claim the Vietnamese population alone exceeds 100,000, in addition to as many as 50,000 Cambodians and 25,000 Laotians.

Inevitably this merging of races and cultures has created problems of adjustment, between immigrant groups as well as with the local population. Internecine strife has flared as the legacy of fear, hatred, and violence that haunted their earlier lives followed some ethnic groups to Los Angeles. Religious organizations and political and social support groups such as the Santana Chirino Amaya Central American Refugee Committee assist immigrants from war-torn and poverty-stricken countries in coping with their painful pasts, present needs, and fears for the future; but needs far outnumber the services available.

Tragically, some immigrants have been ruthlessly exploited by unscrupulous people pretending to help them. Illegal immigrants

have been held hostage until friends or relatives paid ransom for their release. Unethical employers hiring illegals often pay far below minimum wage, even hold some in virtual slavery or turn them in to the INS just before their pay comes due. Immigrants have paid high fees to bogus "legal" advisors and to untrained, unlicensed practitioners in neighborhood "medical" clinics. Some have been victimized by their own, such as the Vietnamese who have been robbed by Vietnamese youth gangs who know their people distrust banks and keep gold, jewelry, and cash in their homes.

In contrast, many of the organizations which assist newcomers are self-help groups formed by immigrants. And Angelenos from a variety of backgrounds have organized to promote understanding and progress among peoples of diverse cultures. The New Majority Task Force, formed in 1989, is comprised of Latinos, Anglos, Asians, and African Americans who work toward economic development in L.A.'s ethnic neighborhoods. Other groups work to open up educational and business opportunities, particularly to young people who often find themselves caught between two cultures.

Some ethnic groups enter the mainstream business community quite easily—such as the educated, affluent Iranians who emigrated after the downfall of the Shah; the English-speaking "invisible" immigrants (British, Canadians, Australians, South Africans, and New Zealanders); and the entrepreneurial Japanese, Chinese, and Koreans.

But hundreds of thousands of immigrants arrive without education, skills, or funds, and this massive influx has strained social and city services, schools, housing, and health programs. The Los Angeles Unified School District faces great challenges in fulfilling its pledge to provide schooling for every child within its jurisdiction.

In 1990 the State Department of Education reported that of the 1.4 million children enrolled in Los Angeles schools, 27 percent do not speak English. Students speak nearly a hundred different languages, and the LAUSD faces the task of finding and training bilin-

gual teachers proficient in those tongues. Spanish-speaking teachers are being recruited in Spain and Mexico, and bonuses are being offered for bilingual teachers.

"To contend with the cacophony of tongues that arrive in the school system each year," says *Los Angeles Times* writer Bob Sipchen, "Los Angeles educators have con-

A wide range of races and cultures works together harmoniously across the entire spectrum of the Los Angeles work force. Photo by Joseph Sohm/Chromosohm

structed a language, in which they speak of FEPs, LEPs and NEPs—students with Fluent English Proficiency, Limited English Proficiency and No English Proficiency." At Hancock Park Elementary School, a multicultural school in the heart of the city, students who need help with English are teamed with others who speak their native language, in a type of "linguistic buddy system." The idea is to teach English while encouraging students to retain proficiency in their own languages.

Los Angeles schools also provide special instruction to a half-million adult immigrants. The Immigration Reform and Control Act of 1986—the "amnesty" program for illegal im-

ENGLISH AS A SECOND LANGUAGE

Los Angeles as Home

Students in the Los Angeles school system speak almost a hundred different languages. Often they are asked to write essays about Los Angeles in English-as-a-Second-Language classes. The following are excerpts from essays written by area students:

"When I came to Los Angeles I saw many, many palm trees. In Poland we don't have palm trees because we have cold climate. I was very surprised how many cars were on the streets."
> **—Rafal Sidorowicz**
> (Poland)

"What I like is the friendship between various peoples in Los Angeles. I like the educational system too. In my country I didn't feel comfortable in school, as I was nervous. I think all the students felt like that and attending school was unpleasant. I think I can thank the American government by my getting education and being one of the clever and helpful members of the society."
> **—Artur Antapkyan**
> (Soviet Union)

"I arrived by airplane. I saw a lot of lights. This sea of lights was a big city called Los Angeles. Was new for me, to see many skyscrapers and many freeways. Another day I went to the ocean where I swam and admired the waves and dolphins. It was a shining."
> **—Maria Purcar**
> (Romania)

"When I first came to Los Angeles I was both happy and sad. I was happy because I came with my mother and I was sad because I left my grandmother in El Salvador."
> **—Jessy Ramirez**
> (El Salvador)

"I saw a lot of buildings, beautiful cars, beautiful girls. . . I heard a lot of kind of musics."
> **—Juan Galeana**
> (Mexico)

"The difference between Los Angeles and my country is that in Guatemala there are fewer people, fewer cars, fewer buildings and it is much smaller."
> **—Yesenia Soto**
> (Guatemala)

"I remember the first day in L.A. I was afraid for no reason, maybe I was taking precaution against the new world. I was standing at home and thinking about my homeland. That was a really hard time for me, but it changed a lot when I went to the school. I started discovering a new world. I thought I was a stranger here, but I wasn't. Everyone was strangers in this world, like pilgrims. My lifestyle changed a lot and I'm proud of myself that I discovered and fought for a new world."
> **—Hong Joo Hyung**
> (Korea)

This racially diverse sixth-grade class at Monlux Elementary School in the San Fernando Valley is fairly representative of the blend of the near future for Los Angeles citizens, who will speak a hundred different languages and observe countless different cultural traditions, while living perhaps only blocks from one another. Photo by Larry Molmud

"I have met many people in Los Angeles and most of them have been very nice to me. One day I went to a store and the owner scolded me because I was touching things. This scared me. But another day I went to another store and the people there gave me a kite and I wasn't scared anymore."
—**Alberto Acosta**
(Mexico)

"When I was in Mexico I didn't know another language and now I can speak English, not so well, but I can translate for my mother English to Spanish. When I grow up I want to be a bilingual teacher and I can help the people or students that don't speak English."
—**Vincent Avila**
(Mexico)

"When I came here I felt very strange. My father's friends came to pick up my family and the first word I learned was 'freeway.'"
—**Sook Hyun "Susana" Choi**
(Korea)

"Of all the people I have met my teachers are the most special. They are special because they are kind and because they are bilingual."
—**Karla Cornejo**
(El Salvador)

"I met here many different people— Chineses, Koreans, Americans. They are a very interesting people."
—**Alexander Kuprin**
(Soviet Union)

"All the people I met here in Los Angeles have different nationality. When I go to church to attend the Sunday Mass, I met a American priest who said he is Mexican and Filipino."
—**Amor Batarra**
(Philippines)

"I was surprised to see how many people live in Los Angeles. I think that the people in Los Angeles are friendly because they smile and laugh a lot."
—**Heidi Arrivillaga**
(Guatemala)

"In El Salvador some people are very important and in Los Angeles the people are good looking. I love Los Angeles."
—**Marleny Granadas**
(El Salvador)

migrants—allows immigrants who have resided continuously in the United States beginning prior to 1982 to apply for permanent residency after their requests for amnesty (temporary residency status) are approved. Residency status is granted to those who meet basic requirements in English and U.S. history. The program has swamped adult community schools and made the demand for bilingual teachers even more acute. In 1989 more than 156,000 students were enrolled in English-as-a-Second-Language (ESL) courses in 26 adult education schools, with thousands more waiting to get in. Evans Community Adult School in downtown Los Angeles is the nation's largest and most internationally mixed adult school in the U.S., with 13,000 students from 80 countries.

Education has traditionally been the key for immigrants and their children to improve their economic standing, and L.A.'s immigrants are gaining higher education in increasing numbers. For the 1990 fall quarter, UCLA had 6,296 international students from 110 countries enrolled in degree programs. Two-thirds of these students were immigrants, and three-quarters of them were graduate students. Thousands more college students at UCLA and other universities throughout the Southland are the children or grandchildren of immigrants.

The wave of immigration which has brought so many changes to Los Angeles has not yet had its full impact on the local political scene, although the huge Latino population is steadily becoming a more powerful political force. However, as ethnic groups establish themselves, they achieve the economic success necessary to turn their attention to consolidating and exercising political clout.

Since its beginnings, Los Angeles has had a large Latino population. And in recent years thousands more have fled poverty or political turmoil in Mexico and Central and South America. Many arrive illiterate, unskilled, and penniless, and—like millions of first-generation immigrants before them—they see the ongoing struggle to survive as their first and only priority. But today

prospects for a stronger political presence are brighter, with more and more Latinos making their voices heard at the polls. As recent arrivals receive their citizenship, the Latino vote continues to grow. And increasing numbers of educated, successful Latinos are taking their place in the political arena.

A key victory came in June 1990 with a landmark court order calling for the redrawing of supervisorial districts, which virtually ensured a Latino seat on the powerful, heretofore Anglo, all-male County Board of Supervisors. The election in January 1991

Education has traditionally been the key for immigrants and their children to improve their economic standing. Photo by Joseph Sohm/ Chromosohm

was a double-barrelled victory when a Latina—former L.A. City Council member Gloria Molina—was elected to the board.

Since many Asian immigrants have lived under governments that swiftly and ruthlessly suppressed any form of dissent, Asians have traditionally sought economic progress through individual efforts rather than through political pressure as a group. That, too, is changing. Asian Americans are now actively running for office—and successfully. In 1985 Michael Woo became the first Asian American elected to the Los An-

geles City Council. Others are being elected to office in smaller communities. More Asian Americans are registering to vote and taking an interest in politics. And the present generation of high-achieving Asian students promises to become a powerful political force in years to come. Whether at the grass-roots level or through L.A.'s most successful ethnic politicians, the various cultures of the Southland are beginning to make their voices heard—foreshadowing movement toward a more appropriate balance of power in a city where a still predominantly Anglo political structure represents a decidedly multiethnic citizenry.

With its huge ethnic population and strategic location, Los Angeles is a prime target for foreign investment, expansion, and business opportunity, especially for Pacific Rim countries. Thousands of foreign professionals transferred by their home offices to U.S. operations live in Los Angeles County and work temporarily on work visas, often the first step toward permanent residency. A foreign firm can file for an extended visa if it feels its employee is needed for a longer period. Also up sharply are requests for temporary work visas, under which foreigners are allowed to work in this country for six years with proof that they are professionals and that a job awaits them.

The Japanese dominate the Pacific Rim business scene in L.A., with real estate holdings, banks, resident corporations, and a major chunk of the import trade. But the two Chinas—Taiwan and now mainland China—are steadily increasing their holdings in Chinatown, Monterey Park, and other areas of the city. After ending its long, self-imposed isolation from the West, the Republic of China has been aggressively acquiring property in Los Angeles as part of its new policy of establishing ties with other nations, especially the United States. Koreans also maintain some business interests in Los Angeles, among them banking institutions and branches of a few large industries.

But the real story of Asian business in Los Angeles is found in Asian immigrant and Asian-American enterprise. For example, Asian-American banks, not to be confused with Asian-based banks, have prospered even during times of financial crisis for larger, mainstream institutions, according to the *Los Angeles Business Journal*. Area Asian-American banks have a history of lending within their own communities, avoiding risky loans, and controlling costs. A survey by California Research Corp. found that 13 of a group of 15 Asian-American banks outperformed many big-name institutions during the first half of 1990, with returns on assets and equity far exceeding the median for California banks.

The *Los Angeles Business Journal* also reports that the numerous small Asian-owned businesses in the region have survived the general economy's vicissitudes better than most. At least 10,000 small businesses—neighborhood grocery stores, gas stations, restaurants, and shops—are operated by Koreans, who are willing to put in the long hours and hard work necessary for success. Grocery and retail is the largest industry for Southland Korean Americans: according to the Korean-American Grocers Association of Southern California, Korean grocery and liquor store owners number 2,700, accounting for 18 percent of the region's grocery and liquor sales. Koreans also own 900 of the 2,000-odd contract shops in the L.A. garment industry. Many Korean-owned businesses are in and near Koreatown, close to downtown Los Angeles. Farther south, the industrious Vietnamese have been just as successful with similar enterprises in Little Saigon and other parts of Orange County.

The San Gabriel Valley is another growing center for Asian immigrant population and business growth, particularly in Monterey Park and nearby communities. Bonnie Culbertson, director of marketing for the Rosemead Chamber of Commerce, points out that about 80 percent of new businesses opened in Rosemead are Asian owned. The chamber works closely with immigrant business owners, many of whom lack know-how but have a strong determination to succeed. Culbertson says, "They're good solid chamber members . . . We want to help them."

Latino entrepreneurship has increased significantly in recent years, striving to keep pace with the phenomenal growth of the Latino population. *Hispanic Business* magazine's 1990 survey of Latino-owned businesses across the nation identified California as the state with the largest number of successful companies—130 of the 500 largest. California ranked second in terms of Latino business revenue in 1990, $1.92 billion to Florida's $2.82 billion. The national growth of Latino enterprise is reflected in another of the survey's results, an 8.1 percent increase in the top 500 companies' sales, for a total of $9.03 billion. Also telling is a U.S. Census Bureau figure showing that the nation's 422,373 Latino-owned businesses represented an 81 percent increase in numbers over the five-year period ending in 1987. Many of the nation's most successful Latino-owned businesses are in L.A.—most in the retail and service sectors, and many in manufacturing.

And there are encouraging signs that the new generation of Latino youth—better educated than their forebears—are preparing to enter the business world. According to *California Business* magazine, "The burden for progress is being borne, for the most part, by the Hispanic community. And there, Latino executives and entrepreneurs are laboring with renewed vigor to open doors for young Hispanics. Established Hispanic organizations like the U.S. Hispanic Chamber of Commerce

Theresa Rodriguez, formerly a newscaster with the Spanish-language broadcasting concern, Univision, is shown reviewing script changes with her cameraman. Rodriguez is now at NBC. Photo by Shelley Gazin

and the Latin Business Association are setting up scholarship funds to send promising Hispanic youths to college." Another group, the National Society of Hispanic MBA, which has a chapter in Los Angeles, offers scholarships and guidance to MBA and Ph.D. candidates from the Latino community.

In addition to the remarkable success of many immigrant entrepreneurs, the ethnic explosion has brought major changes in

Gloria Molina is sworn in as supervisor of the newly-redrawn 1st District in March 1991. She is both the first Hispanic and the first woman supervisor to sit on the board. Photo by Shelley Gazin

marketing strategies and in the L.A. job market. *California Business* rates Los Angeles as the nation's number-one Hispanic market, noting that a Miami-based research group estimates Latino buying power in the L.A. basin at a whopping $22 billion per year. Many Latino-owned businesses have built their success by targeting this immense marget. Of the 10 top-grossing Latino companies in Los Angeles, five target the Latino market, according to the *Los Angeles Business Journal.* They include real estate firm Galindo Financial Corp., Camino Real Chevrolet, and three manufacturers and distributors of Mexican and other Latino specialty foods: Reynoso Brothers Foods, Cacique Inc., and C & F Foods. C & F Foods has built on its success with the Latino market to serve the general population as well,

supplying beans and rice to supermarket chains including Vons, Ralphs, and Albertsons.

Meanwhile, mainstream businesses have become aware of the potential of the Latino market and are beginning to pursue its business. From greeting cards to groceries, companies are courting the Spanish-speaking consumer. Television advertisers who once simply dubbed their English commercials in Spanish now pay for Spanish-language commercials, often shooting separate ads aimed at Mexican, Cuban, and South American audiences. In 1987 the Vons supermarket chain opened its first Tianguis supermarket, catering to the needs and tastes of L.A.'s Latino population. The concept has proven so successful that Vons may open similar food stores in markets outside L.A. And Vons CEO Bill Davila, who was raised in East Los Angeles, is a popular company spokesman in television commercials as well as a role model for area Latinos. Davila, who started at Vons as a floor sweeper and moved up through the ranks, plans to devote more time to serving the Latino community following his retirement in 1992.

Major telephone companies are also providing specialized services for their large Latino clienteles. According to the *Los Angeles Business Journal,* it took lawsuits initiated by Robert Gnaizda, representing groups such as the Mexican American Political Association and the League of Latin American Citizens, to bring the California Public Utilities Commission around. But AT&T, Pacific Bell, and GTE aren't regretting their agreements to provide multilingual phone services now that they've seen the Latino market respond

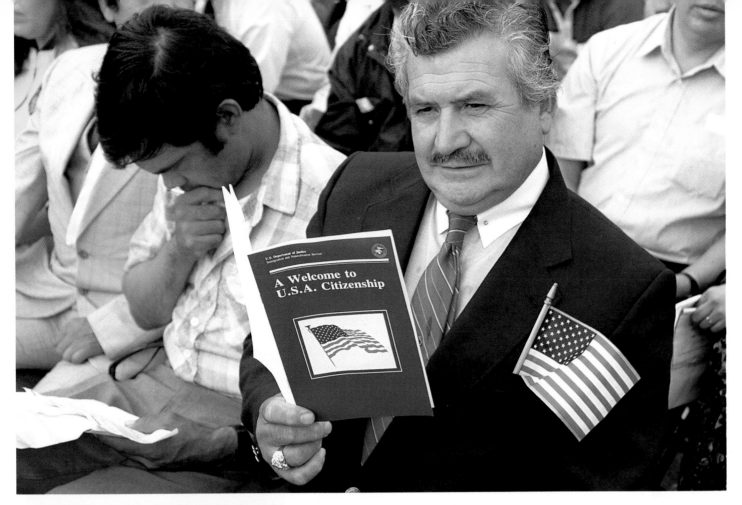

are learning to avoid the pitfalls of stereotyping or inadvertently utilizing taboo topics or translations. Manuel Valencia of Valencia, Maldonado & Echeveste cites Bank of America's new bilingual checks, which feature Latino art, as an example of a positive and successful marketing approach. The bank's automatic teller machines and customer service lines offer bilingual options, as well, and selected branches have bilingual tellers and brochures.

Of course, while Latinos comprise one of the largest of L.A.'s consumer groups, they are one among many ethnic markets in the region. More and more firms now advertise in several languages, and have multilingual staff to serve the newcomers. One San Gabriel Valley car dealership founded by a Filipino immigrant does no advertising, but has a staff which speaks 50 different languages for sales to predominantly Asian customers. More than half of the area's 125 driving schools serve immigrant groups with bilingual instructors familiar with driving conditions in students' native countries. And advertising agency Muse Cordero Chen, owned and operated by a black, a Latina, and an Asian, has achieved striking success in targeting minority markets. L.A.'s increasingly multicultural approach to business has also opened up a variety of jobs for bilingual Angelenos.

to their overtures. And the utilities' new services—such as Pacific Bell's Spanish Yellow Pages—attract not only Latino customers, but also non-Latino companies hoping to target the Latino consumer.

Other types of businesses are also rethinking their marketing strategies. Often with the help of Latino public relations firms, they

Communication is essential in helping non-English-speaking newcomers adapt to their new environment, and the media play a prime role in that process. Within a few years the number of L.A.-area foreign-language publications has grown from a random collection of mostly neighborhood weeklies to nearly 50 native-language newspapers and magazines. According to author Pearlstone, dailies include three in Spanish, three in Japanese, five in Chinese, four in Korean, and one in Vietnamese. There are four weeklies in Korean and four in Vietnamese. L.A. has four Filipino, six Armenian, two Indian, and six Farsi newspapers, and others in German, French, Russian, and more.

Ethnic bookstores, another reflection of L.A.'s diversity, offer consumers reading materials by and about their own, providing a wealth of information not available in mainstream establishments. Specialty bookstores for readers of languages including Tagalog and other Filipino dialects, Armenian, Spanish, French, Chinese, Russian, and Vietnamese also serve as networking centers for their customers, providing support to newcomers as well as cultural memories for the homesick and for those who want to share their heritage with their American-born children. And black bookstores like the Aquarian Book Shop near the Coliseum, said to be the nation's oldest black-owned bookstore, provide black literature ranging from children's books to African-American history texts.

Television also bridges the language and cultural gap for millions of immigrants with news, sports, and dramatic programming in their native tongues. KSCI-TV (Channel 18) has been broadcasting Japanese and Korean programming since 1977. It is now the nation's leading international TV station, with programming in Arabic, Armenian, Cambodian, Chinese, English, Farsi, French, Hebrew, Hindi/Pakistani, Italian, Japanese, Korean, Spanish, Tagalog, Thai, Korean, and Vietnamese. According to the station's general manager, Rosemary Danon, Gallup polls showed that Channel 18 reaches 85 percent of the Chinese and Korean homes in the Los Angeles region. The station's long reign was challenged, however, with the 1990 decision of KAGL (Channel 30) to begin to offer some Asian programming.

Asian-language radio is also experiencing

growing success in L.A. KAZN-AM (K-Asian) went on the air in 1989 and is encountering increasing demand from advertisers eager to tap the Asian market. KMAX-FM, a gospel-music station, also offers some Asian programming; and it airs Spanish-language programming, as well.

The Latino population watches three Spanish-language stations—KMEX (Channel 34), a longtime fixture in L.A.; KWHY (Channel 22); and KVEA (Channel 52). Two new Los Angeles-based Latino cable television stations plan to enter the competition in 1991. Area Latinos also listen to six local Spanish-language radio stations in addition to those beamed up from Mexico.

The approximately 3.5 million Latinos—

Left: Bright sombreros form a still life at Olvera Street's Cinco de Mayo Festival. The celebration commemorates the 1862 Mexican battle that turned back an invading French army and led to Mexico's ultimate liberation. Photo by Joseph Sohm/Chromosohm

Facing page: A *niña* enjoys festivities at Olvera Street's Cinco de Mayo celebration. Photo by Joseph Sohm/Chromosohm

give or take a million or so undocumented immigrants—represent an overall category which includes Mexicans, Cubans, Central Americans, and South Americans. With their country mired in economic problems and with little to stop them from crossing the border, Mexicans are by far the largest immigrant group. They maintain a high visibility, not only because of their sheer numbers

1930 Los Angeles had 368,000 Mexican-born residents, out of a general population of 2 million. Their numbers steadily increased, and by 1940 Los Angeles had the largest Mexican population outside of Mexico City. Like other ethnic groups in the region, Mexicans encountered discrimination, leading to the formation of social and political organizations and the Chicano movement of the seventies.

More than 15,000 Chinese and Southeast Asians live in the Chinatown area. Its markets overflow with fresh, exotic foods, some unfamiliar to Western eyes. Photo by Joseph Sohm/ Chromosohm

but also because they have retained their cultural identity. Many keep in close contact with relatives south of the border and continue to speak Spanish at home.

Mexican culture has had a profound influence on Los Angeles throughout its history. Settlers from Mexico founded the city in 1781, and the Mexican population dominated the Los Angeles area numerically and culturally well into the 1860s, despite becoming part of United States territory in 1848. But eventually the Mexican influence began to fade—and more than a century would pass before L.A.'s Latino population again wielded significant political clout.

In 1910 a wave of refugees fleeing the Mexican Revolution settled in Los Angeles. More fled the turmoil in the 1920s, and by

Today Mexicans make up about 25 percent of L.A.'s population, and their current contributions to the city's political, cultural, and business scenes are commanding respect, as are their contributions to L.A.'s past.

Reminders of its Mexican heritage may be found throughout the city. Famed Olvera Street is the cradle of Mexican culture and a leading tourist attraction. Street signs bear the names of famous families who developed and governed the Los Angeles region during its early years—Sepulveda, Dominguez, Pico, and Figueroa are just a few. And the vibrant culture of Mexico—its food, art, architecture, and music—permeates the Los Angeles scene.

Traditional Mexican events are colorful and well attended. They range from Las

Posadas at Christmas and the Blessing of the Animals on the Saturday before Easter to three-day festivals to celebrate Independence Day in mid-September and Cinco de Mayo. The Independence Day parade, which has been held for some 40 years, now has nearly three times as many entries as the Rose Parade. Cinco de Mayo is not considered a major holiday in Mexico, but in Los Angeles festive throngs jam Olvera Street for the occasion and a spectacular parade attracts thousands each year.

Other Latino immigrant groups are less populous than the Mexicans, but their presence is felt throughout the city. Cubans have been defecting to the United States ever since Castro seized power. Among the early arrivals were many skilled professionals who at first had to take menial jobs but have since progressed in their fields. The first large influx of Cubans came prior to the 1962 Cuban missile crisis when war threat-

ened, and it included 14,000 children who were sent through Operation Pedro (Peter) Pan to live with relatives in the U.S.

Thousands more came in the Mariel boat lift in 1980, and the Cuban Assistance League was formed by those who preceded them to help the *marielito* immigrants adjust to their new location. Today Los Angeles is home to about 125,000 Cubans, who live mostly in the Echo Park and Silver Lake districts of the city.

Many Guatemalans arrived in Los Angeles shortly after World War II and during the 1980s as political refugees, and their numbers—approximately 600,000—have made Los Angeles the second largest Guatemalan city in the world, as it is for a number of other ethnic groups. Most live in the Pico-Union area and Inglewood, and join organized groups of former residents of Guatemalan towns. The Guatemalan community includes about 6,000 Mayans, members of Central America's oldest civilization,

Men gather at a bench in Chinatown to share the news of the day. Photo by Joseph Sohm/Chromosohm

Above: At the 49th Nisei Week Parade, these World War II Japanese-American army soldiers proudly display their colors. Photo by Joseph Sohm/Chromosohm

Facing page: Honoring his heritage, a young musician prepares to drum. Photo by Joseph Sohm/Chromosohm

who speak Mayan dialects rather than the Spanish language. Organizations like the Integration of Indigenous Maya (IXIM), formed by refugees from the Contosal tribe, help the Mayans adjust to their strange new culture.

The Salvadoran immigrant group now numbers about 450,000 in the Los Angeles region. They are the focus of political debate as to whether they are legitimate political refugees entitled to asylum or "economic migrants," as the Reagan administration called them in sending 50,000 back. In any case, bloody civil war has driven many to pay more than $1,000 to be smuggled across Mexico and into Southern California, where they disappear into one of the many Latino communities. Requests for political asylum have increased, but only half who arrived in the U.S. after 1981 qualify for asylum and only about 3 percent of their requests are granted. Under these circumstances, most simply remain among the ranks of the undocumented.

About 50,000 Nicaraguans have emigrated to Los Angeles since 1980 because of political upheaval, internal warfare, and economic decline in their country. Quotas are tight, and many pay to be smuggled across Mexico and into the U.S., then work to finance similar journeys for relatives still in Nicaragua. Loyalty to the opposing Sandanista and Contra factions runs deep and has caused conflict within the Nicaraguan community in

Los Angeles. Recent arrivals from Nicaragua include middle-class professionals seeking a better employment situation as well as political refugees seeking a safe haven.

A groundswell of sympathy for the dispossessed of Central America developed in Los Angeles, and on November 7, 1985, the City Council passed a resolution, sponsored by newly elected Councilman Michael Woo, offering sanctuary to these refugees. Even though it was strictly a symbolic gesture, the resolution challenged federal immigration laws and stirred considerable local controversy. On February 7, 1986, the council approved the Policy on Refugees resolution, a watered-down version of the original which still demonstrated its support for the refugees. A number of local churches and religious organizations acted to provide food, shelter, and counseling to hundreds of homeless immigrants, and such programs continue to offer guidance and support to refugees.

Political unrest and failing economies have been the main reasons for most South Americans' emigration to Los Angeles. The two largest South American groups include approximately 60,000 Peruvians and 45,000 Argentines. Many professionals and well-to-do businessmen came from Argentina during the 1960s; blue-collar workers followed. The Peruvians and Argentines have adapted well to their new environment and live in various parts of the city.

The coup in 1973 brought most of the 16,000 Chilean immigrants to the Los Angeles area. While some have chosen to return now that the conflict in Chile is over, many have adjusted to the American way of life and prefer to stay.

About 7,000 Brazilians have left the uncertain future and failing economy of their homeland and moved to Los Angeles during the past 20 years in search of a better life, and they have brought their special brand of joie de vivre with them. Although small in numbers, they have made a distinct mark on the local scene with their popular music and food, and many are prominent in the entertainment industry and restaurant business.

Like the Mexicans, the Chinese and Japanese have long been a part of L.A.'s cultural mosaic. They were the first Asian ethnic groups to emigrate to America, and their arrival dates back well over a century. Despite having experienced the degradation of virtual slavery and appalling prejudice for part of that century, they have risen to the highest levels of education, government, and the professions.

The Chinese first arrived in the mid-1800s as laborers in San Francisco and the Northern California mine fields during the Gold Rush. They came to L.A. as construction workers on the Southern Pacific Railroad and stayed when the railroad passed through and headed southwest, bringing the Chinese population in Los Angeles to about 4,000 in 1870. Hostility against them was rampant then, and in 1871 a white mob stormed through the Chinese ghetto, leaving 19 dead in the city's worst racial violence until the Watts riots in 1965.

Afraid to compete with whites, most Chinese worked at vegetable farming, peddling, and in laundries and Chinese restaurants. The Federal Exclusion Act of 1902, which permanently barred further Chinese immigration, was not rescinded until 1943. Meantime the original Chinatown was demolished in 1933 to make way for construction of the new railroad terminal. The present Chinatown was established in 1938, and for the first time Chinese were allowed to own land, which they pur-

chased for 75 cents per foot.

Once given the opportunity, the education-minded Chinese soon demonstrated their business skills. With their high-achieving youth as the backbone of their progress, the Chinese branched out into a variety of fields, including medicine, law, and banking.

Today there are approximately 170,000 area residents of Chinese ancestry—a loose-

ly affiliated group. Chinese families here for over a century are thoroughly Americanized, and have little or no connection with China, its politics, or its dialects. Recent arrivals come from Taiwan, the Republic of China, Singapore, or Hong Kong; some struggle with language problems and nearly all have deep political convictions about the present regime in mainland China.

Many Los Angeles Chinese live in and around Chinatown and Monterey Park, al-

Left: Onlookers watch a passing parade during the 49th Nisei Week Festivities. Photo by Joseph Sohm/Chromosohm

Facing page: After enduring the same repressive hostility as most of the other immigrant groups to Los Angeles over the past century and a half, the Asian community has become an integral part of the city's economic and cultural machine. Photo by Jospeh Sohm/Chromosohm

though countless younger professionals have moved to dozens of other suburbs. Chinatown property values have soared with intensive investment by Taiwanese and Hong Kong consortiums, and Los Angeles could well be a prime selection for relocation by wealthy Hong Kong businessmen concerned about what will happen when England surrenders control of its crown colony to the Republic of China in 1997.

Monterey Park, which is over 50 percent Asian—half of whom are Chinese—has a dozen Chinese-run banks, 4 Chinese-language newspapers, more than 60 Chinese restaurants, and several Chinese nightclubs. A short distance away in Hacienda Heights is Hsi Lai Temple, the largest Buddhist monastery in the Western Hemisphere—a 14-acre, 10-building complex housing 40 Buddhist monks and nuns. Chinese New Year in February is always one of the noisiest, most colorful, and most popular celebrations in L.A., with floats, firecrackers, and Chinese dragons.

The other longtime Asian residents of Los Angeles are the Japanese, who arrived after the Chinese and pursued the traditional work they knew best as laborers on large farms all over the state. Several thousand came south after the San Francisco earthquake and fire in 1906; others followed because of growing discrimination in the Northern California farmlands.

A large colony of Japanese fishermen settled in San Pedro shortly after the turn of the century and helped make the Port of Los Angeles the nation's leading fishing port and the world's largest tuna canning center. More than a thousand Japanese lived on Terminal Island, where the women worked in the canneries and the men brought in the catch, until the bombing of Pearl Harbor in 1941. In one of the most disgraceful miscarriages of justice in American history, thousands of loyal Japanese, including all those on Terminal Island, were sent to detention camps, losing everything they owned. A half-century later, the federal government has just begun an attempt to repay them.

Earlier the Japanese had been subjected to the same witless racial prejudice as the Chinese,

and they expanded from farming into whole-saling and retailing within their own community, often through the *tanomishi* underground banking system. Early on, the Japanese owned most of the small businesses in Little Tokyo and worked as gardeners all over the city. Many worked and operated nurseries—and still do—in the Sawtelle Boulevard section of West Los Angeles,

which has been a Japanese enclave for many years. Another large group of Japanese lives in Gardena.

Thousands more Japanese live throughout the Southland, demonstrating success in a wide variety of professions. After being here so long, the Japanese are probably the most thoroughly Americanized of all Asian ethnic groups, although vestiges of Japanese

ranging exhibits. Another annual highlight is the September cultural show which features Japanese art, gardening, and beautiful *koi* fish, many worth thousands of dollars. The ancient Oban Festival, originally a solemn religious festival to honor the souls of the dead, is performed at various Buddhist temples in the area, with a program that recently has been lightened to include entertainment, games, and cultural exhibits.

Hard-working entrepreneurs, the Koreans have made phenomenal progress during the ten years or less that most of them have

Left: The Sree Venkateswara Temple, consecrated in October 1987, is the gathering spot for an estimated 10,000 Hindus in Southern California. It is the largest Hindu temple in the Western Hemisphere. Photo by Joseph Sohm/Chromosohm

been here. The Korean population of nearly 300,000 in Los Angeles—up from a census figure of 60,000 in 1980—is one of the fastest-growing ethnic groups in the city and could total well over a million by the year 2000, according to an official estimate.

Nearly 40 percent of the Koreans in the county live in Koreatown, a prosperous, burgeoning business area concentrated on Olympic Boulevard between Normandie and Hoover. Their business success has been due in part to the Koreans' *kye* banking system for start-up money, their willingness to take over failing non-Korean businesses, and their own dedication. Their persistence and hard work has paid off with a median Korean household income of $41,730 per year and purchasing power that has not been lost on the Anglo business community.

Ironically, the austere routine at the Bud-

Above: Two Hare Krishna initiates pose at the India Festival of Chariots in Santa Monica. Photo by Joseph Sohm/Chromosohm

culture remain and efforts are being made to preserve it, especially by the Japanese American Cultural and Community Center downtown and the Japanese Cultural Institute in Gardena.

The biggest Japanese event of the year is Nisei Week in August, with parades, traditional floats, kimono-clad dancers, bands, races, carnivals, and bonsai and flower-ar-

dhist Dharma Sah Zen Center attracts more native-born Americans than Korean Americans, most of whom are Christian rather than Buddhist. Instead, nearly three quarters of the new arrivals attend some 500 Korean Protestant churches, which also serve as cultural and social centers. The region's Korean network also includes 150 social groups, 86 alumni associations, and 18 Buddhist temples. The Korean community's biggest annual event is a week-long festival and parade in September, in observance of Full Moon Day, which corresponds to the American Thanksgiving.

With the Philippines under American colonial rule from 1898 until their independence in 1946, Filipinos have been emigrating to the U.S. for more than 50 years. Immigration laws which grant citizenship after five years' residency to Filipinos who have worked for the U.S. government for at least 15 years brought in thousands, as well as large numbers who serve in the American armed forces. With an estimated county population of approximately

Angelenos remain fiercely proud of their national origins. Photo by Joseph Sohm/Chromosohm

350,000, Filipinos comprise one of the largest ethnic groups in the area and are considered one of the most affluent after years of being established here.

Despite their numbers, Filipinos here tend to be fragmented socially by the 90 different languages they speak and by their origins in more than 7,000 islands in the

Philippines. Filipinos have melded easily into the mainstream because of their long-time familiarity with the American language and culture. The Filipino community's most important annual celebration is the Philippine Heritage Festival held in May, highlighted by a colorful parade demonstrating ethnic and cultural pride.

Though the census figures are low, there might be as many as 75,000 Vietnamese in the Los Angeles area and at least that many in Little Saigon and other parts of Orange County. The Vietnamese continue to grow in numbers as earlier arrivals establish themselves and bring relatives from Vietnam and the refugee camps of Southeast Asia. Many of the Vietnamese who arrived right after the fall of Saigon in 1975 were skilled, well-to-do professionals who have adapted well to their new life. Since then hundreds of other industrious Vietnamese have joined the business community as operators of service stations, convenience stores, and restaurants, while their children are winning high honors for scholastic achievements in local schools and universities.

Most of the 50,000 Cambodians now living in the Los Angeles area have arrived since 1985 as refugees from the horrors of war and genocide. They have settled primarily in Long Beach, where they number about 40,000 and form the largest Cambodian community in the country. While earlier arrivals in 1979 had the advantage of being trained professionals, Cambodian immigrants in recent years come from small rural communities and often require special help to adjust to American culture. Some have achieved remarkable success with little or no business background. Doughnut shops were among their first business ventures, and Cambodians have since branched out to most of the service industries in Long Beach. The Cambodian New Year in April and *Pchum Ben,* the Festival of Ancestors, in late September are the two major Cambodian events of the year.

In 1977 a small group of Cambodian refugees founded the United Cambodian Community (UCC), established as a self-help group and operated initially with modest funds raised primarily within the refugee community. UCC quickly grew into one of the leading refugee service agencies in the U.S. Today UCC, headquartered in Long Beach, has a full-time staff of over 60 management and program specialists, 80 percent of whom were once refugees. In addition to Southeast Asians, UCC's multicultural staff also counsels and trains people in need from Eastern Europe, Central America, Mexico, and Africa. In little over a decade, UCC has provided job training and counseling for over 25,000 refugees and immigrants and has placed more than 10,000 in permanent full-time jobs.

The estimated 100,000 Thais in the Los Angeles area were not driven from their country by war as were most other Asians, but came here in search of a better life and more opportunity. English instruction in schools has helped them overcome the language barrier, and they have actively entered the business community, primarily in the restaurant field, where Thai food has become very popular. The Thai population lives mostly in the Mid-Wilshire, Hollywood, Long Beach, and San Fernando Valley areas. The three-day Thai New Year observance of *Songkran* is held in April at the Wat Thai Temple in North Hollywood.

The Laotian community of approximately 30,000 in the L.A. area is relatively new among Asian-Pacific groups, but is expected to grow steadily due to secondary immigration—relatives who follow first-wave immigrants. Many Laotians face language and adjustment problems and receive assistance from United Way-supported relief organizations like the International Institute, United Cambodian Community, and others. The Lao population is widely dispersed, with concentrations in the San Gabriel Valley, Van Nuys, and Long Beach.

Among Asia's recent emigres are about 70,000 Indians who have made Southern California home. Most are from southern and western India—students, professionals, and later, the second-wave relatives of professionals—who immigrated to L.A. in the

1960s and 1970s. Today they are active in business and the professions throughout the metropolitan area. A colorful concentration of Indian businesses is located in a section of Artesia known as "Little India." The intricately beautiful Sree Venkateswara Temple in Calabasas serves as a religious and cultural center for some 10,000 Hindus in the re-

Religious worship in Los Angeles is as diverse as its citizens. Churches, mosques, temples, and synagogues coexist side-by-side throughout L.A. Photo by Joseph Sohm/ Chromosohm

gion. Though many Indians have adopted American customs and dress, traditional culture is celebrated on Indian Independence Day in mid-August, at events held throughout the area.

Among the Pacific Islanders, there are an estimated 60,000 American and Western Samoans in the Los Angeles area—a population larger than the entire native population of American Samoa. There is no restriction on immigration for American Samoans, who are United States citizens; most have come because of the limited opportunities at home. Many live in the Carson area, and most Samoan-owned businesses are located there. In 1988 the Samoans held their first Flag Day festival in Victoria Park, Carson, celebrating Samoan independence after 88 years as a territory of the United States.

The Hawaiian community, consisting of about 7,000 in the L.A. area, celebrates its island heritage at the Ho'olaulea Hawaiian Festival in Lawndale's Alondra Park, held annually in July. Other Pacific Islanders in Los Angeles include about 20,000 Tongans, 4,000 Guamanians, and small groups from Fiji and Indonesia.

The overall achievements of the Asian-Pacific immigrants are well documented and little short of remarkable in view of the overwhelming and intimidating problems many faced when they arrived. A survey by KSCI-TV shows that 70 percent of all Southern California Japanese-American and Korean-American heads of households attended college (nearly twice the national average), and 60 percent of that group earns $30,000 or more per year, well over the national average.

In a sense the Asian-Pacific group has been too successful, so that its contributions are recognized while its needs go unmet. A 1988 study of the 10 largest Asian groups by the Los Angeles United Way Asian Pacific Research Development Council found evidence of extreme need within those ethnic

Below: A young lass in traditional Scottish garb enjoys the Highland Gathering and Festival. Photo by Joseph Sohm/ Chromosohm

groups for the elderly, refugees, orphaned children, single parents, and adolescents.

Yet less than half of one percent of all donations from foundations and corporations in the Los Angeles area go to Asian causes, according to a 1990 report from the Asian Pacific Planning Council. Of the estimated $41.7 million allocated by the United Way to

ethnic agencies in 1990-1991, only $2.9 million—or 7 percent—was earmarked for Asian-Pacific groups. "Asians tend to suffer from the stereotype that they are the model minority—the scholars, good incomes, stable family life," a council spokesman says. "This United Way study has identified the other side to that."

Unlike many Asians, who may need time and assistance to adjust to a radically different culture, newcomers to Los Angeles from Europe adjust readily and blend easily into the American scene. The majority are familiar with the American way of life, have few language difficulties, and experience little of

the culture shock which can have such a traumatic effect on many Asian immigrants. Most Europeans speak English well, if not fluently, and they find the American job market similar in many ways to their own.

Europeans in the Los Angeles area include about 100,000 English newcomers, many of whom live near the ocean in Santa

brate half a dozen church-sponsored festivals during the year.

Also, the Los Angeles area is home to well over 150,000 Italians, who are prominent in the professions and run some of the finest restaurants in the area as well as a host of other businesses; about 25,000 native-born Irish and more than a million of Irish descent; well over 100,000 Scandinavians—the Norwegians being the largest in that group, with a century-old Norwegian community in San Pedro—as well as Danes, Swedes, and Finns, and about 200 Icelanders.

The Los Angeles area also claims about 50,000 Scots, whose Annual Scottish Festival at the Orange County Fairgrounds in Costa

Left: Fifty thousand Scots call Los Angeles home. Photo by Joseph Sohm/ Chromosohm

Below: A contestant "throws the hammer" at the Highland Gathering and Festival, held at the Orange County Fairgrounds. Photo by Joseph Sohm/Chromosohm

Monica, where pubs and music halls make them feel at home. About 100,000 Dutch immigrants formed a large community of dairy farmers several decades ago; the community is gone now, but its influence lingers in the Dutch social clubs still in existence. About 50,000 French immigrants celebrate Bastille Day in July, and approximately 30,000 Germans stay in touch through clubs and celebrate Oktoberfest at Alpine Village in Torrance. About 100,000 Greeks, many of whom worship and socialize at the majestic Saint Sophia Greek Orthodox Cathedral on Pico Boulevard, operate hundreds of specialty stores, markets, and restaurants, and cele-

Mesa has been a popular Memorial Day weekend event for years; some 30,000 Yugoslavs of conflicting political views, including about 20,000 Croatians who have lived for generations in San Pedro and were influential in the development of the fishing and canning industries; 10,000 Serbs who work mainly in construction; and many thousands of emigres from the Soviet Union, including a large detachment of Soviet Jews, who gravitated toward the Jewish neighborhood around Beverly-Fairfax.

An Armenian-American population of about 250,000 has been increasing with the arrival of large numbers of ethnic Armenians from the Soviet Union since the Soviets eased their strict policy on exit visas. Despite the size of the population and some concentration in Glendale and Hollywood, the Armenians are not a close-knit group due to their wide variety of backgrounds, homelands, religions, and politics.

Like those who migrated from Europe, most of the 200,000 to 300,000 Arabs and Arab Americans came to the Los Angeles area well equipped to cope with the adjustment to America in terms of language, education, and financial security. Most were trained professionals who could afford to emigrate, and many had attended U.S. universities before moving here permanently. Some arrive with the capital and experience to open new businesses or purchase existing ones, or the qualifications to enter medicine, law, or the other skilled professions.

The seizure of power by the Ayotollah Khomeini regime triggered the wholesale flight of a large segment of Iran's educated elite, who now account for most of the approximately half million Iranians in Los Angeles, including many of the Jewish faith. The Iranians have done well here despite a surge of overt hostility during the hostage crisis from confused Americans who did not seem to realize that these immigrants were outspoken foes of Khomeini and not his followers.

Thriving Israeli businesses have had a

considerable impact on the local economy, and successful businesspeople and professionals comprise a large part of the population of 100,000 to 200,000 Israelis living in the Los Angeles area. In spite of their outstanding achievements in nearly every field, some Israelis remain undecided as to whether to stay or go back to Israel, while their elders mourn the loss of the orthodox religion and traditional Jewish culture among Americanized young Israelis.

Palestinians in the area number about

A young couple enjoy a sunny afternoon in Watts. Photo by Joseph Sohm/Chromosohm

45,000, and although some have had economic difficulties, others have been notably successful in law, medicine, and teaching, and most will remain until a Palestinian homeland becomes a reality.

Though most African Americans are not newcomers to Los Angeles, the area's black population comprises one of its most significant ethnic groups. Black history in Los Angeles dates back to the founding of the city in 1781; 26 of the original 44 settlers were either black or mulatto. In John D. Weaver's

El Pueblo Grande, published in 1973, the author writes:

Young Chicanos see reminders of their heritage in streets named for their forebears and in the tourist attraction Anglos have made of the Plaza, but black children are left in ignorance of their heritage. Few ever learn that the San Fernando Valley and Beverly Hills were once owned by blacks; that Pio Pico, the last of the Mexican governors of California, had a grandmother listed by

census-takers as mulata; *and that one of the first two Americans to settle in Los Angeles was a black man named Thomas Fisher, who came ashore from a pirate ship in 1818.*

Despite this early presence, census figures record a slow increase in the black population in the early years: only 12 in 1850, and 188 in 1880. Nevertheless, a thriving black community developed during the early 1900s. The Los Angeles Forum Club was founded in 1903 to promote a "united effort on the part of Negroes for their advance . . ." And later, the vibrant Sugar Hill neighborhood in the Central-Adams area became home to many successful blacks.

However, racial discrimination, always a bitter fact of minority life, became more virulent in the late 1920s and early 1930s as the black community grew. By 1920 the black population of the county had reached 19,000, and housing restrictions, as previously imposed on the Chinese, Japanese, and Jewish populations, steadily forced blacks into South-Central Los Angeles. Many African Americans started their own companies when white-owned firms declined to do business with them. By 1940 the Golden State Mutual Life Insurance Company was the largest black-owned business in the Western United States.

The major migration of blacks to L.A. began during World War II, when the booming aircraft industry and its enormous demand for workers brought thousands of blacks to the area, most from the South, where industrial progress had devastated agriculture. The majority stayed after the war, and by 1950 the black population had increased to over 200,000. As in other parts of the country, blacks continued to encounter and fight discrimination. The 1965 Watts Riots in L.A. are one painful memory of racial tension during a difficult era.

In the decades which followed, the Los Angeles black community grew in numbers and in social, economic, and political power. The 1990 census lists the Los Angeles County black population at 934,776. L.A.'s postwar economic progress helped bring blacks into the mainstream of politics, business, and other areas. Mayor Tom Bradley, the late Councilman Gilbert Lindsay, and others were among the first African Americans elected to high office in a major American city. In addition, thousands of blacks have used education and affirmative action programs as potent tools in the quest for racial equality, and have reached the highest levels in medicine, law, the arts, industry, and business.

The latest State Survey of Minority-Owned Businesses, which is taken every five years, indicates that there were 23,953 black-owned businesses in Los Angeles County in 1987. In its annual listing of the top 100 black-owned businesses, the national publication *Black Enterprise* lists Shack-Woods & Associates of Los Angeles as the largest black-owned auto deal-

ership in the United States. And Golden West Mutual Life Insurance Company of Los Angeles is the third largest black-owned insurance firm in the country.

The Black Business Association of Los Angeles assists its 300 member firms in bidding for state, federal, and private industry contracts. Black business growth is also fostered by programs ranging from the 101 Foundation, which targets at-risk youngsters and provides them with positive role models, to the Black Business Expo, which helps black-owned businesses network. One outing sponsored by the 101 Foundation in 1990 took 14 disadvantaged teenagers from the inner city on a tour of the Pacific Stock Exchange and West Los Angeles brokerage Oppenheimer & Co. Broker George Arterberry, who grew up in South-Central Los Angeles, offered the youths one example of black professional success.

The Black Business Expo, held for the second year in April 1990, attracted 150 exhibitors, 100 more than in its inaugural year. The Expo at the Los Angeles Convention Center was sponsored by businesses and community groups such as Recycling Black Dollars, a nonprofit organization that encourages blacks to patronize black-owned businesses. Exhibitors included bakeries, radio stations, clothing designers, insurance and real estate firms, gourmet candy makers, security services, and computer consultants, among others.

Black media services are also prospering. The *Los Angeles Sentinel*, published since 1933, is the largest black-owned newspaper in the city, with a weekly circulation of 35,000 and readership of 175,000. Leading black radio stations include KGLH-FM, owned by singer Stevie Wonder; KACE-FM, owned by ex-pro football star Willie Davis; and KGFJ-FM.

Black studies programs in schools throughout the region stimulate pride and interest in preserving African-American heritage. Another reflection of cultural pride is the African Marketplace, a summertime festival organized by the city's William Grant Still Community Arts Center. Storytelling, Yoruba

Facing page: Ferdia Harris, management analyst for the Community Development Department of Los Angeles, chats with neighbors in a South-Central Los Angeles neighborhood. Harris devotes herself to counselling troubled youths, providing job referrals to the unemployed, and beautifying her neighborhood. Photo by Shelley Gazin

"Multiculturalism" is
truly the buzzword for
Los Angeles as the city
enters the twenty-first
century. Photo by Shelley
Gazin

chants, batiks, reggae, and Ethiopian dishes draw blacks from throughout Los Angeles to savor a celebration of their heritage. The Still Community Arts Center features a variety of cultural events, classes, and exhibits—its annual Black Doll Show has been going strong since 1980. Another cultural center is the privately owned Museum in Black in South-Central L.A., which displays a permanent collection of 2,000 traditional African art pieces: masks, statues and figurines, fetishes, textiles, and body adornments.

Many area blacks also celebrate Kwanzaa, a festival created in 1965 to promote black pride. Kwanzaa is the brainchild of Los Angeles activist Maulana Karenga, chairman of US, a black cultural organization, and is celebrated in a variety of ways for the week beginning December 26. Processions, feasts, bazaars, concerts, and family gatherings—featuring traditional values and symbols—honor black heritage.

There are no large ethnic groups from Africa in Los Angeles: the only one of significant size is an Ethiopian population of about 25,000. Next in size would be the Liberian group of about 5,000, including students, followed by Ghanians and Kenyans with some 2,000 each, also including students, and smaller groups from Uganda, Zimbabwe, Senegal, Somalia, Mali, and Tanzania. Other immigrants come to L.A. from even more remote sections of the world; the 50 or so Tibetans make up one of Southern California's smallest ethnic communities.

Inevitably, any attempt to define Los Angeles' multiplicity of ethnic and racial groups is likely to suffer from generalization. The Los Angeles Cultural Affairs Department addresses this issue in its Cultural Master Plan, released in October 1990: "The major racial/ethnic categories provide only an overview of the cultural diversity in the city. Each of the major groups . . . include a collection of highly differentiated ethnic populations, having very different historical experiences and cultural orientations."

The complexity of the city's ethnic population leaves observers straining for metaphors. Certainly the old melting pot

concept—largely a nineteenth-century, and an East Coast, ideal—breaks down when applied to L.A. In the series, "Beyond the Melting Pot," *Los Angeles Times* writer Itabari Njeri states, "Blending in was once considered the ideal. But as the racial and ethnic nature of the nation has changed, so has that ideal. Throughout the nation, and especially in California, *multiculturalism*—the concept of looking at the world through the eyes of more than one culture—is the new end-of-the-millenium buzzword."

"The contemporary ideal is not assimilation, but ethnicity," writes historian Arthur Schlesinger, Jr. "The melting pot yields to the Tower of Babel," as today's immigrants strive to maintain a balance between assimilation and preservation of their identity. Nowhere is this struggle—with all of its conflicts, successes, and failures—more evident than in Los Angeles.

From a sleepy citrus-growing outpost at the turn of the century Los Angeles has metamorphosed on a gigantic scale into one of the great international cities of the world. Waves of immigration have drastically altered its appearance with sharp, bold brush strokes during the past few decades, and its character will become even more diverse in the century to come.

This revolutionary period of change has had a profound effect on all of L.A.'s citizens, from the native-born to the newcomer. Each learns and benefits from the other, and their lives are the richer for it. Even though the local culture might seem overwhelming at first, those immigrants whose hopes and dreams were shackled and oppressed by authoritarian governments in their native lands soon discover here a measure of personal freedom many never knew existed—to speak, to worship, to vote, to plan their lives, and to achieve any social and economic level possible through their initiative and talents.

Already they have added new luster to the cultural fabric of the city, giving it an international ambience unlike that of any other metropolis in the United States. For them, as for all who come here, Los Angeles is indeed the "realm of possibility."

ON WITH THE SHOW

The Arts in Los Angeles

When it comes to the City of Angels, the pundits automatically unload their biggest guns, their choicest epithets, and most bilious metaphors. They either love Los Angeles or they hate it. There is no middle ground. Over time Los Angeles has been described by nearly every adjective in the language—usually in the superlative degree, sometimes in unprintable terms. Among other things, it has been called brash, irreverent, gaudy, bawdy, unorthodox, freewheeling, liberated, capricious, pioneering, theatrical, and adventurous.

To whatever degree they are true, these qualities have combined to create an atmosphere that is remarkably unfettered by traditional restraints. An ideal breeding ground for artistic adventure and freedom of expression. A haven for the uninhibited.

In a cultural sense, Los Angeles was decidedly a late bloomer. Long after the old Eastern cities had the time to consider the aesthetics of civilized living, Los Angeles was still a citrus-growing center sleeping in the sun. "It's a great place to be if you're an orange," cracked Fred Allen. Early on, some of the distinguished names in the arts came here to work in the motion picture industry, but their presence had little impact on local culture, and no sophisticated

"IN EUROPE, EVERYTHING IS HISTORIC; IN LOS ANGELES, EVERYTHING IS JUST BEGINNING."

—ISAAC MIZRAHI, NEW YORK FASHION DESIGNER, 1990

Paul Conrad, *L.A. Times* editorial cartoonist, poses with a drawing of his controversial sculpture *Chain Reaction.* Photo by Joseph Sohm/Chromosohm

Below: Lunch on the Venice boardwalk can consist of seafood, wine, and dessert, with a spectacular view of the Pacific Ocean's crashing waves. The view is always free. Photo by Joseph Sohm/Chromosohm

Angeleno cared to be identified with a disreputable business like the movies.

World War II was directly responsible for the explosive growth of Los Angeles; everything about the city expanded enormously after the war. When the community's intelligentsia finally got around to the dilatory state of local arts and culture, they found very little to work with. Just when this belated attention translated itself into meaningful progress is difficult to define. Even after a quarter century of dispensing insightful and highly literate commentary on area arts and culture, *Los Angeles Times* critic-at-large Charles Champlin still finds it "hard to get a fix on, hard to summarize" that aspect of the city.

"It has been grossly undervalued as an art center for years, the sport of jokes by Fred Allen and others who have bounced in and out of Los Angeles like ping-pong balls," Champlin says. "On the other hand, it has been at least as egregiously oversold by boosters who could hear a Beethoven symphony in a street-corner mouth organist."

He adds: "The Olympic Arts Festival [in 1984] confirmed the existence of a large and sophisticated audience for the arts here. The Music Center itself, the Orange County Performing Arts Center, the Museum of Contemporary Art, and the expanded Los

Facing page: Moran de-Musee adds a new angle to a model of his proposed sculpture, *La Vecchia Mura di Santa Monica,* which won an arts competition sponsored by the City of Santa Monica. Photo by Shelley Gazin

Angeles County Art Museum are, among other structures and institutions, proof that the citizenry will not only consume art but will pay good and continuing money to sustain it."

The 1964 opening of the Dorothy Chandler Pavilion and subsequent completion of the Mark Taper Forum and Ahmanson Theatre in the Music Center complex were sig-

"the colossus on Bunker Hill [would] act like a great cultural sponge, sopping up all audiences, art funds, and creativity in Los Angeles."

It has, in fact, proved to be just the opposite. "The opening of the Music Center gave the metropolitan Los Angeles area a sense of cultural cohesion," Champlin wrote. "It has functioned as a stimulus and catalyst . . .

Left: The Music Center's impact on the ever-changing Los Angeles arts-and-culture scene has been enormous. Photo by Shelley Gazin

Facing page: Ballerina Leslie Carruthers forms a graceful piece of human sculpture before Robert Graham's sculpture, *Dance Door,* at the Music Center. Photo by Shelley Gazin

nificant milestones. The three beautiful new venues were urgently needed for the development of the performing arts in Los Angeles.

In a larger sense, the Music Center's impact has been even more pervasive and far-reaching. In a retrospective on the occasion of the Music Center's 25th anniversary in 1989, Champlin recalled initial concern that

demonstrably enlarging rather than diminishing or merely relocating the amount of theater in the community."

Without question the most remarkable cultural advance in Los Angeles in recent years has been the blossoming of the contemporary art scene from a comatose state of benign neglect to world-class stature within a decade. The amazing renaissance began in

Emmy Award-winning set designer Ray Klaussen's uniquely sculptural designs have graced the productions of stars like Diana Ross, Orson Wells, Martha Graham, Michael Jackson, David Bowie, Cher, and even Miss Piggy. Photo by Shelley Gazin

ARTIFICIAL

ART OFFICIAL

1979 when a small but determined group of private citizens decided to remedy the embarrassing fact that Los Angeles was the only major city in the United States without a significant museum devoted exclusively to contemporary art.

Funding for a new museum came from a Community Redevelopment Agency initiative which required that at least one percent of the budget of any development under CRA jurisdiction be earmarked for public art. Renowned Japanese architect Arata Isozaki was commissioned to design the building.

The new Museum of Contemporary Art (MOCA) staff soon began assembling a first-class collection from gifts and donations and

needed temporary exhibition space. It found that facility in a nearby building that had originally been a hardware store and later a city warehouse and police garage. Named the Temporary Contemporary (TC), it was skillfully renovated by prominent Los Angeles architect Frank Gehry. Everyone loved the TC for its accessibility, informality, and lack of pretension. The *New York Times* called it a "prince of spaces." William Wilson of the *Los Angeles Times* said it "instantly had the hospitable aura of a people's museum."

MOCA presented its first exhibition, comprised of approximately 150 works from eight American and European private collections, in November 1983 at the Temporary

Director Stephen Garrett stands in the Armand Hammer Museum, which opened in the sleek Westside in November 1990. Photo by Shelley Gazin

Contemporary. The exhibition was a resounding critical success and immediately established MOCA as a forceful presence in the world of national and international art.

Under the inspired leadership of director Richard Koshalek, MOCA continued to build an outstanding collection of modern art over the next few years. In December 1986 approximately 800 journalists from all over the country covered the opening of the new MOCA building and its inaugural exhibition of over 400 works by 70 artists. Press notices were almost unanimously favorable, some ecstatic. Michael Brenson of the *New York Times* wrote: "Los Angeles now has one of the finest facilities for contemporary arts in the world."

Sharing the opening accolades and much of the attention was the museum building itself, which already has been called one of the most important new pieces of architecture to appear in Los Angeles in years. Isozaki's striking design of geometric shapes and Indian sandstone stands out in welcome re-

lief among the landscape of high rises in the downtown financial section.

At present MOCA has assembled a permanent collection of post-World War II art that rivals any contemporary art collection in existence. And despite its youth MOCA has been able to attract the finest traveling exhibitions. One of the highlights of its 1990 season was a retrospective of the work of Southern California artist John Baldesseri, a pioneer in conceptual art who achieved extensive honors abroad before receiving belated recognition at home.

By now the city is fully committed to bet-

tering the cultural climate on a broad scale. The Cultural Affairs Department (CAD) has the basic goal of strengthening the quality of life in Los Angeles by stimulating and supporting cultural activities and ensuring access to those activities for all residents and visitors. With a 1989-1990 budget of $9 million and recently increased cultural grants funding of more than $1.4 million, CAD sponsors exhibitions, arts instruction, theater, music, and dance performances; and

photography and folk arts. CAD also monitors the aesthetics of city property and makes decisions on the preservation of historical monuments.

Multiple objectives of the Community Redevelopment Agency (CRA) are to develop a public arts program unique to Los Angeles; increase understanding and enjoyment of public art; provide employment opportunities for artists; encourage collaboration among artists, architects, and engineers; promote artists' participation on design teams for planning public projects; support the city's pluralistic culture; and encourage all variety of art forms. CRA's landmark Downtown Art in Public Places policy requires developers to set aside one percent or more of their total costs to finance cultural and artistic features within their projects, with 40 percent of that one percent deposited in a downtown cultural trust fund to be used for general enhancement of downtown cultural resources.

"There are so many good L.A. art galleries one couldn't even mention them all . . . many showing younger artists who I later see here [in New York]. You feel it's lively there, and I think MOCA helped pick up the whole art community and get it going," says New York art dealer Paula Cooper. With MOCA and the TC beckoning nearby as beacons of hope and encouragement, the industrial Alameda district of the city has evolved into one of the area's most vibrant art centers, with an estimated 2,000 artists living and working there. Warehouses and old buildings have been converted into lofts, studios, and galleries, turning the district into a sort of Soho West, although rents have risen considerably of late since young professionals have made the district a trendy business location.

The Cirrus Gallery on Alameda Street is one of the pioneer galleries in that area, and one of the most prestigious. Cirrus director Jean Milant, who has been instrumental in shaping the downtown art scene, moved there from Melrose Avenue in 1979 because he felt downtown was "going to be the center of things." How right he was! Cirrus showcases some of the best local talent, staunchly dedicated to California artists and sculptors.

The Santa Fe Art Colony, a $3-million, 45-unit complex on the site of a former terrycloth robe plant, was opened in December 1987 as the city's first large-scale subsidized housing

Artist Charles Arnoldi is outstanding in his foundry. Photo by Shelley Gazin

for low-income artists. It was funded in part by a $1.2-million loan from the Community Redevelopment Agency. Applicants must prove they are serious artists and do not earn over $18,000 yearly. They are not evicted if they later exceed the income level, but are allowed to remain to lend encouragement to other artists trying to make a go of it.

Los Angeles took a giant step forward in its public support of the arts in November 1988, when the City Council adopted the Los Angeles Endowment for the Arts, a trust fund that will provide new funding sources for the cultural life of the city. The endowment will eventually increase municipal spending on the arts from $5 million to as much as $25 million a year, in one bold stroke taking Los Angeles from thirty-eighth among U.S. cities to second in the nation in terms of dollar support of the arts.

Much of the credit for the endowment is due to years of effort by Councilman Joel Wachs, who first proposed the increase in 1985, when the city's budget for the arts was $3 million. The endowment's main goals are to serve all facets of the community, take in

Left: Artist Clayton LeFevre's studio was created when the enterprising painter converted a rundown Pabst Blue Ribbon brewery space in East Los Angeles to a rooftop workplace in just seven weeks. Photo by Shelley Gazin

Muralist Judy Baca, a founding director of Social Public Art Resource Center (SPARC), is at work on another creation. Baca, with 215 schoolchildren, painted the world's longest mural, *The Great Wall of L.A.,* along the banks of the Los Angeles River. Photo by Shelley Gazin

THE WRITING ON THE WALL

L.A.'s Famous Streetscapes

Los Angeles is the mural capital of the world. Over 1,500 wall-paintings grace its storefronts, alleys, and street corners. Among the city's muralists are social activists, master's candidates from Otis Parsons School of Design, and *pachucos* (gang members). Their subjects are war, peace, ethnicity, celebrities, and the Olympics—to name a few.

In Venice, Botticelli's masterpiece, *The Birth of Venus,* has been re-created, L.A. style, on the wall of the St. Mark's Hotel at 25 Windward Avenue by local artist "Cronk." Cronk's *Venus* wears gym shorts and rollerskates.

On Skid Row, a wall of the La Jolla Hotel has been transformed into a map for the homeless. The mural titled *The Street Speaks* (721 E. 6th Street and Stanford Avenue) directs displaced persons to food, shelter, and government assistance. Beside it, a sign asks, "Could You Live on $228 A Month?"

"Our multicultural communities are terribly underserved by the arts," says Judith Baca, founder and artistic director of SPARC (Social and Public Art Resource Center) and creator of *The Street Speaks,* who has been painting murals for 20 years. "The people in these communities are not likely to be museum and gallery attendees. We bring our murals to where they live and work."

Unlike museum art, murals brave rain, blistering sun, smog, graffiti, and accidental whitewashing. They crumble when their buildings are gutted. Some, like Wille Herron's *Quetzalcoatl* (Carmelita Avenue and City Terrace Drive) and Kent Twitchell's *Freeway Lady* (Hollywood Freeway, near the Alvarado exit) become obscured by trash bins and newly built hotels. Few remain standing ten years after their creation.

The most famous Los Angeles mural is *The Great Wall,* stretching 2,435 feet along the Los Angeles River in the San Fernando Valley. It is the longest mural in the world. *The Great Wall* depicts the ethnic history of California from ancient times to the 1950s. It was created

by Judith Baca and 215 schoolchildren.

Each neighborhood has its own visual language, style, and iconography. Chicano muralists use pre-Columbian images and popular cultural motifs to convey their messages. Many, like Yreina Cervantez, depict important historical figures to foster community pride.

Cervantez' *La Ofrenda* ("The Offering") (Toluca Street, under the First

Street bridge) memorializes Dolores Huerta, cofounder of the United Farmworkers Union. "She was one of the first strong role models we Chicanas and Latinas had," says Cervantez. "She defied stereotypes and remained a positive force in our community."

Most Los Angeles muralists are influenced by the works of "Los Tres Grande,"—Diego Rivera, Jose Clemente

American neighborhoods are celebrated with murals. In Watts, for example, artist Richard Wyatt painted *Cecil*, a giant face (1727 E. 107th Street), as a tribute to Watts activist Cecil Fergerson. Artist Roderick Sykes created *Literacy* (LAUSD Maintenance Building, 1406 Highland Avenue at Pico Boulevard) as a tribute to hope. "I wanted to show kids in gangs, committing crimes, that there are alternatives."

Across the city in Koreatown, artist Sonia Hahn completed the stylized *Madame Shin Sa-Im-Dang* (1325 S. Western Avenue) to honor the famous poet, writer, and founder of the Yi Dynasty. "She was a good mother, homemaker, and spiritual leader for other women," says Hahn. "These are things we cherish in Asian culture."

And in Hollywood, where celebrity is king, the predominant mural theme is stardom. Richard Wyatt's 26-foot by 88-foot *Hollywood Jazz, 1945-1972* (Capitol Records Building, south wall, 1750 Vine Street at Hollywood Boulevard) features musical pioneers Chet Baker, Charlie Parker, and Nat King Cole. Alfredo de Batuc's *Dolores Del Rio* (1700 N. Hudson Avenue at Hollywood Boulevard) depicts the famous Latina actress surrounded by her movie stills.

Muralists work under conditions that other artists would find unbearable. They labor for minimal fees in rain, smog, and wind, battling noise and continual interruptions. Muralists paint simply because they love their art, and their dedication is legendary.

From 1972 until 1976 artist Kent Twitchell toiled on *Bride and Groom* (Victor's Tuxedo Shop, Broadway and Third Street), a seven-story blue-monochrome mural of a bride and groom in love. Each night, "so I wouldn't have to pay for parking," Twitchell arrived at the wall at 7 p.m. He taped two light bulbs to his scaffolding, climbed several stories up, then painted in the dark, "listening to talk radio," until 8 a.m. the following day.

"Muralists are quite impassioned people," says Judith Baca. "You have to hang from a rope or scaffolding and deal with the elements. But it's thrilling. Because you impact the landscape and you get direct feedback from people as you paint."

Alfredo de Batuc says that when he

painted *Dolores Del Rio*, "People stopped me and asked 'why are you doing it in *that* color?' or told me 'the flower doesn't look too good.' Sometimes they were right. And as I was painting, fans [of del Rio] stopped by and told me stories. They knew her. Some were even on the set when she filmed."

Mural art is not an individual vision. It is a cultural exchange shared by local residents and community youths who often paint alongside the artist. "Murals allow the public to see, touch, and be a part of the process," says artist Roderick Sykes. "Art and community must go hand-in-hand," adds Alan Takagawa, Program Coordinator at SPARC.

Marguerite Garcia's *Deaf Boy Signs Hope* (8th Street entrance to the Harbor Museum) was painted by a crew of deaf children. Yreina Cervantez' *La Ofrenda* was completed by a team of Chicano, Salvadoran, and Guatemalan children. Sonia Hahn's *Madame Shin Sa-Im-Dang* was painted by five Korean youths. "It gave me a chance to reveal our heritage to them," says Sonia Hahn. "We were able to explore our ancestry and values."

Los Angeles' murals are humorous, colorful, playful. They are thoughtful, angry, and accusative. Always, they are provocative.

Witness Eloy Torres' *The Pope of Broadway* (Third Street and Broadway), a seven-story, 60-foot-wide Anthony Quinn dancing Zorba the Greek. Or Kent Twitchell's *Holy Trinity with the Virgin* (Otis School of Design, west wall, Carondelet Street at Wilshire), where a lab-coated father, son, invisible Holy Ghost, and "virgin" hold court. Or the late Tony Yoshida's *Flight to the Angel* (470 E. Third Street), in which Eastern and Western children float arm-in-arm across a dreamscape sea.

"Paintings are small and don't have much energy," says Kent Twitchell. "But a mural is like a cathedral—so powerful. Your head bends back to look up. And you're humbled by it. It reminds us who we are in the grand scheme of things." —*Susan Vaughn*

Orozco, and David Alfaro Siqueires—Mexico's three best-known muralists. They used cubistic and expressionistic renderings to illustrate social injustices in Mexico.

African-American muralists, too, have found inspiration in their roots—African art. They draw upon its iconography to convey ideas and pictures. Community leaders in African-

all disciplines, and reach out to all ethnic and special-interest groups. No other percent-for-arts program in America has that kind of scope. Says Adolfo V. Nodal, general manager of the Cultural Affairs Department, which will administer the endowment: "I think it is potentially the most important civic arts program in this country."

Another oasis for downtown artists and the center of avant-garde art activity is the nonprofit Los Angeles Contemporary Exhibitions (LACE), supported by city funds. In its converted two-level warehouse, LACE gives exposure to emerging young talent—video productions, exhibitions, contemporary dance, new music, and performance art. More than 30 Skid Row artists are receiving free art supplies through LACE's Skid Row Artists Fund. LACE also sponsors two-day tours of artists' studios each spring and an annual auction of 100 pieces by local artists.

Above: Directors Peter Goulds and Kimberly Davis pose outside their L.A. Louver Gallery in Venice. The gallery represents celebrated local and international artists including Ed Moses, David Hockney, and Leon Kossoff, among others. Photo by Shelley Gazin

Right: The J. Paul Getty Museum houses one of America's finest collections of Greek and Roman antiquities. The building itself is a recreation of a first century Roman villa. Photo by Joseph Sohm/Chromosohm

Aside from the downtown galleries, most of the city's scores of art galleries are concentrated in several Westside neighborhoods. Longest established is La Cienega Row, where the city's gallery scene regained its stride after the temporary World War II shutdown, and where the "Monday night art stroll" became a nationally known ritual for art buyers.

Longtime institutions on the Row are the 60-year-old Southern California Contemporary Art Galleries and Zeitlin & Ver Brugge Booksellers, in business since 1928 and a veteran arts patron. The La Cienega-Melrose Avenue enclave also includes the galleries of Hunsaker/Schlesinger, Jan Turner, Rosamund Felsen, Marilyn Pink, Herbert Palmer, Gemini G.E.L., and Simard Halm Shee.

Just a short distance west of the Row is another outstanding cluster of galleries, with

Robertson Boulevard as its main artery, where more galleries dealing with international artists are located than in any other part of town. Prominent here are the galleries of Margo Levin (who has another location in West Hollywood), Asher-Faure, Larry Gagosian, Eliat Gardin, Jeffrey Linden, and Kurland/Summers.

For years the Venice-Santa Monica beach area has provided an appropriately bohemian environment for many artists who live and work there behind blank storefronts, in converted garages, and in tiny beach bunga-

Kohn relocated from the Robertson Boulevard area; Ruth Bachofner came from the La Cienega Row enclave; and G. Ray Hawkins and Roy Boyd came from the La Brea-Beverly-Melrose locale.

The La Brea-Beverly-Melrose corridor is the city's newest gallery district, and one of its most interesting and far-ranging in scope. Located there are the galleries of Jan Baum, Burnett Miller, Fiona Whitney, Jack Rutberg, Tobey C. Moss, Fahey/Klein, Saxon-Lee, Garth Clark, 57th West, and Neil G. Ovsey. "Until they put all those wonderful new Los

Left: A jet sculpture soars skyward at the Frank Gehry-designed California Museum of Science and Industry at Exposition Park. The museum features a DC3, DCB, rockets, satellites, and exhibits on fiber optics, robotics, and high technology. Photo by Bob Rowan/Progressive Image

Facing page: Shops on Melrose, like the La Luz de Jesus Gallery, are often exotic, whimsical, esoteric, and many attract a steady stream of curious tourist and resident shoppers. Photo by Shelley Gazin

lows. A highlight of the colorful beach scene is the annual Venice Art Walk for charity, during which visitors bid on donated art works from among 40 artists' studios.

L.A. Louver is the most prestigious of the Venice-Santa Monica galleries. Others include Blum/Helman, Fred Hoffman, Maloney and Pence (in a single large building on Colorado Avenue), James Corcoran, Karl Bernstein, Angles, Merging One, and Roberts Art Gallery in Santa Monica High School. Santa Monica may be the new hot spot for art galleries. Recent arrivals Daniel Weinberg, Richard Kulenschmidt, and Michael

Angeles art galleries on tour, I'll get myself out there to see them firsthand," says Allen Miller, New York artistic director and filmmaker.

As contemporary art flourishes, the local treasury of classic art grows ever richer. The city's largest monument to the visual arts, the Los Angeles County Museum of Art, has undergone a major expansion program during recent years, with 275,000 square feet of new and renovated space. A principal addition is the handsome new Robert D. Anderson Building, with its Art Deco-inspired glass and terra-cotta design and over 50,000 square feet of galleries for the museum's international collection and special exhibitions. Another important addition is the Pavilion for Japanese Art for the museum's extensive Japanese collection, which now includes the renowned Joe D. Price Shin'enkin collection and a distinguished collection of Japanese netsuke sculpture.

The County Museum of Art received an unexpected setback when industrialist Armand Hammer abruptly canceled the planned donation of his $400-million art collection and instead decided to exhibit it in the new Armand Hammer Museum of Art and Culture in Westwood. Hammer died in December 1990 at age 92, less than two weeks after the museum opened.

The Los Angeles arts and culture scene was considerably enhanced in 1974 with the opening of the J. Paul Getty Museum, the world's richest museum, in Malibu. Even the design of the building caused a stir. A startling departure from modern museum architecture, the Getty is a full-size replica of the floor plan of a luxurious Roman villa near Herculaneum. The villa was buried under volcanic ash in the eruption of Mount Vesuvius in A.D. 79, and was later partially excavated.

With the late oil billionaire's own priceless private collection as its nucleus, the Getty has used its vast financial resources to acquire a definitive collection of Greek and Roman antiquities, paintings and drawings by pre-twentieth-century masters, sculptures, Medieval and Renaissance manuscripts, decorative arts, and European and American photography.

The Getty frequently makes news with its high-priced acquisitions, and it drew worldwide attention and plaudits from the national arts community in 1990 when it purchased Vincent Van Gogh's *Irises.* The art world was delighted that this acclaimed masterpiece, previously owned by an Australian businessman as an investment, will remain in America and on public display.

The Getty's constantly expanding collection already has outgrown its present facility. In order to accommodate the overflow and

provide additional space for lectures and research, the J. Paul Getty Trust has dipped into an endowment in excess of $3 billion to build the new J. Paul Getty Center in West Los Angeles. The campus-like complex of buildings, now under construction on a picturesque 10-acre site overlooking the city and the ocean, is scheduled to open in the mid-1990s.

In addition to some of the most beautiful old homes in the Los Angeles area, the adjacent communities of Pasadena and San Marino boast two museums whose distinguished collections have brought pleasure to Southern California art lovers and scholars for years.

The Huntington Library and Museum, the gift of turn-of-the-century railroad and real estate baron Henry E. Huntington, is a combination of European and American art treasures, one of the world's finest collections of rare books and manuscripts, and a 130-acre botanical wonderland. Artworks include Gainsborough's famed *Blue Boy* and other British portraits, Renaissance bronzes, French sculptures, and Sevres porcelain. The six-million-volume library contains such treasures as a Gutenberg Bible, the earliest known edition of Chaucer's *Canterbury Tales*, George Washington's genealogy in his own handwriting, and first-edition works of Shakespeare and Benjamin Franklin. The gardens include over 9,000 varieties of plants, shrubs, and trees.

In 1974 industrialist/philanthropist Norton Simon reorganized the failing Pasadena Museum of Modern Art as the Norton Simon Museum and assembled a priceless collection, rich in Rembrandts, Picassos, and Rodins. Other notable works include paintings by Rubens, Cezanne, Renoir, Toulouse-Lautrec, and Van Gogh; Degas' paintings and etchings

Above: L.A.'s support for freedom of expression has its limits! But thanks to increasing numbers of community volunteers and hardworking shopkeepers, the ubiquitous scrawl of graffiti is often covered over within hours of its appearance. Photo by Joseph Sohm/Chromosohm

Facing page: Interior designer Janet Polizzi has achieved prominence as a leading Southern California designer through her sophisticated use of materials, space, and color. Photo by Shelley Gazin

of ballerinas; one of the world's largest collections of Goya etchings; and Indian and Southeast Asian art and sculpture representing more than 2,000 years of culture.

The California State Museum of Science and Industry in Exposition Park is rapidly being recognized as one of the world's outstanding educational and cultural centers, with intriguing, multifaceted exhibits on science, technology, aerospace, economics, finance, and ethnic culture. The main hall offers countless wonders for children of all ages, with push-button exhibits and detailed displays. The S. Mark Taper Hall of Economics contains 62 interactive exhibits on the intricacies of the free enterprise system, over half operated by computer. The Hall of Health stars an electronic Circulatory Man which pulsates with fluorescent veins and arteries and a Transparent Woman which lights up its vital organs and explains their functions. The museum's seven-story, 16,000-square-foot Aerospace Complex is the most comprehensive exhibition of air and space travel outside of the Smithsonian Institution in Washington, D.C. The complex

also includes a giant-screen IMAX theater and the outdoor Air and Space Garden.

Also in Exposition Park is the Los Angeles County Museum of Natural History, whose Spanish Renaissance building, erected in 1913, is a splendid historic exhibit in itself. And within its elegant, old-world confines, more than 35 halls and galleries display permanent and temporary collections on people and their environment dating back 500 million years, from the prehistoric dinosaur era through Egyptian, South Pacific, and pre-Columbian cultures, and up to a 1940 model of downtown Los Angeles. The Hall of Gems and Minerals offers a display of over 1,500 raw and uncut stones, and two halls of dioramas contain stuffed African and North American animals in their natural habitats.

One of the area's most unusual historic attractions is the La Brea Tar Pits, the world's richest discovery of Ice Age fossils, adjacent to the Los Angeles County Museum of Art. In 1906 archaeologists discovered that the viscous tar had entrapped 200 varieties of mammals, birds, reptiles, insects, and plants from the Pleistocene Age and preserved them as fossils. In a vivid re-creation of the time, huge fiberglass animals are shown struggling in the sticky tar.

Built into a grassy knoll directly behind the pits is the George C. Page Museum of La Brea Discoveries, which relates the Ice Age beginnings of the land where the modern city now stands. Engrossing holographic displays turn a saber-toothed tiger and a 9,000-year-old woman from fossil to flesh in seconds. Authentic re-creations of ancient ground sloths, American camels, mastodons, and giant condors are found throughout the main hall. Murals depict the Ice Age migration from Asia to North America.

The Southwest Museum, in a Highland Park mission-style building overlooking the Pasadena Freeway, showcases Native American arts and offers a glimpse of what this area was like before Spanish and American colonization. The Skirball Museum, in Hebrew Union College adjacent to the USC campus, contains a reconstructed archaeological dig from the Near East, rare manu-

scripts, ancient Israeli artifacts, and a special exhibit of the five senses as reflected in Jewish ritual art. The Craft and Folk Art Museum is an excellent small museum located across the street from the County Museum of Art.

The tremendous attraction of motion pictures and television has made this area a casting director's dream by creating a huge reservoir of skilled performers in theater, music, dance, and every other form of entertainment—arguably the biggest concentration of such talent anywhere in this country or elsewhere. At any given time, hundreds of actors, actresses, singers, and dancers, from world-famous stars to unknown newcomers, are ready and eager to work.

Los Angeles' thriving performing arts scene is led by the Music Center's downtown venues, which include the Dorothy Chandler Pavilion, Mark Taper Forum, and Ahmanson Theatre. The Dorothy Chandler Pavilion has been the winter home of the Los Angeles Philharmonic, one of the world's highly acclaimed symphony orchestras, as well as home base for the Los Angeles Civic Light Opera, the Joffrey Ballet from 1983 to 1991, and the Los Angeles Master Chorale. Many other distinguished artists, symphonies, and special events like the Academy Awards have kept the Pavilion in almost constant use.

The Mark Taper Forum quickly acquired a reputation as one of America's most adventurous theaters under the aggressive, imaginative direction of Gordon Davidson,

Dozens of international artists joined forces in Los Angeles to record a new Virgin Records single, *Spirit of the Forest*, toward the preservation of the endangered equatorial rain forests. Some of the participants in the fund-raising project, from which all proceeds will go to key organizations and projects dedicated to rain forest preservation, were (this page, clockwise from top) Bonnie Raitt, Thomas Dolby, Joni Mitchell, Amy Sky, and Mick Fleetwood, and (facing page, clockwise from top) Peter Bogdanovich, Charles Fleischer, Rita Coolidge, and Mark Jordan. Photos by Shelley Gazin

opening in 1967 with *Devils,* which was denounced as sacrilegious and obscene by Cardinal James McIntyre, archbishop of Los Angeles, and caused Governor Ronald Reagan to walk out in disgust. The same spirited approach has been taken in the selection of the more than 250 works presented there.

For its first two decades the Ahmanson Theatre presented a series of Broadway hits in limited runs, world-premiere plays, and classics starring well-known movie and television actors. The Ahmanson's viability for the foreseeable future now seems secure, with the record-breaking *The Phantom of the Opera* apparently set to play indefinitely to capacity audiences. At the end of its first year, *Times* theater writer Sylvie Drake pronounced the musical "in rip-roaring shape: a sumptuous, smooth-as-silk super-spectacle."

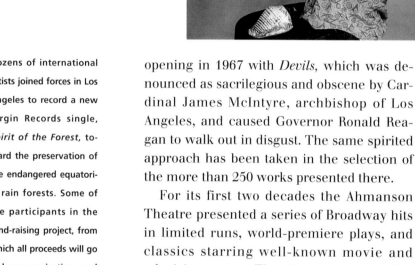

The Music Center will be enlarged in 1994 with the addition of the new Walt Disney Concert Hall, made possible by a $50-million gift from Lillian B. Disney, adjacent to the Dorothy Chandler Pavilion. It will become the new home of the Los Angeles Philharmonic.

An increasingly popular downtown alternative to the Music Center is the Los Angeles Theatre Center, a four-theater complex opened in 1985 in a pre–World War I bank building on Spring Street. LATC presents a full and varied program of serious drama, and led all others with eight 1990 Los Angeles Drama Critics Circle Awards, the Southland's most prestigious honors covering the spectrum of area theater.

Westside theatergoers found a more convenient venue when the plush Shubert Theater opened in 1972 in Century City, with the clout to bring in some of the biggest Broadway musicals and the facility to accommodate them. Its opening blockbuster was *Follies,* with Hal Prince as director and

Michael Bennett as choreographer. The Shubert's long-running hits have included *Evita* (two years), *Chorus Line* (18 months), *Les Miserables* and *Cats* (99 weeks each), and *Dreamgirls* (one year).

The James A. Doolittle Theatre on Vine Street, formerly the Huntington Hartford, has long been a Hollywood landmark. The Doolittle resembles a compact New York theater, with excellent acoustics for its first-class productions, which range from comedy to drama.

The Japanese American Cultural and Community Center in Little Tokyo was built by the local Japanese community to promote the preservation of Japanese culture in Los Angeles, and is the largest nonprofit cultural center of its kind in the country. Within it is the Japan America Theater, a beautiful 800-seat facility which presents the finest in

Japanese performing arts, including Grand Kabuki, Bugaku and Noh drama, Banraku puppet theater, and Western dance and chamber music.

The Ebony Showcase Theatre on West Washington Boulevard was founded in 1950 and is the oldest continuing black theater in the country. Many of L.A.'s leading black stars, including Juanita Moore and John Ames, have appeared at the 300-seat equity theater. Its Annex Theater presents equity-waiver productions.

The vintage Pasadena Playhouse is the grand dame of local theater, dating back to the twenties, when some of the greatest stars in movie history first trod the boards in their climb to international fame. Present-day alumni include Dustin Hoffman, Charles Bronson, Gene Hackman, Raymond Burr, and dozens of others. The Playhouse still presents top-name talent in popular productions.

The Westwood Playhouse usually presents new works in its 500-seat theater, part of a

ROCK TO REGGAE
The L.A. Beat

From scruffy coffeehouses to the open-air romance of the Hollywood Bowl, from earsplitting hard rock to pristine chamber recitals, Los Angeles offers a broad spectrum of musical choices.

A dedicated clubgoer could go out every night for a year in L.A. and not see the same band twice. For an idea of how varied the offerings are, consider one local newsweekly's club and concert listing headings: Country and Folk; Blues, African and Reggae; Latin and Brazilian; Cabarets and Cafes; Dance Clubs; Jazz; and Classical and Experimental.

Every night of the week, nationally known and wholly unknown musical acts offer a variety as broad as the area's demographic spectrum. Thanks to the strong entertainment industry presence and the thriving musical community, musicians from all over the world come to L.A. Many settle here, and whether they support themselves as session musicians (hired guns on soundtracks and the like) or work day jobs and play whenever they can for fun or for that big break, they enrich L.A.'s musical culture.

Rock 'n' roll dominates the local music scene, filling the biggest halls and supporting the most clubs. No U.S. concert itinerary is complete without an L.A. show. The city's performance venues range in capacity from under 100 to over 100,000, and it's possible to trace a band's history just by consulting an itinerary of its L.A. engagements.

The same night Sting fills the Great Western Forum at $30 a head (scalpers and their $200 markups notwithstanding), 50 bands are strutting their stuff in clubs, cabarets, bars, colleges, and even record and guitar stores from Encino to San Pedro.

Three of Hollywood's most popular testing grounds for new talent are the Roxy, an industry hangout where superstars like David Bowie and Madonna sneak in to watch or play; Doug Weston's Troubador, where hard rockers now tread boards Bob Dylan once walked; and the Whisky A Go Go, al-

ways at the center of the action. Over 20 years ago, the Whisky's house band was the Doors; punk rock took over in the late seventies; and hairsprayed rockers claimed it in the eighties. In 1990 the club was restored to the deep red it sported in the sixties for its appearance in the film *The Doors*. What goes around comes around.

Local bars schedule live music several nights a week. Whether presenting hungry young rock bands, Irish folk singers, seasoned blues players, or one-man synthesizer bands, such venues offer intimate settings, low cover and drink charges, and the opportunity to enjoy live music in a relaxed setting. For an even more relaxed, albeit caffeinated setting, many turn to the city's dozen-plus coffeehouses, where espres-

so and eclectic music programs offer up a distinctly Angeleno interpretation of the past. Most charge no cover; some stay open long after the bars close.

As for classical music, aficionados may choose from big-ticket events and oft-surprising smaller shows. Pasadena's Ambassador Auditorium and UCLA both offer world-class concert series featuring internationally known musicians like Peter Serkin, Yo-Yo Ma, the Academy of St. Martin-in-the-Field, and the Kronos Quartet.

Downtown's Music Center is home to the L.A. Philharmonic, but it regularly hosts conductors and orchestras from around the world. In the summer the schedule moves to the Hollywood Bowl, where patrons picnic before the show and watch the stars come out as the evening deepens. While Bowl seats are as low as $2, a more traditional or intimate experience may be found any night or weekend afternoon at professional and semi-pro recitals in theaters, museums, churches, and colleges throughout the city. Opera lovers can savor live arias and Italian food at Verdi in Santa Monica and Sarno's in Los Feliz.

Jazz clubs from the mountains to the sea bop, blow, honk, and slide all week long. Tommy Newsome, lead alto on "The Tonight Show," often plays in Studio City supper clubs, while legends like Dizzie Gillespie and Les McCann come to Hollywood nightspots such as the Vine Street Bar & Grill and Catalina's.

The nearby Cinegrill, restored a few years ago with the rest of the Hollywood Roosevelt Hotel, draws offbeat

Above, left and facing page: Los Angeles is truly a melting pot when the sun goes down and the stage lights go on at hundreds of smaller musical venues around town. The adventurous music and dance fan can gyrate the night away to an overwhelming selection of eclectic world sounds, from Brazilian jazz to Algerian Rai to synthetic Afro-beat funk. Here, the Bonedaddys serve up a frenzied slice of polyrhythmic world fusion at the Music Machine in West Los Angeles. Photos by Joseph Sohm/Chromosohm

performers like Eartha Kitt and Yma Sumac, as well as the occasional singing actress. Dedicated supper clubs compete with restaurants and hotel bars that boost their evening and brunch trade with live jazz.

The maturation of the baby boomer generation has been good for the blues. They're red hot in Los Angeles, opening new clubs and waking up old ones. Country music is also more popular than ever: more than half a dozen country & western bars around the area feature local bands pickin' 'n' grinnin'. The Longhorn Saloon, Silver Bullet,

Palomino, and Crazy Horse are among the favorites, but the biggest stars play mainstream halls like Nederlander's open-air Greek Theater and MCA's Universal Amphitheatre.

L.A.'s proximity to Latin America has drawn a large Latino population that likes to hit the hot spots that offer salsa, merengue, cumbia, flamenco, Afro-Cuban jazz, and other spicy south-of-the-border rhythms. Dance halls and performance theaters catering to these tastes are concentrated in largely Latin East L.A. A few clubs—El Floridita and Candilejas in Hollywood, and Marina del Rey's Miami

Spice, for example—are readily accessible from the Westside as well. The growing popularity of international music has fueled a trend toward Brazilian music, often featured in local bars.

Similarly, Pacific Rim immigrants have imported their customs. Perhaps the best known, karaoke, is an interactive performance experience much loved in Japan, where otherwise conservative businessmen strut and sing to instrumental versions of well-known songs. L.A.'s karaoke bars allow Westerners and Asians to share incomparable displays of pancultural silliness.

There's something for everybody in the entertainment capital of the world. When the sun sets over the Santa Monica mountains and sinks blazing into the blue Pacific, another realm opens up along the city's sparkling boulevards. Los Angeles offers everything from arias to zydeco; the music lover has only to reach out for it. —*Barak Zimmerman*

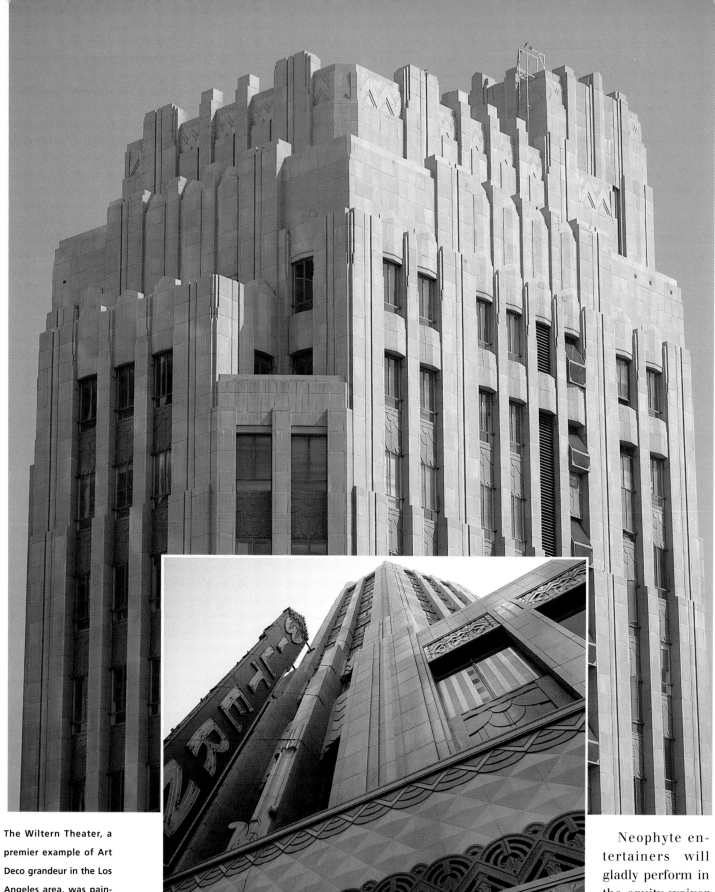

The Wiltern Theater, a premier example of Art Deco grandeur in the Los Angeles area, was painstakingly renovated in the mid-80s, and today showcases contemporary performance events. The building also houses shops, restaurants, and offices in its timeless tower. Photos by Larry Molmud

complex including shops, a restaurant, and an art gallery. The Mayfair Music Hall in Santa Monica offers lively British comedy, slapstick, and song in an authentic old English music hall atmosphere. The offbeat Variety Arts Theater downtown has a main theater for musical shows, a third floor Little Theater for old radio dramas, and Tin Pan Alley, an intimate setting for cabaret shows.

Neophyte entertainers will gladly perform in the equity-waiver houses for little or no pay just for the exposure and the experience. Established performers prefer to remain active and visible, while some of the older stars wouldn't consider an acting assignment out of town but are happy to play a role so close to home. This is the type of virtually inexhaustible talent supply that permited the Canon Theatre in Beverly Hills to extend A.R. Gurney's *Love Letters*, which opened in April 1990, for well over a year, with different well-known stars playing the two leading roles each week.

The plethora of performers has made for an extraordinary amount of activity in the smaller and equity-waiver houses, and for the emergence of promising new actors and playwrights who might otherwise be unable to demonstrate their skills. Rob Reiner and Marian Mercer began their careers at the 80-seat Fountain Theater in Hollywood, and Jason Robards and Nick Nolte began theirs at the Westwood Playhouse.

Bleacher Bums finally ran out of innings after ten years at the Century City Playhouse, the longest run in the history of L.A. equity-waiver houses. The Globe Playhouse company is one of the nation's best Shakespearean groups, performing in a West Hollywood building that is a replica of Shakespeare's original Globe Theatre in London.

Many other small, active equity-waiver houses deserve mention. Callboard Theater has presented over 1,200 productions since its creation from a defunct West Hollywood church in 1938. D.L. Coburn's Pulitzer Prize-winning *The Gin Game* was introduced at the West Coast Ensemble in Hollywood before its run on Broadway. Cast Theater presents award-winning contemporary works at three different theaters on the Westside. After thirty years, Company of Angels Theater is still offering quality productions as the oldest equity-waiver house in Los Angeles. The Tiffany Theatre in Hollywood showcases a succession of regional plays. And the list goes on.

Along with these widespread theatrical offerings, the sound of music—played, sung, and as accompaniment—fills the air throughout the city, outdoors as well as indoors, thanks to our wonderful weather. On the classical side, the Los Angeles Philharmonic has achieved international fame, first under the baton of charismatic Zubin Mehta, then under Andre Previn, and currently under the musical direction of Esa-Pekka Salonen. After wintering at the Dorothy Chandler Pavilion, the Philharmonic plays its summer season at the Hollywood Bowl, one of the world's largest outdoor amphitheaters. A picnic supper before the concert has been a favorite tradition of local concertgoers for years.

The fine Glendale Symphony Orchestra, under noted guest conductors, also shares the winter season at the Dorothy Chandler Pavilion. The renowned California Chamber Symphony performs regularly at UCLA's Royce Hall and at the J. Paul Getty Museum. The Los Angeles Chamber Orchestra gives nine concerts yearly at Ambassador Auditorium in Pasadena, and the Pasadena Symphony Orchestra gives five at Pasadena Civic Auditorium.

The Los Angeles Master Chorale, considered one of the finest choral groups in the world, presents a diverse repertoire, from Bach cantatas to Handel's *Messiah* and Gilbert & Sullivan. Its two Christmas specials at the Dorothy Chandler Pavilion always fill the house. The William Hall Chorale and Orchestra presents four classical performances annually in Pasadena, including an outstanding Christmas program.

Other, nonclassical forms of music—rock, reggae, pop, country, and gospel—saturate Los Angeles so thoroughly that a variety of concerts are available throughout the region on any given weekend. Die-hard jazz buffs who refuse to be rehabilitated still find solace and that old sweet sound at Donte's in North Hollywood, the Lighthouse in Hermosa Beach, Concerts by the Sea in Redondo Beach, Vine Street Bar & Grill, Catalina Bar & Grill in Hollywood, Le Cafe in Sherman Oaks, and the Baked Potato in North Hollywood.

In addition to the Philharmonic at the Hollywood Bowl, some of the biggest names in the field of entertainment draw huge crowds to summer outdoor concerts at the Greek Theatre in Griffith Park, the Universal Amphitheater at Universal City, and venues throughout the region.

A longtime favorite of Los Angeles dance devotees is the homegrown Bella Lewitzky Dance Company, a highly regarded modern dance group which divides its schedule between national and international tours and performances in local concert halls. Another popular group is the colorful 65-member Aman Folk Ensemble, which presents traditional American and international music and dance in performances at the Music Center and other area concert halls and theaters.

In Los Angeles exciting new opportunities abound in nearly every field of artistic endeavor, including motion pictures, where some of the technical work being done today has been elevated to the level of fine art. The decline of the old studio system, under which the majors used their own staff people on an entire production package, from script

T. Coraghessan Boyle, award-winning author and USC professor, strikes a pensive writer's pose. Photo by Shelley Gazin

to props, has brought employment to thousands of highly skilled but nonaffiliated technicians in the film business.

There is little question that this infusion of fresh and imaginative expertise has had a salutary effect on pictures. Writes Charles Champlin in the *Times:* "The independents in recent times have been the most interesting and consistent risk-takers, producing low-budget but quality films that have been in refreshing contrast to the sleek dynamics of the major studios' products."

Writing for the movies has always been one of the most lucrative forms of literary employment, and since the late twenties and early thirties Los Angeles has been a mecca for several kinds of writers. First and foremost and most in need of shelter were the German and British exiles who came here to escape the increasing unrest leading up to World War II. Established English authors like Christopher Isherwood, Aldous Huxley—and Evelyn Waugh for a brief and cranky six weeks—came of their own free will and usually were happy here. More mixed in their feelings were German writers like Thomas Mann and Bertold Brecht, who insisted on never liking Hollywood and fled the U.S. after one disastrous day with the House Un-American Activities Committee in the early fifties.

A large group of America's best-known writers came to Hollywood in the thirties to make their fortune. Humorist S.J. Perelman wrote for the Marx Brothers; Robert Benchley and Dorothy Parker lounged by the pool at the Garden of Allah, hangout of the stars in Hollywood; and William Faulkner made a nightly habit of going behind the bar at popular Musso & Franks restaurant in Hollywood to teach them how to mix mint juleps. Some, like Ernest Hemingway and F. Scott Fitzgerald, found it frustrating to deal with the studio bureaucracy; others found unexpected happiness here, notably Nathaniel West who, despite his grim portrait of Hollywood in *The Day of the Locust,* married happily, went hunting on weekends with Faulkner, and led an idyllic life. On another level, no one captured the seamy side of Los

Angeles in the thirties better than one of the greatest of all mystery writers, Raymond Chandler, a longtime resident.

Those giants of the past have given way to an exciting new generation of home-grown writers, including Judith Freeman, who writes of Los Angeles as the "Alexandria of the Pacific"; T.C. Boyle, who lives quietly in the San Fernando Valley while spinning fabulous tales of America's lost past; futurist Carolyn See, whose stories of nuclear holocaust and trade with other countries on the Pacific Rim point to an entirely new kind of American literature; science fiction writer Ray Bradbury; and many other gifted young writers.

If—as its devotees fervently insist—it all comes together in the City of Angels, it most certainly did in the Los Angeles Arts Festival in September 1990, which Mayor Tom Bradley called "the world's largest showcase of international performing and creative artistry." The Pacific-oriented festival, which had its origins in the 1984 Olympic Arts Festival, presented 350 programs of dance, music, visual art, theater, poetry, film, video, and performance art, mostly free and at locations all over the Los Angeles area. It featured a total of 1,400 performers from 26 Pacific Rim nations, and 900 artists from local groups. Director Peter Sellars and the festival were honored with a special award at the L.A. Drama Critics Circle Awards in 1991.

Distinguished pianist Misha Dicter probably summed up the pulse and pace of the city best in describing a whirlwind visit which included a guest performance at UCLA, a huddle with musicians in town for the Grammy Awards, jogging, an ocean swim, a Beverly Hills tour to show friends where famous musicians once lived, a stand-up street corner lunch, and a gourmet dinner.

"That 24 hours . . . could only happen in Los Angeles."

Press members photograph celebrities at the 62nd Annual Academy Awards. Photo by Joseph Sohm/Chromosohm

GOING FOR THE GOLD

L.A. Plays to Win

No other metropolitan area on earth has so many major attractions and such a glorious climate to enjoy them year-round as Los Angeles. While rain-outs, snow-outs, and glacial weather curtail many outdoor activities elsewhere during a good part of the year, the City of Angels offers a dazzling selection of spectator sports, entertainment, and attractions all year long that no other city can attempt to match.

If there were any doubts, Los Angeles reaffirmed its status as the world's ranking sports/entertainment center as host of the phenomenally successful 1984 Olympics, more than a half century after last holding the games. Despite dire predictions of horrific traffic gridlock, ruinous cost overruns, and possible terrorism, the Olympiad was a masterpiece of logistical planning and execution that went off without a glitch. Furthermore, and most astonishingly, it yielded tremendous financial profits which will benefit the city's social, cultural, and recreational programs for years to come.

In addition to the myriad details involved in arranging and staging hundreds of individual events in far-flung venues from Santa Barbara to San Diego, an extensive program of remodeling, refur-

"LOS ANGELES SPORTS FANS ARE JUST GREAT; THEY'RE AS FAIR AND AS KNOWLEDGEABLE AS YOU'LL FIND ANYWHERE."

—VIN SCULLY, LOS ANGELES DODGERS ANNOUNCER, 1991

While scuba diving at Santa Catalina Island, you can expect to see exotic species of sea life, such as electric perch, saltwater goldfish, and flying fish. Photo by Bo Richards

B y   C h a r l e s   F . Q u e e n a n

bishing, and new construction was completed for the games. One of the world's finest velodromes was built at Cal State Dominguez Hills for the cycling events. McDonald's footed most of the bill for a beautiful new swimming stadium on the University of Southern California campus. New shooting ranges were built at Prado Recreation Area in Chino, and the East Los Angeles College

traffic volume on downtown freeways was actually far lighter than normal; not a single act of political violence disrupted the games; and Los Angeles earned worldwide admiration for the aplomb and cooperation with which it carried off this most complex and prestigious of international events. The 1984 Olympics, first ever to reap a profit, remain the definitive blueprint for future host cities

Facing page: A diver takes the plunge before a crowd of amazed spectators at the Date Festival. Photo by Bob Keeran

stadium was renovated for field hockey. The Los Angeles Olympic Organizing Committee spent $5 million on refurbishing and giving the Coliseum's 52-year-old exterior a facelift to make it an appropriate centerpiece for the main track and field events and the memorable opening and closing ceremonies, as well as $1.8 million on permanent improvements to spruce up adjacent Exposition Park. And that was only a small part of the overall effort.

With millions of residents and their employers adjusting work and commuting schedules to the two-week extravaganza,

on how it should be done.

As a city for all seasons, Los Angeles enjoys an abundance of rich athletic talent in every sport: seven professional teams, including several perennial contenders in their leagues; superstars like Magic Johnson, Wayne Gretzky, and Orel Hersheiser; two collegiate football powers who usually rank among the top 10 in the country; and the granddaddy of all bowl games—the Rose Bowl—which focuses world attention on Los Angeles every New Year's Day.

After years of looking longingly toward the major league circuit in the East, local

Above: Next to L.A.'s Coliseum is the most famous of all public pools still in use. The Exposition Park pool was originally built for the 1932 Olympic Games. Photo by Bob Rowan/Progressive Image

baseball fans saw their dreams come true when the colorful, contentious Dodgers moved from Brooklyn to Los Angeles in 1958. A year later, the team won the World Series in a screened-off section of the Coliseum, the temporary field they used until moving into Chavez Ravine in 1962. To date, the Dodgers have won eight pennants and five World Series here, most recently through their Cinderella heroics in the 1988 playoffs and series sweep over the heavily favored Oakland Athletics.

The Dodgers were firmly entrenched in the city's consciousness by the time Gene Autry fielded his new American League expansion team, the California Angels, in Anaheim. The former movie cowboy has been more than generous in adding such high-priced talent as Nolan Ryan and others to the club in repeated attempts to build a contender. That mercurial combination of hitting and pitching has eluded him so far, but everyone agrees Autry richly deserves a winner after all these years of disappointing near-misses.

Coach John Robinson's Rams made their most serious run at the Super Bowl in years in 1989, only to be defeated in the playoffs by their arch-rivals, the San Francisco 49ers. Nevertheless, the Rams seem to have found the strong-armed quarterback they need to challenge for the title, and recently signed Jim Everett to a mega-million-dollar con-tract to insure his future at that key position. With strength at all vital positions and talent to match any other team in the NFL, the Rams are always exciting to watch.

After much indecision, the Los Angeles Raiders and their owner, Al Davis, decided in 1990 to stay put in the aging Coliseum, which is being extensively remodeled for better visibility. The Raiders have shed the intimidating outlaw image of old and now feature a powerful ground game starring Marcus Allen and versatile Bo Jackson, two of the greatest running backs in the league.

For years the Lakers have been one of the powers in the NBA. They won five league

championships in the eighties, including 1987 and 1988, as the first team to win back-to-back titles since the 1969 Boston Celtics. Earlier, one of the fabulous Jerry West-Wilt Chamberlain-Elgin Baylor teams won a record 33 straight games in 1972 on the way to a 69-13 won-lost record, the best ever in the NBA. Kareem Abdul-Jabbar, one of UCLA's greatest stars during the John Wooden dynasty, anchored the Laker offense for most of the past two decades. Kareem has retired and the brilliant Magic Johnson provides most of the fireworks for actor Jack Nicholson and other Laker fanatics who never miss a game. Sellouts are routine.

Los Angeles' other pro basketball team, the Clippers, have had a tough time of it since moving here from San Diego in 1984, mainly because the dynamic Lakers have provided championship-quality play for so long. However, the Clippers did show marked improvement in 1989, and like the Chicago Cubs' never-say-never faithful, their loyal band of followers can always look forward to next year.

Hockey seemed an anomoly in this Mediterranean environment, and the Kings stirred little interest when they first came to Los Angeles in 1967. The NHL expansion team's caliber of hockey left much to be de-

Above: Gladiators from USC and Michigan State wage nocturnal war at the Rose Bowl. Photo by Joseph Sohm/Chromosohm

Right: Beverly Hills High School football players limber up as the Century City skyline glimmers. Photo by Joseph Sohm/Chromosohm

sired and attendance reflected it. Jerry Buss bought the club in 1979 and eventually decided something drastic had to be done to pull the Kings out of the doldrums. In 1988 he traded away a bundle of unrealized talent for Wayne Gretzky, the most prolific scorer and perhaps the greatest player in the history of the game. "The Great One" continues to shatter all records and has been a tremendous shot in the arm at the box office.

Football Saturdays usually mean a big local game involving either the USC Trojans in the Coliseum or the UCLA Bruins in the Rose Bowl; the classic Notre Dame-USC confrontation in alternating years; and the climactic UCLA-USC showdown in November, when tens of thousands of alumni from both schools come out and cheer themselves hoarse for their teams. With several generations of USC and UCLA graduates still in the area, the crosstown rivalry remains as intense as ever, and the outcome can make or break the season for both teams. It is a rare year indeed when one or the other isn't in the Rose Bowl. In what has become a seasonal ritual, groups of alumni attend all of their team's home games and, thanks to a

benevolent climate, have made pregame tailgate and parking lot luncheons extremely popular.

While college football monopolizes the headlines and draws the biggest crowds, some of the nation's finest baseball players, track stars, and men's and women's basketball players perform for area schools before going on to the professional ranks. UCLA and USC, as well as Pepperdine, Loyola Marymount, and Cal State Long Beach regularly produce teams and all-star talent to rank with the best in the land. In addition, Los Angeles-area high schools continually turn out a wealth of gifted young athletes, and it isn't unusual to discover that an All-American candidate at a distant university or an emerging major-league baseball star is a local boy who played for one of the L.A. region's high schools, like Don Drysdale, Darryl Strawberry, George Brett, and dozens of others.

For racing fans, there are celebrities in attendance and plenty of exciting thoroughbred racing at Santa Anita and Hollywood Park. For the trotter crowd, there's harness and quarter-horse racing at Los Alamitos. The Forum, home of the Lakers and Kings, also holds championship boxing matches twice a month.

But unless age and infirmity make it impossible, most Angelenos feel an irresistible compulsion to get out there and join in the action themselves. For fitness buffs and the enthusiastic hordes who actively participate

Tennis anyone? Playing courts are abundant in Los Angeles. Lincoln Park (Santa Monica), Griffith Park (Los Angeles), and Barrington Park (West Los Angeles) offer well-maintained, well-lit surfaces for beginners and aces alike. Photo by Bob Rowan/Progressive Image

in various outdoor sports, the sky is literally the limit in this land of perpetual warmth and sunshine. Satellite photos of the area show a landscape peppered with tennis courts, golf courses, and swimming pools—one-fifth of all the swimming pools in this country are in Los Angeles County alone.

As might be expected in this climate, golf and tennis are the most popular year-round participant sports, with hundreds of public and private golf courses, and thousands of tennis courts at nearly every school, park,

and hotel or motel of any size. The city operates 13 public golf courses in addition to the 15 run by Los Angeles County. There are dozens of private courses throughout the suburbs, as well as the better-known courses like Riviera Country Club and Los Angeles Country Club. The city also operates 287 public tennis courts, 238 of which are lighted for nighttime use.

It sometimes seems that half of the population is out jogging in a bizarre variety of sizes, shapes, and attire. Dozens of 5k and 10k races for amateur runners are held every weekend, and tens of thousands create a mob scene at the start of the Los Angeles and Long Beach marathons, which also attract world-class runners.

Cycling has its own fast-growing army of enthusiasts, with the city steadily extending and improving bikeways throughout the area. The longest and most scenic bike path, also used extensively by roller skaters, extends from Pacific Palisades to Redondo Beach, much of it along the oceanfront. Los

Cyclists prepare for the Beverly Hills Subaru Cycling Race. Photo by Joseph Sohm/Chromosohm

FAST GETAWAYS

L.A.'s Urban Wilderness

Somewhere in L.A., just this minute, a pack of coyotes is stalking a helpless rabbit. A hawk is catching thermals high above a rugged canyon. A bobcat is slinking through a field mottled blue and yellow with lupine and mustard blossoms. While the wheels of commerce and pleasure spin unendingly through the great metropolis, a more primal life, unseen by most visitors, endures.

It's the most heartening of Los Angeles' many contradictions and juxtapositions: wildness not only endures; it thrives here. And it's never far from wherever the freeways and boulevards may lead. In fact, the very course of those trademark rivers of tarmac is determined by the mountain range that runs through the heart of the city.

The Santa Monica Mountains extend 46 miles westward from Griffith Park near downtown L.A. to Point Mugu in Ventura County. The mountains average 12 miles in width. Even the urbanized sections of the range retain a wild beauty. The character of Beverly Hills, Bel Air, and Brentwood, and the canyon communities of Laurel Canyon and Beverly Glen, all maintain a degree of wildness and rugged contour endemic to the mountains they inhabit. It's not uncommon for a Beverly Hills jogger to see a coyote slink across a street and into a stand of thick chaparral.

But the real treasures of the mountains lie in the parklands that preserve their nature. And those parklands are considerable, beginning with Griffith Park. The lowlands of Griffith Park are the usual playing fields and picnic tables, plus the zoo and a golf course. But the upper reaches are wild, another world, where dozens of hiking trails lead through oak woodlands and chaparral, the dense scrub that's characteristic of the entire range.

On a clear day Griffith Park reveals the great anomalies of Los Angeles. Hike to the top of Mount Hollywood (1,625 feet)—there are the famous Hollywood sign, and the vast basin of broken dreams and fantasies fulfilled that

the sign represents. But turn around, and high, often snow-capped, mountains loom to the north, (more about those later); and to the west, the extension of the Santa Monica mountain range: a series of rugged, rocky peaks and deep folds of canyons extending to the ocean in Santa Monica, then for another 36 miles along the beaches of Malibu.

After Griffith Park, the mountain parklands are variously in city, county, state, and federal hands, collectively known as the Santa Monica Mountains National Recreation Area. The scattered parcels total 65,000 acres. Nearly completed is a trail that connects many of the jigsaw-puzzle tracts of park—the Backbone Trail, meandering 65 miles from Will Rogers State Park in Pacific Palisades to Point Mugu State Park. The trail stays high much of the time, well over 2,000 feet along the mountain spine, and ascends to the crown of the range, 3,111-foot Sandstone Peak. Portions of the trail, and many other trails in the range, are wide fire road, suitable for mountain biking and horseback riding.

The Santa Monicas are delightful any time of year. In spring an effusion of wildflowers erupts. Summers are often foggy in the morning and evening. Clearing fog makes for spectacular views from coastal ridges such as those traversed by Overlook Trail in Point Mugu State Park. Fall and winter are often brisk and windy, and the visibility is crisp, revealing the distant contours of the Channel Islands 30 or so miles offshore.

Access to the mountains is best from the canyon roads that cleave the range, especially Topanga Canyon, Malibu

Canyon-Las Virgenes, and Kanan-Dume. Another road, Mulholland Highway, travels the entire length of the mountains, and is a classic Sunday drive. Sunset Boulevard and Pacific Coast Highway run along the southern slopes near the ocean.

Now, about those higher mountains to the north, so vivid when winds sweep the basin clean of pollution. (And so alluring to New Year's Day watchers of the Rose Bowl.) These are the San Gabriel Mountains, which lord over the northern fringes of the metropolis. The

Casey Patterson, a legend among endurance cyclists, challenges the Santa Monica Mountains. In 1987 she broke the women's division record for a 3,117-mile bike race from San Francisco to Washington, D.C. Photo by Shelley Gazin

foothills of the San Gabriels are a melange of suburbia and chaparral; the higher slopes are pine covered and undeveloped, lying largely within the Angeles National Forest.

The San Gabriels rise abruptly behind the foothill towns of Glendale and Pasadena and extend eastward behind

Upland and Ontario. The crown of the closest section of the San Gabriels is Mount Wilson (5,710 feet), topped by an observatory and a nest of high-tech antennae. Nearby peaks like Mount Lowe and Mount Harvard are less trammeled.

The Angeles Crest Highway (State Route 2) leads to the Mount Wilson Road and on through to numerous national forest campgrounds, picnic areas, and trail heads. Access to the nearest local skiing is also from the Angeles Crest.

The landmark peak of the San Gabriels is massive Mount Baldy (10,064 feet). Baldy is not the mountain's true name, but try asking directions to Mount San Antonio and you'll draw blanks. Call it Baldy, and find it north of Claremont, off I-10 (Mountain Avenue to Mount Baldy Road). The summit of Baldy is snow covered much of the year, roundish and barren in the warmer months.

Just as the tentacles of the metropolitan area are long-reaching, so are the natural areas they embrace. Besides the Santa Monicas and San Gabriels, Angelenos also favor the San Bernardino Mountains, farther east. Home of lakes Arrowhead and Big Bear, the San Bernardinos' piney slopes also provide excellent hiking and skiing. At the eastern edge of the range is Southern California's tallest peak, San Gorgonio (11,499 feet).

South of San Gorgonio, Interstate 10 rushes through a gap between the San Bernardino and San Jacinto mountains. With San Gorgonio, Mount San Jacinto (10,804 feet) forms a dramatic portal to the metropolitan area for visitors arriving from the east. A tramway from Palm Springs ascends San Jacinto and provides an easily earned, panoramic view of mountain and desert.

Farther south, Orange County dwellers escape to Cleveland National Forest in the Santa Ana Mountains and to the coastal mountains of Crystal Cove State Park near Laguna Beach.

More than pollution, the hurly-burly of city life tends to obscure the vast natural areas so close at hand to the metropolis. Their denizens, though, are undeterred; the coyotes, bobcats, and hawks go about their daily business. Visitors who join them are well rewarded. *—Bob Howells*

Dog walking in Topanga Canyon is a perfect diversion for nature-loving Angelenos. Photo by Amy Seidman-Tighe

Angeles Wheelmen was organized in 1882 and is believed to be the oldest cycling club in the U.S. The most prestigious annual cycling event is the Wheelmen's Double Century, a 200-, 300-, or 400-mile ride in 24 hours, and there are dozens of local rides and races nearly every weekend. Many bike shops offer full schedules.

With more than 70 miles of coast, the somewhat chilly Pacific offers sand, surf, and sunshine on more than a half dozen beaches from Malibu to Long Beach for swimming, surfing, fishing, boating, sailboarding, snorkeling, and scuba diving. Some of the best snorkeling and scuba diving is found in the crystal-clear waters around Catalina Island and the Channel Islands.

Not surprisingly, saltwater fishing is a favorite leisure-time pursuit for thousands of residents who relish the challenge of the deep in an invigorating fresh-air environment. Shore fishing is generally excellent on many area beaches, and bait-and-tackle shops on Santa Monica, Malibu, and Redondo Beach piers provide everything needed—except luck—to hook dinner from those vantage points. For more ambitious fisherfolk, sportfishing charters are available at accessible areas like Redondo Beach, Mal-

Dirt biking through L.A.'s craggy hillsides is a favorite pastime of college students. Photo by Bob Rowan/Progressive Image

ibu, Long Beach, San Pedro, and Dana Point.

Hikers and campers find plenty of open space to roam free and commune with nature in Griffith Park, Cleveland National Forest, Angeles National Forest, and the San Gabriel and San Bernardino mountains. Hiking trails honeycomb the hills, and supervised camping sites are available throughout the mountains. With 4,107 acres, Griffith Park is the largest city park in the United States and a veritable entertainment center in itself. In addition to the park's 53 miles of hiking and bridle trails, two of the park's most popular attractions are the Griffith Park Observatory/Planetarium and the 113-acre Los Angeles Zoo, which houses over 2,000 birds, mammals, and reptiles. The Los Angeles Zoo is noted for its breeding of endangered species, and its Ahmanson Koala House is of particular interest to many visitors.

In addition to Griffith Park, the city operates four other large regional parks: Elysian overlooking downtown L.A., Harbor in Harbor City, Sepulveda in Sherman Oaks, and Hansen Dam in Pacoima. L.A.'s parks offer basketball and volleyball courts, hiking and equestrian trails, and plenty of picnic and barbecue facilities.

During the winter months, Los Angeles is probably the only urbanized desert center offering skiing within a short drive of the city. California-born children often have their first physical contact with snow and winter sports in the nearby mountains. Residents who moved to Los Angeles years ago to escape winter conditions sometimes take nostalgic trips to Big Bear in the San Bernardino Mountains just to tramp around in foot-deep drifts again, secure in the knowledge that sunny warmth is only an hour or two away.

Any discussion of theme parks in the Los Angeles area has to begin with Walt Disney's all-time international favorite. Disneyland has long been an American institution, a must-see on the itinerary of visiting royalty and heads of state as well as for millions of parents and children. Disneyland's shrewd strategy of introducing new rides and attractions nearly every year has enabled the park

to retain its strong return trade and enduring popularity. True to form, the company will add dozens of new attractions in a massive expansion over the next decade.

Meanwhile, for all its dominating position, Disneyland still has lively competition right in its own backyard from Knott's Berry Farm in nearby Buena Park. Originally made famous by Mrs. Knott's home-cooked dinners and preserves, Knott's has grown into a 150-acre complex of more than 100 rides, 60 eating places, a like number of shops, top-flight entertainment, and ice show extravaganzas. Another popular attraction, Movieland Wax Museum, is a few blocks from Knott's Berry Farm.

The third major theme park in the area is

Six Flags Magic Mountain in Valencia, with the biggest collection of thrill rides of them all. The park features the awesome Colossus roller coaster and the first stand-up roller coaster in the West; a white-water ride and a ride over a 50-foot waterfall; and numerous looping, revolving rides to test the visitor's resistance to motion sickness. Magic Mountain also offers shops and eateries, a puppet theater, celebrity revue and rock concerts, and high-diving shows.

Universal Studios-Hollywood is certainly one of the most spectacular attractions in town, especially for those who have never been near a movie studio. The five-hour tour offers a close-up, behind-the-scenes look at sets, props, and makeup. Special effects in-

Many of California's beaches rate with those of Hawaii and Australia as the world's finest for surfing. The sport was first promoted in Los Angeles in 1907 to boost weekend passenger traffic for the Pacific Electric Railroad. Photo by Bo Richards

clude the parting of the Red Sea, an avalanche, a flood, a collapsing railroad bridge, a 30-foot King Kong, an attack by the killer shark from *Jaws*, and demonstrations by movie stuntmen. The tour also covers the New York Street set, rebuilt since the original was destroyed in a $25-million fire in November 1990, and the latest addition, Lucy: A Tribute, which pays homage to the late, great comedienne.

The *Queen Mary* and the *Spruce Goose,* Long Beach's biggest tourist attraction, has finally become a profitable venture after

years of rough sailing. While area theme parks are family-oriented operations, the *Queen* is very much a nostalgia piece for those who remember it from its glory years before World War II as the largest and most luxurious passenger ship ever built at that

The Matterhorn at Disneyland, although perhaps overshadowed by more modern roller coasters, is still big, fast, and always a popular draw. Photo by Bob Rowan/ Progressive Image

time. The vast floating palace is still maintained in beautiful condition and visitors have the run of its 12 decks. In addition to its seagoing equipment, the ship contains Jacques Cousteau's Museum of the Sea, several fine restaurants, meeting and ballroom facilities, and the Queen Mary Hotel, where guests can stay in the ship's first-class cabins.

Eccentric millionaire Howard Hughes began building the *Spruce Goose*, the largest wooden airplane ever made, as a troop transport and hospital plane in 1942, when Nazi submarine wolfpacks were ravaging shipping in the Atlantic. Even though the submarine threat abated, Hughes kept at it, completing the giant aircraft in 1946, a year after the war ended. The plane made its first, brief, and only flight in 1947, when Hughes gunned the engines and took off to an altitude of 85 feet while supposedly taxiing

around the harbor to check equipment. Today the self-guided tour covers the cockpit, cabin, and cargo areas. Also housed under the 12-story dome is Time Voyager, a time and space travel show for children.

Hollywood still enjoys its international reputation as the movie capital of the world, although that literally isn't true anymore, now that mostly the "deals" are made there. Movie production has scattered to the four corners of the earth, since cardboard backgrounds won't do anymore—audiences demand the real thing and get it.

However, Los Angeles and its environs remain the longtime favorite location of film producers for the weather, convenience, and cost savings, dating far back to the silents when Rudolph Valentino melted female hearts in *The Sheik of Araby*, filmed in the sand dunes behind the beach in El Segundo. Movie and television companies are con-

Above and facing page, top: A 30-foot-tall, dark, and handsome King Kong awaits visitors at Universal Studios. Photos by Bob Rowan/Progressive Image

"Star maps" are for sale at Hollywood and Beverly Hills street corners. They lead the curious past the mansions and manicured lawns of the rich and famous. Photo by Bob Rowan/Progressive Image

stantly shooting in and around Los Angeles, the harbor area, the Santa Clarita Valley, and the San Fernando Valley, and part of the fun of living here is in recognizing familiar streets, buildings, and landmarks in shows filmed locally.

Television production occupies many of the landmark properties where Chaplin and Laurel and Hardy once cavorted and Rhett and Scarlett fled the burning of Atlanta. Ownership has changed hands many times and some of the back lots have been carved up for development, but many of the original studios are still there, as are ornate entrances like the Paramount gate. Studio tours are available; so are tickets to a number of television shows which have live audiences, such as the "Tonight Show" and other talk shows. A list of nearby locations where movies and TV episodes are being filmed is available at the Los Angeles County Film Office on Hollywood Boulevard.

Hollywood Boulevard features its Walk of Stars, with the names of the famous and not-so-famous embedded in the sidewalk. Near the Hollywood Wax Museum is Mann's Chinese Theater, scene of many a spectacular world movie premiere. Mann's forecourt features the footprints and handprints of movie greats embedded in cement, a tradition that began during the theater's construction in 1927, when actress Norma Talmadge accidentally slipped and put her hands down into the wet cement.

A number of tours take visitors past the homes and former homes of the stars. Successful business executives now occupy most of the old stars' homes on the palm-lined streets of Beverly Hills, but that well-heeled community has never lost its aura of elegance and affluence. Rodeo Drive, with its designer labels and stratospheric prices, is regarded as one of the world's most exclusive shopping districts. Beverly Hills restaurants like the Bistro, Chasen's, La Scala, Mateo's, and a half dozen others attract a polyglot clientele which

Professional skateboarder Dee Dee Devine pops a wheelie at Venice Beach. Photo by Amy Seidman-Tigh

typically includes celebrities, film producers, and pop music idols.

Recognizable stars are sometimes seen dining, shopping, and behaving like ordinary mortals, though many have fled the city to reside on outlying ranches and estates. Among favorite stopping places when they are in town are the secluded Bel Air Hotel and the Beverly Hills Hotel, where the Polo Lounge has been the scene of some of film-dom's most highly publicized romantic trysts and major movie deals.

In direct counterpoint to Los Angeles' frenetic pace and flamboyant image as jet-age trendsetter and innovator, centuries-old relics of the city's humble Spanish origins still stand as silent reminders of the past. Downtown, El Pueblo de Los Angeles Historical Park marks the original site where 44 Mexican peasants founded the tiny pueblo in 1781, and much of it has been restored and preserved to re-create the atmosphere of early California. Within the park are the Avila Adobe, the city's oldest existing residence, built in 1818, and its oldest religious building, Our Lady Queen of Angels, completed in 1822 and still an active parish church. Familiar to many Angelenos is Olvera Street, with its lively collection of stalls and handicraft shops, which erupts in a riot of color and music on Cinco de Mayo.

In the immediate Los Angeles area are two of the 21 missions established by the early Spanish to bring God and civilization to the Indians—whether they wanted it or not. Closest to the city are Mission San Fernando Rey and Mission San Gabriel, both of which often serve as backgrounds in movies and TV series. The pious but eminently practical padres from San Gabriel were the first traders in the Bay of San Pedro, exchanging food and hides with smugglers for basic comforts the Spanish authorities refused to send them.

Farther south, in Orange County, is Mission San Juan Capistrano, founded by Father Junipero Serra in 1776 and devastated by an earthquake in 1812. Still, there are the ruins of the original church and the only remaining altar where Father Serra said Mass. Capistrano's unique attraction is the legend of the swallows, which brings thousands of visitors from all over the world to the mission on St. Joseph's Day, March 19. Although some cynics claim the swallows have long since subcontracted their annual appearance to other species, the lovely legend survives.

Valuable historic landmarks have been painstakingly restored and preserved in the San Pedro-Wilmington-Long Beach harbor

area 20 miles south of downtown L.A. They are vivid reminders of the halcyon days of Spanish rule, when enormous land grants were bestowed on Spanish soldiers for service to the king. The entire Palos Verdes Peninsula was only part of the 74,000-acre land grant which became Rancho San Pedro, first of the great California ranchos. Still standing and open to visitors are the adobe ranch houses full of priceless memorabilia of Rancho Los Alamitos and Rancho Los Cerritos, which together form the site of present-day Long Beach. The immaculately maintained mansion of Phineas Banning, "Father of the Port of Los Angeles," and the Union Army's Drum Barracks, a block apart, welcome visitors in Wilmington.

The harbor today is a major attraction. While the freeways provide quick and easy access to the bay, a far more picturesque route is via the towering Palos Verdes Peninsula, with its breathtaking views of the vast

61-year-old John Feyk runs a treadmill to test aerobic capacity, oxygen capacity, and carbon dioxide levels at USC, during a study of exercise's effect on aging. Photo by Shelley Gazin

Facing page: Gary Siegrist, a manager of Gold's Gym, works out at the Venice facility. Gold's is the haunt of L.A.'s most serious muscle builders, including such health-minded luminaries as Arnold Schwarzenegger, Lou Ferrigno, Jane Fonda, and Carl Weathers. Photo by Shelley Gazin

Below: Jogging is an extremely popular Los Angeles pasttime. Photo by Joseph Sohm/Chromosohm

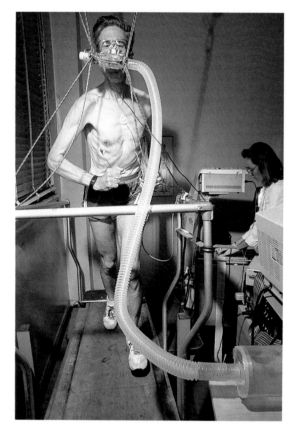

sweep of ocean and Catalina Island. A favorite stop on the way is the glass-and-redwood nondenominational Wayfarer's Chapel. Designed by Frank Lloyd Wright and perched on a hillside overlooking the sea, it is a romantic setting for the many weddings performed there.

San Pedro retains the atmosphere of a small town, although it has completely altered its old waterfront image, much to the relief of longtime residents. During World War II, thousands of servicemen returning from long, hazardous duty in the Pacific swarmed to Beacon Street with its bars, strip joints, fleabag hotels, and brothels.

Massive redevelopment has replaced the old eyesore. Today's landside attractions are conveniently concentrated along the Main Channel, where a steady parade of everything from tiny sailboats to giant oceangoing vessels passes in and out of the port. Located off Harbor Boulevard near the end of the Harbor Freeway is the World Cruise Center, where lead-in shots and many scenes were filmed aboard the *Pacific Princess*, the "Love Boat" of the popular television series. A short distance down the boulevard, at the entrance to Ports O' Call Village, is the Los Angeles Maritime Museum, the former municipal ferryboat building. The museum is crammed with wonderful historic photos of the early days of the sailing ships and other maritime memorabilia.

From its beginning as a single restaurant, Ports O' Call Village has grown into a 24-acre complex of cobblestone lanes and quaint New England-style shops and restaurants. The village is now one of Southern California's leading tourist attractions.

Catalina Island is just 22 miles off the coast, and for those who find the lure of the island irresistible, numerous cruise ships make the two-hour trip daily from San Pedro and Long Beach. Besides Cabrillo's stopover in 1542, Catalina has sheltered an assortment of col-

orful characters, including sun-worshipping Indians, Russian fur trappers in search of otter skins, pirates, smugglers, and, more recently, film crews and movie stars, who like to sail over and tie up for a weekend of privacy—or whatever. Catalina's diversions include scenic natural terrain, the quaint town of Avalon, and sparkling, crystal-clear waters for scuba diving, snorkeling, and glass-bottom boat tours. Once owned by the Wrigley chewing gum family, Catalina has some unusual wildlife, including a flourishing herd of buffalo which were first brought to the island for the filming of *The Vanishing American* in 1924 and apparently liked it there.

One offbeat source of waterborne enter-

Avalon Harbor at Santa Catalina Island is abrim with cruise ships and pleasure craft. Photos by Bo Richards and John Gale

tainment, especially intriguing for visitors from inland states, is whale-watching. From December through mid-April, when the huge mammals migrate south along the coast to their breeding waters off Baja California, sportfishing centers offer a daily schedule of whale-watching trips to observe the gentle giants as they cruise surprisingly close to shore. The animals' progress is carefully tracked by helicopter and radio, and chances are usually good that at least one whale will be seen on each trip. Boats are strictly forbidden to get too close, but even at a distance it is a thrilling sight to see one of the stately leviathans flip its enormous tail skyward as it plunges toward the ocean bottom.

Even with an exhausting year-round agen-

da fairly bursting with variety, Los Angeles also hosts an exciting lineup of special events throughout the year, in addition to a large number of ethnic festivals.

Nothing can top the year's opening act: the incomparable, century-old Tournament of Roses Parade, which was the first event broadcast on national radio in 1927, on national television in 1951, and in color on national TV in 1954. The annual parade of lavish floats, marching bands, and equestrian teams reaches a worldwide audience of over 100 million.

More than any other single event, the Rose Bowl Game is responsible for a sudden increase in the local population each year. These are the more resolute souls among the snowbound millions around the nation who have watched the game played in brilliant sunshine and have decided they want to live permanently in this Eden of eternal summer.

Sports for the spectator and participant continue to attract crowds during the first few months of the year. In January the inimitable Harlem Globetrotters bring their sleight-of-hand to the Forum, and the Sunkist Invitational Track Meet at the Sports Arena brings together 500 world-class athletes with sights set on the next Olympics.

The top pro golfers assemble here in February for the Los Angeles Open, and the lady pros compete at the LPGA Treetop Classic in March. After only a few years the Los Angeles Marathon has become a major event, with thousands hitting the pavement downtown and following a serpentine course through the city to its end at the Coliseum.

Another notable March event is the annual Academy Awards ceremony, first presented in 1930 at the Coconut Grove in the Ambassador Hotel, where an unknown young singer named Bing Crosby first appeared in Los Angeles. The Academy Awards have since been held at a number of large venues in the area. As proof of the enduring magic of the movies, the awards ceremony and the Tournament of Roses Parade in Pasadena always draw the largest worldwide television audiences of the year.

The striking Crystal Cathedral in Garden Grove draws large crowds during the Easter season with its annual religious pageant, "The Glory of Easter," which features live animals, flying angels, and elaborate special effects. Also, leading choirs, symphony orchestras, soloists, and prominent speakers participate in a moving two-hour sunrise service on Easter morning

at the Hollywood Bowl.

In spite of widespread doubts that it would be possible to stage a top-flight auto race with almost no straightaways to speak of, Toyota's Grand Prix of Long Beach has achieved the stature of a national racing event, and thousands jam the city for it each year. Leading international drivers compete in the 150-mile, 75-lap run through downtown Long Beach in what is the only grand prix race on city streets in this country.

Cinco de Mayo means fiesta time all over the city as the area's huge Latino population turns out en masse, along with many non-Latinos, to observe that favorite Mexican holiday. Also in May, the Renaissance Pleasure Faire in San Bernardino County re-creates the atmosphere of an old English country fair, with costumed performers, artisans, and an eclectic variety of food.

The summer months mean fewer orga-

This young entrant in Venice's Soap Box Derby is preparing for a future as a Los Angeles freeway pilot. Photo by Joseph Sohm/Chromosohm

nized events and more time outdoors. With perfect weather virtually guaranteed, multitudes of sun worshippers descend on the beaches. The world's finest surfers ride the waves at the International Surf Festival at various beaches in July, and the World Championship Volleyball two-man team competition is held on a weekend in Septem-

Pasadena's Doo Dah Parade presents an annual cavalcade of the odd, exotic, and comical, marching proudly alongside similarly ridiculous floats. Photo by Larry Molmud

ber. Also in September, the Los Angeles County Fair attracts more than one million visitors during its 17-day run at the Pomona Fairgrounds.

The Fishermen's Fiesta in Los Angeles Harbor in October, highlighted by a visit by the Catholic Cardinal of Los Angeles to bless the harbor and the fishing fleet, began as a small community affair after World War II. By the 1950s it had grown to rival the Rose Parade and had become so large, unwieldy,

and commercial that it was discontinued twice and finally revived on a much smaller scale in 1981.

The Hollywood Christmas Parade launches the holiday season in November with a celebrity grand marshal, floats, equestrian units, dozens of TV and movie stars, and more than 20 bands. The parade is televised nationally and to 86 foreign countries. Another November highlight is the utterly silly, fun-filled Doo Dah Parade in Pasadena, a

nutty takeoff on the Rose Parade and conclusive evidence that Los Angeles has more than its share of mad geniuses out there waiting to be discovered.

As December winds down, various Christmas boat parades present a brilliant spectacle and a charming seasonal event at Marina del Rey, San Pedro, Newport Beach, Huntington Harbor, and Dana Point. Processions of boats decorated with thousands of Christmas lights cruise slowly through the darkened

harbors, reflecting a festive, kaleidoscopic glow off the surrounding waters.

For many years Los Angeles has been a mecca for tourists and star-struck newcomers drawn by the city's climate, laissez-faire aura, and stimulating recreation scene. Unfortunately, L.A. has also been saddled with a somewhat unflattering reputation as a glitzy, glamorous, superficial amalgam of free spirits, itinerant dreamers, and adolescent sun worshippers, more show biz than substance—hardly a fitting or balanced image for the second largest population and business center in the United States.

But L.A.'s image is changing, and the city is being taken more seriously, even in the realm of sports and recreation. With the 1984 Olympics, Los Angeles achieved a new

level of maturity and respect in the eyes of the nation and the world. Being chosen as the site of the quadrennial Olympiad is a signal honor, but it also places enormous pressure on the host city to organize and present perhaps the most difficult and complicated international extravaganza efficiently and without inflicting financial ruin on itself. The fact that Los Angeles was able to turn that gargantuan event into an unprecedented success rightfully earned the metropolis esteem and admiration on a global scale. The message was clear and unmistakable: Los Angeles had truly come of age as a city whose horizons are limitless.

A Renaissance Pleasure Faire-goer adopts a Puckish disguise. Photo by Larry Molmud

THE BUSINESS HOURS

Angelenos at Work

Tom Geniesse, 27, didn't grow up with a movie camera on his shoulder, like Steven Spielberg, and his family didn't know anyone in the entertainment industry. Four years ago Geniesse vacationed in Los Angeles and, like others before him, fell in love with the movie business. "It's the only work that mixes the oil and water of art and business, so I decided to stay. I called my parents in Washington, D.C., and could hear their jaws hit the floor 3,000 miles away," he explains.

Armed with letters of introduction from the Colorado senator he'd been working for, Geniesse landed his first job as an unpaid intern for a producer. Next, he worked as a paid assistant at a production company and spent a year answering phones. After one more year as an assistant at Fox Broadcasting Company, today he is director of development at Reeves Entertainment, a large television production company.

Geniesse offers a bit of advice about how to move up in the entertainment industry. "What you end up being in Hollywood depends on the amount of energy you devote to the job, aside from answering the telephone."

"Like its surfers, southern California has ridden one wave after another; farming, oil, movies, aerospace and electronics. Now its economy is growing so fast that Los Angeles hopes to ride the ultimate wave into the next century, and to rival New York as America's business capital."

—*The Economist,* 1988

Frank Alonzo, president of Spectra Star, Inc., the largest manufacturer of kites in the world, plays with some of his high-flying samples. Alonzo produced a 1,500-foot-long kite— the world's largest to be successfully flown. Photo by Shelley Gazin

B y   E l l e n   H o f f s

The vast numbers of people who flood the Los Angeles area each year are testimony to the quality and number of job opportunities the city offers. State employment projections back up the city's reputation as a choice job market, among the best in the world. The state Employment Development Department (EDD) predicts that by 1992 all categories of jobs are projected to grow at an average rate of 13.8 percent. The services industry will have the greatest percentage of growth.

With over 1.3 million of the 4.3 million employees in Los Angeles County, services is the county's top industry in terms of employment. Manufacturing ranks second in number of jobs, according to data gathered by the state and based on standardized industrial classifications, followed by retail trade, government, and wholesale trade. Finance, insurance, and real estate—which EDD considers a single industrial group—is the state's sixth largest employer; transportation and public utilities are seventh, and construction is eighth. Agriculture and mining, which EDD regards as related, completes the list.

The *1990 Economic Report of the Governor* ranks motion pictures as the fastest-growing subcategory of California's services industry. "The Business," as insiders refer to the movie industry, employs about 118,000 people directly and 116,000 indirectly, in jobs like hairdressing and catering, throughout Los Angeles County.

But the movie industry's impact goes far beyond the number of people employed. Each year film, television, and commercial production companies pump more than $5 billion into the local economy, about 95 percent in Los Angeles County, says Michael Walbrecht, director of the California Film Commission. The entertainment industry returns millions more to the economy indirectly. Angelenos feel the loss of those dollars during an industry strike. When the merry-go-round of Hollywood meetings stop, restaurants are empty and limos are stalled. If it's possible to say that a city has feelings, Los Angeles feels depressed when "Tinseltown" is out of work.

Big rigs are frequent sights on Los Angeles' highways and roadways, transporting goods and comestibles to local business owners. Photo by Bob Rowan/Progressive Image

The people who work in Hollywood and the dollars they contribute to the economy are significant. However, the less glamorous industries such as manufacturing, retail trade, and finance are the backbone of the region's booming economy. These industries are spread throughout the county. Separate industry rankings are not available for the city of Los Angeles. However, data provided by EDD shows that the city's workers make up about 40 percent of the county's work force.

Monthly employment data does not count the self-employed, so their exact number is unknown. But there are significant numbers of independent contractors throughout the Los Angeles area, most notably in the service sector. Ranging from financial planners and computer programmers to interior designers and screenwriters, these self-employed individuals often work at home. Thus the service industry is likely to include an even bigger portion of the work force than state figures suggest.

Entrepreneurs are a thriving band of workers included in the employment rolls but not counted as a separate category. *Los Angeles Times* columnist Harry Anderson lauds the role of entrepreneurs in California. Entrepreneurship, he writes, "is the new underpinning of the California economy. It supports the growing population; its miraculous diversity protects us against cyclic downturns in the bigger industries. And the legendary ability of California to nourish small, young businesses (the business failure rate here is well below the national average) keeps new investors pouring in."

Entrepreneurs are attracted to Los Angeles because of its unparalleled acceptance of new ideas. Small companies, with 50 or fewer employees, make up 94 percent of the businesses in California. Their success is particularly striking in Los Angeles. Here young companies with fewer than 10 employees rank high on the 1990 *Los Angeles Times* list of California businesses with the highest return on equity over two years.

Entrepreneur Michael Moretti hopes to make that list someday. Moretti grew up and went to school in Northern California and moved to Los Angeles to take advantage of business opportunities in the area. In 1985 he began selling computer hardware from the rented room in which he lived. Today his business is located in an executive suite, and his company, Ideal Technologies, provides software designed to enhance the compatibility of computer products. Moretti gives the city of Los Angeles some of the credit for his success. "Opportunities are great in this densely populated area. I have access to sup-

pliers and a vast number of professionals."

Entrepreneurs throughout Los Angeles have their own version of Moretti's success story. Some, like Moretti, followed the independent route taken by entrepreneurs for generations. Others pursued local educational and governmental resources.

Above: Hollywood director/producer Taylor Hackford was the creative force behind *An Officer and a Gentleman, Against All Odds,* and *Everybody's All-American.* Like the classic Hollywood hero, Hackford began his career as a mailroom clerk at KCET television. Photo by Shelley Gazin

Left: A TV cameraman focuses on an L.A. story. Photo by Bob Rowan/ Progressive Image

The Mayor's Office of Business and Economic Development offers the Counselors on Urban Entrepreneurship (CUE) program. To begin the program, CUE volunteer entrepreneurs, who are actively carrying on their own businesses, advise budding entrepreneurs. During the program's second stage, a member of the staff helps the entrepreneur develop a business plan. If the entrepreneur needs financing, city programs are available for qualified applicants. Other programs are available for established companies.

Educational opportunities abound for the

(UCLA) is one of the largest graduate programs in the nation. UCLA's Entrepreneur Association runs 24 different student activities such as a student investment program. Other programs are available at more than 10 local universities, including Loyola Marymount University, California State University, Los Angeles, and Pepperdine University.

Be they entrepreneurs, nurses, or lawyers, it is likely that there are more of each occupation and profession in Los Angeles County than anywhere in California. For example, the 10,000 members of the Los Angeles County chapter of the California Society of

Los Angeles entrepreneur. The Entrepreneur Program at the University of Southern California is the nation's oldest and largest program. About 700 graduates and undergraduates are enrolled in the program each year. With almost 400 students, the Entrepreneurial Studies Center at the John E. Anderson Graduate School of Management at the University of California, Los Angeles

Certified Public Accountants make up the organization's largest membership in the state. The California Board of Registered Nursing counts almost 55,000 registered nurses in Los Angeles County, more by far than the closest runner-up, Orange County, with 20,000 nurses.

Los Angeles County has the largest number of attorneys in the state, according to the

California State Bar Association. Almost 37,000 lawyers practice in the county. East Coast lawyers consider Los Angeles so important that by 1987 some 40 New York law firms had opened branches in Los Angeles. Litigation drives Los Angeles law, says Rex Heeseman, a litigator with Adams, Duque & Hazeltine. He cites several reasons why. First, the California Supreme Court was a trailblazer in legal opinions extending legal rights. Also, he says, litigants in Los Angeles have received punitive damage awards, and their success encourages further litigation.

As the field of law grows, so does the paralegal profession. State economists forecast that paralegals will have the highest percentage of job growth of any profession—42 percent by 1992. New government regula-

Up-and-coming Hollywood agent Patrick Dollard shoots hoops while negotiating deals and helping budding writers and filmmakers get their projects started. Photo by Shelley Gazin

tions are in the works that will force paralegals to follow tougher guidelines. Mary Margaret FitzGerald, a member of the Los
Angeles Paralegal Association's Board of Directors, points out that Los Angeles offers
the largest job market for paralegals in the
nation.

But paralegals don't have a monopoly on
job growth. According to state economists,
service jobs are the fastest-growing segment
of the work force, with health care and
"business services" leading the way. "Business services" takes in about two dozen industries, including advertising.

Though long considered a trendsetter, Los
Angeles did not become a player in the nation's advertising market until the 1980s. As
usual, when the city started to move, it mus-
cled in fast. Today Los Angeles ranks as the
third largest advertising market in the nation, after New York
and Chicago. Fueled
by foreign automobile
and entertainment in-
dustry advertising, Los
Angeles is growing
faster than either of
its competitors, says
Cleveland Horton,
West Coast bureau
chief for *Advertising
Age* magazine.

Public relations
firms profit from the
entertainment indus-
try, too, though large
local agencies special-
ize in every aspect of
the business. Margaret
Mathis made her mark
in consumer public re-
lations before relocat-
ing to Los Angeles. An
account supervisor
with Manning, Selvage
& Lee, Mathis explains
why she decided to
work in the area. "I
came here after slav-
ing away to build my
career in Atlanta and
New York, which is the
most competitive of all
markets. The motivat-
ing factor to move
here was the fact that
Los Angeles was still a
major market for pub-
lic relations but of-
fered a better quality

Left: Tressa Miller, First Vice President and Director of Cultural Affairs of Security Pacific Corporation, routinely defies convention by purchasing "unconventional" art that brightens Security Pacific's corporate spaces, making Security Pacific Corp. one of the world's largest collectors of contemporary art. Photo by Shelley Gazin

Below: Michael Diamond, managing partner of the multinational law firm Skadden, Arps, Slate, Meagher & Flom, prepares to ride into the sunset on his BMW motorcycle. Photo by Shelley Gazin

of life. I felt I wanted more of a balance between personal and professional life. The work environment here is more relaxed, and that's a function of the Los Angeles life-style. The pressure is not as great."

In spite of L.A.'s renowned laid-back lifestyle, people living in the area have their share of health problems. Businesses are trying to hold down health care costs, but the industry has mushroomed due to an aging population and new medical technology that extends life. Health care is the county's largest service employer, with more than 266,400 health specialists working in the industry. Allied industries have grown also. For example, almost 10,000 area workers manufacture medical/surgical supplies.

More than 50,000 nurses work in the county, and the health care system needs more, says Gwen Umen, chairperson for the California Nurses Association. There is demand for nurses with specialized skills such as transplant surgery, pediatric care, and cancer care. Opportunities are greatest for nurses with master's and Ph.D. degrees.

"At the other end of the spectrum, there's growth in the home health care industry," Umen explains. "More patients need home care because the prospective payment system is causing people to be discharged from the hospital quicker and sicker."

The Los Angeles life-style and career opportunities at top medical institutions have attracted more than 20,000 physicians to Los Angeles, says Robert Calverley, spokesman for the Los Angeles County Medical Association. Physicians gravitate to Los Angeles for many reasons. One is California's lower medical malpractice insurance premiums. The state's Medical Injury Compensation Reform Act has contained medical malpractice insurance premiums by placing limitations on lawyer's contingency fees and capping awards for pain and suffering.

Physicians also settle in the Los Angeles area to be where medical advances are taking place. "Lots of firsts occur here, such as transplant centers with advancing medical technology. Also, a critical mass develops. When you get all these teams of talented people together they attract other professionals and patients," Calverley says.

Tourists coming to Los Angeles also want to be in the city where the action is. The Los Angeles Area Chamber of Commerce ranks tourism second on its list of the five top industries. In 1990 Los Angeles hosted 12 million tourists. While entertaining themselves, the tourists slept in 86,140 local hotels and motels and pumped at least $4.3 billion into the economy, says Michael Collins, vice president of public affairs for the Greater Los Angeles Convention and Visitors Bureau. California economists estimate that more than 48,000 people work in the lodging business in Los Angeles County. New luxury hotels will have a positive impact on the industry.

Bill Lucas, managing director of the Westin Bonaventure Hotel in downtown Los Angeles, has worked at nine different hotels during his 16-year career. He says that the hospitality business is different in Los Angeles. Labor costs are high here, he explains. This forces businesses to become more efficient than in other cities. While unskilled labor is abundant, skilled labor is harder to find because of competition from other industries.

Also, hotel marketing differs in Los Angeles. "Without question Los Angeles requires the most diverse marketing approach in the country," Lucas says. "We market globally. East for us is the entire United States and Europe. West is the Pacific Rim. Visitors come from Europe, the Pacific Rim, Mexico, and the entire United States."

Since 10 percent of the city's visitors come from Europe and 25 percent come from the Pacific Rim, some hotel employees must speak either Japanese, Korean, German, French, or Italian. Also, multilingual menus, service directories, and translation services must be available.

Attracting travelers who live in the U.S. is also a priority. To increase the number of convention bookings in the 1990s, Los Angeles has splurged to double the size of the Los Angeles Convention Center, on South Figueroa Street in downtown Los Angeles. The $485-million project is likely to be the most expensive convention center expansion in the country. Civic leaders are not scrimping and waiting to see if excitement about the center generates spontaneously. The city is investing $4.6 million in a preopening

Left: Health-conscious celebrities and ordinary folk alike come to Ron Teeguarden for his comprehensive stock of herbal teas and elixirs available at his Tea Garden Herbal Emporium in Venice. Photo by Shelley Gazin

Facing page: Keith Alway, owner/president of Long Beach-based Bio-Legal Arts, creates "demonstrative evidence" for the legal community, ranging from eight-foot scale models of freeways to videotapes depicting the daily hardships of the disabled. Photo by Shelley Gazin

marketing campaign to tell the world about the advantages of booking their conventions in Los Angeles. To date, the efforts have been successful. Eleven conventions have already been booked for 1993, the year the expansion is scheduled to be finished.

Los Angeles has no need to entice students. Education is a favorite pastime in Los Angeles, and jobs are plentiful in the educational sector. The Los Angeles Unified School District, which covers an area larger than the city of Los Angeles and is independent of the city government, employs more than 78,200 people. State economists predict that jobs in education will increase as immigrants are assimilated into the system. Presently the county contains more than 50 school districts that serve more than 500,000 elementary and secondary students. Enrollment at the nine community colleges is around 100,000 students. Los Angeles Coun-

ty's *Economic Resource Profile* lists 58 schools of higher education. In addition, the *1990 California Private School Directory* lists 740 private accredited elementary and high schools throughout L.A. County.

Brenda Lakin-Clapp is a professor of education at California State University, Northridge. For as long as she can remember, she wanted to be a teacher.

"My mom was a teacher. My aunts were teachers. And for black women in my mother's days, and in the era I grew up in, teaching was a reasonable notion."

Lakin-Clapp began teaching the sixth grade in the Westside of Los Angeles in 1961 after earning a Bachelor of Arts degree from UCLA. Three years later she was training student teachers, and by 1972 she had accepted a tenure-track position as an assistant professor of education at Cal State Northridge. Nine years later she became a full professor.

Landscape architect
Richard Powell has creat-
ed lush floral gardens
for Joni Mitchell, Steven
Spielberg, Barbara Streis-
and, and Madonna.
Photo by Shelley Gazin

Left: Packard Bell investors Jason Barzilay and Alex Sandel's Woodland Hills-based business, specializing in semiconductor and computer peripheral distribution, grosses more than $500 million annually. Photo by Shelley Gazin

Facing page: The *President Polk*, an oceangoing vessel bound for Oakland, California, docks at the Port of Los Angeles. Photo by Bo Richards

Below: A battalion of new Japanese imports are parked dockside, awaiting delivery to their Southern California dealerships. Photo by Bo Richards

WORLD-CLASS PORTS OF CALL

L.A.'s Maritime Commerce

A scant 50 years after Columbus recorded his discovery of a new continent, Portuguese navigator Juan Rodriguez Cabrillo sailed north from Mexico along the other coast of that continent on another voyage of discovery. On October 8, 1542, he landed in a shallow, crescent-shaped inlet and claimed it for the Spanish crown.

After several name changes the inlet would be called the Bay of San Pedro, and centuries would pass while that swampy landfall served as a primitive port-of-call for early Spanish missions, ranchos, and the tiny pueblo of Los Angeles.

Almost no one had heard of San Pedro until Richard Henry Dana immortalized it bitterly as "the hell of California . . . in every way designed for wear and tear on sailors" in his classic, *Two Years Before the Mast.*

Today that desolate marshland has been transformed into not one, but two of the largest, busiest, and most profitable man-made ports in the world, sharing the same continuous waterfront in direct competition with each other. Between them, the ports of Los Angeles and Long Beach dominate West Coast maritime commerce, and more decisively with each passing year.

Together the two ports achieved a historical milestone in 1988 when they became the busiest harbor in America, with a total of 7,106 ship arrivals, compared with 5,579 for the giant New York-New Jersey Port Authority—and exceeded the New York-New Jersey complex in customs collection, $2.8 billion to $1.8 billion, with the gap widening each year.

The present Port of Los Angeles is comprised of 28 miles of waterfront and 7,500 acres of land and water, fairly teeming with round-the-clock activity. As a landlord port, it leases its precious property to more than 100 tenants, ranging from individual stalls for local fish merchants to 100-acre container terminals for international shipping firms. Its waterfront footage is as valuable as any in the world.

Worldport of L.A., as the port calls itself, has an enormous impact on the regional job market in all five counties in the Southland. Directly or indirectly, the port generates employment for approximately 203,000 people, or one out of every 32 employees in the region. In fiscal 1988-1989, port-related activity led to $20.7 billion in industry sales, $5 billion in wages, and $725 million in tax revenues.

During the 1990 fiscal year, L.A.'s port handled trade with more than 100 different countries. Its largest trading partners have been Japan, Taiwan, and South Korea, as the focus of maritime shipping has shifted from the Atlantic to the Pacific with the continuing development of the Pacific Rim countries. Notable among them is the People's Republic of China, which has ended its long isolation and now seeks to restore relations with the West.

As the gateway to the second largest concentration of population and business in the United States, the Port of Los Angeles has been growing steadily in size, traffic volume, and income, especially since the mid-1980s, when its main waterways were dredged from a depth of 35 feet to 45 feet to handle the world's biggest container ships.

Other factors have contributed to the increase in traffic. More than half of arriving imports are destined for the Los Angeles megalopolis and are therefore off-loaded at the bay. Another factor is the increasing tendency to land goods on the West Coast and ship overland instead of using the Panama Canal, with its delays, rising rates, political unrest, and locks too narrow for some of today's biggest ships.

Thus the increases have been truly dramatic during the past decade. The port's 66.3 million metric revenue tons of cargo handled in 1989 marked a 26-million-ton increase from 1980. General merchandise tripled from 12.5 million metric tons to 36.7 million metric tons, as did container movement, from 657,000 units to 1.85 million units, while revenues increased from $59 million to $146 million during the same period. The value of cargo handled in fiscal 1989 totaled $45 billion, the highest on the West Coast.

For all the dazzling statistics, the massive movement of commercial goods through the port's wharves and terminals is only part of its diverse activities and functions. Besides its eight container and three omni terminals, the

tion as the home port for the "Love Boat" of television fame, L.A.'s port leads all West Coast ports in passenger traffic with its new World Cruise Center, which has docking space for five large vessels. In fiscal 1989 cruise ship arrivals totaled 387, or 10 percent of all vessels calling at the port, and the record 582,602 passengers who embarked and disembarked represented a 29 percent increase in passenger traffic from the previous year. Under an unusual management arrangement, the port allows a consortium of the seven cruise lines that use the center regularly to manage it.

A short distance down Harbor Boulevard is the old ferry building which has been converted into the Los Angeles Maritime Museum. Farther south is one of Southern California's leading tourist attractions, the Ports O' Call Village, which now draws nearly 3 million visitors annually.

South of the village is the sprawling new West Channel Cabrillo Beach Recreational Complex, which is becoming another major tourist attraction. The centerpiece of the 370-acre complex is a series of marina basins which will accommodate more than 1,000 pleasure craft.

Resolutely independent and competing aggressively for every potential tenant and consignment of cargo, the ports of Los Angeles and Long Beach have rarely collaborated on anything, but one issue they had to address together was the future expansion of the bay and what to do about it. Present facilities are taxed to capacity and both ports are short of space. In 1985 it was predicted that the volume of cargo passing through the two ports would triple by the year 2020. And it is already well ahead of that pace.

Working with the Army Corps of Engineers, the two ports have devised a program to meet increased demand. Called the 2020 Plan, it will require enormous increments of man-made land which will forever alter the appearance and configuration of the harbor. The only place such quantities of new land can be created is within the bay, and the plan calls for almost a quarter of the open water now surrounding the two ports to be filled in, requiring 1,104 acres of landfill in Los

Angeles Harbor and 1,496 acres on the Long Beach side of the bay.

When completed, the 2020 Plan is expected to create at least 50,000 new jobs and add $80 billion to the region's economy.

Unlike many port cities whose harbors are an integral part of the community, Los Angeles is more than 20 miles from its harbor. City fathers paved the

Above: Nightfall at the Port of Los Angeles finds a lone sailor scaling his ship's rigging, preparing for debarkation. Photo by John Gale

Left: The *Shin-Kashu Maru* of Tokyo pays another visit to the Port of Los Angeles. Photo by Bo Richards

way to ownership of the harbor in 1906 when they annexed the "shoestring strip," a mile-wide belt of land leading to the waterfront, along what is now the Harbor Freeway. It was a clever move and it served its purpose, but because of even that brief distance a surprising number of Angelenos have never visited their harbor. Those who haven't would find it well worth the short trip to enjoy the harbor's many recreational facilities and see how their world-class, international port operates.
—*Charles F. Queenan*

Port of Los Angeles accommodates the World Cruise Center, commercial fisheries, shipyards and boat repair yards, and a constantly expanding pleasure and recreational complex.

After gaining international recogni-

A NASA jet prepares for flight in the Mojave Desert. Photo by Bob Rowan/Progressive Image

Lakin-Clapp describes the educational climate in Los Angeles as "challenging." The challenge is in addressing the needs of the region's changing population.

"If you have abilities and interests, there are a lot of opportunities, if for no other reason than that we have such a diverse population. People can find a niche here." One of those niches is in special education. Cal State Northridge has one of the largest deaf student populations in the nation, second only to Gallaudet University, a center for deaf students in Washington, D.C.

Those not interested in service jobs may find their niche in Los Angeles County's vast manufacturing sector, the largest in the na- tion. One of every five employees in the county works at manufacturing everything from aircraft parts and wetsuits to pickles and paper. Manufacturing jobs are good for the county. Each manufacturing job creates two or three others in warehousing, truck- ing, management, finance, accounting, and sales.

California economists estimate that dur- ing the second quarter of 1990, 18,377 pri- vately owned manufacturing firms dotted Los Angeles County. Orange County was the closest runner-up in the state with 5,492. Los Angeles leads the nation in the number of production jobs in high tech/aerospace tech- nology. The American Electronics Association reports that 1,260 electronic companies are spread throughout the county. These companies are more diverse than in Silicon Valley. In Los Angeles computer manufacturers and software companies work alongside companies manufacturing machinery for defense and aerospace.

Even when it comes to high tech Los Angeles is king. More high-tech industries do business in Los Angeles County than in Silicon Valley. Weather, location, and life-style are the obvious reasons why industries choose Los Angeles. Not so obvious is the enormous and broad-based labor pool. Motivated unskilled laborers and highly skilled workers make up the county's 830,000 who work in manufacturing. The nation's largest concentrations of mathematicians, scientists, engineers, and skilled technicians work in Los Angeles County.

Also, manufacturers opt to settle in the area because of excellent access to international trade. The Port of Long Beach and the Port of Los Angeles, on San Pedro Bay, form the trade gateway to the Pacific Rim. Import-export cargo at both ports increased by $6 billion to nearly $111 billion in 1990, a rise of 6 percent. The increase is particularly impressive considering that in five years exports and imports have almost doubled. In 1986 they totaled $61.8 billion. Currently more than one in 10 of the nation's international trade dollars is shipped in or out of the Los Angeles area.

In 1990 the Port of Los Angeles surpassed New York in number of containers handled. The Port of Long Beach is the busiest port on the West Coast. Foreign cars are top imports at both ports, followed by electrical machinery and equipment and office machines.

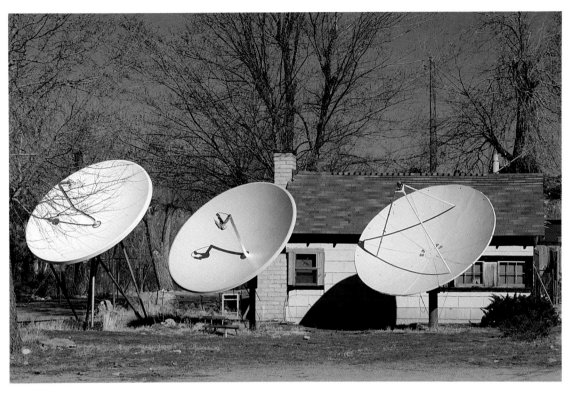

Prime exports include electrical machinery and equipment and aircraft and spacecraft. Nearly 54 percent of the nation's West Coast imports pass through the ports of Los Angeles and Long Beach.

Japan is the number one trading partner for the Los Angeles Customs District. The district includes Los Angeles International Airport (LAX), the ports of Los Angeles and Long Beach, and Port Hueneme in Ventura County. In addition to the Pacific Rim nations, 15 nations do one billion dollars or more in two-way trade with Los Angeles, writes Jack Kyser, chief economist for the Los Angeles Area Chamber of Commerce, in a 1990 update to *Marketplace of the World.*

Several occupations have benefited from L.A.'s trade boom. First, the number of employees handling exports and imports has jumped. And the number of manufacturers who export and import products has skyrocketed. Dollars generated from the port have helped build the city of Long Beach and produced added income for LAX. Most important, international trade has created 255,000 jobs for Los Angeles County, according to Kyser.

In 1989 the area's high-tech/aerospace industry exported $8 billion in high tech and

The occupant of this home may be unsatisfied with L.A.'s cable and network programs. Photo by Bob Rowan/Progressive Image

aerospace technology from Los Angeles ports. Since the early 1950s Los Angeles County has led the nation in defense, space, and commercial airplane development and manufacturing. During the Persian Gulf War the region demonstrated its continuing leadership. Along with radar equipment and overhead reconnaissance systems and missiles, the pinpoint accuracy of the F-117 Stealth Fighter, manufactured by Burbank-based Lockheed Advanced Development Projects, awed the world.

"Technology developed in Los Angeles has been a major contributor to the success of the Persian Gulf War," says Wolfgang H. Demisch, U.S. director of equity research at UBS Securities, Inc., in New York.

Demisch sees future growth in commercial airplane manufacturing, pointing out that some 3,000 or so older and less efficient planes will have to be replaced in the next 10 years. However, along with most experts polled, he is not bullish about future military expenditures.

Demisch explains, "The Southland has performed an outstanding job in providing the nation with its defense system. Nevertheless, the standard American tradition is to give the heroes a parade and send them back to civilian life. To a certain extent that is happening in the aerospace industry."

Los Angeles County will receive rewards for its technological expertise. Robert K. Arnold, CEO at the Palo Alto-based Center for the Continuing Study of the California Economy, believes that changing national priorities and a shrinking federal budget make defense cutbacks likely. Other expen-

ditures will replace these cutbacks, Arnold predicts.

Today about 8 percent, or 245,200, of Los Angeles County's employees work in high tech/aerospace jobs. A substantially larger 14 percent worked in the industry in the 1970s when defense cutbacks rocked the local economy. The defense industry is preparing for every eventuality by setting dollars aside for job retraining. The economy's diverse opportunities hold the promise of new jobs for workers caught in the squeeze of defense cutbacks.

The $10-billion apparel industry is a bright spot in Los Angeles' manufacturing economy. State economists estimate that in L.A. County more than 94,000 employees work in clothing and textile production. Most garment companies are small to middle sized. But the industry will continue to grow. The state forecasts a 43.6 percent increase in the manufacturing of men's and boys' apparel by 1992.

Los Angeles is the nation's second-largest furniture manufacturing region, runner-up only to North Carolina. Location and fine craftsmen brought the industry to the area. Formerly, major furniture manufacturing

Facing page: The metamorphosis of a Los Angeles high rise is revealed. Photo by Joseph Sohm/ Chromosohm

Are they cars? Are they planes? No, they're Minute Man Messenger Jets, guaranteed to turn heads as they speedily maneuver along the streets of downtown Los Angeles. Photo by Bob Rowan/Progressive Image

SOLID GOLD

The Music Business in Los Angeles

When people think entertainment, they think movies. And when people think movies, they think Hollywood. But Hollywood is also home to the music industry, which outdistances film's higher profile with substantially higher annual revenues: roughly $6.5 billion to film's $5 billion in 1990.

As one of the country's main music centers (with New York and Nashville), Los Angeles naturally sees a good chunk of the profit. Yet impressive as that figure is, it only covers sales of CDs, prerecorded cassettes, LPs, and music videos. Music and related businesses bring much more money—and many more jobs—to the L.A. area.

They also bring people. Like the silver screen, gold and platinum records are powerful magnets. As actors flock to Los Angeles for screen work, musicians are drawn by the city's active club scene and the possibility of a career in music. The Hollywood local of the Musicians Union boasts 11,000 members—mainly professional musicians for hire on sound tracks, orchestral, and other commercial jobs—not the street-level hopefuls.

Each year, 1,200 such hopefuls study at Hollywood's Musicians Institute of Technology, where they shell out $6,000 for a 12-month course of study with working musicians. The student body is 40 percent foreign and just 10 to 15 percent native Angeleno. Related engineering skills are taught at other schools in the area.

Aspiring musicians patronize rock-star fashion outlets, fast food joints, and of course, the 120-plus instrument stores listed in the Greater Los Angeles Yellow Pages.

You can see these kids cruising the famed Sunset Strip on weekend nights, checking out bands, striking poses, and reeking of hairspray, all in hopes of becoming next year's Van Halen, Guns N' Roses, Poison, Motley Crue, or Warrant—all success stories that started in Los Angeles.

But for those who don't catch the golden ring, music offers other opportunities. Some go to work at record companies. The Burbank-based music divisions of Warner Bros.—record companies, music publishing, special products, and product distribution—employ more than 850 people in the L.A. area alone.

Over 75 record companies—or "labels"—large and small, base their operations in L.A. Virtually all other labels of consequence maintain a Los Angeles office to preserve an essential West Coast presence. Some of these operations have become fixtures on the local landscape. The cylindrical Capitol Records building, a bold abstraction of a stack of records, is a Hollywood landmark.

The nineties ushered in a fertile growth period for record companies. Inspired by the spectacular sums many labels fetched in a foreign buyout wave, a dozen or more new ones have been formed—many in L.A.—and represent the hopes of both the entrepreneurs starting them and of the musicians they may sign.

Some were created to diversify existing record companies, others to tap the talents of heavyweight free agents. In the latter category are former MCA head Irving Azoff's new Giant Records, ex-Island honcho Lou Maglia's Zoo Entertainment, and Chrysalis founder Terry Ellis' Imago Records.

Increasingly, Hollywood's film and music communities cross-pollinate. Record moguls like David Geffen and Quincy Jones turned to the screen years ago. More recently, film producer Ted Field founded his Interscope Records; and actor Michael Douglas is part owner of Third Stone Music, an offshoot of his film company, Stonebridge Productions.

And music supports other enterprises in L.A.: nightclubs, recording and rehearsal studios, law practices, management firms, publicists, printers, publications, and a host of luxury services, among others.

Nightclubs serve several functions on L.A.'s music scene. For the technicians and servers who work steadily in them, they're reasonably solid income. For musicians they're better and worse than cash; they're the big chance. L.A.'s record execs scout talent in clubs; later on the road to success, labels and managers

sometimes rent nights at clubs to showcase new music for the press or industry.

Recording studios, like rehearsal spaces, fetch high hourly rates, as do the engineers who operate their complex electronics.

Yet far from the smoky late-night jam sessions, music pays for the lifestyles of the rich and obscure. Music law doesn't stop at bailing rowdy rockers out of jail. It extends to contracts, copyrights, and even the executive suite. Among the lawyers who have jumped over to record companies is Peter Paterno, who left his Westside law firm for the top rung at Disney's new pop label, Hollywood Records.

Managers also help guide artists' careers in a variety of ways, from choos-

ing lawyers, labels, and development strategies to setting up dinner reservations and weekly allowances.

The image-intensive music industry supports a wide array of enterprises: restaurants, hotels, limousine services, caterers, florists, and high-end imported car dealerships.

Some businesses—like the Sunset Strip's famed Le Dome restaurant—cater largely to the music business. Others—like the Music Express and Record Time messenger services—do so almost exclusively. And several national music trade papers are published in L.A., including *Radio & Records, Cashbox,* and *HITS.*

Of course, the end product of all the deals and hopes—the music itself—sells

as well or better in L.A. than anywhere else. Record stores, concert promoters, and ticket brokers all do strong business in Los Angeles, where a youthful, mobile, and diverse population provides fertile ground for an amazing hybrid of musical successes.

Angelenos consider the entire metro region their concert hall. As Fred Rosen, chief executive officer and chairman of L.A.-based Ticketmaster, the world's largest ticket service, points out, "You're dealing with a population base of 25 million and distance is not an issue—people do travel half an hour for dinner."

People travel even farther to hear the music of their choice. And the diversity of their choices supports an equally eclectic range of concerts and

Graham Nash (center) and sound engineers mix music during a recording session at The Complex in West Los Angeles. Photo by Shelley Gazin

clubs. Rosen adds: "You have more clubs here than anywhere else in America, more kinds of music . . . [L.A. has] a very healthy, active, young population, and music is a very important part of the life here. There are L.A. bands that sell great in L.A. and don't do that kind of business anywhere else in the country."

Which is why the music industry will continue to boom in Los Angeles, pumping up the economy and issuing its siren call to guitar-bearing hopefuls across the nation. —*Barak Zimmerman*

areas in the U.S. were located on the north side of the Rocky Mountains and far from the West Coast. As the population grew, manufacturers wanted to be closer to their buyers. Also, many European emigrants who settled in Los Angeles worked with wood and opened furniture factories in the region.

Today the furniture industry's approximately 2,500 independent companies directly employ about 33,800 production workers

Everyone—including locals—is a tourist in Los Angeles. Within its borders, something new and surprising is always happening. Photo by Joseph Sohm/Chromosohm

throughout the county. They ring up $2.5 billion a year in sales, and are hoping to increase sales by exports to Japan, according to Stephen Wise, chairman of the Export Council of the Western Furniture Manufacturers Association and president of Los Angeles-based Furniture Profiles. "Japan is essentially the largest growing market in the world for home furnishings. We are making a breakthrough, and they are changing their distribution system to buy our furniture. The Japanese love the California life-style, and Japan is a natural export market because it's on the Pacific Rim," he maintains.

The printing industry is another economic success story. California is the largest print-producing state in the nation. Sales in the Los Angeles metropolitan area add up to about $4.5 billion and account for some 65 percent of the state's print production, says Bob Lindgren, president of the Printing Industries Association, Inc., of Southern California. Lindgren estimates that about 2,700 businesses are spread throughout Los Angeles County. Companies average 10 to 11 employees and supply work to a total of about 27,000 people.

When it comes to publishing, the *Los Angeles Times* has the largest newspaper circulation in the nation. More than 13,000 people work to put out four editions of the newspaper in Los Angeles, the San Fernando Valley, Orange County, and San Diego. Every Sunday 1.5 million people buy the *Times.* In 1989 the city's other metropolitan newspaper, the *Los Angeles Herald Examiner,* closed its doors. The *Times* and suburban newspapers such as the *Daily News* in the San Fernando Valley took up the slack.

Traditionally the area's magazine publishers have focused on special-interest publications that meet the needs of particular groups. Catering to the region, *Los Angeles* is the nation's most successful city magazine. And *L.A. Style,* which celebrates the city's fabled trendiness, has been so successful that it was recently purchased by American Express.

As a media city, Los Angeles has global reach. Each day television brings Los Angeles into the living rooms of the world.

Eighty-seven percent of the nation's syndicated television shows are shot in Los Angeles County. A breakdown of the close to $5 billion that the film industry spends in the county yearly shows how much the television industry contributes to local coffers: $2.1 billion is spent on films; $1.5 billion goes for commercials; and the television industry spends $1.4 billion.

The region has the fastest-growing cable market in the nation, states David Billnitzer, project manager for the Southern California Cable Marketing Council. In 1987 cable penetration in Los Angeles was a little over a third. By 1990 half the homes in Los Angeles had cable.

"We're seventh in the country as far as cable penetration goes," Billnitzer says. "The main reason we're not first is cable's competition with the California life-style. In other

Joe Weider, patriarch of a fitness magazine empire, relaxes at home with his wife Betty (holding cat) and nationally renowned cyclist Casey Patterson. Photo by Shelley Gazin

ON THE CUTTING EDGE
Designer Kevan Hall

When he was seven years old Kevan Hall was sitting in front of his TV set in Detroit, redesigning the wardrobes of stars from Martha Reeves and the Vandellas to Marlene Dietrich. At 26, he was one of 10 top designers chosen to dress Ethel Bradley, the wife of Los Angeles' mayor, for the 1984 Olympics.

Today Hall's designs are featured in department and specialty shops throughout the nation. His staying power is no small feat in the precarious fashion industry. A share of the credit for Hall's inspiration and success goes to Los Angeles.

"Flowers blooming all over the city are often an inspiration. I can be driving down the street and see a beautiful hibiscus, and go back to my studio and use the flower in a design. Colors are more intense in Los Angeles because of the light. And I love the weather and the quality of life here," he adds with a smile.

Also, the city is a practical place for a young designer to begin. "Even when times are bad," Hall explains, "you can survive in Los Angeles because overhead is low. In New York you may pay $25 a square foot for space. Here a young designer can find a storefront for $2 to $4 a square foot."

Los Angeles has always been a positive environment for manufacturers and designers to get started, says David Morse, managing partner of the CaliforniaMart, a giant complex with showrooms leased by garment makers or their representatives.

"There are very good financial resources in Los Angeles' $10-billion-a-year fashion industry. Working conditions are good in terms of being able to get labor and suppliers of fabrics. Young designers can find a representative here, so they don't have the overhead of a showroom. Also, they're able to link into a variety of market activities that are unavailable in

Kevan Hall is a prime example of one shining star who rose to prominence in the dynamic Los Angeles apparel design and manufacturing scene. Photo by Shelley Gazin

other parts of the country," Morse says.

Representatives from every major retailer and significant specialty shops visit Los Angeles at some time during the October launching of the spring lines. Morse estimates that buyers make over 100,000 trips through the CaliforniaMart. Buyers are attracted to the mart by fashion shows, promotions of young designers, and travel discounts on airfare, hotels, and parking.

Besides coming to see the newest designs, buyers visit Los Angeles to take home merchandising techniques from the region's trendsetting fashion communities. Nowhere else can they find the diverse shopping available at Sunset Plaza, Rodeo Drive, Venice Beach on Sunday afternoons, and Main Street and Montana Avenue in Santa Monica.

"Los Angeles has evolved during the last 15 years from what once could have been considered a regional marketplace into a truly international fashion center," says Morse. "We've seen an evolution that focuses on our life-style and gets translated into fashion that is worn worldwide. Our strengths are focusing on the Sunbelt states as well as the major metropolitan areas. I'd say the only things that Californians don't manufacture is apparel for the New England winter climate."

That wasn't the case in 1983 when Hall spotted a void in the Los Angeles fashion market. No one was designing affordable special occasion dresses, suits, and evening wear. Hall stepped in with a line of sleek couture after-five wear that featured luxurious velvets, taffetas, and beaded laces. The classics were an immediate sellout. Today Hall is renowned for his apparel that can be worn from day into evening. This year Hall has launched a new label, Kevan Hall Studio. The less expensive sportswear line is being shown at one of the 2,000 showrooms in the CaliforniaMart.

In his downtown Los Angeles loft, with his wife and studio manager Debbie by his side, 33-year-old Hall exudes confidence. Clippings from newspapers and magazines showing Hall's fashions are pinned to the wall. And for inspiration there's a picture of French designer Givenchy's chateau.

Hall moved from Detroit to Los Angeles at 17 to enroll in the Fashion Institute of Design and Merchandising (FIDM) after placing in the school's "Designers

of Tomorrow" contest. Later a school-sponsored European study tour influenced his work.

"We went to Dior, Givenchy, and Pierre Cardin, and that whetted my appetite to do special couture, fabulously constructed and elegant designs that are modern and young. That's the concept our collection has taken."

Hall graduated from FIDM with a Peacock Award for outstanding design in a fashion show presentation. Just out of school, he worked for big-name designers like Harriet Selwyn during the day. At night he would return to his apartment and design clothes aimed at the executive woman. It took a year of nights and weekends, using Debbie as a model, to produce 18 samples of sportswear with the Kevan Hall Couture label.

"We were up until three and four in the morning, cutting and prepping everything for the sewing contractors. I remember one time the Santa Ana winds came up and the lights went out in the whole area. I had to get these things cut, so we lit candles all over the house and cut by candlelight," he says with a wistful smile.

With samples in hand, Hall managed to get orders from the city's highest-priced and most fashionable boutiques. Not satisfied with local sales, he took a few days off work and carted his collection up to San Francisco, where he rounded up more orders. When it came time to go into full production, he quit his regular job, but found he was still working until three and four in the morning, cutting and prepping for the sewing contractors.

After his line was completed, he decided to try his luck in New York. Few designers are able to sell to the big stores without a representative doing it for them. So his friends in the fashion industry were amazed when on his own Hall persuaded major department stores such as Henry Bendel and Bergdorf Goodman to purchase his clothes.

For the nineties, Hall has plans to expand his Studio collection to include coats and rainwear. Influenced by animal rights activists, he is working on a special project in which he will design a line of fake fur coats with quilted linings.

"Los Angeles is a glamour city. Lots of celebrities will be wearing our fake furs to opening parties," Hall says with confidence earned from experience.

—*Ellen Hoffs*

L.A. fashion designer Glenn Williams poses with a model. Williams' women's wear is feminine and sleek, and comes in exotic shades like "cactus blooms" and "cracked clay." Photo by Shelley Gazin

places in the country, people just stay home and watch television, especially during the winter. Here, there are lots of other things to do all year round."

The largest number of radio advertising dollars in the nation changes hands in Los Angeles, says Gordon Mason, president of the Southern California Broadcasters Association. In 1989 that totaled $415 million, about 10 percent more than New York. Los Angeles County has the greatest number of radio stations in the state, with 44 commercial radio stations using the airwaves. Half

are FM stations, and about 75 percent of the radio audience tunes in to FM radio.

Media jobs go to experienced and tenacious professionals. But almost any Angeleno can get a job in retailing, declares Sheila Speer, owner of Alley, a trendy women's clothing store specializing in Los Angeles designers. From the street-corner vendor to the salesperson on Rodeo Drive, more than 649,000 people work in retail trade, the county's third largest industrial group in terms of employees. State economists project that one out of four new jobs in the county

Sandy Cruze, pictured, owner and creator of the Mohair Salon, a Pasadena haircutting establishment where hair and art collide, holds frequent art exhibits. Photo by Shelley Gazin

WORKING 'ROUND THE CLOCK

L.A.'s 24-Hour Day

It's 10 p.m. and the cast and crew of the film *December* break for what they jokingly call "lunch." They've been gathered around a pool at the University of Southern California since 5 p.m. to film a tense reconciliation scene between actor Wil Weaton *(Stand By Me)* and Brian Krause *(Return To Blue Lagoon)*. If all goes well, they'll get to go home at 5 a.m.

Welcome to workaday—or better yet, workanight—L.A., a city as unconventional about its working hours as it is about its fashion, cars, and architecture. Based on U.S. Census and Bureau of Labor Statistics data, Dr. Murray Melbin, a professor of sociology at Boston University, estimates that as the clock strikes midnight in the greater Los Angeles area, nearly 500,000 people are out making a living. While every city has its share of "graveyard shift" workers—namely, police, fire, and hospital personnel as well as airport, newspaper, and TV and radio station employees—the dynamics of the Los Angeles economy have allowed for especially large inroads into what Melbin calls "the colonization of the night."

The film business, in particular, with its erratic shooting schedules and uncompromising deadlines, is completely divorced from any notions of 9 to 5 regularity. As any of *December*'s 30 crew members—camera operators, actors, grips, catering staff, and more—working this evening can attest, there is no such thing as a "typical working day."

"We chose to shoot at night," explains Don Pemrick, *December*'s producer and casting director. During one portion of the production, Pemrick says they shot 10 nights in a row. "The movie takes place after dark, so that's when we shoot," he says. While Hollywood has the technical know-how to turn day into night in some situations

and vice versa, in today's budget-driven film environment Pemrick, his eyes fixed on the bottom line, finds that it's cheaper to work with nature than against her. Plus the results, aesthetically, he says, are better.

The TV and film satellite industries also function without regard for time of day. Companies that develop motion picture film, dry clean costumes, or edit videotape must operate 'round the clock, taking in what's shot in one day and having it ready before the cameras roll on the next. Nowhere is the relationship between time and money so strikingly clear as in Hollywood, where equipment rental, location fees, and salaries can easily reach tens of thousands—even

Radio host and experimental musician Brent Wilcox explores new frontiers in electronic world and fusion music over the nocturnal airwaves, broadcasting from public radio station KCRW at Santa Monica City College. Photo by Shelley Gazin

hundreds of thousands—of dollars a day.

Over on the other side of the entertainment industry—the music recording business—things aren't much different. Recording studios typically remain open 24 hours every day.

"In this business, the artist is everything," says Mark Stebbeds, a recording engineer at Lion Share recording studios in West Hollywood who has helped such megastars as Dionne Warwick,

John Cougar Mellencamp, and Whitney Houston lay down their tracks. "And they," Stebbeds continues, "are typically night people."

Agents, record company A&R executives, and even attorneys find that they, too, must adjust to the music performers' rhythms. After spending the day in the conservative atmosphere of his Century City office, music attorney Gene Salomon, of the law firm of Mitchell, Silberberg & Knupp, will spend many evenings meeting with his clients in the raucous and decidedly noncorporate environment of a rock club.

But it is not only in the glitzy milieu of show business that work carries on into the late night and early morning hours.

One of Southern California's biggest employers, the aerospace industry, keeps its facilities churning from early morning until midnight. When civilian and defense contracts are high, these plants expand production, and the airplanes, rockets, jet engines, and helicopters come off the assembly line nonstop.

Also, as Los Angeles comes into its own as an international business center, such sober institutions as banks and investment houses keep their corps of traders active well before the morning rush hour.

"We start trading with Europe at 3 a.m.," says Frank Baxter, president of the Los Angeles-based investment firm, Jefferies and Company, Inc. At the other side of the dial, firms tied to Asian markets (4 p.m. Los Angeles time is 9 a.m. the next day Tokyo time) find themselves working well into the night, keeping an eye on the financial action in the Far East. "As the world gets smaller," Baxter concludes, "the hours get longer."

L.A.'s leadership in the shift to an information-based economy creates even more imperatives for expanded business hours. The massive computers and data bases that form the core of these information-based enterprises are expensive. Businesses can ill afford to keep them idle. In some cases, this has led to corporations rethinking the entire concept of the work week.

One example of that can be found at

TRW Information Systems in Orange. The giant data base here stores credit information on 170 million Americans, each of whom has an average of eight credit relationships. To keep up with what Susan Murdy, manager of Public Affairs of TRW Credit Data Division, calls "the ongoing stream of information that comes in from credit granters throughout the U.S.," TRW abandoned the idea of an eight-hour-a-day, 40-hour work week for many of its employees. Instead, technical support and data entry personnel work three 12-hour shifts a week, alternating between day and nighttime work every three months. Murdy says the new system has resulted not only in greater employee productivity, but also in reduced burnout and turnover, problems that plague many companies with graveyard operations.

If business no longer stops at 5 p.m., then industries that service businesses and their employees must also adjust to meet these new realities. Restaurants, messenger services, and computer repair companies are becoming increasingly available, expanding the nocturnal work force even further. One company, the Janway Agency in Century City, even specializes in providing temps, from word processors to multilingual attorneys, to businesses on an hour's notice—any time day or night.

Finally, there's what Professor Melbin calls "the invisible work force" —the hundreds, perhaps thousands, of screenwriters, songwriters, artists, graphic designers, and other creative individuals who call Los Angeles home. "These people want to do their work during uninterrupted blocks of time," he says. For many, that means the midnight hours, when street noise is subdued and the phone seldom rings.

There's nothing subdued about midnight on the set of *December,* however. Here it's business as usual, and the swimming pool buzzes with activity, as grips adjust lights, the director of photography plans the next camera move, and the makeup artist puts a few last-minute dabs on actor Wil Weaton's face. Then for a few seconds—after director Gabe Torres yells, "ACTION!" but before the actors begin their dialogue— the silence and tranquility normally associated with the late-night hours is allowed, briefly, to descend.—*Mark Ehrman*

will be in retail trade in the 1990s. Moreover, these jobs will increase by 28 percent between 1985 and 1995.

Speer, who has been a Los Angeles merchandiser for 25 years, says, "Los Angeles designers understand that local women need soft, unstructured clothes." Only in the last five years, she adds, has New York finally looked to Los Angeles for designers. Now even New York-based *Women's Wear Daily,* the fashion industry journal, features major sections on Los Angeles.

Los Angeles County is the top county in the nation in retail sales. According to the U.S. Department of Commerce, the Los Angeles-Long Beach area rang up $63 billion in sales in 1989. Chicago came in a not-so-close second with more than $46 billion. As might be expected in Los Angeles, automobiles rank first in dollar sales.

One reason local consumers are big spenders is that they have money to spend. Los Angeles County is home to more families with incomes above $50,000 than any other county in the nation, according to estimates from *Sales & Marketing Management* magazine. Also, county residents' income is 15 percent greater than the national average.

In Los Angeles competition is fierce in every sector of retailing, as businesses vie for a share of the consumer dollar. Grocery stores often stay open 24 hours a day. And Los Angeles County's 20,000 restaurants, more per capita than anywhere else in the nation, compete vigorously to serve a clientele that eats out frequently.

Yet there's always room for a restaurant that has a new concept or a personality chef, contends Marvin Zeidler, owner of Citrus in West Hollywood, and president and general partner of the Broadway Deli in Santa Monica. Los Angeles restaurants thrive on the region's growth and diverse population, Zeidler says.

"We have the European along with the Hispanic influence. And people here do a great deal of traveling. When they come home they want to reexperience things here that they did on their travels," Zeidler explains. "People are more adventuresome in

Southern California. This is the land of experimenters."

Los Angeles would be an ideal travel destination even if the city was made up of nothing more than its ethnic restaurants and markets. They represent almost every ethnic group in the world. And there is variety within each group. Restaurantgoers can choose from 10 Ethiopian restaurants and as many as 100 Salvadoran restaurants. And adventurous diners can sample the countless ethnic markets where locals from every culture buy their food.

"Most of these places make their living from their own people. But they are thrilled when someone from outside their culture ventures in," says Ellen Melinkoff, author of *Flavor of Los Angeles.*

Local ethnic restaurants, retailers, manufacturers, and markets receive their goods from the thriving wholesale industry, the county's fifth largest industry after government. More than 300,000 people make up the wholesaling work force. Many work in prominent Los Angeles landmarks such as the Pacific Design Center and Design Center

Citrus Restaurant is celebrated not only for the exceptional cuisine of its chef, Michel Richard, but also for its fine art program. Here, Richard has effectively reproduced the fruit depicted in a painting by Astrid Preston, held by program creator and curator Heidi Von Kahn. Photo by Shelley Gazin

South, which specialize in furniture. Or they sell flowers and fresh fruit and vegetables at the Los Angeles Flower Market and three Los Angeles wholesale produce markets. Other well-known wholesale centers are the downtown jewelry center and the wholesale toy area, nicknamed "Toy Town."

The CaliforniaMart, another landmark wholesale center, illustrates the influence of Los Angeles' apparel industry. Within the Mart's 2,000 showrooms, 10,000 apparel lines are represented. Many West Coast apparel manufacturers locate in Los Angeles just to be near this wholesale center. Some designers have found new ways to wholesale their clothing.

Designer Harriet Selwyn chooses not to wholesale her fine line of women's clothing downtown. She works in a vintage white California adobe bungalow in West Hollywood. Selwyn explains, "The life-style here is kind and nice. I like the work environment."

Selwyn's apparel has influenced a generation of young designers. The city's weather has served as a major source of inspiration for Selwyn. After leaving New York, Selwyn settled in Los Angeles and soon realized that she felt cold in the morning and sweltering in the afternoon. She found herself adding or subtracting layers of clothing to make herself comfortable. Selwyn made her first fashion splash in 1971 with thin jerseys and chiffons that could be worn in layers for warmth and style. Selwyn is a creative businesswoman as well as a designer. Today she is designing, manufacturing, and wholesaling her own line of clothing.

After wholesaling, the county's next largest number of employees works in finance, insurance, and real estate. And about half of those 293,000 employees work in the financial sector. The state credits a rise of employment in finance to Saturday banking hours and increased use of part-time help.

Banks are big business in Los Angeles, which has eclipsed both San Francisco and Chicago to become the nation's number two money center in terms of total bank deposits. California commercial bank deposits totaled almost $213 billion in June 1989, the most recent period for which data is available. Los Angeles County's share was $74 billion, with

Facing page, bottom: Frieda Caplan is the brains behind Frieda's Finest, a Los Angeles firm specializing in "the world's weirdest produce." Caplan, who is happiest educating consumers about spikey orange kiwano fruits, pineapple-scented basil, and yellow-fleshed watermelon, was named by Governor George Deukmejian as one of California's Outstanding Women in Business. Photo by Shelley Gazin

STOCKING UP
The Markets for Produce

For 52 years the Tanaka family has sold fruits and vegetables to celebrities, socialites, and just plain folk from their store on Montana Avenue in Santa Monica. The street that used to be lined with mom-and-pop grocery stores and service establishments has been transformed into one of the trendiest shopping streets in the Los Angeles area. Yet Tanaka's Quality Produce has remained the same. No gimmicks. No diet books. Not even a book about vegetarianism. Just fine produce.

Throughout the years the Tanakas have traveled downtown six mornings a week to buy their produce at Los Angeles' wholesale produce market. The trip took an hour before the freeways were built. Now it takes only half an hour, but the changes in the produce business have meant more to Tanaka's Quality Produce than saving travel time.

Until four years ago Eddie Tanaka had the option of shopping at the City Market or the 12-acre Los Angeles Union Terminal Market, both built in the early 1900s. In 1986 the Los Angeles Wholesale Produce Market opened, and he had a new 32-acre market to explore each morning. The new produce market is considered one of the largest and most modern in the nation. Together the city's three produce markets encompass more than 50 acres, offering a choice of more than 200 varieties of fruits and vegetables that are flown, shipped, or trucked in from more than 30 states and 30 countries. Market sales top one billion dollars a year.

Since 1953, when his father died and he started buying for the store, Eddie has arrived at the market around 5 a.m. each day. The market opens at midnight, so the parking lot is already filled by the time he arrives. Eddie makes his purchases and visits with old friends at two of the city's three produce markets, and is back in Santa Monica by 9 a.m. The market closes an hour later, at about 10 a.m.

A seemingly infinite number of new and exotic varieties of fruits and vegetables are constantly becoming available. Several years ago Japan began exporting the now popular Fuji apples and Fuji pears. And today tiny baby vegetables are as much a staple at Tanaka's as lettuce and tomatoes.

There were four years during which the Tanaka family did not shop at the produce market. From 1942 to 1946 the family was held at Manzanar, an internment camp in Central California where the U.S. government sent Japanese-Americans during World War II. The Tanakas were given two weeks to prepare to leave and not told how long they'd be held at the camp. So they sold their store to the first buyer for $800. When Eddie's parents were released they returned to Santa Monica to buy back their store. This time they paid a whopping $10,000. With a promise not to return to the West Coast, Eddie had been released from Manzanar two years earlier than his parents. He joined the U.S. Army, and in 1947 he returned home to his family and the store.

Today Eddie and his daughter Candy are partners. Eddie works behind the scenes, and Candy works out front taking care of customers. She remembers the market as always being part of her life. At 14 she was going to the wholesale produce market with her father.

Eddie has always loved his work. He still gets a thrill from finding a new fruit or vegetable. He's even more delighted when he finds it at a bargain price, or buys out a small farmer who has come in from out of town to sell his produce. Candy says that the market is a place where her father can search for treasure each day. She explains, "Like when he sees the first figs of the season. My Dad wants to go to the market every day, because his biggest joy is finding that one thing that hasn't been there before." —*Ellen Hoffs*

The Tanaka family has sold top-quality produce to Angelenos from their Brentwood shop for five decades. Photo by Shelley Gazin

Sunset Strip is a windy, hilly stretch where billboards tout new movies, records, celebrities, and clothes above comedy clubs, restaurants, and razzle-dazzle shops. Photo by Bob Rowan/ Progressive Image

San Francisco a distant runner-up at $20 billion, according to the Federal Deposit Insurance Company (FDIC) in Washington, D.C.

The County of Los Angeles is the leading savings and loan center in the nation. There was a time when that was cause for boasting. More recently, most financial analysts have been watching to see which of the nation's S&Ls will survive the crisis.

Economist Kyser notes, "There has been the savings and loan debacle, but several of the leading savings and loans in the Los Angeles area are very sound financially and will be survivors, either as savings and loans or as banks. Low stock prices will make some savings and loans bargains for those wishing to get into the Los Angeles market."

About 84,000 people work in the insurance industry in L.A. County alone. Small and medium-sized businesses are common, and offer the insurance industry sales opportunities because small companies do not always provide employee benefits. Steve Mellinger, general agent for Northwestern Mutual Life, explains further why selling insurance is easier in Los Angeles than in other cities in the nation.

"In other major metropolitan areas only a few people control the business. Los Angeles is spread over many communities, so we don't have the old boy network. Young organizations are developing all the time, and they force the business community to stay open," he maintains. "The opportunity to leverage or network is easier in Los Angeles."

The same holds true for the 62,700 employees who work in the county's real estate industry. The rising price of Los Angeles real estate has created a challenging and exciting market. Alexander Auerbach, public relations representative for the Los Angeles Board of Realtors, explains, "Los Angeles has gone through a number of cycles in demand, but the trend over time has always been for housing prices to increase. Homes that were considered extravagant 30 years ago at $15,000 are now considered extravagant at $300,000 to $500,000," he says.

"Since 1980 commercial real estate has

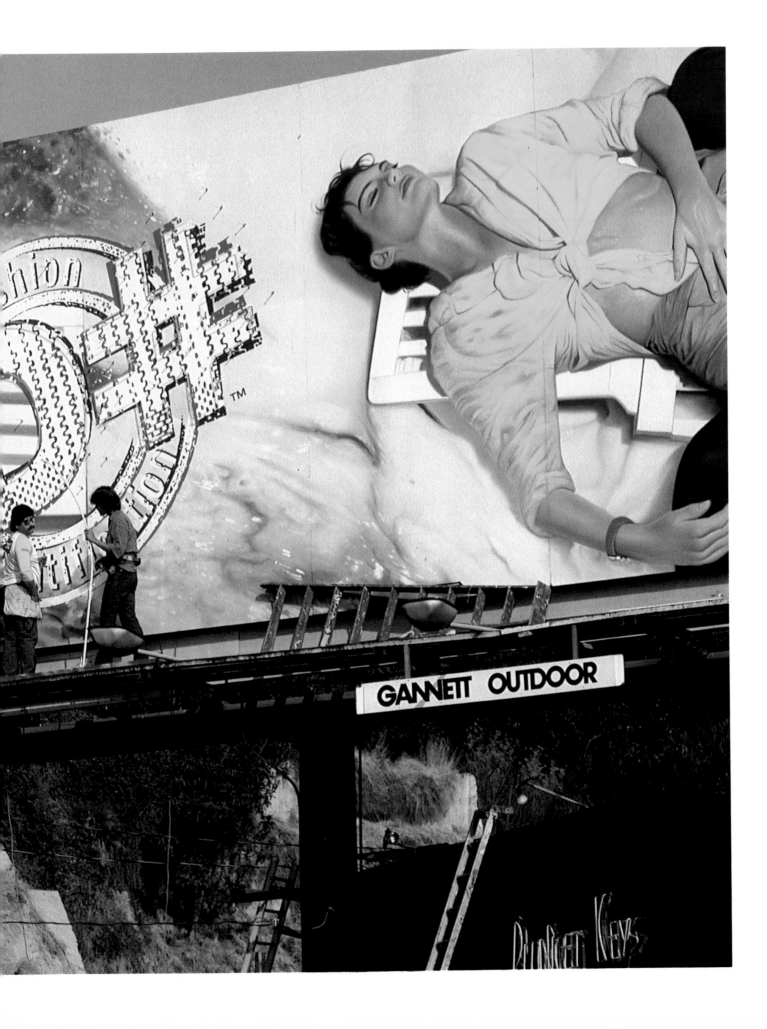

Drilling for oil in Torrance is big business. Photo by Joseph Sohm/Chromosohm

grown by a yearly 6 percent compounded," points out Dennis Macheski, director of research for the real estate group at Price Waterhouse. "That's double the national average. Even during the economic downturn in 1990, tenants occupied 4.3 million square feet of new office space," Macheski says. "By 1993 fewer commercial buildings will be available, and vacancy rates will drop."

Anyone flying into Los Angeles International Airport (LAX) on a clear night sees the lights of the city's lofty new office buildings and the transportation system that drives the region. In addition to the famous freeways and LAX are the ports of Los Angeles and Long Beach, and three railroads: the Southern Pacific, Union Pacific, and Santa Fe. With about 222,000 employees, the seventh ranking industry is transportation and public utilities. Close to half work in transportation and more than 46,000 in communications services, mainly telephone, with 25,000 others working in utilities and sanitary services.

Los Angeles' energy, water, and communications infrastructure is excellent and provides the means for growth. Natural gas is supplied to 531 cities directly by the Southern California Gas Company. The Los Angeles Department of Water & Power provides the city of Los Angeles with electricity, while Southern California Edison is the main supplier for other parts of the county. Among its many services to the community, Edison provides the utility's largest industrial and commercial customers with a contact representative to coordinate services. Local telephone service is provided by Pacific Bell Telephone and General Telephone Company of California. The Metropolitan Water District of Southern California is chiefly responsible for bringing water to the county. Employment in the utilities is stable.

However, transportation employment is

sure to increase. The people of Los Angeles County used their vote to guarantee better transportation facilities in the future. Angelenos first cast their vote for transportation in 1980 with Proposition A, a half-cent sales tax that generates more than $400 million a year for transportation. Thirty-five percent of the funds devoted to construction has paid for the newly built Long Beach-Los Angeles section of the Blue Line train system. In 1990 Angelenos voted to tax themselves another half cent to bring the transportation bounty to $800 million a year.

"We are way ahead of everybody else in terms of the people taxing themselves for transportation purposes. The federal govern-

ment has indicated that they are impressed with our program because the people of Los Angeles are committed to improving transportation service," says Claudette Moody, administrator of state affairs for the Los Angeles Transportation Commission. She adds, "We're committed to greater mobility and cleaning the air for the county."

On the state level, Californians sent a clear message to California lawmakers that they want to continue the state's leadership in transportation. The 1990 passage of propositions 108, 111, and 116 will pump $20.5 billion into highways, freeways, and mass transit projects throughout the state. The propositions will support the state's

"The Stack," perhaps the most famous highway interchange in the United States, provides passage for commuter and commercial vehicles alike. Photo by Joseph Sohm/ Chromosohm

largest public works projects since the freeways were built in the 1950s. The money will support 270,000 direct jobs and 480,000 indirect jobs in California through the year 2000. The propositions will pay for backlogged road building plans and rejuvenate repair projects that may have been abandoned due to lack of funding.

"Not only will people and goods gain improved mobility. A large number of jobs will also be created," economist Jack Kyser predicts.

Air transportation continues to grow. Four commercial airports and noncommercial general aviation airports serve Los Angeles County. LAX is the world's third busiest airport. Even the county's local airports set records. With 528,000 takeoffs and landings a year, Van Nuys Airport is the busiest noncommercial airport in the nation.

The county's commercial giant, LAX, transports 45 million passengers a year. Eighty percent of those passengers either start or end their flights in Los Angeles. International passengers totaled almost 10 million in 1990. After New York, LAX ranks second in quantity of air cargo, with almost 1.3 million tons a year. The financial impact of LAX is staggering. At $28.6 billion, LAX may have a greater financial impact on the community than any airport in the world, according to an airport spokesperson. The airport is likely to expand in the future, Kyser predicts.

Such an expansion would boost jobs for the 151,000 who work in construction, says Ben Bartolotto, research director of the Construction Industry Research Board. Bartolotto forecasts a construction slowdown in the early 1990s; however, he sees a possible boom for the rest of the decade. Contributing to the potential increase will be older households with money to spend on construction and apartment building construction, especially for high-income residents.

Sanford Goodkin, executive director of KPMG Peat Marwick/Goodkin Consulting, foresees increased construction triggered by a housing shortage in the 1990s. By 1992, he says, the housing inventory will have deteri-

Stockholders of a more tangible kind, the State Meat Packing Company provides the raw materials for a backyard California barbeque. Photo by Shelley Gazin

Left: Real estate developer Jerry Snyder has been building homes and offices in Southern California for 41 years. Snyder's latest project is "The Water Garden," a $450-million, 1.3-million-square-foot office complex under construction in Santa Monica. Photo by Shelley Gazin

Below: Tim and Barbara Leach have spent seven years remodelling their La Cañada Flintridge home. Here, with sons Austin and Andrew, they install drywall. Photo by Shelley Gazin

orated and created a shortage for first-time buyers. That will mean job opportunities in construction.

Los Angeles' economy is the most vibrant in the nation. The region is the foremost manufacturing center and the nation's third largest wholesaling center. It rings up more retail sales than the New York City metropolitan area. Even if one industry declines, the region's fabled versatility moves the economy forward because no single industry dominates. With the thrust of an increasing population, Los Angeles may emerge as the primary economic powerhouse in the nation by the twenty-first century.

THE INNOVATORS

Creating New Horizons

Since its founding Los Angeles has been a city based on an entrepreneurial dream. The first 44 settlers who arrived here in 1781 endured an arduous seven-month journey across the Mexican desert and the Gulf of California, as well as exposure to smallpox, just for the opportunity to till a piece of their own land in this alien spot.

During the nineteenth century, wildcat oilmen, railroad tycoons, and land speculators amassed fortunes by seizing opportunities others were too timid, too dull, or (in some cases) too scrupulous to grasp. In the process, people like oilman Edward Doheny, transportation baron Phineas Banning, and publisher Harrison Gray Otis set an entrepreneurial stamp on Los Angeles that endures to this day.

Innovation has been another major thread running through the tapestry of the city. Cut off from large population centers in the East, early Angelenos were obliged to be more resourceful, to invent what they did not have. From orange-crate labels to hula hoops and seismographs, this inventiveness has put a unique "spin" on the products, trends, and styles emerging from the L.A. region.

"CALIFORNIA IS LOADED WITH PEOPLE GOING PLACES AND MAKING

SPEED TO GET THERE . . ."

—RAYMOND CHANDLER, THE PENCIL, 1959

Dr. Robert Gale, associate professor of medicine and head of the bone marrow transplant unit at UCLA Medical Center, gained international attention in 1986 when he administered round-the-clock aid to Chernobyl radiation victims in the Soviet Union. Photo by Shelley Gazin

B y   A .   D o n a l d   A n d e r s o n

Today Los Angeles is still truly a city of entrepreneurs and innovators. The economy is dynamic and diverse, with more people self-employed here than in any other city in America. One out of eight small businesses in the United States is located in this region. Ninety-five percent of the firms doing business in Los Angeles employ fewer than 50 persons. The reservoir of venture capital (both human and financial) to fuel this engine of creativity seems bottomless.

During the early part of the century, most of the city's creative energies were directed toward issues of survival—finding enough

A UCLA physicist pursues the mysteries of the mechanical universe in his laboratory. Photo by Shelley Gazin

water, developing adequate port and rail facilities, and building streets, sewers, and water mains for the sprawling megalopolis that was taking shape.

Real estate speculation, which had been a mainstay of the Los Angeles economy since the 1880s, became more frenzied in the first decade of the twentieth century. The hectic trading in land and buildings created huge demands for investment capital, which in turn led to the formation of new banks and investment houses.

During World War I Los Angeles began growing into a major Western commercial center, a funnel for the burgeoning agricul-

tural production beginning to pour from the rich valleys to the north. Drawn by clement weather and open spaces, many pioneers of aviation began to set up shop in the area, the start of what would become the multibillion-dollar Southern California aerospace industry.

Two of the city's major centers of learning and research—the University of Southern California and the California Institute of Technology (initially called Throop University)—were already up and running by the onset of World War I, and in 1927 they were joined by a third, the University of California at Los Angeles, which moved from its original campus on North Vermont Avenue to a vast open space in Westwood in 1929.

Caltech vaulted into world prominence as a scientific research center in 1921, when Dr. Robert A. Millikan, the leading authority on the nature of electricity, agreed to become its administrative head. Two years later he won the Nobel Prize, and over the next 25 years he attracted many of the world's most eminent scientists to the faculty, opening up breathtaking new avenues of scientific study.

Los Angeles industry entered the age of high technology during World War II, when it became a major center for military aircraft production. Companies like Lockheed and Douglas Aircraft provided the nation with much of its air might from 1940 to 1945, with planes like the Lockheed P-38 *Lightning* fighter, the *Hudson* bomber, and the C-47 military version of Douglas' reliable DC-3 transport.

As the world entered the Cold War era, the nation again looked to Los Angeles for technological expertise, and the city swiftly responded. Lockheed's famed research director, the late Kelly Johnson, set up the world-renowned "skunk works" at the company's corporate headquarters in Burbank, where a series of aviation firsts—including the high-altitude U-2 and SR-71 reconnaissance jets and the F-117 Stealth Fighter—were developed.

Other high-tech (and often hush-hush) advances, such as cutting-edge electronic gear for navigation, communications, and

aerial surveillance, were spawned at Los Angeles-based companies like Northrop, Hughes, TRW, Rocketdyne, Litton, and Rockwell International. The first military rocket guidance and propulsion systems were also developed locally.

In a very real sense, the Space Age had its beginnings here as well. Much of the theoretical work leading up to the massive rockets that later transported men to the moon was carried out at Caltech in the 1930s by Theodore von Karman. Von Karman tested his experimental engines at a remote spot in the Arroyo Seco north of Pasadena, near the present site of Caltech's Jet Propulsion Laboratory division.

In 1958, only 66 days after getting the go-ahead to design and build it, JPL launched *Explorer I,* the nation's first successful satellite. Since then, JPL has led the world in the exploration of the planets, directing a number of NASA programs, including the deep-space probes, *Voyager, Mariner,* and *Galileo,* which have sent back astonishingly clear photos of planets barely discernable by ordinary telescopes.

Caltech's leadership in exploring the cosmos via telescope is unchallenged. Starting with its 100-inch Mt. Wilson Observatory telescope in the 1930s, the institute has been the operator of the world's largest optic instruments. In 1948 Caltech unveiled the 200-inch Mt. Palomar telescope, and in 1991 it began joint operations (with the University of California) of the 400-inch Keck Observatory Telescope on 13,500-foot Mauna Kea on Hawaii's Big Island.

At UCLA, meanwhile, researchers are digging into a wide variety of scientific, medical, and philosophical issues that have puzzled mankind for centuries.

• Dr. Jared Diamond of the Medical School is engaged in pioneering work on the biological nature of human creativity.

• Richard Weinstein of the Graduate School of Architecture and Urban Planning is leading research into ways to make our cities function more smoothly and to improve the lives of the people who live in them.

• Management Professor Arthur Geoffrion's work on the corporate planning process may help restore American industry to its once-dominant role in the world marketplace.

• Dr. Philippa Foot, Griffin Professor of Philosophy, examines contemporary moral issues in the light of traditional philosophical concepts.

Computer guru Peter Norton has turned his canny sights toward art collecting and philanthropy. Norton enjoys funding adventurous and offbeat art projects that would otherwise have trouble finding sponsorship. Photo by Shelley Gazin

Fourteen-year-old whiz kid Ray Bateman addressed the American Federation for Clinical Research about the effects of 5-Fluorodeoxyuridine, an experimental cancer drug. Photo by Shelley Gazin

At the University of Southern California, oldest of the city's higher education institutions, research is afoot on a myriad of questions whose answers may help us deal with population growth, aging, and how we educate our youth.

• Dr. Maurice D. Van Arsdol, Jr., head of USC's Population Research Laboratory, using a massive demographic and economic data base, is able to analyze where population growth is likeliest to occur, which age groups will dominate, and where and how often people are likely to move domiciles.

• Psychobiologist Richard F. Thompson is codiscoverer of important new data about the physical nature of memory and learning, which could help in future treatment of mental disorders.

• Dr. George Olah, scientific director of the Loker Hydrocarbons Research Institute, has developed a family of "superacids," millions of times stronger than normal acids, that may prolong the planet's stores of energy and make them safer for the environment.

Whether attached to major research centers like Caltech, working for major corporations, or operating alone in suburban garages, the innovators and visionaries of Los Angeles continue to leave their mark on the character of this most enterprising city. Who are these creative few, and where is their inspiration leading them—and us?

In 1986 the atomic reactor at Chernobyl in the Soviet Ukraine blew up, scattering nuclear waste across a wide area of Europe. Of the 299 persons in the immediate vicinity, two died in the blast, and another 29 died over the following months from burns and radiation.

More than 135,000 people living within a 20-mile radius of the explosion and another 450,000 downwind from the blast were evacuated to other parts of the Soviet Union. Another 20 towns in Byelorussia, where fallout was unexpectedly heavy, have been evacuated. Much of the land surrounding the reactor will remain uninhabitable for the foreseeable future.

Within hours of the Chernobyl explosion, Dr. Robert P. Gale, associate professor of hemotology-oncology at UCLA, was on a plane heading for Moscow. He had been invited by the Soviet government to advise the medical team treating the casualties and to oversee a massive program to monitor the long-term consequences of the accident on persons exposed to heavy doses of radiation.

Already a leading authority on the effects of radiation on living tissue, Dr. Gale was thrust into the international spotlight by Chernobyl, and he has hardly been out of it since. In the days following the explosion, he focused much of his effort on 35 persons who received the heaviest doses of radiation, performing several bone marrow and fetal liver transplants using massive doses of antibiotics to fight off infections. Most of these patients survived.

Today Dr. Gale remains heavily involved in the critical follow-up to Chernobyl—closely following the medical progress of the 270 survivors most seriously exposed at the plant as well as the status of the hundreds of thousands of Soviet citizens who were relocated from the region. He travels to Moscow on the average of six times a year and is in touch by phone and fax machine on a weekly basis.

Meanwhile, Dr. Gale's work as a researcher and physician at UCLA continues. At the moment his cancer research team is trying to unlock the genetic secrets of a key leukemia virus that he hopes will lead to more effective ways to treat leukemia and related types of cancer. The team has isolated the virus—the first time this has been achieved—and may be close to a major breakthrough in controlling it.

In addition, Dr. Gale chairs an organization that is building a global data base on bone marrow transplant patients. The International Bone Marrow Transplant Registry keeps vital information on potential marrow donors around the world, easing the task of matching recipients with donors and speeding delivery of the vital marrow to where it's needed.

This program serves another purpose. "No single center has done enough marrow transplants to draw solid clinical conclusions about success rates, complications, and so on—information we need to move the technique forward," says Dr. Gale. "The registry enables us to pool information from centers all over the world, shortening the learning curve tremendously."

Somehow, in the midst of these career pressures, Dr. Gale has found time to write a novel, *Final Warning,* which describes a Chernobyl-type nuclear accident. A television motion picture based on the novel and starring Jon Voigt as a character based loosely on Gale was filmed in the Soviet Union in 1990 and was shown in the U.S. and USSR in early 1991. Dr. Gale also played a cameo role in the 1990 release, *Fat Man and Little Boy,* starring Paul Newman.

Despite his close association with history's worst nuclear accident, Gale believes atomic energy should play a growing role in the world's future energy scheme. "I don't regard technologies as inherently good or evil," he explains. "It seems to me the rest of the world will need this form of power, even if the United States doesn't. If we're truly worried about global warming, and we should be, how can we reject nuclear energy out of hand?"

As one intimately familiar with the effects of radiation on the human body, Dr. Gale thinks we need to put the threat of radiation into context. "We are radiated all the time from a number of sources," he points out, "and only a miniscule portion of it is man-made. People living in Denver receive four

On the other hand, Gale believes nations must do more to reduce the threat of nuclear weapons, and has written several articles urging a speedup in nuclear disarmament. "Atomic weapons, as opposed to atomic energy, are the real threat to mankind, it seems to me."

As for curing cancer, Robert Gale believes science may be on the threshold of a major breakthrough. "I've always felt that in science and medicine there's a time for things—a point when it's possible to achieve success," he says.

"The Manhattan Project could not have succeeded five years earlier because they didn't have the knowledge they needed to create a chain reaction. I think we now know enough about the nature of cancer to make the breakthrough we need."

Blockbuster miniseries producer David Wolper, a devoted collector of Picasso artwork, donated his collection to LACMA. Photo by Shelley Gazin

While researchers like Gale are focusing on health issues of global concern, others of L.A.'s own are working to resolve the multiple challenges facing the Los Angeles region. For most of this century, the power structure of Los Angeles was dominated by white businessmen,

times the natural radiation as someone living at sea level, yet most Denverites would not dream of moving, even to reduce their dosage by 75 percent. Yet many people would stop all nuclear energy just to eliminate a small fraction of one percent of the radiation we now receive."

chiefly from the downtown area. In the 1960s, with the city's outward expansion well under way, this coalition began to fray, and by the beginning of the 1980s, it had completely unraveled.

Today the city's power structure is spread across a wide geographic spectrum, from the Palos Verdes Peninsula to the northern reaches of the San Fernando Valley. And the movers and shakers are no longer exclusively (or even predominantly) male, white, or rich.

Instead, the people who make things happen in Los Angeles in the 1990s reflect a rainbow of ethnic backgrounds, are often women, and increasingly come from nonaffluent parts of the community—the barrio of East Los Angeles, the black neighborhoods of South-Central, or the Asian enclaves of Koreatown and Little Tokyo.

Harnessing the energies of these disparate communities to work toward common goals has mostly been an exercise in futility for the urban planners of Los Angeles. Too often, it seems, each geographic, ethnic, or special interest has come first, to the detriment of the city as a whole.

In the last few years, however, a number of visionary individuals have begun building the kinds of coalitions that may one day crack the knotty problems confronting Los Angeles. Through vehicles like United Way, the Community Redevelopment Agency, the Los Angeles Area Chamber of Commerce, and other ad hoc organizations, a network of public-spirited citizens is beginning to make things happen.

Symbolic of this evolving order is Jane Pisano, an energetic urban analyst who has become one of the community's most visible and thoughtful proponents for positive change. As the president of Los Angeles 2000 Partnership, Pisano heads up an ambitious effort to bring order and common sense to the often chaotic process of planning urban growth.

"Part of my job is to build and work with networks of people who can effect change," she says. "Our challenge and our goal is to create a multicultural society that works, to harness the enormous energies within this community, and use them to improve the quality of life for everyone."

Pisano, a mother of three, was named by Mayor Tom Bradley in 1986 to convene a two-year colloquium of leaders from government, business, labor, education, and the

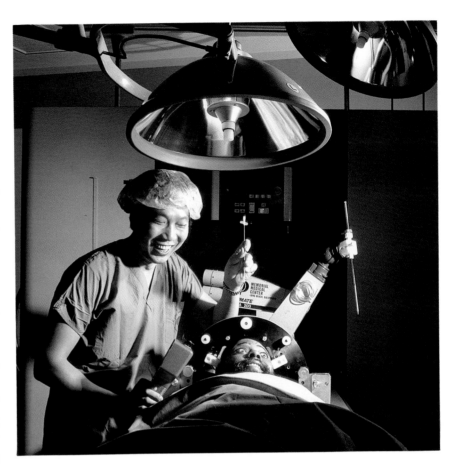

nonprofit sector to produce a vision of what Los Angeles should be in the year 2000. Hundreds of the city's leading lights were eventually involved in the project, including Roman Catholic cardinal Roger Mahony, Bank of America executive vice president James Miscoll, and Warren Christopher, chairman of the prestigious law firm of O'Melveny and Myers.

Pisano proved eminently capable of challenging the energies (and egos) of this high-powered committee through its two years of work, which produced a widely acclaimed report, *L.A. 2000: A City for the Future*, in the fall of 1988. The report depicts the city, as it is and as it could be, in six areas: the environment, education, ethnic diversity, urban growth, the arts, and government and finance.

Since the report emerged, Pisano has turned to Phase II of Project L.A., an implementation effort called the 2000 Partnership, in which a "shadow" committee of her earlier group will develop a comprehensive action plan to achieve the vision of L.A. 2000.

That vision is perhaps best summed up in

Yik San Kwoh, inventor of the computer-controlled "surgeon," with his remarkable invention. The robotic arm is capable of conducting brain surgery within an accuracy of 1/2,000 of an inch. Photo by Shelley Gazin

the report itself, which describes the Los Angeles of tomorrow as "a kind of international city of cities that has never existed before," or as one chapter of the report describes it, "A Crossroads City," rich with opportunity and diversity.

"We want this project to be the catalyst that brings about concrete changes in our community," says Pisano. "I think we can achieve it, because in addition to individual commitment from our committee members, I sense a widespread belief that time is running out."

Even so, can Los Angeles overcome its propensity for the laissez-faire approach to the future? "If people perceive the process of change as fair," says Pisano, "then I think they're willing to work within it, and not subvert it for their own ends. People seem willing now to compromise on the small things in order to achieve the big ones."

And while people like Jane Pisano are rethinking L.A.'s big picture, others are redesigning specific aspects of the L.A. scene, such as its icon, the automobile. But even though he's probably one of the world's foremost experts on the subjects, Ron Hill either can't say, or won't say, what the cars of the future will look like.

For the last several years, Hill's Industrial Design department, which he chairs at prestigious Art Center College in Pasadena, has been turning out a major share of the world's top automotive designers. Hill himself was a leading factor in formulating the "look" of U.S. autos when he headed the design programs at the Chevrolet, Pontiac, and Buick divisions of General Motors during the 1970s and 1980s.

So he would seem eminently qualified to predict what cars will look like, say, five years from now.

But he demurs. "I'm afraid it's impossible to anticipate what the 1997 models will look like," Hill says. "In fact, that's one of the things this department is trying to figure out right now. We should have the answer in about five years."

Hill is fairly confident that the "aerodynamic look" of the current auto crop will continue throughout the 1990s, partly because of fuel economy requirements imposed by the federal government. But the cars may have some "wrinkles" that don't show from the outside.

Whatever they look like, however, automobiles will continue to be a major passion of the American consumer well into the twenty-first century. Through wars, depressions, and energy crises, they remain (after housing) the number one consumer expenditure in America, with more than 8.5 million new passenger vehicles sold in 1990 at a cost of around $110 billion.

What's behind the enduring love affair between Americans and their automobiles?

Sociologists could probably cite a dozen reasons—from a desire for freedom to a hunger for power—but certainly one of the factors can be traced to Ron Hill and his disciples at Art Center. Americans love glitz.

And that's why graduates of the Art Center like Jack Telnack, head of design for Ford Motor Company of North America, or Mark Jordan, who designed the fabulously successful Mazda Miata, can command the kinds of six- and seven-figure salaries and commissions they now enjoy.

Along with the Center of Creative Studies in Detroit and the Royal College of Art in London, Art Center College has been recognized for nearly four decades as one of the world's leading sources of automotive design talent. And Ron Hill comes as close as anyone to being the profession's Mr. Chips.

In addition to transportation design, Hill's portfolio at Art Center includes product design and environmental design studies—the folks who will be giving shape to the VCRs, toasters, pencil sharpeners, ergonomic chairs, and computer workstations of tomorrow.

But automotive design is the glamour field, the one that is consistently oversubscribed and most sought after. "We have a little over 100 students enrolled in transportation design at any one time," explains Hill, "out of perhaps 300 or more who originally apply."

"Out of the 30 or so who graduate each

year, perhaps 10 will end up actually designing cars. The rest will find their ways into related design fields, or into fields completely separate from transportation. This is the single most competitive area of design."

The upside of these figures is the rewards that the top auto designers of the world can achieve. Those who go to work for one of the major manufacturers (Art Center has alumni in every major auto company in the world outside the former communist bloc) do well enough, but those with the talent and drive to go independent can do even better.

Three times each year the Art Center's transportation design group holds an exhibit for auto company recruiters, who come from as far as Tokyo and Stuttgart in search of new talent and new ideas—a novel dashboard treatment, a high-tech wheel cover, a daring silhouette. They generally find them.

"When we screen applicants for our department," says Hill, "we look for kids who *love* automobiles. Not just like them, but *love* them. If they say, 'I think cars today are great, I just want to refine them,' we tell them they've come to the wrong place. We're looking for people who can't stand today's products and want to do them better. Then we provide the tools for them to achieve that."

On the wall behind Hill's desk are perhaps a hundred drawings and photographs of student designs, looking every bit as futuristic as one might expect at this mecca of automotive revolution. One drawing shows what Hill calls a "deconstructed" car with two profiles—a sleek, aerodynamic look for highway cruising, and an "exploded" silhouette that turns the car into a kind of Sydney Opera House on wheels. The "exploded" version, says Hill, offers driver and passengers greater interior freedom and comfort.

Part of the job of Hill and his teaching staff is to nurture this kind of innovative thinking while helping their students deal with the realities of the marketplace.

"Automotive designers are constrained by several factors," Hill says, "including engineering needs, government regulations—safety requirements, for example—and of course public tastes. You can't get too far ahead."

On the other hand, he adds, automakers whose designs are too conservative will lose out in the long run. "If consumers are entirely comfortable with your new design, you're probably in trouble. Because they'll drop you for the first appealing new idea that comes along."

By encouraging their students to remain innovative—what test pilots call "pushing the envelope"—Hill and his graduates probably stand in no immediate danger of being forced off the highway by other people's appealing new ideas.

Even less predictable than the car of the future is the precise date of Los Angeles' next big quake. On an average of every 20 years or so in this century, the Los Angeles area has experienced an earthquake of sufficient magnitude to cause widespread property damage and loss of life. The last serious jolt was in 1987, when a portion of the Elysian Park Fault slipped, severely shaking the community of Whittier and much of the rest of Southern California.

The region around Los Angeles is crisscrossed by several faults, or fracture

Mayor Tom Bradley meets with Jane Pisano, president of the 2000 Partnership, a privately funded, nonprofit organization which develops strategies and agendas for Los Angeles' future. Over 200 top civic, academic, and corporate leaders participate in goal-setting for the twenty-first century. Photo by Shelley Gazin

Dr. Kerry Sieh, professor
of geology at Caltech,
seeks out and studies the
real movers and shakers
of the Los Angeles area.
Photo by Shelley Gazin

points in the earth, but the granddaddy of them all is the San Andreas, which runs nearly the length of the state, from the Gulf of California to San Francisco Bay and along the Northern California coast.

Unlike other local faults, where small pieces of the earth's crust press against one another, the San Andreas is a break between two of the planet's giant continental plates. Instead of pressing toward each other, the two plates are slipping in opposite directions along the same line. Most people believe the San Andreas, which caused the great San Francisco earthquake of 1906, will also bring the next "Big One" to Southern California.

Dr. Kerry Sieh, professor of geology at Caltech, isn't so sure. As a student at Stanford 20 years ago, he wondered out loud what was known about the geology of the San Andreas Fault. When he heard the answer—"not much"—he decided to find out more. He has spent most of the last two

decades doing just that, and in the process has become arguably the world's foremost authority on earthquakes.

Employing tools both primitive (picks, shovels, backhoes) and sophisticated (computers and radio-carbon dating instruments), Dr. Sieh has in effect done a CAT Scan on the southern end of the San Andreas Fault to learn its history and its configuration, as well as its possible future.

"There are substantial benefits in learning more about earthquake faults, even if we can't closely predict when they'll slip," says Dr. Sieh. "Knowing the potential threat of the San Andreas Fault can help us plan and prepare." Partially as a result of his work on the San Andreas, the city of Los Angeles has beefed up its building codes, requiring older masonry buildings to be reinforced with "earthquake rods" that strengthen external walls. Around 15,000 such buildings have been identified.

What is the nature of the beast Dr. Sieh has been studying these last 20 years? One of the most important discoveries he has made is that the San Andreas is composed of several sections from 50 to 100 miles long, and that the segments seem to slip independently of one another.

The last major quake (Richter magnitude 7.5 or above) in the Mojave segment of the fault, northeast of the Los Angeles Basin, probably occurred around 1857 and may have been the final event in a "cluster" of quakes over a period of 100 years or more. These clusters, explains Sieh, seem to be separated by quiet periods of around 300 years.

"If this is so, and research points that way, then this section may be in the midst of an interregnum that could last another 150 to 200 years," he says. "On the other hand, we believe the Palm Springs segment has a fairly high probability of slipping in the next century. We're continuing to dig along the fault to see if we can confirm this pattern."

Dr. Sieh spends about half his time from September to June digging and poking at the San Andreas, alternating with work behind the computer or at his desk at Caltech. In the summer he takes a busman's holiday, traveling to the Mammoth Lakes area to study volcanic activity there.

"I plan to spend another couple of years on the San Andreas," he says, "and then I think I'll move on to other things. I'd like to take a look at some interesting formations in Sumatra and China, and maybe the Aegean."

The world, Sieh observes, is only superficially understood from a geological standpoint, and he'd like to help deepen that understanding. "There are still a lot of surprises out there," he says. No doubt he will discover some of them himself.

Another Los Angeles researcher is uncovering mysteries of another sort—the secrets of the human brain, especially as it affects the aging process. In a curious reversal of past trends, America today is an aging society. While demographers expect the U.S. population to grow by around 20 percent by the year 2014, the number of people over age 65 will more than double—a result of the graying of the Baby Boom generation. The question is, will this be good or bad?

The answer depends largely on the physical health of the new aging population. If its members are beset with illness and fragility, then the trends are ominous indeed. The costs of maintaining such a population could be huge, and this burden would fall squarely on the young.

On the other hand, if the elderly population is healthy and robust, it could make a significant contribution to the well-being of the society at large. Its members would represent a vast repository of knowledge, experience, and wisdom from which the young could draw and benefit. Active seniors would also become a vibrant consumer market. Someone for whom these antipodal visions have special significance is biologist Caleb Finch, a professor at USC's Andrus Gerontology Center, whose work over the last 20 years has been dedicated to making the last fourth of human life as fruitful and satisfying as the first three. He believes the key to bringing this about lies in our genes.

"I think we're on the threshold of knowing whether life expectancy can increase significantly, or whether the species has 'hit the wall' from a longevity standpoint," he says. "I'm betting we can improve not only the length of human life over the next several years, but its quality as well."

To better understand the mysteries surrounding these issues, Dr. Finch and his team have been probing the innermost functions of the brain, producing studies rife with terms like "imipramine binding," "calmodulin compartments," and "neuroendocrine dysfunctions."

What they are finding, in oversimple language, is that subcellular changes in our brains—changes so subtle they elude the most sophisticated medical tests—may end up totally altering our personalities and possibly devastating our lives. Alzheimer's disease is a primary example.

Dr. Finch has focused much of his recent energies on the nature of Alzheimer's, the seemingly progressive deterioration of brain function, primarily in the elderly. Until the last few years, the cause was a complete mystery, but thanks to findings by Dr. Finch and others, the mystery is coming unraveled.

Dr. Finch holds out a fuzzy photograph of what could be a moray eel or an understuffed sausage, twisted and bent in a weird configuration. In fact, it's a neuron in a human brain cell, with a thin bind of white along one side.

"We think that's the culprit in Alzheimer's," Finch says. "We still don't know the nature of it."

Finch and his research colleagues around the world may finally be closing in on the problem, which appears to be at least partly genetic in origin. This has important implications for the future health of the estimated 10 percent of the population who will eventually contract the disease, as well as for their families.

In addition to his role at the Andrus Gerontology Center at USC, Dr. Finch heads a cooperative program among four Southern California universities studying Alzheimer's. The Alzheimer Center Research Program, involving USC, UCLA, UC Irvine, and Caltech, pools clinical and research information on the disease, exchanges ideas, and carries on joint research.

"No single laboratory can master all the technologies that will be required to get to the bottom of this mystery," says Dr. Finch. "By collaborating, we cover many more bases. In this case, the effect is greater than the sum of the parts."

How does a young scientist come to take up this area of study? In a recent article for *The Scientist,* Dr. Finch recalled: "As a child I was intrigued by how differently people age, so that some retained mental clarity and memory into advanced old age, while others began to fail 20 years earlier. Was this mostly hereditary, or also the result of nurtured expectations for high mental performance throughout life?"

He's been working out the answers ever since. Fortunately, Finch seems to have inherited genes that will enable him to carry his work forward for a long, long time. "My forebears tended to be long-lived," he says. "I remember how thrilled I was hearing their accounts of the days before 1900. Once I calculated that the Roman Empire had ended only 80 generations before mine."

When he is not fiddling in his lab or with one of his computers, Caleb Finch is apt to be fiddling with a fiddle. His passion away from biology is early American music ("Dixie," "John Henry," and "Cotton-Eyed Joe"), which he studies and plays with a trio called the Iron Mountain String Band. The group has made several albums, the most recent of which is *Songs of Old Time America,* for Peach Bottom Records.

Long-lived relatives and early music notwithstanding, Dr. Finch spends most of his time looking forward rather than back. He envisages a day when people will live longer, more productive lives far beyond the age we now regard as "elderly."

"Creatures tend to die for reasons having nothing to do with their general health," Finch explains. "Flies die when their wings wear out. Lions die because they wear out their teeth. But the rest of them is built to last a lot longer.

"It seems to me we can identify those things that shorten life and eliminate or restrict them—from our environment, our diets, our life-styles. There's no magic bullet, and life is ultimately finite, but it's plausible to think we can extend the span of healthy, productive existence. That's what this is all about."

The innovative work of Caleb Finch and countless others makes Los Angeles a global center for discovery: innovation and a willingness to take risk are distinctive, if not unique, hallmarks of the L.A. experience. These qualities have been pivotal in creating the California life-style, products, and contributions that are so widely imitated and

sought after around the world.

There is no evading the indictment that Los Angeles has given the world more than its share of hula hoops, day-glow paint, hot rods, and diners shaped like hamburgers. But creativity doesn't fit into neat boxes, and kitsch is often the by-product of a probing mind.

And so are the guidance systems and rocket engines that took human beings to the moon, the genetic engineering break-

throughs that are revolutionizing medicine, and the microcircuits that have brought such astonishing computer power into our schools, homes, and offices.

The city's creative and entrepreneurial spark produces film and fine art, amusement parks and museums, small businesses and giant corporations, volunteer organizations and potential cures for cancer. There is no question that L.A.'s diverse population of thinkers and doers will continue to dazzle the world community by making its visions of the future tangible.

Bob McKnight, Jr., owner/creator of L.A. sportswear manufacturer Quiksilver, is a former surfer who built his company from a small casual-wear concern to the eighth largest income-producing company in California. Photo by Shelley Gazin

MAKING THE DREAM WORK

These final chapters spotlight many of the organizations whose innovation and drive have put Los Angeles on the forefront of the national and international business scene.

MAKING CONNECTIONS

Los Angeles Networks

Maintaining a dynamic and consistent flow of power, people, and data both inside and outside Los Angeles is the responsibility of energy, transportation, and communication suppliers.

L.A.'s freeways may be congested but as this multitude of bicycles in Venice shows, Southern Californians enjoy using healthy, alternate forms of transportation. Photo by Mark E. Gibson

MISSION ENERGY COMPANY

As the twenty-first century approaches, many industries are rapidly changing to compete in a global economy. Among these is the electric utility industry, evolving from a regulated system to being more market-driven and competitive. At the same time, the industry faces a growing concern for the environment and hastened demand for new electric resources. These challenges provide significant opportunities for innovative, state-of-the-art energy solutions in meeting the world's growing energy needs.

Mission Energy, one of the new private electric power companies involved in the development, ownership, and operation of electric power plants domestically and abroad, is one of the largest independent power producers in the world. The company offers electric utilities and other industries, new environmentally sound options for supplying the energy needed for economic growth and expansion.

Mission Energy is a wholly owned subsidiary of SCEcorp, a Southern California-based *Fortune* 100 company which also owns Southern California Edison, the second-largest electric utility in the United States.

At year-end 1990, Mission Energy's portfolio of 21 commercial electric generating facilities provided 2,349 megawatts (MW) of electric power from a variety of different fuel sources, including gas, oil, coal, biomass, and geothermal. Mission projects are capable of delivering nearly 18 billion kilowatt-hours of electricity annually to industrial, commercial, and residential customers through local electric utilities. In addition, many of these generating facilities supply thermal steam energy to neighboring industry for a variety of commercial and industrial production processes.

If Mission Energy were an electric utility, it would rank among the top 50 regulated, investor-owned electric utilities in the country, based on sales. By 1995 Mission Energy is expected to have 16 additional generating facilities representing 1,700 megawatts of electric power in operation. This will boost annual electricity available to consumers to more than 30 billion kilowatt-hours, or enough to supply more than 2 million households. This anticipated growth would place Mission Energy among the top 30 regulated, investor-owned electric utilities.

Looking back, major changes in domestic electric power markets began in 1978, following the second Arab oil embargo. Congress enacted legislation aimed at conserving the nation's energy resources and enouraging alternate and renewable power production. It also provided incentives to independent power suppliers to compete with investor-owned electric utilities. From the beginning, Mission Energy has been one of the pioneers of the independent power industry using a high efficiency, century-old technology known as "cogeneration."

Cogeneration produces two forms of energy—electricity and steam—from a single fuel source such as gas or coal. Traditional utility generation produces only one: electricity. For certain applications, cogeneration is nearly twice as fuel-efficient as traditional utility generation. It also becomes an increasingly cost-effective alternative as the cost of fuel rises. Consequently, cogeneration has accounted for the majority of new electric generation capacity built in the United States during the later half of the 1980s. As the world's fuel supply tightens and competition increases, cogeneration is likely to emerge as one of the desirable alternatives for serving the energy appetite of various commercial and industrial economies throughout the world.

Several of Mission Energy's commercial generating facilities employ cogeneration to satisfy the needs of a broad range of industries that use large amounts of electricity and steam in their production processes, including the oil, chemical, food, and forest products industries. Other commercial users include mines, hotels, shopping centers, universities, and hospitals.

The Watson Cogeneration facility, one of the largest cogeneration projects ever constructed at a refinery, utilizes state-of-the-art pollution control equipment to reduce air emissions equivalent to the exhaust of 160,000 gasoline-powered vehicles, while providing a reliable source of electricity for more than 400,000 homes in Southern California. Photo courtesy of Gregory Igers' Photographic Art Studio

One of the largest cogeneration projects ever constructed at an oil refinery in the United States is the Watson Cogeneration Project at Atlantic Richfield Company's Los Angeles refinery, representing roughly 10 percent of California's entire refinery capability. Completed in 1988 through a partnership between subsidiaries of Mission Energy and ARCO, the 385-megawatt facility delivers thermal energy in the form of high quality, high pressure steam to facilitate the refinery's processing of crude oil. In addition to

meeting the steam requirements for refinery processing, the Watson Cogeneration Project delivers enough electricity for the local electric utility to serve the equivalent of more than 400,000 homes.

The Watson Cogeneration Project also employs state-of-the-art emission-control technologies to remove pollutants from the air equivalent to the emissions of more than 160,000 gasoline-powered vehicles.

While cogeneration provides significant benefits to utilities and other industrial customers, demand for new electric generation facilities far exceeds the capacity for economic cogeneration facilities. In the years ahead, utilities will need substantially more electric power to meet growing consumer demand.

Mission Energy works with electric utilities to supply both reliable and environmentally responsible electricity to their customers. Because Mission Energy can offer cost advantages and other benefits to regulated electric utilities, the opportunity to own and operate utility-grade power plants presents significant growth potential for the company.

Mission's privately owned electric generation facilities are designed and built to produce electricity in the same way as utility-built power plants. They offer consumers a reliable source of electricity at prices competitive with those charged by utilities. Additionally, plants developed, owned, and operated by Mission Energy offer other benefits to consumers. Unlike utility-built generating facilities, Mission Energy assumes the risk of development, ownership, and operation. Because Mission Energy can also achieve certain cost advantages over regulated utilities, these benefits can be shared with consumers.

Mission Energy is developing power projects for a number of electric utilities in different parts of the United States. With strengths in power con-

tracting, construction management, and operation of clean and efficient power plants, Mission Energy has expanded its focus to international markets as well. In 1990 the company expanded its business development activity into Great Britain, the Pacific Rim, and Europe. Mission's power plants now being developed will supply an additional 1,700 MW of electricity, with the flexibility to serve one or several electric utilities to meet growing demand.

While top-quality, low-cost power generation is important to Mission Energy's business prospects, the company is also well diversified. Through special purpose subsidiaries—Mission Energy Fuel Company and Mission Operation and Maintenance, Inc.—Mission Energy provides a full range of energy services to its clients. To provide a hedge against rising gas prices and guarantee fuel supplies for its projects, Mission Energy has interests in proven, producing natural gas and oil reserves. With the international marketplace for independent power growing, Mission Energy is positioned to participate.

A leading nonutility geothermal energy producer, Mission Energy harnesses the internal heat of the earth to generate clean, reliable electric power at nine geothermal power facilities in California and one in Nevada. Photo by Lonnie Duka

Through a variety of measures—safeguarding endangered species, choice of environmentally preferred fuels, and technically advanced pollution control technologies—Mission Energy delivers new energy resources to balance regional economic and environmental concerns. Photo by Lonnie Duka

SOUTHERN CALIFORNIA EDISON COMPANY

S outhern California Edison Company traces its roots back to the nineteenth century. The company is proud of the traditions of technological innovation and customer service that have kept it in the forefront among public utilities throughout the twentieth century.

In 1896 a group of four men organized the West Side Lighting Company in Los Angeles. A year later, through a merger, it became the Edison Electric Company of Los Angeles and began a program of expansion in which it acquired a number of smaller, local companies. Three of them, all founded in 1886, were located in Visalia, Santa Barbara, and Highgrove and are considered Edison's earliest ancestors.

During the first decade of the twentieth century, the firm grew rapidly, and by 1909 was serving more than 600,000 customers. In July of that year it was reincorporated as Southern California Edison Company, with capital of $30 million.

Over the years, as California's economy has become the most dynamic and prosperous in the nation, Southern California Edison has kept pace. Today its 17,000 employees serve more than 4 million customers in a 50,000-square-mile area covering much of Central and Southern California.

Yet the most exciting part of the Edison story does not lie in the past or even the present, but in the future. For here is a company whose major focus is on the twenty-first century as it faces such issues as energy conservation, alternative power sources, cost containment, and environ-

mental and social considerations—issues its founders could never have imagined.

True to the firm's history of technological innovation, Edison people are hard at work, devising creative solutions to the challenges that lie ahead. While focusing on all segments of its customer base, particular emphasis is being placed on meeting the needs of commercial and industrial customers.

One of the biggest challenges is air quality. Edison's territory includes the area covered by the South Coast Air Quality Management District (AQMD), which has the most stringent requirements in the United States. Most heavily impacted by these requirements are commerce and industry. In 1989 the AQMD approved a clean-air plan designed to bring the region encompassing Los Angeles, Orange, Riverside, and San Bernardino counties into compliance with federal standards

by the year 2007.

To help meet this goal, Edison has agreed to cut its nitrogen-oxide emissions 76 percent by the year 2000, by investing $680 million in added emission controls for its generating units in the Los Angeles Basin.

As part of its plan, the AQMD has mandated that, by 2010, 6.7 million motor vehicles in its district must be replaced by electric vehicles. As a result, more than two-thirds of Southern California's smog would be eliminated.

Edison has taken a giant step in meeting that challenge. For several years it has led pioneering efforts to develop electric-powered vehicles, and today its own fleet includes a number of electric vehicles called G-Vans. Produced by a group of firms comprised of General Motors Corporation, Magna International Inc., and Chloride EV Systems, the G-Vans have a range of 60 miles or more at a top speed of 55 miles per hour.

Edison emphasizes the use of electric vehicles in local commercial fleets. The utility has begun a program to lend its G-Van to 50 public and private fleet operators in Southern California to demonstrate their effectiveness and to encourage these entities to purchase them for their fleets. Easy to

Far Left: Southern California Edison corporate headquarters is located in Rosemead, California.

Left: Southern California Edison Company is always ready to meet the present and anticipated needs of its customers.

operate and economical to maintain, the G-Vans can be recharged during non-peak evening and night hours. Edison is convinced that as the technology improves, future generations of electric vehicles will serve much more of the driving public, well beyond the fleet market.

Electric transportation is by no means limited to electric automobiles, trucks, and vans. It includes electric trolleys and buses, electric light and heavy rail, electromagnetic-levitation trains, and even electric highways, where subsurface cables will supply the power to move vehicles. One electric roadway has already been built and is being tested in the Los Angeles area.

Edison, which historically played an important role in the development of electric rail transport by supplying power to the famous Red Car and Yellow Car systems, is convinced that electric transportation is the wave of the future.

Another major tool provided by Southern California Edison for commerce and industry is its

Customer Technology Application Center (CTAC), a 23,000-square-foot facility opened in 1990 in Irwindale. Built at a cost of $4 million, CTAC houses a Residential Technology Center, an Industrial Technology Center, a Commercial Technology Center, a Commercial Cooking Center, a Lighting Design Center, and a Learning Center. It was designed to introduce advanced electrotechnologies into the marketplace by demonstrating for manufacturers, restaurant operators, small-business owners, and home builders the efficient use of electricity in industrial, commercial, and residential operations.

Very much a hands-on facility, CTAC allows customers to touch, feel, and see how electrotechnologies apply to their businesses. Visitors can test equipment using their own products and experiment with new processes, while learning how to use energy more efficiently.

The Industrial Technology Center examines new electrotechnology solutions that not only improve productivity but also address air emission challenges. Showcased technologies include ultraviolet curing, infrared heating, and dielectric heating and drying. Applications on display can benefit a multitude of industries, including petrochemical, aerospace, paper, metals, printing, construction materials, furniture, wood products, and textiles.

The Commercial Technology Center promotes efficient end-use technologies with proven value to commercial customers. Displays include a Commercial Cooking Center with both functional and demonstration capabilities, a Lighting Design

Center complete with a storefront merchandising area, and an office mock-up.

Other technologies on display include high-efficiency heat pumps, energy management systems, thermal-energy storage systems, and internal combustion engine replacement with electric motors.

The Residential Technology Center focuses on new developments in energy-efficient appliances and equipment to help reduce energy costs without sacrificing comfort and convenience. Included is a 1,000-square-foot House of the Future, incorporating all the latest technologies. Parked in its garage is an electric van from Edison's fleet.

The Learning Center, with a capacity of 80, is designed to accommodate seminars, conferences, group presentations, and training sessions. It includes a multipurpose conference room and a central exhibit area to promote the exchange of information among vendors, trade and professional associations, commercial organizations, public policy groups, and Edison customers and employees.

Southern California Edison is committed to

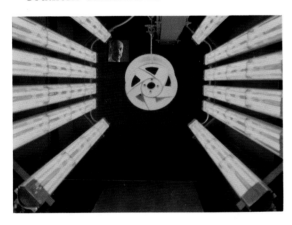

serving its industrial and commercial customers in many other ways as well. For years electric rates regulated by the California Public Utilities Commission (CPUC) subsidized residential customers at the expense of commercial and industrial customers. But recently, with the support and cooperation of the CPUC, the company has made substantial progress in achieving a more equitable rate structure. Edison has also been given the flexibility to negotiate special rates and services for large customers who might otherwise generate their own electricity.

To further serve major customers, the firm has developed a highly trained group of professionals who serve as personal contacts with the 250 largest accounts, which generate 20 percent of its revenues. These Edison representatives advise customers on ways to cut costs, suggest economic alternatives to installing customer-owned generating facilities, and help provide means of meeting the increasingly stringent air-quality

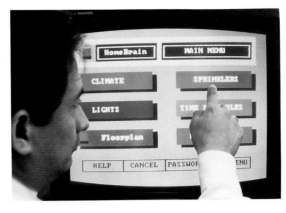

The Hypertek Touch Screen Home Automation System is one example of the kind of electrotechnologies introduced by Edison into the marketplace.

standards in Southern California.

The results have been dramatic. Recently the company helped a major customer in the aerospace industry cut its electric bills more than $4 million annually, by adapting its system to use higher voltage service. Two industrial customers saved one million dollars and $150,000, respectively, by following the recommendation of an Edison representative to replace gas-fired equipment with new electric technologies.

Edison has been a longtime leader in the research and use of alternative energy sources. It has developed nine different generation resources, more than any other utility company in the world, giving it great flexibility in adjusting to unforeseen changes in world energy markets. These resources are oil and gas, nuclear, coal, hydro, geothermal, solar, wind, and biomass. Through its massive research activities, Edison is discovering new ways to utilize these resources safely, cleanly, efficiently, quietly, and cost-effectively.

As the twenty-first century draws near, Southern California Edison Company stands ready to meet the present and anticipated needs of its customers, as it has done for more than 100 years. It remains committed to providing energy-efficient, state-of-the-art, quality service to its customers at reasonable costs and helping them meet their energy needs through improved electrotechnologies, while making a significant and beneficial environmental impact on the dynamic and growing region it serves.

Far Left: The Customer Technology Application Center's infrared heat chamber.

The Lighting Design Center is part of Edison's Customer Technology Application Center.

LOS ANGELES DEPARTMENT OF WATER AND POWER

As Los Angeles approached the end of the last century, it was by no means clear that it would be able to grow much further. With a population of just over 100,000, the city was rapidly running out of water.

It had been regularly involved in water wrangles almost since its founding in 1781, when settlers depended on the uncertain flows of the Los Angeles River and fought to keep upstream natives from diverting its water for their own uses.

Over the years the city built systems to store the runoff from winter rains, which helped stabilize supplies. But as the population began to grow rapidly in the late 1800s, it was clear something more was needed.

Enter William Mullholland. This rugged, mustachioed engineer for the municipal water company realized in 1905 that the city's salvation lay 250 miles north, in the seasonal water runoffs from the eastern slope of the Sierra Nevada Mountains.

Thus was born the Los Angeles Aqueduct project, a nine-year effort in which the city bought up vast acreage and the accompanying water rights in the Owens Valley, captured the snowmelt that flowed into this watershed, and diverted it south through a gravity-flow aqueduct that still—some 80 years later—provides more than half of the city's water supply in normal years.

This is the heritage of today's Los Angeles Department of Water and Power (the "power" came a few years later, when the city bought private electricity suppliers and began producing its own power from hydroelectric generators along the aqueduct).

Today's DWP is the largest municipally owned utility in the United States, with annual revenues of more than $3 billion. The DWP contributes more than $100 million each year to the city treasury. It employs 11,000 people and serves some 1.35 million electric and 645,000 water customers.

Keeping up with the power needs of Los Angeles over the past half-century has been as challenging as meeting its water requirements. The task was seriously complicated in the 1970s, when air pollution rules made it increasingly difficult to generate power in the Los Angeles Basin.

By that time the city's early dependence on hydroelectric power from aqueduct generators and Hoover Dam had given way to electricity generated by fuel oil and natural gas. With smog rules getting tougher, the DWP had to find ways

Los Angeles Department of Water and Power is taking a leadership role in supporting the use of electric vehicles to reduce air pollution in the Los Angeles area. The goal is to have 10,000 electric vehicles in Los Angeles by 1995.

to reduce emissions from its generating stations in the basin, but more critically to find ways to import power from outside.

Over the next 20 years the DWP became a partner in coal-fueled generating stations in Arizona, Nevada, and Utah, and a nuclear power plant in Arizona, while building massive transmission systems to bring the electricity here. Today around 75 percent of the power Angelenos consume is generated out of the state.

Meanwhile, the generating plants in the basin are being upgraded with the latest pollution-control equipment to meet ever-tightening standards. They are also being made more efficient, to conserve fuel and keep costs as low as possible.

As a result of such long-range planning and investment by the DWP, Los Angeles utility customers enjoy some of the lowest rates in the nation, well below those paid by neighboring communities in Southern California.

As an indicator of its financial strength, Department of Water and Power revenue bonds—sold to raise money for future expansion—are rated among the safest in the public utility field and are highly coveted by investors.

No metropolis as dynamic as this one can live without uncertainty, and (as it was in the early 1900s) one big question mark hanging over the city's future is water. With access to outside sources becoming more difficult, the DWP is leading an effort to conserve and recycle the water we have.

The department has carried on a far-reaching public information campaign, tied to promotions of water-saving devices like low-flow shower heads and ultra-low-flush toilets.

The DWP also implements water-conservation measures passed by the city council, which limit water use by home-owners and businesses in the city. As a result, water consumption in the city fell nearly 17 percent during one three-month period in 1990.

"In many ways, Los Angeles has become a great metropolis in spite of the limits imposed on it by nature," says one DWP authority. "Despite our placement between a desert and the world's largest body of salt water, we have managed to create a livable and thriving environment."

Large thyristor valves convert direct current to alternating current. These valves are a part of the Sylmar Converter Station which has a capacity to convert up to 3,100 megawatts of power from the Pacific Northwest. This power is enough to serve 4 million customers.

UNOCAL

Unocal chief executive officer and chairman Richard J. Stegemeier poses with some of the more than 8,000 old, heavily polluting cars destroyed under the company's SCRAP program.

T he first automobile had not yet appeared in the west when Union Oil Company of California was founded on October 17, 1890. The oil industry was barely 30 years old. Headquarters for the new company were established in Santa Paula, in the heart of the state's oil country. In 1990, when Unocal celebrated its centennial, the original two-story building was renovated and became the Unocal Oil Museum.

To form Union Oil, cofounders Lyman Stewart, Thomas Bard, and Wallace Hardison merged their holdings. Although they could not have foreseen the tremendous impact the automobile would soon have on oil demand, they were aware of oil's potential as an industrial and transportation fuel. True entrepreneurs, they worked to expand the uses for fuel oil in factories, steamships, and railroads. The company often assigned its own mechanics and technicians to convert power or heating systems to use oil instead of coal in order to demonstrate fuel oil's superiority—and earn the goodwill of future customers.

In 1891 Union Oil opened the first petroleum research laboratory west of the Mississippi with the initial aim of developing a process to extract nonsmoking kerosene from the heavy California crudes, much less suitable to such use than the lighter, cleaner eastern oils. While the goal eluded Union Oil chemists, that rudimentary lab began a long tradition of research that has served the company well.

By the turn of the century, only one of the three cofounders remained: Lyman Stewart. In 1901 the company moved its headquarters to Los Angeles—which Stewart referred to as that "great city of the future."

Stewart served as president until 1914, when his son Will stepped into the job. Lyman continued to play an active role as chairman until his death in 1923.

Together, father and son guided Union to a position of prominence in the western United States. Recognizing the importance of building an integrated company, the Stewarts created an effective refining and marketing organization backed by a solid resource base.

In Santa Paula, the building where Union Oil Company of California was founded on October 17, 1890, was renovated and reopened 100 years later as the Unocal Oil Museum.

By 1913 there were nearly 123,000 automobiles in California, prompting the company to open its first service station—or "gas stand"—on the corner of Sixth and Mateo streets in downtown Los Angeles. As the number of automobiles mushroomed, the company worked hard to keep pace. By 1925 Union had more than 400 service stations on the West Coast.

In 1930, with the death of Will Stewart, leadership passed to Press St. Clair. As the Great Depression deepened, St. Clair drastically cut back company operations. The bright spots in that dark decade were the introductions of the first 76 gasoline and Triton motor oil. Both products helped motorists get better performance to keep their cars rolling until better times. The 76 marketing symbol was destined to become one of the most recognizable and enduring corporate symbols in the nation.

As the world went to war in the late 1930s, Union—with a dynamic new leader in former steel man Reese Taylor—beefed up production and refining to pour out fuels to support the Allies. The company's growth continued into the booming postwar era as Union expanded in all directions: discovering the first natural gas in Alaska and the first oil in Australia; taking a lead position in offshore development in the Gulf of Mexico; building a thriving chemicals business; and developing a revolutionary refining technology—Unicracking—that became the most widely used in the world.

When Reese Taylor died unexpectedly in 1962, Cy Rubel, who had led the expansion in oil and gas exploration and production, came out of retirement to take over. He named a successor, Fred Hartley, two years later.

Hartley moved quickly to assure the company's future. In 1965 Union Oil merged with The Pure Oil Company of Illinois, lifting the company from regional to national status with operations in 37 states. The new Union Oil had the financial clout to expand its international petroleum search.

In the next 25 years Union became the major

oil producer in the Gulf of Mexico. Overseas, the company discovered the huge Attaka offshore oil field in Indonesia, developed fields in the rugged North Sea, became the world's largest geothermal energy producer, and—despite technical difficulties—developed the nation's first commercial-scale plant to produce oil from shale in Colorado. Union made the first commercial discoveries of natural gas in the Gulf of Thailand, helping create a hydrocarbon industry that has played a major role in Thailand's economic revolution.

In 1983 Union Oil Company of California was reorganized, becoming an operating subsidiary of a new holding company, Unocal Corporation. Two years later Union began doing business as Unocal. The name quickly gained headline status when the company was targeted for unfriendly takeover. Unocal survived, but with a heavy burden of debt. When Dick Stegemeier was named president in late 1985, he, Hartley, and their executive team faced enormous challenges in streamlining the company. They reduced the debt from

$6.1 billion to less than $4 billion by mid-1990. Stegemeier succeeded Hartley, who retired as chairman and chief executive officer before the end of the 1980s.

The history of Unocal has been marked by tenacity and technological leadership. The company is an efficient finder and producer of oil and gas, a pioneer in alternative energies, and a leader in the development of technology that improves refinery operations and reduces emissions.

In 1990, with environmental challenges becoming an international concern, Unocal made an aggressive commitment to finding innovative solutions with immediate impact. Unocal and the San Diego Gas & Electric Company announced a facility to provide compressed natural gas (CNG) as an alternative vehicle fuel, the first such joint effort in California by an oil company and utility.

Unocal also launched its South Coast Recycled Auto Project (SCRAP)—the first of its kind in the nation. The company paid $700 each to owners of more than 7,000 pre-1971 cars, which were scrapped and the metal recycled. Tests showed these older vehicles emitted more than 60 times

the amount of hydrocarbons as new models. Imaginative and highly successful, SCRAP drew participation from other companies to take more than 1,000 additional older cars off the road.

Another program—76 Protech Patrol—involved fleets of Unocal trucks in several California cities providing free assistance to motorists stranded in rush-hour traffic. A key objective was to reduce congestion and the resulting pollution.

Unocal people work in many ways to improve the quality of life in their communities. More than a century ago Lyman Stewart helped organize the Union Rescue Mission in Los Angeles and raised money for the local YMCA. He founded the Bible Institute of Los Angeles, which evolved into Biola University.

Succeeding generations followed Stewart's example. For more than 40 years Unocal has been a partner with the National 4-H organization, sponsoring an annual public-speaking contest that involves nearly 200,000 young participants.

Unocal is also a major supporter—both through contributions and volunteer efforts—of United Way and similar fund-raising efforts. Across the nation, such activities act as clearing houses for donations to a wide variety of organizations serving people in need.

In the 100 years from its modest start in 1890, Unocal has become a leading *Fortune* 500 company with more than 17,000 employees worldwide and annual revenues in excess of $11 billion. At the time of its centennial in 1990, Unocal was one of only 22 surviving industrial companies among the top 100 companies operating in the early 1900s—and looked forward to a second century of technological innovation, productive growth, and community leadership.

GTE

For generations, California has been a place where inge-nuity and hard work paid off, a place where dreams come true. People come to California from every corner of the globe, often bringing little more than the clothes on their backs, their en-ergy, and their aspirations.

Since World War II Califor-nia's population has exploded, swelling the state's borders with nearly 30 million people by the dawning of the twenty-first century. This massive influx of people has created a great diversity of life-styles, ranging from free-spirited Venice Beach to the sedate, stately mansions of Palm Springs, from the peaceful hideaways of the wine country to the freeway beehives connecting the Greater Los Angeles area.

Tying this together is GTE California, a com-pany whose growth, ethnic diversity, and innova-tion match the nature and pace of the legendary Golden State itself. In many ways, GTE's tele-phone operations mirror California's spirit of savvy and progressiveness, and its story is punc-tuated with firsts and breakthroughs in American telecommunications:

• The first independent telephone operation to have a million phones in service.

• The first telephone operation to use fiber-optic technology to transmit telephone calls.

• The first independent local exchange com-pany to build and operate its own long-distance switching centers.

• GTE is conducting the nation's largest test of advanced communications in Cerritos.

GTE California's success story began in 1929 when its forerunner, Associated Telephone, Ltd., took over six smaller telephone companies oper-ating in Long Beach, Redondo Beach, Covina, Huntington Beach, Laguna Beach, and San Bernardino. Associated would eventually evolve into the nation's largest independent telephone operating company.

Between 1932 and 1977, Associated purchased 12 more local telephone companies, giving the company almost 2 million customer lines as the 1970s drew to a close. Along with its new cus-tomers, Associated adopted a new name in 1953—General Telephone Co. of California.

As dramatic as the company's first 50 years had been, a turning point came with the telecommuni-cations industry's deregulation in the 1980s. GTE responded to this challenge by offering customers new products and services through retail outlets called GTE Phone Marts. In 1985 the company formed GTEL, a wholly owned subsidiary that con-tinues to handle its deregulated business activities. GTEL's mission is to meet the telecommunication equipment needs of customers, from the largest private network to a single residential telephone.

The mid-1980s were a time of huge technologi-cal investments for GTE California. Spending more than $3.4 billion over five years, the company con-verted its network and switching facilities to the latest in telecommunications technologies. Today GTE serves all customers with advanced electronic or digital technology. The company has a higher percentage of digital lines than any other local telephone company in the state.

GTE is also a leader in applying new technolog-ical developments to its telephone business. The

company installed computerized equipment to routinely analyze thousands of telephone lines each night to spot and correct potential problems before they affect telephone service. Customer billing is state of the art, with computerized billing centers that give operators instant access to customer account records when handling billing inquiries.

In 1988 General Telephone Co. of California changed its name to GTE California.

As the 1990s began, the company's 10,000-square-mile franchised service area included 20 counties and 330 communities. Most of GTE's telephone operations are in Southern California, but the company also serves several important markets in the central part of the state, including Los Gatos in high-tech Silicon Valley and Kenwood in the world-famous wine country.

Even as GTE helped shape the California of yesterday and today, the company is a leader in the state's future.

GTE California was the first telephone company to use fiber optics on the public telephone network, when it linked its Artesia and Long Beach switching centers with glass cables in 1977. With fiber optics, there is the potential for a virtually unlimited number of laser-beamed telephone conversations to be carried simultaneously over a single pair of hair-thin strands of glass.

The most important telecommunications breakthroughs in decades are being pioneered in Cerritos, where GTE has built a fiber-optic network of the future and is conducting the nation's largest test of advanced communications services. The project is a marketing and technology test of three transmission mediums—fiber optics, coaxial cable, and traditional, twisted-pair telephone wires.

The test project, which required a special waiver from the Federal Communications Commission, is a partnership among the City of Cerritos, GTE Service Corp., GTE California, and Apollo CableVision, which holds the city's cable television franchise. Apollo leases bandwidth on GTE's networks to provide 36 channels of cable service citywide. GTE uses the rest of the network to test a broad range of services delivered straight to consumers' homes using leading-edge technologies.

As well as providing regular telephone service over fiber optics into customers' homes, GTE is offering video-on-demand television and two-way switched video, which lets customers send, as well as receive, video signals. Another test offers Cen-

A GTE California linesman. A vast range of worker skills are required to maintain the telephone network. Courtesy, Andrew Rodney Photography

ter Screen, the largest pay-per-view system in the world. A few of the other areas being explored are educational services, home banking, shopping, travel arrangements, and access to city services.

While technology is a major force at GTE, the company's first concern is people. GTE California is a leader in providing business opportunities for women and minorities, and company employees are active in civic, charitable, and cultural organizations in every community GTE serves.

The company actively supports many worthwhile community activities, including the Adopt-A-School Program, the United Way, National Public Radio, scholarship programs, and much more. The company has also sponsored major cultural and sporting events, including Los Angeles County Museum of Art exhibits, the Los Angeles Times Indoor Games, and the GTE West Classic, an annual stop on the Senior PGA Tour.

The company is also responsive to the needs of the various ethnic groups it serves. Bill inserts are multilingual, and a Language Assistance Center offers help for non-English-speaking people.

GTE California's parent company is GTE Corp., based in Stamford, Connecticut. The GTE family is one of the nation's largest corporations, with operations in 46 states and 41 nations, and 160,000 employees.

With a past filled with stellar accomplishments, GTE California continues to set a rapid pace as a telecommunications leader and corporate citizen. GTE will continue to innovate and evolve as it emerges as a major economic force in California, and also as a leader and gatekeeper to the burgeoning Pacific Rim.

GTEL

n the early 1980s the Federal Communications Commission and the California Public Utilities Commission delivered a one-two blow to the comfortable status quo of the telecommunications business:

• The FCC ordered a historic split between the telecommunications equipment business and the telecommunications service business; the marketing of equipment was deregulated and thrown open to competition, while transmission service providers continued under regulated, government-granted monopolies.

• The California PUC followed up the FCC order by telling GTE California—which was in both businesses—that if it wished to remain a marketer of equipment, it would have to form a completely separate subsidiary to do it.

GTE California had no intention of abandoning the customers who for decades had depended on the company for all their telecommunications needs. It accepted the challenge of creating a subsidiary with the creativity, aggressiveness, and quick reflexes demanded by a wide-open market—and in 1985 GTE California launched GTEL, a wholly owned subsidiary.

GTEL was a curious mix of regal corporate pedigree and venture capitalist feistiness, and still is. The customer premises equipment (CPE) market is the telephone business' Bermuda Triangle—a lot of companies enter it and disappear. But five years after its inception, GTEL is not only surviving, but prospering.

The secret of GTEL's success is that it refuses to be intimidated by anything. It has consistently tackled projects that seemed too big and ideas that seemed too new. And flying in the face of conventional wisdom has paid off handsomely.

The most illustrative, dramatic, and lucrative example of this trait is the vast telecommunications network GTEL is building for the state of California—CALNET. The only American public institution larger than the state government of California is the federal government, and the state's telecommunications and information management needs were commensurate with the scope of its operations.

GTEL, as usual, was unruffled by the challenge. It conceived a statewide network that would vastly upgrade quality and the range of available services, and save money while it was doing it. It put together an

Above: At its headquarters in Thousand Oaks, GTEL is meeting the telecommunications needs of large to small customers.

Right: The Federal Building is one of GTEL's large complex customers who has varied telecommunications needs.

all-star team of subcontractors—IBM, MCI, Northern Telecom, and GTE Telecomm. It staged a spectacular, real-life demonstration of CAL-NET's potential that impressed state experts. And it faced down the competition, including a court challenge.

The result is a state-of-the-art, cost-effective new network for the state of California and another improbable but undeniable win for GTEL.

And CALNET is merely one very visible example of a long list of high-wire walks, including:

• Reinventing the concept of the GTE Phone Mart—GTE's national, 120-location retail chain for CPE—by creating the "Multi-Mart," an innovative approach to serving both residential and small-business customers in the same store.

• Leading the rest of the telecommunications industry into the "electronic funds transfer" business—ATMs. ATMs were generally regarded as a financial business until GTEL planners took a second look and saw that they were computers wired to data bases and to each other. That, they realized, is a telecommunications business, and GTEL leaped in.

•Acquiring a videotex business in San Francisco before most of its competitors had learned how to spell "videotex."

However, at GTEL, death-defying feats of entrepreneurship don't overshadow a more venerable GTE value: a fierce commitment to customer service. While GTEL's sales force is confounding the competition, its highly trained, highly experienced technicians—with an average tenure in the business of 15 years—are making sure that everything works as promised.

An uneasy combination of gleeful adventurousness and salt-of-the-earth conservatism? Absolutely. GTEL wouldn't have it any other way.

And neither would five years' worth of satisfied customers.

PACIFIC BELL

Were Alexander Graham Bell alive today, he would surely be astonished at how his brainchild has grown and the level of sophistication it has achieved. Back in 1876 when he placed the very first telephone call, he could hardly have imagined that, within the next century, his invention would become the linchpin of the Age of Information and Technology in which we live today.

The Bell Telephone Company was founded in 1877, and over a span of more than 100 years grew to become American Telephone & Telegraph Company (AT&T), one of the largest and most successful organizations in history, known far and wide as "Ma Bell." Then the 1980s brought a series of regulatory decisions that would forever change the industry. Those changes are best summed up in the words "divestiture" and "deregulation."

A 1983 ruling by the Federal Communications Commission (FCC) deregulated the manufacture and sale of telephone equipment, opening that portion of the industry to competition. Telephone service was unaffected by the ruling and continues to be regulated by the FCC and various state agencies.

In 1984 the settlement of a lawsuit by the U.S. Department of Justice against AT&T resulted in the divestiture by the company of the various components of the Bell System. Suddenly Ma Bell was no more, and in its place were a number of so-called "Baby Bells," each a very substantial company in its own right. Even the industry itself took on a new identity. The word "telephone" no longer adequately described it and the much more accurate term "telecommunications" soon came into vogue.

Among the new entities created was the San Francisco-based Pacific Telesis Group, comprised of several companies, one of which, Pacific Bell, bears the name of the man who started it all back in 1876. Since 1984 Pacific Bell has been serving the needs of its customers throughout California, and at the same time investing in the technology that will allow it to continue meeting the growing needs of a growing state through the remainder of the 1990s and into the twenty-first century.

Much of that investment is in optical fiber, capable of carrying enormous amounts of voice, data, and video communications simultaneously. With its high performance and cost efficiences, it has quickly become the telecommunications medium of choice in the markets served by Pacific Bell. The company first proved the value of innovative fiber telecommunications technology at the 1984 Olympic Games in Los Angeles, and again at the Democratic National Convention in San Francisco the same year.

Recently the company further enhanced the already high reliability of fiber optics with the introduction of a system called Fiber Rings. Recognizing the need of many businesses for an uninterrupted flow of information, Pacific Bell's fiber optics team designed the Fiber Rings system, which connects each location on a network with two separate, diversely routed fiber cables.

If trouble occurs on the primary route, the secondary route activates immediately, assuring uninterrupted service. Other innovative products aimed primarily at serving business accounts include the Advanced Digital Network (ADN); Centrex; Centrex IS; and VideoWindow. The ADN is a digital private line network for banks, stores, campuses, hospitals, and other organizations that need to send and receive data. Applications include electronic funds transfer, automatic teller machines, network management, video teleconferencing, inventory management, order entry, and information retrieval.

Pacific Bell's Centrex business system is a central-office-based switching system for business customers who require call transport management capabilities as part of their telecommunications systems. In December 1989 the company introduced Centrex IS, combining Centrex reliability with the simultaneous voice/data/video capabilities of its Integrated Services Digital Network (ISDN).

The Centrex IS system provides unprecedented interactive links to all types of data resources and is ideally suited to a broad range of industries, including financial services, health care, high-tech manufacturing, distribution, professional services, and transportation, as well as public sector applications.

VideoWindow, an integrated audio/video interactive teleconferencing system, allows people in two different places to talk to each other and exchange information almost as though they shared adjoining offices and a connecting window.

In 1990 Pacific Bell made a major advance in meeting the needs of California's small business community by making its Centrex system available to them. Once limited to customers with 20 or more telephone lines, the system now accommodates businesses with as few as two lines. The full line of Centrex features is available, including Centrex IS, electronic telephone features, and Pacific Bell Voice Mail, which allows users to send, store, and receive messages in the sender's own voice.

In 1990 the company greatly expanded its 800 service with the introduction of Custom 800, allowing businesses of all sizes to tailor an 800 number arrangement that meets their specific needs, at a 20 to 60 percent lower cost than existing 800 services. Pacific Bell was the first local telephone company to offer an 800 service with the ability to customize calling areas and call routing, making it especially attractive to small businesses.

Well aware of the ethnic diversity of its market areas, Pacific Bell has been at the forefront in providing multilingual services to its business and residential customers. It was the first telephone company in California to offer bilingual services for the state's 115,000 Hispanic businesses, who can order service anywhere in the state by calling a toll-free number.

Residential customers can place orders, change telephone features, and have their questions answered in Spanish, Korean, Cantonese,

Mandarin, or Vietnamese. The service is available toll-free throughout the state for nearly seven million Hispanic residents and more than one million Asian residents.

Pacific Bell's commitment to innovation, state-of-the-art technology, and outstanding service to its rapidly growing, ethnically diverse customer base is matched by a long-standing commitment to community involvement. Pacific Bell employees have traditionally played active volunteer roles in civic, cultural, educational, and charitable organizations throughout California.

In Los Angeles, one example is "Efficacy in the Classroom," a partnership program with the Los Angeles Unified School District. The plan was designed to reverse the pattern of low achievement at 10 predominantly African-American and Hispanic schools, by teaching a set of ideas that can improve performance and help students achieve a better quality of life.

A grant from Pacific Bell made the program possible and the participation of more than 40 company managers who volunteer their time to teach "Efficacy" classes has kept it going. It illustrates well the spirit of the people of Pacific Bell, whether they're installing the latest telecommunications equipment or reaching out to help a neighbor in need.

Above: Pacific Bell serves the metropolitan Los Angeles business customers with high-reliability, high-speed fiber optics. Pacific Bell's fiber optics team designed a Fiber Rings system that connects each location on a network with two separate, diversely routed fiber cables.

Far left: Pacific Bell's 24-hour network management center maintains near-normal operating conditions in the face of unusual demands or emergency situations that would otherwise result in traffic slowdowns or service failures.

ROTARY CLUB OF LOS ANGELES

The history of the Rotary Club of Los Angeles closely parallels that of Rotary International itself. The worldwide organization was born in 1905, when founder Paul Harris gathered a few men together in Chicago to explain his concept of a club whose members would be encouraged to do business with one another. Membership would be limited to one man from any particular type of business or profession. Thus began the Rotary Club of Chicago.

It remained a single club until 1908 when a Chicago man visiting San Francisco told a local attorney named Homer Wood about it. Wood was excited by the concept and quickly began organizing a club in San Francisco, and another in the tri-cities area of Oakland, Alameda, and Berkeley.

The two new clubs began in November 1908 and February 1909, respectively. Wood also contacted his brother, Walton J. Wood, a Los Angeles attorney, urging him to start a club there.

The latter joined forces with Jerry Muma of the Travelers Insurance Company and began planning a Los Angeles club. At about the same time a Seattle club was being formed, and was organized just prior to the one in Los Angeles. When the Rotary Club of Los Angeles was officially organized on June 25, 1909, with Jerry Muma as its first president, it became the fifth Rotary Club, and continues to proudly bear the designation "Club #5" or "LA 5."

The new club literally got off to a flying start. Less than three months after it was organized, it sponsored the first aviation meet ever held in America. The meet was a huge success, highlighted by a flight from Dominguez Field to Pasadena and back. That 20-mile trip broke the existing long distance record for airplanes.

The Rotary movement grew rapidly, with numerous clubs opening across the country, including many in the Greater Los Angeles area. A National Association of Rotary Clubs was formed, and at its 1913 Convention in Buffalo, New York, it was announced that the Los Angeles Club #5 was the largest, with 310 members.

As Rotary grew and matured, the focus on networking diminished, replaced by a commitment to service. Rotary International now includes more than 1.1 million members in almost 26,000 clubs in more than 170 countries. The Moscow Rotary Club was chartered in 1990 and Eastern Europe is again opening up.

Simply stated, the object of Rotary is "Service Above Self." It connotes a commitment to worldwide service, perhaps best expressed by a Rotary program called Polio Plus, designed to rid the world of the disease which still cripples nearly 500,000 of the world's children every year. The members of Rotary International have pledged millions of dollars for massive immunization projects to stamp out polio by the organization's centennial year of 2005.

Locally, the men and women of the Rotary Club of Los Angeles have demonstrated that same spirit of service in hundreds of ways. The largest service club of any kind in California, with 659 members, it contributes more than $250,000 annually for worthwhile community projects and student scholarships, over and above its major financial commitment to the Polio Plus Program.

In recent years the club has provided $100,000 in annual support to DARE. Substantial financial assistance and member involvement are also provided to a variety of community service organizations and charitable programs. The newest major project is the Child Victims in Court Foundation (CIVIC) to benefit abused and neglected children at the new Childrens Court of Los Angeles County.

The members of the Rotary Club of Los Angeles, many of them the community's top civic, business, and professional leaders, are justifiably proud of their role in making the Greater Los Angeles area a better place for all its people for nearly a century. For them, "Service Above Self" is more than a motto; it's a way of life.

TIMES MIRROR

Times Mirror, headquartered in Los Angeles, is a media communications company with annual revenues of more than $3.5 billion. The company was incorporated in 1884, but actually began in 1873 with the establishment of the Mirror Printing and Bindery House, which began publishing the *Los Angeles Daily Times* in 1881.

The newspaper, later renamed the *Los Angeles Times*, flourished with the growth of Southern California. In terms of circulation, today it is the nation's largest metropolitan daily newspaper and, since 1955, has been the world's leader in advertising volume.

Times Mirror began to diversify in the 1960s; today it focuses on three lines of business: print media, electronic media, and information-based professional publishing. It is the nation's leading publisher of large-circulation newspapers, serving affluent markets with such highly respected dailies as *Newsday* and the *Baltimore Sun* newspapers. The company also owns network-affiliated television stations in several major cities and is among the largest cable television operators in America.

As a publisher of law and medical books, it commands sizable market shares and is the world's leading provider of navigational information for aircraft pilots. Times Mirror also publishes consumer magazines and is a leading provider of courseware for industrial training.

With all its far-flung enterprises, Times Mirror has maintained close ties with Los Angeles for more than a century and has played a major role in the growth and development of the region. Its largest property, the *Los Angeles Times*, was first published on December 4, 1881, as a four-page paper selling for a penny. Circulation in its first year was less than 1,000, a respectable number for what was then a dusty town of 12,000 people.

Harrison Gray Otis arrived in Los Angeles in 1881, and in 1884 he wrote of "a mighty Pacific empire, with a population numbering millions where we now see only thousands, and possessing a measure of wealth, civilization, and power now inconceivable."

Acquiring *The Times* and the Mirror Printing and Bindery House, which printed both the newspaper and the first telephone directory in Los Angeles, Otis set out to turn his dream into reality.

By 1900 *The Times* led all local competitors in both circulation and revenue. Circulation reached

90,000 by 1920 and 300,000 by 1945. The one-million mark was first reached in 1970.

Today the *Los Angeles Times* is consistently ranked as one of the best and most respected newspapers in the United States. It has been the recipient of numerous honors, including 18 Pulitzer prizes, journalism's highest honor.

Both *The Times* and Times Mirror, now international in scope, remain very much in spirit Los Angeles enterprises, fully committed to the ongoing growth and prosperity of the community. A major expression of that commitment was the completion, in 1990, of *the Times'* $230-million Olympic production plant on a 26-acre site at Alameda and 8th streets. The nearly 700,000-square-foot plant is one of the world's most modern newspaper production facilities.

Times Mirror fully recognizes the key role Los Angeles plays as the hub city of the dynamic and rapidly expanding Pacific Rim and is well aware

The dramatic entry arch to the new *Los Angeles Times* Olympic plant, situated on a 26-acre site in downtown Los Angeles.

of the future communications needs of the area as this growth continues. The Olympic plant is designed to meet those needs for many years to come.

Times Mirror's deep commitment to Los Angeles and the other communities it serves is expressed in other ways as well. Both as a company and through The Times Mirror Foundation, it makes charitable contributions of nearly $10 million a year, supporting civic and community programs, culture and art, health and human services, and educational programs and activities.

In Times Mirror, Harrison Gray Otis' dream of more than a century ago has indeed come true. Although now publicly owned—in 1964 it became the first newspaper-based company listed on the New York Stock Exchange—its board continues to include Otis' descendants, many of whom have played vital roles in the company over the last four generations.

LOS ANGELES BUSINESS JOURNAL

In recent years, "innovation" and "growth" have become the watchwords at the *Los Angeles Business Journal*, propelling it to its current position as the leading business publication in Los Angeles County and the fastest-growing business journal in the United States.

The weekly newspaper was founded in 1979 and its first issue appeared in August of that year. It was the third in a chain of papers launched by Cordovan Publications, headquartered in Houston, Texas. Later Cordovan was acquired by Scripps-Howard, which sold its interests to American City Business Journals, based in Kansas City, Missouri, in 1986.

In 1988 the *Los Angeles Business Journal* and the *San Diego Business Journal* were acquired by their present owner, CBJ Associates, Inc., which has since purchased a third publication, the *Orange County Business Journal*, based in Newport Beach.

The editorial focus of the *Journal* is on business news not generally covered elsewhere about companies headquartered or operating in the

CBJ Associates publishes the *Los Angeles Business Journal* and its affiliated special publications.

Greater Los Angeles County area. Published every Monday in a tabloid format, it includes articles about some of the fastest-growing companies in the area.

In addition to local business news, the *Journal* covers business trends, executive profiles, and information written for the Los Angeles area executive. Subscribers are primarily top and upper-middle-level managers in a wide range of large and small companies. Industries covered include advertising and marketing, banking, aerospace, high technology, retailing, agribusiness, international trade, real estate, finance, manufacturing, entertainment, telecommunications, education, hospitality, accounting, media, transportation, and health care.

One of the most popular features in the *Los Angeles Business Journal* has always been its weekly listing of an industry or institutional segment, with each issue focusing on a different industry or profession, and including important statistics and other data on each company, in summary form.

In addition to being of great reader interest, the lists have become an important marketing tool.

Once a year the *Journal* publishes the *Book of Lists* that contains not only the lists published in the last 52 issues but others compiled exclusively for the annual edition. Also included are lists of the 100 largest public companies and 75 largest private companies in Los Angeles County. Begun in 1987, the *Book of Lists* has become an indispensable aid for virtually all marketing organizations in the Los Angeles metropolitan area.

The list is but one of several popular features of the *Los Angeles Business Journal*, which prides itself on providing a great deal of practical, useful information for its upscale readers. Based on recent surveys, the most-read features (all 75 percent and above) are the "Journal Profile," "Newsmakers," "the List," the "Extra" sections, and columns on real estate, advertising, and marketing, and a personal finance column called "You and Your Money."

Under its present management and with a top-quality staff, many of them award-winners, the *Journal* has made giant strides, as evidenced by dramatic increases in advertising space, circulation, and revenues. Of even greater significance has been the stature and respect the paper has gained as the chronicler of the Los Angeles area business markets and as a strong advocate and supporter of a wide variety of worthy community endeavors.

The philosophy of the *Los Angeles Business Journal* is perhaps best expressed in a book it recently copublished with City National Bank, called *Founding Fortunes of Southern California*. Its introductory message includes these words: "[We] believe strongly in Southern California business—past, present, and future. Like so many others in this dynamic, exciting marketplace, our fortunes have paralleled the Southern California experience. And, like many others, we take pride in boosting local and regional businesses and business people in every way we can . . . we commend the impressive business leaders of today who foster the region's continued growth and pave the way to an even more exciting tomorrow."

KCET

The remarkable story of public television station KCET, Channel 28, began in Los Angeles more than 25 years ago. In 1964 a group of distinguished community leaders formed the Committee for Educational Television to launch a television station serving all the people, "dedicated to the cultural and educational development" of its audience, and one that would "help viewers understand and appreciate the American way of life."

KCET has grown dramatically since its birth in 1964 and is now the largest public television facility on the West Coast. Its service area stretches from Santa Barbara to Palm Springs, and from Bakersfield to La Jolla. On average, more than 2.5 million southern and central California households tune in weekly. Its programming includes the finest in exciting drama, informative news, stirring musical and dance performances, provocative current affairs, enlightening children's and family fare, and amazing scientific and nature adventures.

KCET has served the changing cosmopolitan region of Southern and Central California throughout the years with a wide variety of locally oriented programming and community outreach activities that respond to the needs of Los Angeles and its surrounding communities.

From the 1968 broadcast of "Cancion de la Raza," a 65-part series dramatizing the daily problems of Mexican Americans, through the 1990 celebrations of Black History Month, Hispanic Heritage Month, and Asian Pacific Heritage Week, KCET has continually served its multicultural viewing audiences with award-winning programs.

Other popular and acclaimed series produced by KCET for its local audiences have included the magazine-style shows "Off Ramp" and "Citywatchers" in the 1960s; a news broadcast, "28 Tonight," in the 1970s; and most recently the documentary series, "KCET Journal," the weekly "California Stories," the compelling "L.A. History Project," and the lighthearted "Videolog." KCET has also produced "By The Year 2000," the only weekly local public affairs series in Los Angeles airing in prime time.

For these and other local production accomplishments, in 1990 KCET was awarded a record-breaking 14 local Emmy Awards from the Academy of Television Arts and Sciences, more than any other Los Angeles television station.

Strategically located at the heart of the world's entertainment industry, KCET also produces or presents many programs aired nationally on PBS stations. The most recent projects include the long-awaited, internationally filmed series, "The Astronomers," introducing the scientists and technologies that are revolutionizing our current knowledge of the universe; "Millennium," a com-

The popular children's show, "Sesame Street," has been educating and entertaining youngsters of all ages with such well-known characters as Big Bird, shown here visiting KCET President William H. Kobin.

pelling, multi-part series that examines tribal cultures around the world and their impact on modern life; and numerous landmark dramatic productions for the award-winning series, "American Playhouse."

KCET strongly supports, and is strongly supported by, the community. Nearly 350,000 people have become individual members and contributors, supporting the station with annual gifts. More than 3,000 volunteers donate as much as 43,000 hours of time annually, performing a broad variety of functions that serve station activities. An active Community Advisory Board serves as the liaison to a number of community constituencies.

KCET gives back to the community as much as it receives. Its Community Relations division works closely with the programming department to further understanding of and appreciation for the diversity of cultures and the variety of issues in the community. Broadcasts on such critical issues as literacy, child care, AIDS, aging, and the disabled are supported by ancillary off-the-air activities, including the wide distribution of brochures and other resource materials.

KCET has won a host of local, national, and international honors, both for its programming and community involvement. Proud of its history, it is looking forward to a bright future as it continues to serve both the audiences within its community and throughout the nation with the finest in television programming.

KCET, located in the heart of Hollywood, has been providing its viewers with quality programming for more than 25 years.

KNX NEWSRADIO

Two words that perhaps describe Los Angeles radio station KNX (1070 AM) better than any others are consistency and excellence. In an industry where stations are regularly bought and sold, where managers come and go, and where formats seem to change with the seasons, KNX has remained a model of consistency.

CBS Inc. acquired KNX in 1936 and has been broadcasting from the same facility at 6121 Sunset Boulevard since 1938. The Newsradio format for which it has become famous was introduced in 1968 by George Nicholaw, who had joined the station as general manager a year earlier.

Today Nicholaw is vice president of the CBS Radio Division and continues as general manager of KNX. News Director Robert Sims, who joined the station a year after Nicholaw, is another example of the stability and consistency that enables KNX to maintain its leadership year after year.

The clearest evidence of KNX's commitment to excellence can be seen on its office walls, which are literally covered with honors and awards. KNX has been honored more than any other radio station in America and has won more awards for news excellence than all other Los Angeles stations combined.

Since 1971 the Radio-TV News Association of Southern California has presented KNX with its coveted Golden Mike Award for Best Newscast every single year. In one recent, typical three-month period, the station received 10 Golden Mike Awards, nine top APTRA awards from the Associated Press, 10 out of 14 of the top broadcast journalism awards from the Greater Los Angeles Press Club, and the distinguished Sigma Delta Chi Award from the Society of Professional Journalists.

KNX, the first continuously operated radio station in the Los Angeles area, was founded in 1920 by a former shipboard wireless operator named Fred Christian. The original call letters, 6ADZ, were changed to KGC in 1921. By broadcasting orchestra performances from the California Theatre, KNX became the first station in the area to air live music.

Christian sold the station in 1924 to Guy Earle, publisher of the *Los Angeles Evening Express* newspaper. In 1932, when KNX was owned by Western Broadcasting Company, power was boosted to 10,000 watts. In 1934 it was granted a clear channel of 50,000 watts, which it still utilizes. As such, it is one of just two area stations at that power level and enables it to blanket all of Southern California.

KNX is one of the Southland's most popular stations, with some 1.5 million listeners; it continually ranks at or near the top in audience rating estimates. KNX/CBS Newsradio reaches more adults 25 and older than any other radio station in the western United States. In Southern California it ranks highest with that audience both at home and during peak driving times, as well as with home owners, those with college and advanced degrees, and households with high incomes. Of the more than 10,000 radio stations in the United States, only seven have more listeners—six of them are in the New York metropolitan area.

KNX's more than a half-century affiliation with CBS has been of great benefit to both organizations. Officially debuting in 1929, the CBS Radio Network now comprises about 400 stations, only seven of which are in the 50,000-watt category. KNX has one of the largest broadcast-journalist staffs in the nation, and much of the Southern California news aired on the network originates with KNX people. With the nation's ever-growing interest in international events, the news-gathering abilities of KNX, strategically located at the heart of the Pacific Rim, become more important to the network all the time.

General manager George Nicholaw gives the credit for the station's success to his staff. "We have developed a reputation for integrity, quality, and reliability," he says, "and our peo-

George Nicholaw, vice president, CBS Radio Division, and general manager of KNX.

The KNX newsroom is always a hubbub of activity.

ple are dedicated to maintaining it. They are very good journalists and take great pride in what they do."

Because of its nationwide reputation, KNX is viewed as a career goal for many in broadcast journalism, enabling it to pick the brightest, most talented people available whenever an opening occurs. "Once they get here," says News Director Robert Sims, "they tend to stay."

To help its people do their best, KNX provides the most technologically advanced equipment available. For example, it was the first radio station in Southern California to computerize its newsroom and the first to have its own satellite uplink. A jet helicopter enhances its on-the-scene coverage of local news events.

With its slogan, "All you need to know," KNX is on the air 24 hours a day. Its broadcast schedule includes coverage of all late-breaking news events, traffic and weather reports, market and business news, sports reports, entertainment news, and a variety of consumer-oriented features.

KNX offers exclusive radio sports coverage of USC football and basketball, various NFL football games, and post-season college football bowl games. It also broadcasts major league baseball, including the All Star Game, league playoffs, and the World Series, as well as horse racing, tennis, and golf. It has been the official radio station of the City of Los Angeles

Marathon, the largest event of its type in the nation.

KNX is the only radio station in the United States to air editorials seven days a week and one of the few that endorses political candidates. Such features can alienate rather than attract listeners, but it represents a long-standing policy at KNX that responsible programming and community service are as important as building an audience.

At KNX public service is given high priority. It actively supports a variety of community and charitable causes and regularly honors outstanding people of the community with its Citizen of the Week award. Community problems are covered in the award-winning "Assignment" documentary series, and weekly "On the Scene" reports feature interviews with community leaders about areas of concern. Rounding out the KNX broadcast schedule are such CBS features as "News on the Hour," "The World Tonight," "The Osgood File," and "Dateline: America."

In the ever-changing world of Los Angeles radio, KNX has been providing its NEWSRADIO format to a weekly audience that has averaged more than 1.3 million listeners for nearly 25 years. Its emphasis on consistency and excellence has enabled it to continue its role as the leading news station in Southern California.

KBIG-FM

Radio station KBIG-FM, known throughout Southern California as "K-BIG," is well named. It is a perennial leader in the biggest radio market, based on revenues, in the United States. In an average week, more than one million listeners—big by any standards—turn their radio dials to 104.3 FM. K-BIG's signal, with 105,000 watts of power, is the biggest in Los Angeles and one of the most powerful in the nation. It is owned and operated by an even bigger organization, Bonneville International Corporation, based in Salt Lake City, Utah.

side and its "core values" on the other. Those values are integrity, excellence, service, profitability, leadership, and sensitivity.

K-BIG's own mission statement reflects those values: "K-BIG is a radio station that entertains and informs with integrity through excellence in programming. Recognized as a leader in serving and enriching our community, K-BIG maintains an atmosphere that creates growth and profitability."

The K-BIG offices and studios, which include state-of-the-art broadcast equipment, have been

During an average week, more than one million listeners tune in K-BIG, which plays adult-contemporary music.

K-BIG received its license and began broadcasting in the Los Angeles area in 1959. A decade later it was acquired by Bonneville, which also operates two television stations, 11 other radio stations, a full-service advertising agency, two film and video-production houses, a broadcast music service, a data service company, a news bureau in Washington, D.C., a signatory and corporate sales company, and a satellite transmission company. Formed in 1964, its broadcast stations serve nine major metropolitan areas—Los Angeles, San Francisco, Seattle, Salt Lake City, Dallas, Kansas City, Chicago, Phoenix, and New York City.

Bonneville describes itself as a "values-driven company composed of values-driven people." It takes that description very seriously. Each year the firm publishes a "Values Report" in much the same manner as most companies prepare annual financial reports. Every employee receives a wallet-size card describing the firm's mission on one

located in a building it owns at 7755 Sunset Boulevard in Los Angeles since 1969. Its transmitter is strategically located at an elevation of 5,800 feet atop Mt. Wilson in the San Gabriel Mountains. Its coverage extends north to Santa Barbara and south to San Diego and includes Los Angeles, Orange, San Bernardino, Riverside, Ventura, and Kern counties. It has a staff of approximately 50 people and broadcasts 24 hours a day, seven days a week.

K-BIG's programming features adult-contemporary music, and the station has been a market leader for many years. Among the more than 80 radio stations in the Los Angeles area, K-BIG has consistently ranked within the top 10. Its music programming is supplemented by periodic newscasts, traffic reports, and weather updates. The station also features life-style reports, entertainment news, and other information of interest to its listeners.

An exclusive daily feature, "The California Report," presents a unique view of California's growth potential and examines how expansion and the opportunities it presents will impact the future for the business community and residents alike.

In addition to its regular programming, K-BIG presents numerous special features that contribute to the community. As with all broadcast stations, it is licensed by the Federal Communications Commission, which requires it to operate ". . . in the public interest, convenience, and necessity." K-BIG is keenly aware of that responsibility. It is the official Los Angeles radio station for the March of Dimes' most important fundraiser, the WalkAmerica Campaign; it introduced the "Radio Love Network" for muscular dystrophy; and it is involved with many community organizations on an ongoing basis.

Dedicated to being the "number-one radio station for community service and public awareness," K-BIG supports many other leading charities in the Los Angeles area. It advocates literacy and anti-drunk-driving campaigns, and promotes patriotism and other worthwhile causes through public service announcements tailored to

its listening audience. It annually donates more than $2 million in air time for public affairs programming and public service announcements.

K-BIG's commitment to community service and its overall programming have brought the station numerous awards. It has received several Angel Awards, given by Religion in Media, and PIRATES Awards, given by the Public Interest Radio and Television Educational Society, among others, all recognizing K-BIG's contributions to the community. It also has been honored by the International Radio Festival of New York as "The Best Adult Contemporary Radio Station."

K-BIG's impact on the community extends well beyond its on-the-air activities. The station's employees are actively involved in more than two dozen civic and charitable organizations outside the workplace, volunteering approximately 1,000 hours per year in support of a broad variety of worthwhile causes.

The people of radio station KBIG-FM are proud of their heritage of programming excellence and community service and have every intention of maintaining K-BIG's reputation as an innovative, exciting, and successful station and a leader in the highly competitive Los Angeles radio market.

K-BIG's commitment to the community extends beyond the airwaves and is evident in its association with such organizations as the March of Dimes.

KFWB

When radio station KFWB News 98 announces that it broadcasts "All News, All the Time," that's exactly what it means. Twenty-four hours a day, every day, KFWB broadcasts news, and only news. And more than 1.5 million listeners tune in each week.

In 1924 motion picture mogul Sam Warner bought the station, and KFWB's call letters stood for "Keep Filming Warner Brothers." KFWB's first broadcast occurred in 1925 when the station was only 250 watts strong. Many of the future stars of the entertainment industry made their debuts on KFWB, including Ronald Reagan; Roy Rogers on the "Sons of the Pioneers" show; Bing Crosby; George Burns and Gracie Allen, who appeared on KFWB in the 1940s when Big Band music was heard on the station; and Alan Ladd, among others.

KFWB was the first station to broadcast several events, including the Hollywood Santa Claus Lane Parade, and pioneered coverage of the Tournament of Roses Parade and the Rose Bowl Game during the 1930s. With the wartime spirit that swept the country in the 1940s, the KFWB epigram was changed to "Keep Fighting . . . Warner Brothers." During this period "Preview Theatre," a series that dramatized famous novels, was particularly popular.

After Sam Warner's death in 1951, the station was sold and under the new ownership began broadcasting the "American Dance" program and "Strictly From Dixie." Crowell Collier bought KFWB in 1956, and the station became a giant in

the market, being the first to broadcast top-40 songs while it billed itself as "Color Radio." "Channel 98" was the rage from the late 1950s to the mid-1960s. Well-known personalities such as B. Mitchell Reed, Sam Riddle, Gary Owens, Wink Martindale, Gene Weed, and Bill Ballance all launched their careers on KFWB at that time.

In 1966 Westinghouse Broadcasting Company, a pioneer in the industry, purchased KFWB. The format they instituted was an adult-oriented popular music format which ranked among the top in the market. Lohman and Barkley were two well-known favorites on KFWB at that time.

KFWB left its music history behind in 1968, and became Southern California's only all-news radio station, a format which Group W had recently installed at WINS, New York, and KYW, Philadelphia. This continued the Westinghouse news tradition established 48 years earlier by its Pittsburgh station, KDKA, which became the first commercial radio station in the U.S. when it broadcast the results of the 1920 Harding-Cox election.

All-news radio station KFWB quickly became known as the radio news leader, and today the station broadcasts in AM stereo to Los Angeles and Orange counties and parts of Ventura, Kern, San Bernardino, and Riverside counties, and consistently ranks among the top stations in the Los Angeles market.

Because of its long history in the market and commitment to consistency, people know exactly what to expect, and when to expect it, from KFWB. A new 20-minute news program begins on the hour and at 20 and 40 minutes past every hour. Each cycle opens with news, sports, and business headlines plus traffic and weather information. Detailed reporting follows the headlines.

KFWB broadcasts traffic reports around the clock. Listeners can tune in every 10 minutes of every day to learn of the latest road conditions, and to get the information they need to get to their destinations on time. It also uses two aircraft—a jet helicopter and an airplane—to provide the most up-to-the-minute, accurate traffic coverage possible. *Jet Copter 98* and *Air 98* are

supplemented by a large mobile-phone force, comprised of loyal listeners who telephone in, traffic problems they encounter on the freeways.

To ensure that its listeners are constantly abreast of the latest news, dozens of newsroom employees gather data from myriad sources, and use a specially programmed computer to prepare each 20-minute segment. Those sources include CNN, ABC, and the Associated Press, as well as reporters at the state capitol in Sacramento, and at news bureaus in Washington, D.C., and Orange County. Mobile units blanket the area, providing live reports on newsworthy events any time of day or night.

KFWB's unique, comprehensive, and consistent programming continues to bring it numerous awards from such organizations as United Press International, the Associated Press, the International Radio Festival of New York, and the Radio and Television News Association of Southern California, to name a few. The awards cover virtually all the station's features, including newscasts, business, sports, investigative reporting, special

reports, profiles, community portraits, and overall reporting.

KFWB is as proud of its many contributions to the community as it is of its award-winning record. It is a faithful supporter of the City of Hope, the March of Dimes, the American Cancer Society, the American Heart Association, and many other local institutions. To encourage students to pursue higher education, in 1989 the station launched a scholarship program in which it provides scholarship aid to graduating high school seniors each year.

The employees of KFWB, more than 100 strong, make no distinction between such activities and their work responsibilities. "We provide significant community service all the time," says one employee, "and we very much enjoy

that role." When major news stories break, the station is quick to suspend all commercials, often for 24 hours or more, in order to keep its listeners aware of every development . . . that's what KFWB's commitment to delivering news is all about.

Sports anchor Randy Kerdoon interviews Los Angeles Raider Greg Bell.

(From left) KCAL TV anchor Jerry Dunphy, Los Angeles Mayor Tom Bradley, and Chris Claus, KFWB's vice president and general manager, pose with copies of KFWB and KCAL's video cassette, "The Great Quake Hazard Hunt."

1990 KFWB scholarship winners with members of the KFWB staff.

A WEALTH OF ENTERPRISE

Business and Finance

Business and financial institutions, accounting firms, and computer technology combine to put some impressive numbers on Los Angeles' ledgers.

In the midst of palm trees and sunshine, the city's thriving business community works diligently to ensure a high level of productivity. Photo by Mark E. Gibson

TOWERS PERRIN

What do the names TPF&C, Cresap, and Till- inghast have in common? All are units of the worldwide management consulting firm known as Towers Perrin. Founded in Philadelphia in 1917, when it designed one of the first private pension plans in the United States, the firm was formally established as Towers, Perrin, Forster & Crosby (TPF&C) in 1934. Today it is an international orga- nization of management consultants and actuaries specializing in total compensation (pay and bene- fits), actuarial, communication, and related human resource consulting services. TPF&C has given advice to thousands of organizations of every size in virtually every industry, as well as in the public and nonprofit sectors, on evaluating, developing, financing, communicating, and ad- ministering human resource programs.

nesses, nonprofit organizations, and government agencies. A fourth Towers Perrin division, TPF&C Reinsurance, is one of the major reinsurance in- termediaries in the United States.

Today Towers Perrin, which is headquartered in New York, has more than 60 offices worldwide and more than 5,000 employees. It is the second- largest privately owned management consulting firm in the world. Towers Perrin is owned by ac- tive employees who have a vested interest in en- hancing the quality of the diverse consulting services the firm provides.

The firm, from its offices in the United States, Canada, Latin America, Europe, Australia, and the Far East, serves more than 8,000 clients world- wide. It has more than 400 clients among the *Fortune* 500 industrial companies, including nearly all of the top 100. Its clients, many of which have been with the firm for more than three decades, in- clude more than 80 percent of the largest American and Cana- dian industrial firms and a signif- icant number of major national and multinational firms and gov- ernment-owned enterprises in the United Kingdom, Europe, Australia, and the Pacific Rim. The firm serves many small and mid-size organizations as well.

The Southern California prac- tice, which opened its office in Los Angeles in 1966, was the eighth established by Towers Perrin. Encouraged to come to Southern California by a major client with a substantial presence in the area, the firm opened the office with two senior consul- tants. Today the Southern Califor- nia practice, with over 200 employees, is one of the five largest in the firm and has offices located in Los Angeles, Irvine, and San Diego. It has by far the largest pension actuarial practice in Southern Cal- ifornia, with three times as many large clients as its closest competitor. Much of its growth is due to its strategic position in what has become one of the major business centers in the world as well as the headquarters of the Pacific Rim.

In the firm's more than a quarter-century of doing business in Southern California, its mem- bers have participated enthusiastically in a vari- ety of civic and philanthropic activities that include leadership positions in the United Way, the L.A. Music Center, and numerous other organizations.

Offering both a general management perspec- tive and specific functional and industry

A Towers Perrin consult- ing team on its way to a progress meeting with a client's task force. Pho- tographs by Ed Honowitz Photography

Cresap, founded in 1946 as Cresap, McCormick & Paget, has enjoyed an outstanding reputation for many years. Acquired by Towers Perrin in 1983, Cresap, the general management consulting divi- sion of Towers Perrin, consults with clients throughout the world in strategy and organiza- tional effectiveness. Its services, supported by strong capabilities in information technology and manufacturing, are provided to large organiza- tions in both the public and the private sectors.

Tillinghast, formerly Tillinghast, Nelson, and Warren, was acquired by Towers Perrin in 1986. An international organization of management consultants and actuaries, it has, for more than 40 years, provided actuarial services and manage- ment advice to the insurance industry and related industries, and risk management services to busi-

expertise, the Southern California office of Towers Perrin is fully staffed to handle every aspect of all assignments it receives. It also has available the full resources of the worldwide organization, including computer facilities accessible from any office in the world. Towers Perrin maintains a broad data base of information, culled from thousands of assignments, that provides a vast pool of knowledge that any consultant can use to help point the way toward a solution to a client's unique problem. Towers Perrin also employs a large research, information, and technology staff to support its consulting efforts with studies of economic trends, business developments, and human resource practices throughout the industrialized world.

One of those studies, a "CEO Compensation Survey," was included in a special executive compensation supplement published by *The Wall*

Street Journal. The special section features a report by the firm on the salaries, bonuses, and long-term incentive awards paid over a three-year period to the chief executive officers of more than 300 of the leading corporations in the United States. Media representatives frequently seek out Towers Perrin professionals to obtain information on executive compensation, benefits, and other aspects of the firm's services.

An unwavering commitment to quality has been the driving force behind the rise of Towers Perrin to its preeminent position in the management consulting profession. That commitment encompasses, in the firm's own words, "objectivity in identifying, analyzing, and fulfilling client needs; providing practical solutions that can be put into action efficiently and cost-effectively; establishing and maintaining good working relationships with clients; complete independence, which allows the firm to offer counsel and guidance based solely on

the issues involved; ability, demonstrated by the high caliber of the consulting staff and the results of their work, the professionalism of technical and support staff, and the effectiveness of its computer resources; and curiosity, satisfied by a search for broader and deeper knowledge."

A major portion of the firm's assignments either are with existing clients or are referrals from existing clients, which is clear evidence of the firm's commitment to quality and its success in meeting clients' needs. Despite that success, Tower Perrin continues to seek new ways to grow and to serve its clients more effectively. Much of its research today concerns what changes await the world's economy in the twenty-first century and how to prepare present and future clients to deal with those changes, which include an aging work force, zero population growth, and the emergence of a global marketplace.

Then, as now, Towers Perrin stands poised to meet its clients' needs with the innovation and quality that have long been its hallmarks.

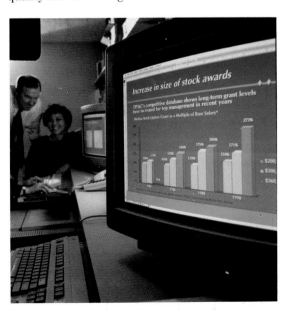

A consulting team reviews the final presentation describing a client's newly designed benefits program.

Far left: Consultants from Cresap (Towers Perrin's general management consulting organization) often work on-site as they develop operational strategies for clients.

State-of-the-art technology helps Towers Perrin consultants illustrate competitive trends in long-term incentives for a client report.

PAYDEN & RYGEL

Cofounder Joan A. Payden. Photo by Steve Crise

It was during the early 1980s that Joan A. Payden and Sandra J. Rygel, in classic entrepreneurial fashion, decided to fill a niche they had identified in their investment management profession. The niche was investment counseling that focused exclusively on management of short and intermediate fixed-income securities. In 1983 they resigned the senior positions they held at the major firm where they had spent a combined 36 years and launched Payden & Rygel.

The two women had identified their niche well. Within less than a decade, the Los Angeles-based organization had grown to approximately 50 employees, with assets under management of close to $10 billion. It ranks among the top 100 investment firms nationally, the top 10 in California, and the top three in Southern California. It is also the largest independent firm specializing in short-term fixed-income securities.

More than half of Payden & Rygel staff are professionals with extensive experience in all areas of investment. Many of them, including the founders, have earned the CFA (Chartered Financial Analyst) and CIC (Chartered Investment Counselor) designations.

The paths of Joan Payden and Sandra Rygel first crossed in 1970. It was a case of East meeting West. Payden, president of the firm, was born in Connecticut and spent much of her early life in Indonesia. Returning to the eastern United States, she earned her Bachelor of Arts degree at Trinity College in Washington, D.C. Later she did graduate work at Columbia University and the Harvard

Business School. Before venturing forth on her own, she had risen to the post of managing director of the Los Angeles office of the nationwide firm she joined in 1960.

Sandra Rygel joined the same firm in 1970, becoming a vice president in 1980. A California native and a "cum laude" graduate of the University of California at Los Angeles, she serves as executive vice president of Payden & Rygel. Joan Payden and Sandra Rygel own a majority of the corporation's stock. The only other shareholders are senior members of the firm.

It was a series of dramatic changes in the fixed-income securities, or debt instrument markets that first caused Payden and Rygel to take notice. One was a substantial increase in the volume, type, and complexity of short-maturity assets.

Another change was the increase in the returns produced by these assets that often made them competitive with other financial assets. Other changes included greater market price volatility, usually only associated with equities and longer-term assets, and expanding markets in the United States and around the world. A growing conviction that these changes had created a need for specialized counsel and management led directly to the formation of Payden & Rygel.

The organization has developed a unique approach to the management of fixed-income securities. It concentrates on securities with maturities of up to five years that provide both high quality and liquidity. Portfolios are actively managed, and selling prior to maturity is emphasized, in order to improve returns and reduce volatility. The firm's wholly owned subsidiary, PortFolio Systems, provides a computer hardware/software service to enable clients to directly access the portfolio and reporting system.

Payden & Rygel's expertise is by no means limited to domestic markets; foreign bonds play a

Cofounder Sandra J. Rygel. Photo by Steve Crise

Sandra J. Rygel (left) and Joan A. Payden are actively involved with their clients on a regular basis. Photo by Steve Crise

major role in the firm's investment strategies. Very much a global firm, Payden & Rygel represents both domestic and foreign clients, including many with multinational operations.

Among its client base are major pension funds, foundations, credit unions, *Fortune* 500 corporations, and individuals. Close interaction is maintained between the firm and its clients.

Internationally, Payden & Rygel utilizes a team approach, with portfolio management, trading, and reporting all closely aligned to ensure that client needs are met and effectively communicated.

The ongoing personal communication between firm and client is supplemented by the publication of a *Quarterly Review* and a *Performance Index of Short-Maturity Assets*, also published quarterly, with monthly updates. The *Review* covers various segments of the domestic and international economy and markets, as well as significant market events. The *Performance Index* measures the total return of a variety of short-maturity fixed-income securities.

In addition to providing the highest level of investment counseling and management to its clients, the firm gives professional organizations' concerns a high priority. The two founders and virtually all the senior members of the firm are active in various professional groups. Payden serves on the board of directors and the executive committee of the Los Angeles Area Chamber of Commerce. She is also on the board of directors of the Society of Experimental Test Pilots and the Asia Pacific Museum.

Payden & Rygel is also deeply committed to helping meet the needs of the community through such organizations as The United Way and other charitable groups that serve the sick, the poor, and the homeless. Rygel, for example, is a member of the advisory board of the Academy of Finance, a program offering a two-year course of study in business and finance to local high school students. Combined with a summer intern program, it provides challenge and opportunity to young people who might not otherwise attend college.

Having risen to the top ranks of their profession very rapidly, Payden and Rygel have no intention of resting on their laurels but continue, on behalf of their clients, to explore favorable short-maturity fixed-income opportunities all around the world. At the same time, they are justifiably proud of Payden & Rygel, which stands as a tribute to the vision and courage of two women who dared to turn their dream into reality.

The firm has established itself as a major player in the international arena through its representation of both domestic and foreign clients.

BANK OF AMERICA

Few organizations, including government, have done more for the people of California than Bank of America. Beginning on that day in 1904 when A.P. Giannini founded a different bank, one that would serve the needs of all people, Bank of America has brought beneficial banking services to all, and has done it so well that the entire banking industry has followed its lead.

When the great San Francisco earthquake and fire devastated the city in 1906, many bankers wanted to stay closed for six months. Giannini set up a makeshift desk the next morning on a waterfront wharf and began making loans, with no collateral except a strong handshake.

The bank was the first in the nation to create a statewide system of branch banks to gather small deposits into larger sums and move them around the state where they could be put to work building communities. Other bankers scoffed, then tried desperately to stop it, but the idea prevailed. Bank of America thus played the major role in helping free California farmers from the stranglehold of Eastern bankers and higher rates.

During the depths of the Great Depression, the bank launched a major, widespread "Back to Good Times" campaign to help break the prevailing mood of self-defeat and bought local bond issues to put people to work. For example, the bank bought the first bonds for the construction of the Golden Gate Bridge.

From its earliest days Bank of America has helped practically every California community find a market for its bond issues. From small housing programs to such huge projects as Hoover Dam, Bank of America has been involved, helping to build California into the dynamic and robust economy it is today.

Bank of America has been a major real estate lender throughout its history, taking the leadership position in America for making home loans after Congress passed the Federal Housing Act in 1934. Today it makes real estate loans on everything from single-family homes to major residential, commercial, and industrial projects.

Nowhere has Bank of America had a greater impact than in Southern California, a marketplace that has long been its single most important one. A Los Angeles office, opened in 1913, was its first in the entire southern part of the state. The bank serves all segments of the market, including small and medium-size businesses, global corporations, individual customers, and government agencies at city, county, and state levels.

Bank of America has particular expertise in serving specialized needs in Southern California in the areas of advanced technology, agriculture, tourism, media, and entertainment. From the earliest years, the bank led the way in developing the movie industry, helping United Artists, Columbia, and Twentieth Century get started, and financing independent producers such as Cecil B. DeMille, Sam Goldwyn, David O. Selznick, and Frank Capra. It was Bank of America, in 1936, that helped a young cartoonist named Walt Disney by financing a project others called "crazy" —a feature-length animated film called *Snow White and the Seven Dwarfs*.

Bank of America has had a major role in pioneering consumer loans, credit cards, student loans, SBA financing, retail lending, cash management, and foreign trade and investments. The bank is backing its commitment to local communities with strong support for housing and community development loans in low and moderate-income areas.

But it is much more than financing that has distinguished Bank of America. Through its BankAmerica Foundation, Employee Matching Gift Program, High School Achievement Awards Program, and other projects, it has helped support civic, charitable, and educational activities in California and elsewhere. The bank has had an active paper recycling program since 1971 and has set forth environmental principles to guide its decisions and practices worldwide.

For its efforts, Bank of America has been honored by the president of the United States, the U.S. and local chambers of commerce, *Fortune* magazine, and others as one of America's most socially responsible organizations.

FIRST INTERSTATE

First Interstate Bancorp, with assets of more than $50 billion, is one of the largest banking companies in the United States. It is the modern version of a multistate banking organization conceived by A.P. Giannini during the early years of the twentieth century. When federal legislation enacted in 1927 restricted the operation of any one bank to a single state, Giannini formed Transamerica Corporation the following year to serve, in part, as the beginning of a national banking system.

The first bank that eventually would become a First Interstate Bank was acquired by Transamerica in 1930. By the 1940s Transamerica also owned banks in Arizona, California, Nevada, and Washington. By year-end 1955 Transamerica owned seven banks with 208 banking offices in five states. In 1956, facing the imminent passage of the Bank Holding Company Act, which was designed to restrict bank holding company activities, Transamerica completed a $52-million stock offering and used the proceeds to buy 18 additional banks in six states.

Passage of the act, however, caused management to split Transamerica into two parts, banking and nonbanking. In 1958 Firstamerica Corporation took over operation of 23 Transamerica banks in 11 western states. The following year Firstamerica acquired California Bank, which in 1961 was merged with First Western Bank and Trust Company to form United California Bank (UCB). Also in 1961 Firstamerica changed its name to Western Bancorporation and by the close of the 1960s had more than 600 offices in 339 communities in 11 states. Assets exceeded $10 billion.

The ultimate move to unite all the banks in the then 11-state territory came with the adoption of a new and common name. On June 1, 1981, Western Bancorporation and its 21 banks became known as First Interstate Bancorp. The nearly 900 offices in 450 communities, plus 40 offices in

First Interstate Bancorp Chairman and Chief Executive Officer Edward M. Carson.

major cities around the world, unveiled new signs identifying them as First Interstate banks.

In 1982 First Interstate made banking history by introducing the nation's first bank franchise program. Under the program, franchised banks would use the First Interstate name, advertising, signs, common products, and computer services, while retaining local ownership and management.

In January 1985 First Interstate Bank of California was restructured to segregate the two traditional lines of banking—retail and wholesale—into two separate entities. Today First Interstate Bank of California focuses on the California retail and corporate middle markets. A new bank, First Interstate Bank, Ltd., delivers wholesale banking services throughout the First Interstate system worldwide.

First Interstate has consolidated its expansion across the western states and currently operates 20 affiliate banks in 13 states: Alaska, Arizona, California, Colorado, Idaho, Montana, Nevada, New Mexico, Oregon, Texas, Utah, Washington, and Wyoming. In addition, franchised banks operate in Colorado, Hawaii, Iowa, Louisiana, Montana, North Dakota, South Dakota, and Wyoming.

Today First Interstate is a banking company that utilizes more than 1,100 domestic offices and 31 international offices in 16 countries to serve consumers and business customers. It serves more than 5 million households in some 626 communities in the western United States.

First Interstate's 20 banks in 13 Western states extend their services through one of the most extensive ATM networks in the country. First Interstate has also expanded its reach to an additional eight states through a unique franchise program involving 29 banks.

A. Foster Higgins & Co., Inc.

A. Foster Higgins & Co., Inc., is, technically, a fairly new firm, having been officially formed on January 1, 1988. Nevertheless, Foster Higgins, as it is generally known, has a long and distinguished record in human resources consulting, with a primary focus on the role of employee benefits.

The firm is a wholly owned subsidiary of Johnson & Higgins, a privately owned, internationally prominent general lines insurance company. Founded in New York in 1845, Johnson & Higgins has been in the employee benefits field since 1925. Foster Higgins was formed when Johnson & Higgins spun off its employee benefits department into a new subsidiary. On the day it was formed, the new firm—named after Andrew Foster Higgins, one of the founders of the parent company—already had a history of more than 60 years of experience in the human resources consulting field.

Foster Higgins is based in New York but is nationwide in scope, with 10 regional centers across the United States. These regions are supported by a national research office located in Princeton, New Jersey. The firm has been in California since 1925, with regional offices in San Francisco and Los Angeles. The latter, home of the Southwest region, has a satellite office in Costa Mesa.

Foster Higgins specializes in designing, implementing, and maintaining all types of employee benefit plans ranging from basic medical and dental coverage to highly sophisticated executive packages. Its services are divided into seven practice areas: retirement income, flexible compensation, communication, retiree health care, health and welfare, health care delivery systems, and human resources administration.

Critical to the firm's client mission is the ability to identify emerging benefit issues and foresee their implications.

The Foster Higgins legal research group maintains constant contact with Capitol Hill and key agencies to anticipate the actions of Congress and regulatory agencies. The group interprets legal and regulatory activity and provides technical materials to support the work of the firm's consulting staff. The firm's offices are kept up-to-the-minute on news and background details by its BeneNet information network. Regular publications keep clients thoroughly briefed on compliance issues and other key topics.

Foster Higgins also conducts several annual surveys, including the *Health Care Benefits Survey*, widely recognized as the most authoritative in the field. This survey gives the firm's consultants and clients a wealth of current data for assessing the effectiveness of cost-management measures and tracking trends in program design.

The firm's Southwest region has a staff of more than 100 people. About two-thirds are professionals, including actuaries and attorneys. The client base primarily includes corporations in the financial, industrial, and service fields, many of which are *Fortune* 500 and/or prominent Los Angeles-based companies. Some have been Foster Higgins clients for decades. At least one major relationship dates back more than a half-century.

Foster Higgins consultants specialize in human resources and employee benefit programs. Yet as a firm they make a point of stepping back to take in the broader view. They see the implications of the changing world economy for their clients' business and human resources planning, this year and years from now. They help clients visualize a new role—one based in reality—for employer-sponsored benefit programs.

Whether involved in direct consulting assignments or in monitoring industry developments, the people of A. Foster Higgins & Co., Inc., are dedicated to helping clients achieve their business objectives through the most effective use of their human resources.

Since its inception in 1988, Foster Higgins has maintained an exceptional record in human resources consulting.

IBM wafers and chips.
Photo by Erich Hartmann-Magnum

SANWA BANK CALIFORNIA

As the seventh-largest bank in the state, Los Angeles-based Sanwa Bank California is recognized as a solid competitor among the state's top tier of banks. While it offers a blend of services that rivals banks of any size, its corporate philosophy emphasizes the kind of service that is usually associated with community banks. To understand these "best of both worlds" characteristics, one need only consider Sanwa's affiliation with one of the world's largest banks and its long history of friendly acquisitions of smaller banks that retained their culture of local branch autonomy and personal attention.

Sanwa's commitment to California dates back to the last half of the nineteenth century, when previous banks were opened in San Francisco and such Southern California locations as Santa Ana and Pasadena. Today, after a series of mergers and acquisitions, the bank has over $7 billion in assets and more than 100 branches throughout the state. Given the importance of California in international commerce, the relationship between the parent bank, The Sanwa Bank, Limited, and its California subsidiary will clearly become even stronger as Pacific Rim trade expands.

Sanwa's new headquarters since January 1991 is an office tower at the corner of Figueroa Street and Wilshire Boulevard, in the heart of the downtown financial district. The bank occupies 220,000 square feet of space and is the anchor tenant in the 52-story building, which commands a key position in the Los Angeles skyline. When announcing the move, Mark Yoda, president and chief executive officer, said that it emphasized the bank's growing, long-term presence in California and demonstrated its commitment to Los Angeles. This is particularly important in light of the city's prominence as the focal point of business activity in both Southern California and the statewide market, and as the gateway to the Pacific Rim.

Business banking accounts for most of the bank's loan portfolio. With such a large commitment to business over the years, Sanwa Bank has been an active participant in the broad-based and vigorous economy that has characterized California throughout recent history.

Although perhaps best known for middle-market commercial lending, the bank also has specialized expertise in personal trust services, employee benefit trust, interim construction financing, international services, cash management, and treasury management. Whether it is the acquisition of manufacturing equipment and other capital goods, or financing for multifamily residential developments, industrial facilities, and office buildings, Sanwa Bank has the capacity to meet most borrowing needs and the wherewithal to structure financing packages for businesses large and small.

Meanwhile, with its philosophy of fast, courteous service, the bank attracts increasing numbers of individuals throughout the state, including the Greater Los Angeles and Orange County areas, where it has a network of more than 60 offices. Additional offices are planned for the future.

With its long history of customer service, Sanwa Bank California could well become the bank of choice for more and more Californians, whether longtime residents or new arrivals to the Golden State.

Sanwa Bank's new headquarters at the corner of Figueroa Street and Wilshire Boulevard.

1st Business Bank

From the beginning, the four bankers who founded 1st Business Bank knew exactly what they wanted to do—build a bank that would focus on one market and service it better than anyone else. Robert W. Kummer, Jr., Joseph P. Sanford, W. Peter Bohn, and Thomas F. Savage, were career bankers who had spent some 20 years each at a major California bank.

All were experienced in serving mid-sized companies, a market they felt was badly neglected. As Kummer explains, "Major banks focus mainly on *Fortune* 500 companies and the consumer market. Middle market business is usually handled at the branch level by less experienced officers, while senior officers work with the major customers. In addition, bank officers are often promoted and transferred, precluding the formation of the personal, long-standing relationships that business owners long to have."

Displaying the same entrepreneurial instincts as the customers they served, 1st Business Bank's founders left their senior-level positions, put together a business plan, and within a mere two months raised $8.5 million in capital. On May 1, 1981, the new bank welcomed the first customers to its headquarters on the ground floor of the completely restored One Bunker Hill building in downtown Los Angeles, an historic 13-story structure built in 1931. The building has since been renamed the 1st Business Bank Building and its granite walls and marble interiors epitomize the bank's traditional style of business banking.

Kummer became chairman of the new bank, with Sanford as president and Bohn and Savage as executive vice presidents. They continue to hold those titles, which are a bit misleading, inasmuch as they function more as a team of equals, with all four serving on the bank's board of directors. In conversations they frequently refer to each other as "my partners."

A fifth "partner" joined the team in 1989, when John E. Anderson purchased all the outstanding stock for $86 million, three times its book value. One of California's most prominent and successful business leaders, Anderson is an attorney, a certified public accountant, and holds a master's degree from the Harvard Graduate School of Business. He founded and is the sole owner of Topa Equities, Ltd., a diversified holding company with major interests in more than 20 companies. He is also well known for his many civic and philanthropic activities, as exemplified by the Anderson Graduate School of Management at UCLA, which was named in his honor in 1988.

As founding director, Anderson shared management's concern about the possible acquisition by a major foreign or domestic bank and a resulting change of focus. The acceptance of his offer to buy it guaranteed the continued independence of 1st Business Bank and its unswerving commitment to become, in Kummer's words, "one of the best independent business banks in the country."

After completing its first decade, 1st Business Bank was already well on its way to meeting its lofty objective. Profitable from its first month of operation, it has grown impressively, setting records year after year in deposits, assets, and earnings. During the 1980s it posted gains of 20 percent or more in assets and earnings for nine consecutive years, and recorded 34 consecutive increases in quarterly earnings.

By virtually every yardstick used to measure the performance and stability of financial institutions, 1st Business Bank stands out. It consistently ranks among the top 25 percent of its peer group in performance statistics published by the Federal Deposit Insurance Corporation and the Federal Reserve. With capital and reserves nearly double the industry standard, it is one of the nation's best capitalized banking companies. It is also frequently cited as a role model for other independent banks. Management is justifiably proud of what it calls its "fortress financial statement," a symbol of strength that is one of the five basic concepts that form the foundation of its operating philosophy.

The bank has achieved these results without venturing into such areas as brokered CDs; deposit concentrations; or foreign, energy, or leveraged

The 1st Business Bank management team, from left to right: Thomas F. Savage, executive vice president; Joseph P. Sanford, president; John E. Anderson, vice chairman; Robert W. Kummer, Jr., chairman; and W. Peter Bohn, executive vice president.

of excellence has continued into the 1990s and has earned 1st Business Bank "A Quality" and "Premier Performing" ratings by the Findley Reports and an "A+" rating by Sheshunoff & Company, the highest awards given by these respected rating services. The bank is also listed by Sheshunoff in *The Highest Rated Banks in America.*

Another of the bank's basic concepts is its "clear market focus" on a single market—midsize companies. These are typically owner-managed businesses with annual sales ranging between $3 million and $100 million. The bank serves more than 1,000 such companies,

buyout loans. Its loan to deposit ratio remains at the extremely sound 50 to 60 percent level, and nearly half of 1st Business Bank's assets are invested in highly liquid U.S. Government securities, government guaranteed mortgage-backed securities, and short-term money market instruments.

about equally divided among manufacturers, service and professional organizations, and wholesalers and distributors.

They include some of the best managed and most successful companies in the state. Nearly all

Loan performance has also been excellent. In the 1980s loan losses averaged less than $50,000 a year, placing its portfolio in the top 5 percent among the more than 12,000 banks in the U.S. The reserve for loan losses is more than double the industry average, which is especially impressive in view of the bank's minimal loan loss record. The bank has also done an exemplary job of controlling loan delinquencies and nonperforming loans through varying economic cycles during the past decade.

This remarkable across-the-board record

have come from major banks, attracted by 1st Business Bank's reputation for service and responsiveness, and by the same entrepreneurial management style that characterizes their own operations. As one customer puts it: "They think more like businesspeople than bankers."

To these customers the bank delivers the same high quality service that major banks reserve only for General Motors or IBM. Delivering *"Fortune 500 services"* is another of the five basic concepts, has led more than one observer to dub 1st Business Bank as "the J.P. Morgan of the middle market," a high tribute indeed.

A wide range of borrowing programs is offered, including loans for general working capital purposes, equipment purchases, construction and commercial mortgage financing, as well as accounts receivable financing; revolving credit agreements; lines of credit; and equipment leasing.

The bank also provides its customers with complete international services, sophisticated cash management programs, and investment and consulting services. Special services range from daily messenger pickup to individually designed operating services and accounting systems based on state-of-the-art technology. The bank's personal banking services are also designed uniquely for professionals, business owners, and corporate executives.

A fourth basic concept is hiring and retaining "superior bankers." The bank motivates its people with a highly professional environment, performance bonuses, and special awards for customer service. As a result, morale is high, turnover is minimal, and every employee has a vested interest in the success of the bank's clients.

The fifth trademark of 1st Business Bank is "hands-on management." Despite rapid expansion and growth, the members of the senior management team each continue to have face to face contact with the bank's customers and are always available to help any client solve a problem or discuss an important business decision.

1st Business Bank has also established an excellent record of community service. It was a founding member of the California Community Reinvestment Corporation, a consortium of banks formed to finance low-income housing projects. It also makes regular contributions to a variety of worthwhile civic and charitable inner-city groups, and many of its officers and directors hold leadership positions in nonprofit organizations, dedicated to improving the Los Angeles community.

The growth of the bank has taken place without merger or acquisition. During the 1980s it opened regional offices in Orange County, the South Bay, and the San Fernando Valley. Additional offices are planned for Century City, the Inland Empire, San Diego County, and eventually Northern California. A trust department is also planned to serve as trustee of the pension and profit sharing plans of its client firms and to meet the personal trust needs of business owners and professionals.

The bankers who founded 1st Business Bank back in 1981 are proud of the remarkable performance that has vaulted it into the ranks of the top 10 percent of both U.S. and California banks. But Bob Kummer, Joe Sanford, Peter Bohn, and Tom Savage have no intention of resting on their laurels or riding off into the sunset. All have management contracts extending well into the 1990s.

Before the turn of the century, they, along with owner and partner John Anderson, fully expect to pass the one-billion-dollar mark in total assets, without deviating from the philosophy that has brought them so far so quickly.

The historic 1st Business Bank building, built by Southern California Edison Company in 1930, stands at the gateway to the Los Angeles downtown financial district.

SEARCH WEST

As a new division president of international giant Hansen Industries PLC, Keith Niemann was eager to show results quickly. "We met with him on a Friday," relates Search West President Bob Cowan, "and he described his pressing need for a V.P. of manufacturing for the Southern California operation. The difficulty was that he was leaving on a business trip the following Wednesday, and had to conduct initial interviews before his departure."

Four days later Niemann was in Search West's private offices interviewing five highly qualified candidates for his confidential opening. Three of them were invited to meet him at the plant when he returned from his trip and within a few days he hired his first choice.

"I was recruited for my position by another firm, but I was so impressed with the professionalism of Search West that I decided to work with them instead," says Niemann. "They personally visited my facility and took the time to understand our needs. Believe me, there was no sacrifice in quality in their urgent response to our problem."

A short time later, Niemann again turned to Search West to find a V.P. of marketing and a V.P. of sales, and has recommended Search West to other divisions of his company as well.

Search West was founded in 1966 by Lawrence and Robert Cowan, both graduates of the prestigious Wharton School of Finance at the University of Pennsylvania. While neither had been involved in executive search before, they had worked in service-oriented businesses.

"From our experience, we knew that satisfying the client means everything," comments chairman/chief executive officer Larry Cowan, "and our background helped us understand the needs of a variety of industries and business environments."

This client-centered orientation has been a major factor in building Search West into the largest executive search firm in Los Angeles County. In addition to their facilities in Century City, Encino, and West Covina, the company operates large regional offices in other areas of Southern California, including Ventura, Orange, and San Bernardino counties. In 1984 the company started their successful San Francisco branch.

The firm's original staff of about a dozen search professionals has now grown to more than 200. While the bulk of their recruiting efforts are confined to California, positions have been filled across the country and abroad. Because of its strategic position on the Pacific Rim, Search West sees Southern California playing an ever-increasing role in the world economy, and has already served a number of Asian companies in the U.S.

With its large staff of recruiters, Search West offers client companies expertise in a wide range of industries and disciplines. The firm has specialties covering virtually all manufacturing industries, including high-tech electronics and computers, major food and chemical companies, metal fabrication, plastics, printing and publishing, and consumer products of all kinds.

In addition, the firm has numerous clients in the burgeoning service sector, encompassing banking, insurance, retail, health care, hospitality, entertainment, and financial services. Search West account executives fill positions in engineering and production, financial control, administration, data processing/MIS, sales, and marketing.

President Bob Cowan emphasizes that one corporate goal of Search West is to "become an integral part of recruiting and job search strategies to help client companies grow and advance candidates' careers."

That means working closely with decision makers throughout the entire recruiting process, from establishing initial search parameters to assuring a smooth transition when the candidate steps into the new position. In addition to identifying and screening qualified candidates, the firm provides counsel and advice to employers on how to conduct interviews and develop compensation packages to satisfy the particular needs of each recruit.

Search West founders Larry and Bob Cowan (standing) discuss recruiting strategies.

Search West also maintains interview rooms in its own offices to provide clients with complete privacy during the initial screening process. In this way, employers can use their time most efficiently by seeing three or four prospects without interruptions, and make immediate, back-to-back comparisons of their qualifications. Candidates also appreciate meeting employers initially on "neutral ground" where they know confidentiality will be preserved.

After 25 years, the most gratifying part of the executive search business to Larry and Bob is the way that their company has significantly touched the lives of so many people. "Over the years, many executives placed by Search West have returned to the company for help in recruiting key professionals for their own departments," observes Larry. "That's the best evidence that we're doing the job right."

THE CAPITAL GROUP

The Capital Group, headquartered in Los Angeles, is one of the oldest and largest money management organizations in the world. For six decades it has served millions of investors—individuals as well as leading corporations and institutions throughout the world. Among them, the companies in The Capital Group manage some $60 billion in stocks, bonds, and convertible securities, with about $10 billion of that huge sum in international or global investments.

Most of those assets are under the supervision of two firms, Capital Research and Management Company and Capital Guardian Trust Company, which are based in Los Angeles. There are seven investment management companies in all—four headquartered in the U.S. and three outside the U.S. They draw on the organization's global research network, made up of five research companies, for most of the information on which their investment decisions are based.

The Capital organization has research and investment management offices in cities around the world, including Tokyo, Hong Kong, Singapore, Geneva, London, New York, Washington, D.C., San Francisco, and Los Angeles.

There are three other companies in The Capital Group, each fulfilling essential functions: American Funds Distributors is the national distributor for the mutual funds managed by Capital Research; American Funds Service Company, based in Brea, California, and San Antonio, Texas, provides services to the shareholders of those

mutual funds; and Capital Management Services is a venture capital manager.

The Capital Group, which is employee-owned, traces its roots to 1931 and to a man named Jonathan B. Lovelace. As the 1920s drew to a close, Lovelace, a partner in a Detroit investment firm, differed sharply with his partners as to the investment outlook. He considered 1929 prices greatly inflated.

Lovelace left that organization in 1929 and moved to Southern California, forming the firm that was to become Capital Research and Management Company. Today Capital Research oversees some $35 billion in assets, primarily for the shareholders of The American Funds Group of mutual funds. These shareholders include over 2 million individuals as well as thousands of corporations, banks, trust companies, insurance companies, and retirement plans.

Capital Guardian Trust Company, organized in 1968, provides fiduciary and investment management services to institutional accounts in a number of countries. It manages assets of more than $20 billion. The firm's distinguished list of clients includes many *Fortune* 500 companies as well as prominent foundations and college endowment funds. Nearly half of America's 50 largest corporate retirement plans have selected Capital Guardian to manage part of their assets.

The Capital Group organization has been active internationally since the mid-1950s. Capital International S.A., the first of its non-U.S. invest-

Left to right: Jon B. Lovelace, chairman of Capital Research and Management Company; Robert G. Kirby, chairman of Capital Guardian Trust Company; and Robert B. Egelston, chairman of The Capital Group.

ment management companies, was formed in Geneva in 1963. Capital International, Inc. (U.S.), Capital International Limited (London), and Capital International K.K. (Tokyo) were formed more recently to help meet the growing needs of institutional and individual investors around the world. Together the four companies supervise assets of more than $4 billion, including mutual funds, pension funds, and government accounts in many nations.

In recent years the Capital organization's activities—and its assets under management—outside the United States have increased at a particularly fast pace, and that trend may well continue. As a result of its global involvement for so many years, the firm is uniquely positioned to take advantage of rapidly changing economic conditions worldwide.

Few organizations can match Capital's extensive, time-tested research capabilities. Over 30 years ago it began building a worldwide research effort staffed by its own people. One-third of its more than 100 investment professionals are based outside the United States. An annual research budget in excess of $35 million finances thousands of visits to companies in more than 40 countries.

Fluent in over 20 languages, Capital's investment people travel millions of miles each year interviewing corporate executives, industry specialists, economists, and government officials. They examine financial statements, reports, and

publications for facts and opinions on companies and the economic and political environments in which they operate. The results of this comprehensive effort are available only to the organization.

That depth of commitment to research has been one of the most important factors in the consistent success of The Capital Group. A second has been a focus on value. The firm's investment philosophy has been to seek fundamental values at reasonable prices.

Another key factor that has contributed to the organization's investment record is a unique method of portfolio management—the multiple portfolio counselor system. Each fund's investment portfolio is divided into several segments, and each segment is managed by a different individual. This enables each counselor to invest according to his or her strongest convictions, within the fund's objectives. Other key factors include the concentration of a large staff of proven professionals on a small number of accounts, and Capital's ability to attract and retain key people.

More than two-thirds of the key decision-making professionals who have joined the organization over the past 20 years are still there. It is these men and women who have brought The Capital Group to its preeminent place in the investment management field through their commitment to value and research, the foundation stones put in place by Jonathan Lovelace half a century ago.

The scope of Capital's global activities can be seen from this map. It shows the countries where its professionals made more than 4,000 research calls on companies, government officials, and other experts in the past year. The red dots show Capital's major offices.

PRICE WATERHOUSE

Were they alive today, Samuel Lowell Price and Edwin Waterhouse would probably not recognize the accounting firm they founded in the mid-nineteenth century in London, England. In the closing years of the twentieth century, Price Waterhouse stands as a leading worldwide professional organization of business consultants, tax advisers, management consultants, accountants, and auditors.

Through a global network of firms practicing in over 400 offices in more than 100 countries, Price Waterhouse professionals provide advisory services to major global companies, growing businesses, individuals, nonprofit organizations, and government entities. In the United States alone, where the firm opened its first office in 1890, there are more than 100 offices offering a range of professional services designed to meet the needs of almost any size company in virtually every industry.

There are more than 13,000 Price Waterhouse men and women in the U.S. offices, and more than 40,000 in more than 400 offices worldwide. Annual revenues exceed $2.5 billion. Considered by many business observers as the preeminent firm in its profession, its client list includes more of the Dow Jones Industrials and *Forbes* 100 largest multinationals than any other firm.

The growth and success of Price Waterhouse is primarily the result of the operating philosophy to which it has long been committed. First and foremost is what senior partners of the firm refer to

as "an obsession with client service." It means thinking, eating, breathing, and living client service, and it is expressed in three ways: professional excellence, with services provided by recognized specialists in various fields; personalized attention, by anticipating, identifying, and meeting or exceeding client needs; and creating competitive advantages for clients, contributing to their growth and profitability.

That commitment to client service led directly to the opening of a Los Angeles office in 1911. Many clients of the San Francisco office, opened seven years earlier, had Los Angeles operations, and in 1911 Price Waterhouse decided to open a branch office to better serve them. In addition, Los Angeles was beginning to come into its own as a business center. At this time Los Angeles encompassed an area of 61 square miles and had a population of about 300,000 people.

A man named Ismay Graham Pattinson from the Price Waterhouse London office was dispatched to Los Angeles and, aided only by a typist, began operating from an office in the Title Insurance Building on Spring Street. Price Waterhouse thus became the first national accounting firm to open a Southern California office. Today more than 1,000 Price Waterhouse professionals serve the Los Angeles community.

Early Los Angeles clients included Southern California Edison, Southern California Gas Company, Eastman Kodak, National Cash Register, the California Institute of Technology, and the Los Angeles Department of Water and Power. Los Angeles

was also becoming the home of the fledgling entertainment industry, and many of its pioneers became Price Waterhouse clients. The firm was retained by the Academy of Motion Picture Arts and Sciences in 1927, and seven years later began handling the balloting process for the Oscars, to assure objectivity, secrecy, and credibility. The relationship continues to this day.

During the 1930s Price Waterhouse began its association with a then-unknown cartoonist named Walt Disney. Other movie industry clients included Charlie Chaplin, Douglas Fairbanks and Mary Pickford, and the Samuel Goldwyn Company.

The 1932 Olympic Games in Los Angeles brought the firm another unique challenge: establishing financial systems and controls for ticket sales. They worked so well that, out of a total of 3 million tickets, only 142 remained unaccounted for, and the net cash difference was a mere $125.90.

Price Waterhouse has long recognized that its success, and the success of its clients, is dependent on its ability to anticipate the expanding, full-service requirements of companies competing and growing in complex and multifaceted business environments. At first, the Los Angeles office dealt primarily with partnerships, attorneys, and start-up firms. But, as Southern California has continued to grow and diversify, the firm has kept pace. Its tax practice, begun as a service for wealthy people in the motion picture industry, was one of its early areas of specialty. Another, providing management advisory service, was first offered on a formal basis in 1954. As high technology came to Southern California, Price Waterhouse expanded its capabilities in order to serve such high-tech companies as Bell Industries, Ashton-Tate, and Caltech's Jet Propulsion Laboratory. The Los Angeles practice

is headed by L. Dale Crandall, managing partner, who oversees the offices located in downtown Los Angeles, Century City, Woodland Hills, Long Beach, Newport Beach, and Riverside. Also headquartered in Los Angeles is Kenneth G. Docter, managing partner of the firm's 22-office West region, which comprises Alaska, Arizona, California, Hawaii, Idaho, Montana, Nevada, Oregon, Utah, Washington, and Wyoming.

With more than 70 partners, Price Waterhouse Los Angeles provides a wide range of specialized services, in addition to accounting, auditing, tax, and information systems consulting. They include entertainment and media, real estate, financial services, aerospace and government contracting, high technology, retail, Japanese/Pacific Rim and international businesses, litigation consulting, employee benefits services, strategic management consulting, valuation services, and mergers and acquisitions. A full range of business and industry-specific services are available for most Southern California businesses.

The firm has had a long-standing tradition of involvement in professional, community, and charitable organizations. Staff members at all levels are encouraged to give back to the communities generous portions of their time, talents, and financial resources.

The firm's early commitment to the Los Angeles area bodes well for the future. With California's emergence as a world economic center and with the growing importance of the Pacific Rim, Price Waterhouse is uniquely positioned to provide knowledge and experience to businesses of all sizes entering the international marketplace through Southern California.

(Left to right) Japanese business partners Richard H. Izumi and John J. Bonacci, Jr.

(Left to right) Tax partners Bruce A. Daigh, Eugene I. Krieger, and J.J. Coneys.

ROCKWELL INTERNATIONAL CORPORATION

Skill and teamwork are the hallmarks of Rockwell's heavy-duty transmission facility at Laurinburg, North Carolina.

An edition of the *Los Angeles Times* rolls off a Rockwell Colorliner press at a rate of 75,000 copies an hour.

ockwell International Corporation, based in El Segundo, California, is a diversified, $12-billion, high-technology company engaged in four principal businesses—electronics, aerospace, automotive, and graphics. These diverse businesses are leaders in the major markets they serve, and each makes important contributions to the company's growth.

Rockwell's aerospace business includes military aircraft, manned and unmanned space systems, rocket engines, and advanced space-based surveillance systems.

Electronics operations cover a broad range of commercial and defense electronics systems and products principally for precision guidance and control; tactical weapons; command, control, communications and intelligence; precision navigation; avionics; telecommunications; semiconductor and other electronic devices; and industrial automation.

Automotive includes various components for heavy- and medium-duty trucks, buses, trailers, and heavy-duty off-highway vehicles. The company is among the world's leading producers of these components. Automotive also manufactures and markets components and systems for light trucks and passenger cars.

The automotive operation is a global one, with development, production, and marketing facilities in 15 countries.

In its graphics activities, Rockwell manufactures and markets high-speed printing presses and related equipment for newspapers and the commercial printing market. Rockwell leads the world in the manufacture of newspaper production systems. Two of every three daily newspapers in the United States are printed on presses manufactured by the company, and the largest and most prestigious newspapers in 95 other countries are printed on Rockwell's Goss presses.

Rockwell operates some 150 plants and research and development facilities worldwide, and employs more than 100,000 people. About 20 percent of them are based at its facilities in 24 foreign countries. Rockwell ranks in the top 35 among the *Fortune* 500 companies.

A number of Rockwell businesses, founded by pio-

neers in their respective fields, can trace their heritage to the formative years of such industries as high-speed newspaper printing, radio, aircraft, trucking, rockets, and space exploration.

Major predecessor firms of Rockwell were North American Aviation, Inc., a prominent aircraft manufacturing firm founded in 1928, and Rockwell-Standard Corporation, an independent producer of automotive components established in 1953. These two companies merged in 1967 to become North American Rockwell Corporation. The name of the company was changed to Rockwell International Corporation in 1973.

Other well-known American industrial enterprises that became part of the company include Miehle-Goss-Dexter, Inc., formed in 1957; Collins Radio Company, founded in 1933; and the Allen-Bradley Company, formed in 1903.

Building on the strengths of these pioneer enterprises, Rockwell has evolved from a collection of separate companies into a major, multi-industrial international corporation.

The Rockwell name comes from Colonel W.F. Rockwell, who reorganized a bankrupt Oshkosh, Wisconsin, axle company in 1919. Nearly wiped out a few years later due to a downturn in the automotive market, Rockwell vowed never again to allow the problems of one business to nearly ruin him, thus launching the philosophy of diversification that remains the company's cornerstone. Today it is clearly evidenced by the balance that exists between Rockwell's government and commercial customers.

Domestically, Rockwell has facilities scattered across 47 states. While the headquarters of a number of its major businesses are elsewhere, the Greater Los Angeles area has been home to its aerospace and aircraft operations for more than a half century. North American Aviation, founded in 1928, opened a new plant in Los Angeles in 1936 to manufacture planes for the U.S. Army Air Corps and has been building military aircraft ever since.

Today all three of the major aerospace divisions are Southern California-based. North American Aviation is based in El Segundo, the

Rocketdyne Division in Canoga Park, and the Space Transportation Systems Division in Downey. Rockwell is one of the five largest employers in Los Angeles County and ranks second in Orange County.

In space, Rockwell has established itself as a leader in the development of spacecraft and propulsion systems. The company had a major role in the Apollo program for which, under contract to the National Aeronautics and Space Administration (NASA), it provided the Apollo command and service modules that carried men to the moon and back; the second stage of the three-stage Saturn V launch vehicle; and all of the rocket engines on Saturn V.

The company continues to play a prominent role in the United States manned-flight space program. Rockwell is the builder of the Space Shuttle *Orbiter* and its main engines, and performs mission support operations for NASA's Johnson Space Center in Houston.

The next U.S. man-in-space program, the Space Station, is currently scheduled to begin operating during the late 1990s. Rockwell will supply the Space Station's electric power generation and distribution system.

Many of the company's aerospace programs are pointed toward the twenty-first century. One such program involves the National AeroSpace Plane (NASP), a national initiative managed by the Department of Defense and NASA. NASP would advance the state of air travel by operating at speeds of up to 25 times the speed of sound in the upper atmosphere or functioning as a space vehicle by ascending into low earth orbit. Rockwell is the leader of a consortium of companies chosen to develop the NASP.

The eyes of the people of

Rockwell are focused on the future in other ways as well, as evidenced by its commitment to the environment and to the communities where it operates. The company has adopted a detailed and specific environmental plan, outlining its goals, policies, and programs, as "an expression of our concern for the physical health and safety of our employees and neighbors, and for the well-being of our common environment."

Rockwell and its people are determined to take actions that contribute to the vitality of community life and are involved in a broad range of activities, many of them focused on education. One such program is the Rockwell-sponsored Advanced Career Training in which high school students are offered a head start in the business world. Working in a real business environment, students operate sophisticated equipment and learn high-technology skills from volunteer instructors who are experts in their career fields.

Annually the company, its employees, and the Rockwell International Corporation Trust contribute millions of dollars for education, the United Way, culture and the arts, civic and community projects, human services, and health projects all across the United States and in foreign countries.

The well-known slogan of Rockwell International Corporation is ". . . where science gets down to business." But that's only part of the story. The rest is summed up in these words from a recent Community Involvement Report: "Our efforts boil down to being responsible and caring. Getting personally involved. Working in partnership with our communities. Reaching a little higher."

Flight testing of the X-31 enhanced maneuverability aircraft began in October 1990.

The Space Shuttle *Discovery* successfully deploys NASA's Hubble Space Telescope.

BATEMEN EICHLER, HILL RICHARDS

The Los Angeles-based securities brokerage firm of Bateman Eichler, Hill Richards (BEHR) traces its origins to two firms, both formed during the early 1930s. In 1931 Carey S. Hill and John R. Richards founded Hill Richards, and two years later Henry M. Bateman and Rudolph J. Eichler launched Bateman Eichler.

For more than 30 years the two firms, located just one block apart on Spring Street in Los Angeles, grew at an almost equal rate. During that period Bateman Eichler had acquired a number of smaller firms, while most of the Hill Richards growth had been internal. In 1966 the two firms merged and became Bateman Eichler, Hill Richards, Incorporated.

In 1982 the firm was acquired by a subsidiary of Kemper Corporation, Kemper Financial Companies, Inc. (KFC), a nonoperating holding company with other major subsidiaries in life insurance, property/casualty insurance, and reinsurance. KFC, headquartered in Chicago, operates a life insurance company, several asset management and financial products companies, and five regional broker/dealer and investment banking firms, including Bateman Eichler, Hill Richards.

As a member of the Kemper family, Bateman Eichler can offer its clients the security and credibility that come with being part of a giant financial organization. Overall, Kemper Corporation assets exceed $14 billion, and Kemper Financial Companies manages more than $60 billion in assets. The Kemper organization, long recognized as a pillar of strength in the insurance industry, has a reputation for conducting its activities in a highly ethical, lawful, and responsible manner. Its conservative yet innovative image is consistent with the reputation enjoyed by Bateman Eichler and its sister firms.

In 1990 Kemper announced a major restructuring of its broker/dealers, establishing each broker/dealer as a separate division under the Kemper Securities Group, Inc. This included Bateman Eichler, Hill Richards and its four other sister divisions: Blunt Ellis & Loewi (Milwaukee), Prescott Ball & Turben (Cleveland), Boettcher & Co. (Denver), and Lovett Underwood Neuhaus & Webb (Houston). Together these five divisions comprise the 11th-largest network of broker/dealers in the country. Each member firm enjoys a unique advantage in today's marketplace, a locally based, autonomous management team with the strength and resources of the Kemper organization behind them.

Bateman Eichler operates in seven states, with 29 offices located in California, Washington, Oregon, Alaska, Hawaii, Nevada, and Arizona. Nearly 500 account executives serve its client base, which has grown steadily over the years. It places a major emphasis on hiring and retaining quality people by offering superior accessibility to the management of the firm and its headquarters support personnel.

An essential element in the success of any investment firm is the development of reliable market information. Kemper Security's well-respected research department has focused its attention for many years on a broad range of industries and

In all its dealings with clients, BEHR emphasizes five important investment essentials: tradition, stability, investment opportunities, market information, and personal service.

businesses throughout the Pacific Rim, including aerospace, biotechnology, entertainment, and financial services. It regularly publishes its recommended list, which offers recommendations on the most promising companies.

The firm's own proprietary research activities are supplemented by many well-known secondary research sources.

The services offered by Bateman Eichler are by no means limited to stocks and bonds. The firm also provides a full range of both personal and corporate investment services. For the individual investor, those services include cash-management accounts, money market funds, mutual funds, unit investment trusts, certificates of deposit, insurance and annuities, limited partnerships, retirement plans, commodities, precious metals, and portfolio evaluation.

The firm also has an assortment of investment services available to help corporations, institutions, and small businesses achieve their financial objectives. Its investment banking services include public offerings, private placements, mergers and acquisitions, leveraged buyouts, bridge financing, advisory services, fairness opinions, partnership management, valuations, real estate finance, and leasing and secured asset financing. Other Bateman Eichler corporate

services include consulting, pension plans, and stock option financing.

For municipalities and public institutions, the firm's services include certificates of participation, tax and revenue anticipation, notes, equipment leasing, and a broad range of bonds.

The people of Bateman Eichler, Hill Richards have a strong commitment to the communities in which they serve. The firm has lent its support to numerous community events. For example, it was instrumental in bringing to Los Angeles the annual Wall Street Basketball Challenge for the benefit of the Multiple Sclerosis Foundation.

In all its dealings with clients, BEHR emphasizes five important investment essentials. These include such qualities and services as tradition, stability, investment opportunities, market information, and personal service, the most important being personal service, defined as an abiding concern for the client's needs, commitment to the client's best interests, and timely communication.

It is a combination that has been working successfully since 1931. Today, firmly entrenched in one of the world's soundest and most rapidly growing economic areas, the people of Bateman Eichler, Hill Richards and Kemper look forward to building the firm's future on those same essential ingredients of success.

Bateman Eichler, Hill Richards provides a full range of both personal and corporate investment services.

U.S. TRUST

T he name "U.S. Trust Company" may be an unfamiliar one to many Southern Californians, but it is, nonetheless, the oldest and among the most highly respected trust companies in the nation. Founded in 1853, U.S. Trust Corporation, a publicly owned company headquarted in New York, is a leading financial institution providing investment management, trust, and banking services to individuals, corporations, foundations, and endowment funds throughout the country. U.S. Trust is premier among the trust companies of its size, with a long history of steady growth while remaining independent.

Rather than competing across the entire spectrum of financial services, U.S. Trust focuses on opportunities in tightly defined specialty markets. In addition to being the oldest corporate fiduciary in the United States, it is among the largest managers of personal wealth in the nation and one of the leading institutions in the private banking market.

With the rapid and dynamic growth of the western United States and its emergence as a major international economic center, U.S. Trust began seeking expansion opportunities in California as part of its overall goal of becoming a nationwide organization.

In December 1986 U.S. Trust acquired Summit Management Corporation, headquartered in Los Angeles. Summit, founded in 1983, specialized in managing assets for a mix of clients similar to those of U.S. Trust in New York. U.S. Trust Com-

pany of California, N.A., headquartered at 555 South Flower Street in Los Angeles, was granted a national charter in November 1987. It combines the investment expertise of Summit with the custodial and trust services of U.S. Trust to offer a full range of investment, trust, and private banking services.

Those services offered in Los Angeles and New York fall into four main categories: asset management and fiduciary services; private banking; corporate trust; and institutional asset services. The largest of these is investment management. Of the more than $200 billion of assets held in custody by U.S. Trust nationally, about $17 billion is managed by the firm, placing it among the largest investment advisors in the United States. Some two-thirds of its total revenues are derived from investment management and custodial services.

For its clients, the firm constructs carefully diversified portfolios that reflect client needs, preferences, and financial goals. It does not function as a broker/dealer nor does it earn commissions from buying or selling securities. Investment advisors work with clients on an ongoing basis, reviewing portfolios, assessing new investment opportunities, and reevaluating strategies as market conditions or client objectives change.

U.S. Trust is a strong advocate of balanced portfolios, allocating assets in a mix of stocks, bonds, and cash equivalent investments.

Most of the portfolios managed by U.S. Trust are on a discretionary basis, as clients generally experience superior results when timely investment decisions are made on their behalf by the firm. For example, the performance of its discretionary stock portfolios has been significantly better than the Standard & Poor's 500 and places U.S. Trust nationally among the top 25 percent of personal advisors and managers over most 3-year, 5-year, and 10-year periods.

U.S. Trust is also an acknowledged leader in the area of private banking. As a bank with more than $2 billion in assets, it has the resources to furnish a full range of deposit and credit services to individuals, families, and professional firms

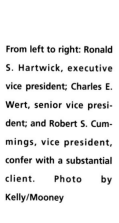

who prefer a more personal style of banking. Each client is assigned a personal banking officer who has the authority to immediately approve and execute even the most complex credit transactions. Clients rarely visit the bank, with most business handled via telephone. When signatures are required, account officers often bring the documents to the client's home or office.

For a number of years U.S. Trust has ranked among the 10 largest corporate trustees in the United States, with an aggregate par value in excess of $70 billion. It grew into the corporate trust business as a result of its skills as a personal fiduciary and it is now among the nation's most experienced trustees. It routinely participates in a broad spectrum of transactions that are diverse in credit rating and type.

The Corporate Trust and Agency Division offers a variety of trustee services that include both secured and unsecured corporate debt, municipal debt, and equipment leasing. It also serves as paying, conversion, and fiscal agent, as well as registrar. Other activities include serving as escrow or exchange agent, and pro-

viding tender offer depository services.

In its fourth principal line of business, institutional asset services, U.S. Trust is a leader in serving employee benefit funds, endowments and foundations, insurance companies, commercial banks, thrift institutions, brokers, dealers, and corporations. It is one of the largest providers of custody and master trust services to institutional investors, with more than $50 billion of assets under supervision.

U.S. Trust Company of California offers its clients a full range of services in addition to the strength, stability, and tradition of an organization that has been providing a superior level of financial expertise to people with substantial resources for nearly 150 years. Under the leadership of President and Chief Executive Officer Franklin E. Ulf, it is an autonomous organization capable of reacting quickly to events on a local level.

The people who comprise the U.S. Trust Company of California are a close-knit group of experienced, highly skilled, professional men and women committed to values such as personal responsibility and integrity in serving their clients in the western United States and the countries of the Pacific Rim.

The portfolio managers at the ARCO Plaza Fountain. From left to right: Lois G. Ingham, vice president; William L. Hildeburn, managing director; John S. DeGroot, senior vice president; Robert M. Raney, managing director and chief investment officer; and William H. Doheny, Jr., managing director.

Sitting from left to right in the conference room: Mark K. Talt, vice president, Asset Management Department; Dwight Liu, vice president and controller for CEO office; Franklin E. Ulf, president and chief executive officer; William R. Barrett, Jr., senior vice president and head of Private Banking; and Jean V. Keatley, senior vice president and director of research.

EXPERTISE AND INSIGHT

The Professions

The business and professional community is an integral part of the city's infrastructure. By providing a wealth of service, expertise, and insight to Los Angeles, this sector enables continued growth and stability.

The professional sector is a city within a city, a plethora of eye-catching architectural structures where a variety of services are available. Photo by Mark E. Gibson

ALSCHULER, GROSSMAN & PINES

The Century City-based law firm of Alschuler, Grossman & Pines enjoys an excellent national reputation for vigorous and creative advocacy in complex business litigation and business transactions. It is recognized within the legal community for introducing effective tactics in difficult business disputes and is respected as a capable and aggressive law firm providing full services to its clients in its practice areas.

In 1964 name partner Marshall B. Grossman joined the firm, which was founded in 1952. Grossman has a national reputation as a litigator of complex business transactions. Having served many years as a member of the California Coastal Commission, he is actively involved in the professional and civic organizations of Los Angeles.

The other name partner of Alschuler, Grossman & Pines is Burt Pines, who joined the firm in 1981 after serving two four-year terms as the city attorney of Los Angeles. He is also a former Assistant U.S. Attorney and chaired the California Commission on Personal Privacy.

The firm's clients include major public utilities, multinational banks and accounting firms, and leading *Fortune* 500 corporations, as well as emerging businesses. Its practice areas include business and securities, real estate and land use, environmental law, business litigation, financial institutions, taxation, bankruptcy, labor,

estate planning and probate, intellectual property, insurance coverage law, and administrative law.

The firm counsels clients in a full range of business matters. It also practices before government regulatory agencies such as the Securities and Exchange Commission. Its real estate practice includes commercial and residential transactions with particular emphasis on the purchase, exchange, and sale of real property, construction financing, commercial and ground leasing, and development.

The environmental law practice at Alschuler, Grossman & Pines includes local, state, and federal compliance, toxic waste disposal, asbestos abatement, and clean air and water matters.

Business litigation matters include securities, antitrust, unfair competition and trademark, real estate, environmental, and shareholder/management disputes.

The firm provides a full range of services to financial institutions engaged in commercial and secured lending. It also counsels clients respecting bankruptcy and creditors' rights matters in business transactions. In its labor practice, the firm represents employers in a full range of management/labor relations issues.

Drawing on years of experience in the public sector, Alschuler, Grossman & Pines is often called upon to assist clients in the advocacy of their administrative and legislative agendas. It also represents clients before government regulatory, licensing, and disciplinary agencies.

The working atmosphere at Alschuler, Grossman & Pines is one of interaction. Collaboration among firm members with different specialties is the rule rather than the exception. The firm has a policy of steady but controlled growth and now counts more than 40 attorneys among its ranks.

The firm's practice is both national and international in scope, which has led to the establishment of relationships with leading law firms in the United States, Europe, and the Far East. Attorneys take particular pride in the representation of local, Los Angeles-area clients.

Alschuler, Grossman & Pines is a member of the International Association of Commercial Lawyers, a group of major law firms located throughout the world, with which it works on a cooperative basis. These relationships give the firm the access necessary to effectively represent clients' interests in out-of-state and foreign jurisdictions.

Whether representing a major multinational corporation or a small, emerging company, the firm uses a "hands-on" approach, determined to see that each client receives the expertise and personal attention that Alschuler, Grossman & Pines has to offer. At least one partner is involved in

The firm's practice is both national and international in scope. Marshall B. Grossman (right) and Burt Pines (left) with managing partner Bruce Warner (center).

every case and the judicious use of support staff and state-of-the-art technology help reduce time billings and expenses, and produce cost-effective results.

The firm is proud of its long-standing relationships with its clients, many of which it has helped grow from small companies to large corporations. For example, the firm organized and brought public what was then a small local bank and is today the California headquarters of a major multinational financial institution. The firm also assisted a major public utility in its most significant real estate transactions, including the acquisition of its corporate headquarters.

Because of their broad legal or commercial significance, and because of the creativity Alschuler, Grossman & Pines brings to the process, some cases have received considerable public attention.

The firm, for example, served as lead counsel for the victims in various major securities fraud cases. In one, the recovery exceeded $60 million—an unprecedented result at the time. In another widely reported case the firm successfully defended a leading New York Stock Exchange company in a bitterly contested proxy contest. It also obtained a multimillion-dollar recovery on behalf of the former chairman of a major motion picture film studio in litigation alleging breach of his employment contract. The firm recently concluded the defense of a leading international accounting firm with a large trial defense verdict on all counts.

The firm's commitment to excellence in the practice of law is matched by its commitment to professional, community, and philanthropic involvement. Its members have held leadership posts in a wide range of professional organizations, including the Beverly Hills Bar Association, the Association of Business Trial Lawyers, the California Young Lawyers Association, the Century City Bar Association, and the Southern California Chinese Lawyers Association.

The Adopt-a-Family program, in which more than two dozen Los Angeles area law firms now participate, was launched by Alschuler, Grossman & Pines in 1983. Needy families are identified by teachers in the Los Angeles Unified School District and referred to the Los Angeles Police Department, which assesses the level of need. Each holiday season, dozens of families are adopted by law firms, who give generously of their time, money, clothing, food, and other materials to brighten the lives of less fortunate members of the community.

The firm also formed the Alschuler, Grossman & Pines Charitable Foundation to assist various local causes. For example, the firm joined with KCET, the public service television station in Los Angeles, to produce 10,000 copies of a brochure called "Environmental Impact," which was distributed without cost to community groups and organizations, school districts, local politicians, and public leaders. Deeply committed to environmental matters, the firm also sponsored a series of five programs on KCET to educate the public on environmental issues.

Other organizations the firm has assisted include the Western Center on Law and Poverty, the Constitutional Rights Foundation, the Greater Los Angeles Partnership for the Homeless, the City of Hope, Cedars-Sinai Medical Center, the Los Angeles Committee of Concerned Lawyers for Soviet Jewry, the American Heart Association, the Boy Scouts of America, and the United Way.

Alschuler, Grossman & Pines firmly believes that involvement in such activities not only enhances the effectiveness of its attorneys but strengthens the community of which it has been an integral part since 1952.

Whether representing a major multinational corporation or a small, emerging company, the firm uses a "hands-on" approach, determined to see that each client receives the expertise and personal attention that Alschuler, Grossman & Pines has to offer.

LOEB AND LOEB

J oseph P. Loeb and his brother, Edwin J. Loeb, were in their early twenties and practicing law in Los Angeles when they decided to strike out on their own. In 1909 they formed the firm now known as Loeb and Loeb, which quickly established its niche in the Los Angeles legal marketplace and became what is today the third-oldest law firm in the community.

While Joseph Loeb laid the foundation for the firm's extensive banking and commercial practice, his younger brother became involved with a fledgling industry, an involvement that would have a major influence on the future of the firm. The industry was motion pictures, and Edwin Loeb was a key player in the development of Hollywood's "studio" structure.

In 1927 Edwin Loeb helped found the Academy of Motion Picture Arts and Sciences. In fact, he personally drafted the Academy's bylaws; according to some accounts, he suggested the idea that became the world-famous Oscar Awards. In 1931, at the insistence of leading producers in Hollywood and studio executives in New York, he was appointed sole arbiter over the western activities of the industry as an official of the Motion Picture Producers and Distributors of America, Inc.

Louis P. Eatman (left) is a member of the management committee and a partner practicing in the Real Estate Department; Andrew S. Garb is the managing partner of the firm and practices in the Tax, Trusts, and Estates Department.

After practicing law for six decades, the Loebs retired during the 1960s. Edwin Loeb died in 1970 at the age of 83; Joseph Loeb in 1974 at age 90. Yet the firm they founded continued to grow, expanding its motion picture practice to all phases of the entertainment industry and simultaneously becoming a leading real estate, litigation, and general commercial firm.

In 1986 Loeb and Loeb merged with a leading New York firm, Hess Segall Guterman Pelz Steiner & Barovick, which traces its origins to 1907. This merger made Loeb and Loeb the law firm with the nation's largest private practice entertainment department. Today the firm has approximately 200 attorneys. In addition to its entertainment, real estate, and litigation departments—each containing about one-fifth of the firm's attorneys—Loeb and Loeb's other major practice areas include corporate, tax, insolvency and workout, labor, and trusts and estates.

Loeb and Loeb's downtown Los Angeles offices are located in the landmark 1000 Wilshire Building. From this building's conceptualization through its construction, Loeb and Loeb handled every significant legal issue confronted by its developer. The firm's other offices are located in Century City and New York; in 1990 Loeb and Loeb became the first American firm to open a full-service European office in Rome.

Loeb and Loeb's real estate department represents major institutional investors, real estate investment trusts, large developers, and individual investors in the acquisition and sale of commercial real estate throughout the United States. The department also serves as counsel to many commercial banks, life insurance companies, pension plans, and real estate investment trusts in their real estate-secured lending operations. It also is active and has recognized expertise in development projects, commercial leasing, like-kind exchanges, and general real estate matters.

In transactions of major significance to the Los Angeles community, the real estate department represented the lenders on some of the area's largest recent projects. They include the construction financing for the 73-story First Interstate World Center, the tallest building in downtown Los Angeles; the acquisition financing of Playa Vista, the largest single piece of undeveloped land in any metropolitan area in the United States; and the permanent financing for Phase I of Citicorp Plaza, which is comprised of an office tower and subterranean shopping center, a unique concept in retail design in California.

The litigation department's primary areas of emphasis include the representation of banking and financial institutions; securities litigation and related matters; antitrust; real estate litigation; entertainment, sports, and intellectual property litigation; constitutional and civil rights litigation; and appellate advocacy. In conjunction with the firm's labor department, it also represents employers in connection with wrongful termination claims. The litigation department also represented the dissenting shareholders in the largest appraisal proceeding involving a privately held real estate corporation in American legal history. It also represented the plaintiffs-investors in one of the nation's largest securities fraud cases.

The department represents directors and officers in several lawsuits brought by federal regulatory authorities for alleged mismanagement of failed thrifts and banks. It also represented one of California's largest multi-family housing developers in construction arbitrations, and frequently represents the producers of major television programs and motion pictures in cases alleging copyright infringement, breach of contract, and defamation. Loeb and Loeb's litigation attorneys also regularly defend the constitutional and civil rights of various media clients, individuals, and nonprofit entities.

The firm's entertainment department represents a client base that extends throughout the United States, Canada, Europe, Japan, and Australia, with primary practice areas in distribution, production, talent, music, lending, finance, and professional sports. Among its clients are prominent independent theatrical and home-video distributors, major institutional lenders, a leading pay television network, television syndication and distribution companies, motion picture and television production companies, and foreign-sales agents.

The entertainment department also serves as counsel for many prominent talent clients, including writers, directors, actors, and producers. It represents some of the world's most renowned recording artists, performers, songwriters, and composers, as well as music publishers and record companies. The department's clients also include a number of major professional sports franchises, athletic associations, and individual athletes.

Loeb and Loeb's attorneys are also actively involved in a wide array of major pro bono public litigation, either as counsel of record or as a friend of the court. These cases have raised issues under the U.S. and California constitutions and under the Freedom of Information, Privacy, Voting Rights, and Unruh Civil Rights Acts. A

The firm's library in its downtown office.

number of the department's lawyers participated as co-counsel for the Hispanic plaintiffs in the Los Angeles County supervisorial redistricting litigation.

In addition to handling a wide range of nonlitigation matters for various nonprofit organizations, partners in the firm hold major leadership positions in many of them, including the Arthritis Foundation, the American Jewish Committee, the City of Hope, the John Wayne Cancer Foundation, the American Jewish Congress, Cedars-Sinai Medical Center, the ACLU Foundation of Southern California, the National Foundation for Ileitis and Colitis, Hebrew Union College, Hathaway Children's Services, and the National Parkinson Foundation.

For nearly all of the twentieth century Loeb and Loeb has served its community and its clients well. Today, strategically positioned in major commercial centers on both the East and West coasts, as well as in Europe, Loeb and Loeb plans to continue its tradition of growth, community involvement, and comprehensive, innovative, quality legal services.

MILBANK, TWEED, HADLEY & McCLOY

Very few, if any, law firms operating in Los Angeles can trace their roots back to the middle of the nineteenth century. There is, however, at least one exception. Andrew Johnson was president of the then 36-state nation when the firm of Milbank, Tweed, Hadley & McCloy was founded in New York in 1866 as Anderson, Adams & Young. Today the firm has more than 475 lawyers, with an extensive worldwide practice in banking, corporate, litigation, real estate, bankruptcy and reorganization, trusts and estates, and tax law. Its 75-lawyer Los Angeles office, opened in 1987, is its newest addition joining its offices in New York, Washington, London, Tokyo, Hong Kong, and Singapore.

Over the 125 years since its founding, many successor firms were created through the addition of new partners and the retirement or death of others. In 1931 it became Milbank, Tweed, Hope & Webb, and in 1962 it adopted its present name. The men whose names the firm bears were Albert G. Milbank, Harrison Tweed, Morris Hadley, and John J. McCloy. The four, who died in 1949, 1969, 1979, and 1989, respectively, were not only distinguished in the legal profession, but had compiled outstanding records of community service.

However, it was John McCloy, described in an obituary as "lawyer, diplomat, and adviser to seven presidents," who achieved the greatest fame. Prior to joining the firm in 1946, he had served for five years as Assistant Secretary of War. He later served as president of the World Bank, High Commissioner of Germany, chairman of Chase Manhattan Bank, and chairman of the Ford Foundation. He returned briefly to the firm in 1961 before his appointment as special assistant on disarmament to President John F. Kennedy. He returned to the firm in 1962, serving as a general partner until his death.

The firm has always had its roots planted deeply in the Wall Street area, having opened its doors on Nassau Street in 1866. Sixteen years later, it moved to offices across the street from the New York Stock Exchange (which it has represented for more than a half-century) and then, in 1961, to its present headquarters at One Chase Manhattan Plaza.

Originally, much of the firm's activities centered on real estate and investment banking, which brought in such clients as John D. Rockefeller, Sr., and John D. Rockefeller, Jr., and their interests, including the construction of Rockefeller Center and Radio City Music Hall and the Williamsburg restoration. Today the firm has become very much of an international law firm, with clients worldwide served by offices in the United States, Europe, and Asia.

The Tokyo office opened in 1977, 10 years earlier than any other American law firm. The Hong Kong office opened later that same year, followed by London in 1979, Washington in 1980, Singapore in 1985, and Los Angeles in 1987. It was the firm's strong Asian practice as well as the dynamic California economy that led directly to the opening of the Los Angeles office.

For a number of years, the firm had been

Milbank was the recipient of several awards for his services as a director or trustee of numerous civic, charitable, and educational institutions. Tweed, among other activities, was president of the American Law Institute, the Association of the Bar of the City of New York, the Legal Aid Society, and Sarah Lawrence College, and he was the recipient of awards from the City of New York, New York State, and American bar associations. Hadley, son of a former president of Yale University, was president of the board of trustees of the New York Public Library for 15 years.

In Los Angeles, the banking and finance practice is led by Francis D. Logan, a top-rated banking lawyer who transferred from the New York office in late 1988. He is well known for his representation of Chase Manhattan Bank over many years. The Los Angeles office represents many major California banks as well as overseas banks with California operations. It also represents, in its general corporate practice, investment banks and commercial enterprises ranging in size from some of the world's largest corporations to many medium- and small-size companies. Its litigation practice emphasizes representation for corporations, financial institutions, and professional firms in complex economic and financial cases including antitrust, securities, professional liability, and international trade matters. The litigation practice is headed by partner Richard J. Stone, who joined the firm in mid-1988 after being engaged in complex major-case litigation in Los Angeles for more than a decade.

When the decision was made to establish a Los Angeles office, the partners of the firm set out to establish a meaningful presence in California to provide a broad spectrum of legal services to corporations, financial institutions, and individuals located not only in Southern California but throughout the western United States and the Pacific Basin. Today Milbank, Tweed, Hadley & McCloy has indeed established its presence and become a significant factor among the law firms in Los Angeles.

asked by Asian clients, some of whom it had represented since 1917, to establish a West Coast office. Recognizing the need to serve those clients and to establish a practice in what had become one of the world's major economic centers, the firm recruited Guido R. Henry, Jr., a well-known and respected corporate lawyer who practiced law with one of the city's finest law firms for 22 years, to open and manage its Los Angeles office. Henry was soon joined by six lawyers from the New York office, including bankruptcy partner David Frauman whose practice has included corporate reorganizations in various cities across the country. Frauman now heads the bankruptcy practice in Los Angeles and Henry heads the corporate practice.

From that small beginning in January 1987, the Los Angeles office now has about 75 lawyers, most of whom have practiced law in California for their entire careers. Early in 1991, on the firm's 125th anniversary, the Los Angeles office moved from its 50,000-square-foot quarters at 515 South Figueroa Street into new 80,000-square-foot facilities in the just-completed 52-story Sanwa Bank Building at Figueroa at Wilshire. In a very short time, it has become a major factor in Southern California and is the second biggest Los Angeles office of a New York-based firm.

Milbank, Tweed, Hadley & McCloy is perhaps best known for its banking and finance practice. It has long been recognized as a top banking firm internationally. With offices strategically located in the world's money centers, the firm has positioned itself to achieve its goal of becoming the preeminent financial services firm in the nation.

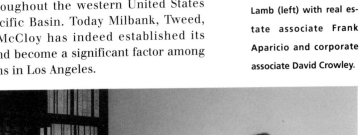

ARGUE PEARSON HARBISON & MYERS

Among the law firms in Los Angeles, Argue Pearson Harbison & Myers is relatively small and relatively young. Yet there are few firms, regardless of size, whose roots are deeper, whose contributions are greater, or whose members practice better law or play a more active leadership role in community activities.

The firm was founded in 1972. John C. Argue, Don M. Pearson, Stephen F. Harbison, and Louis W. Myers had been practicing law in Los Angeles prior to that time. All but Pearson came from Flint and MacKay, which had been formed around the turn of the century and represented many prominent people in early Los Angeles history, including William Randolph Hearst. Argue Pearson has continued with a client base that includes many old-line organizations and New York Stock Exchange companies, and with a tradition of significant client contact and quality service.

The firm has a general business and litigation practice. Its major practice areas include real estate, litigation, corporate and securities, taxation, labor/employee relations, and estate planning. Originally located in the State Mutual Savings Building at 626 Wilshire Boulevard, in 1983 the firm members became partners in the ownership of the building at 801 South Flower Street that the firm now occupies. This entrepreneurial spirit is pervasive throughout the firm and in the approach of its lawyers to the practice of law.

The members of the firm have many close ties to Los Angeles and an enviable record of participation in professional and community activities. Senior partner John Argue practiced law early in his career with his father, J. Clifford Argue. The firm name, Argue & Argue, earned them mention in "Ripley's Believe it or Not." John Argue is a past chairman or president of the Los Angeles Area Chamber of Commerce, the American Heart Association, Verdugo Hills Hospital, Town Hall of California, Chancery Club, the California Club,

and USC Associates. He serves as vice chairman of L.A. 2000 and Pomona College and on the board of trustees of the University of Southern California and as a director of several major Los Angeles-area companies.

Despite these and numerous other activities, Argue is best known for his involvement in the Olympics, an involvement that came very naturally. His father competed in the 1924 Olympic Games in Paris, later made famous in the film *Chariots of Fire*. In 1971, John Argue became president of the Southern California Committee for the Olympic Games (SCCOG). Primarily due to his efforts, the International Olympic Committee awarded the 1984 Games, the XXIII Olympiad, to Los Angeles. When the city's bid was approved in 1978, Argue also became founding chairman of the Los Angeles Olympic Organizing Committee, a post he held until turning the reins over to his hand-picked successor, Peter V. Ueberroth.

Argue's role in what proved to be the most successful games in Olympic history brought him numerous awards and broad recognition as the man "who was most responsible for bringing the Olympic Games to Los Angeles." Nevertheless, not being one to rest on his laurels, Argue continues as SCCOG president and chairman of the Los Angeles Sports Council and hopes to bring the Olympic Games back to Los Angeles early in the next century.

Other members of the firm share Argue's commitment to service. Don Pearson, who earned his law degree from Harvard Law School, *cum laude*, has been involved with various educational, community, religious, and business organizations in the Los Angeles area. He has served as chairman of the City of Glendale Planning Commission, as president of the board of trustees of Flintridge Preparatory School, as a Trustee of the Beverly Foundation, as a Bishop in The Church of Jesus Christ of Latter-Day Saints, and as a District Chairman of the Verdugo Hills Council of the Boy Scouts of America. Pearson, who authored the "Attorney's Guide to California Stock Qualification and Exemption," is a past chairman of the Taxation Section of the Los Angeles County Bar Association, an instructor in the master of business

John Argue with client
Magic Johnson.

taxation program at the University of Southern California, and a frequent lecturer and writer on tax and corporate subjects.

Stephen Harbison was born in Santa Monica and received both his undergraduate and law degrees from Stanford. His community involvement includes service as director of the Los Angeles Master Chorale Association, director of the Carmel Bach Festival, and as a trustee of the First United Methodist Church of Santa Monica and of the National Methodist Foundation for Christian Higher Education. He has also served as president of the Stanford Law Society of Southern California and as a director of the Los Angeles Junior Chamber of Commerce and the Stanford Club of Los Angeles County.

Louis Myers is a Southern California native and a third-generation Los Angeles attorney. His grandfather, Louis W. Myers, who served as chief justice of the California Supreme Court in 1925, came to Los Angeles in 1889 and was a cofounder of the law firm of O'Melveny & Myers. Lou Myers has distinguished himself in transactional real estate law with particular expertise in hotel and resort properties.

The other partners share an equal dedication to community services. Joseph Lazara was the founder of the Glendale Youth Orchestra. Mark Spraic helped organize the Los Angeles County Sheriff's Foundation, serves on the Board of the East Los Angeles Alcoholism Commission and is an active member of the Pasadena Tournament of Roses Association. Bill Jones, who was on the heavyweight crew at Princeton, and Jerry Staub, who played on two NCAA championship baseball teams at USC, are active as coaches with youth baseball, basketball, and soccer teams.

With their many achievements in community activities, the members of the firm feel the greatest pride in their accomplishments in the practice of law. They continue to emphasize personal contact with their clients and quality service. They seem to thrive on being one of the smaller firms in downtown Los Angeles where the clear trend is toward institutional firms. Having all come from larger firms, they appreciate the flexibility and creativity of a small one, and the opportunity to spend more time with their families and to become more involved in community activities.

Their clients represent a broad range of business entities engaged in a variety of endeavors, including health care, hospitality and lodging, real estate, securities brokerage, manufacturing, automobile dealerships, and sports. In the last-named category, clients include individuals and firms in such diverse sports as golf, horse racing, windsurfing, and basketball. The most prominent among them is undoubtedly the Los Angeles Lakers' star basketball player, Magic Johnson.

Whether representing a prominent athlete, structuring a new business, teaching a course on taxation, winning a bid to host the Olympic Games, or guiding a client through the intricacies of a multimillion-dollar real estate transaction, the attorneys at Argue Pearson Harbison & Myers are proud of the contributions they have been privileged to make to the dynamic and growing community of Greater Los Angeles.

Partners Stephen F. Harbison, Don M. Pearson, and Louis W. Myers discuss firm business.

HAIGHT, BROWN & BONESTEEL

T oday's society features rapidly advancing technologies, from new drugs and medical devices that help us live longer to improved electronics that enhance our daily lives. This environment is also often litigious, with an increased volume of complex cases resulting in cumbersome and laborious fact finding, making traditional litigation costly.

Haight, Brown & Bonesteel distinguishes itself by having more top-level litigators than most firms in the country and the specialized resources and sophistication needed to handle complex issues both successfully and cost efficiently.

This broad experience in all areas of civil litigation enables the firm to analyze every option—from arbitration to jury trial—based wholly on client goals.

Attorneys for this Santa Monica-based firm are prepared to know how and when to avoid trial, how to seek a suitable solution for the client, when to pursue a jury trial, and how to achieve a favorable verdict or other result.

"We rely on teamwork inside and outside of any lawyer or team of lawyers assigned to a case because we believe the best work comes from lawyers who learn from and draw upon the resources of other lawyers," comments one of the firm's partners. "The result for the client is a well thought out strategy that consistently delivers desired results."

Haight, Brown & Bonesteel's senior partner is Fulton W. Haight, a fifth-generation California lawyer who joined the firm in 1952 after serving as senior deputy city attorney for Los Angeles. Haight's great-great-grandfather was one of the first federal judges in San Francisco, and that city's Haight Street was named after him and his pioneer brothers. Haight is also a descendant of Henry H. Haight, governor of California from 1867 to 1871.

During the firm's early years in the 1930s, 1940s, and 1950s, its foundation was insurance defense. But as the theories of liability expanded throughout California, and later throughout the nation, the firm rapidly developed expertise in product liability and business matters, as well as other specialized areas of litigation.

The practice of litigation remains the firm's major focus, with an average of more than 50 cases tried to conclusion each year. Of course, many times this number of matters are resolved through other means each year as well.

Litigation activities are conducted in a variety of areas. One of these is environmental law and toxic tort litigation, where the firm is deeply involved in the defense of numerous substances alleged to be environmentally or personally harmful. The firm is also involved in toxic waste site cleanup issues and the myriad issues presented by regulatory enforcement of the emerging body of law governing these property sites.

The firm handles cases involving chemical spills, groundwater contamination, and toxic

waste litigation. The firm has represented several major clients in mass litigation, handling more than 3,000 local asbestos cases for one client and more than 1,200 lawsuits for a consortium of asbestos producers and insurance companies.

In its corporate product litigation practice, the firm represents and has successfully defended matters for the manufacturers of a wide variety of products, including automobiles, farm equipment, construction equipment, and household appliances. The firm is also frequently retained to advise foreign manufacturers of potential product liability problems, including product reviews and the development of maintenance, use, and warning literature.

Haight, Brown & Bonesteel is also well represented in the fields of pharmaceutical products and medical devices, acting as local, regional, or national counsel for some of the nation's largest manufacturers. Over the years the firm has successfully defended such products as anesthetics, polio and DPT vaccines, prosthetic devices, intrauterine contraceptive devices, and nonsteroidal, anti-inflammatory drugs.

The firm is well known for its expertise in the defense of attorneys, accountants, architects, engineers, and other professionals involved in errors and omissions cases. It has played an important role in the development of the California law governing the duties of attorneys. The organization has also represented physicians, convalescent homes, and medical corporations in a variety of cases and arbitrations.

As support services to its clients, the firm has a fully staffed Appellate Department, a Business Transactions Group, and an Internal Investigation

Unit. The firm's extensive experience in the area of appellate law is exemplified by a senior partner who has more than 100 published appellate decisions, probably more than any other attorney practicing in this area in California today.

Additional fully staffed litigation practice areas include commercial and real estate litigation, insurance coverage and bad faith litigation, and insurance defense. The firm has represented insurance companies since its founding and has client relationships in that industry dating back more than 50 years.

Once a very small firm, it now has more than 135 attorneys and a total staff of more than 350. All the growth has been from within, without benefit of merger or acquisition. In addition to its Santa Monica office, the firm has an office in Santa Ana.

Many of the firm's partners and associates are actively involved in continuing education through seminars offered by the American College of Trial Lawyers, the Association of Southern California Defense Counsel, the Defense Research Institute, the Federation of Insurance, and the Corporate Counsel-Product Liability Advisory Council's Pharmaceutical Litigation Section and Medical Devices and Equipment Committee.

Throughout the firm's history, as the practice has grown in size and scope, Haight, Brown & Bonesteel has remained focused by its strength in litigation.

Front row: Wayne E. Peterson, Roy G. Weatherup, Steven L. Hoch, George Christensen, Michael J. Leahy. Back row: William G. Baumgaertner, William K. Koska. Courtesy, David J. Lans Photography

Standing: Michael J. Bonesteel. Seated in chair: Fulton Haight. Seated on stool: Harold H. Brown. Courtesy, David J. Lans Photography

SHEPPARD, MULLIN, RICHTER & HAMPTON

Sheppard Mullin senior partner Gordon F. Hampton, outside Los Angeles' Museum of Contemporary Art. Hampton is a proud founding member and trustee at "MOCA" and a longtime friend and supporter of contemporary art in Los Angeles.

Sheppard, Mullin, Richter & Hampton was founded in 1927 at the height of the Roaring Twenties. The firm practiced law for 48 years at 458 South Spring Street before moving to its present quarters in 1975. On five floors near the top of the Security Pacific Bank Building, it is now the fifth-largest firm in Los Angeles and the 13th-largest in California. Nearly 250 attorneys span the Golden State, from San Diego and Orange County in the south to San Francisco in the north.

The firm has acquired a reputation as a "client's law firm" by its continual awareness of the importance of serving its clients, many of which are based in California. Its strong commitment to clients coupled with stability gained from more than 60 years of practice, and a long-range view of the Golden State's evolving role in a world economy, has led the firm to the forefront of the challenging California legal market.

Founded in 1927 as Haight, Mathes & Sheppard, the firm first adopted its current moniker in 1961, reflecting the personalities that led the firm to the present day: James C. Sheppard, who passed away in October 1964, J. Stanley Mullin, George R. Richter, Jr., and Gordon F. Hampton. The latter three remain active with the firm.

The largest segment of the firm's attorneys practice in the litigation area, including commercial civil litigation, antitrust, white collar crime, government contracts, qui tam actions, and environmental litigation. The firm's litigators represent such diverse clients as Security Pacific National Bank, Wells Fargo Bank, First Interstate Bank, Bank of America, Northrop Corp., Honeywell Inc., American Airlines, Farmers Insurance, Sundstrand, and Atlantic Richfield Company.

Perhaps the oldest and best known segment of the firm's practice remains one of its largest—banking and finance. The 50-plus attorney department represents numerous banks, asset-based lenders,

The Los Angeles office of Sheppard Mullin relocated to the Security Pacific building in 1975. The building, located high atop Bunker Hill, is distinguished by the Alexander Calder arch at its entrance. A Los Angeles landmark, the building often appears in background scenes of downtown L.A.

and other financial institutions in all aspects of complex financial transactions, ranging from initial lending, restructuring transactions, leveraged buyouts, corporate reorganizations, and bankruptcy.

Real estate has been one of the fastest-growing practice areas in recent years, expanding from 2 lawyers in 1977 to more than 30 in 1991. The department represents a collage of related interests, including development and financing. In Los Angeles, the firm has represented the developer of the Citicorp Plaza and Seventh Street Marketplace project, as well as Merv Griffin in his purchase of the Beverly Hilton Hotel. The firm also represents numerous banks in real estate lending transactions.

The Corporate and Securities Department specializes in representing California companies, such as *La Opinion*, the daily newspaper for the Southern California Latino community. The 25-lawyer group specializes in mergers and acquisitions, as well as asset-backed securities and venture capital financing, to service the large number of emerging companies founded by California's entrepreneurs.

The 20-plus attorney Labor and Employment Law Department specializes in representing employers such as Nordstrom, Mervyns, and Neiman Marcus, as well as State Farm Insurance, The Gillette Company, and Honeywell Inc. And the 15-attorney Tax and Estate Planning Department fulfills the vital role of servicing the tax needs affecting most transactions and litigation

handled by the firm.

Although Sheppard Mullin is organized into departments, clients are also served by practice groups drawn from the various departments to service needs in environmental law, government contracts, white collar crime, and entertainment law.

Sheppard Mullin has established three outlying offices to facilitate the delivery of cost-effective legal services to business in other regions of California that might be best served by a member of that community. In 1977 the firm opened an office in expanding Newport Beach, which now has 30 attorneys. In 1981 the firm established a presence in San Francisco, which now has 26 attorneys. In 1986 the firm opened an office in San Diego, one of the state's fastest-growing areas. The San Diego office now has 40 attorneys. Sheppard Mullin has made a practice, as well, of being an active member of its community. It has been recognized in Los Angeles and San Diego as a leader in the provision of legal services to the poor. In its home region, the firm strives to build a better community for everyone, by serving as a benefactor to the Los Angeles Union Rescue Mission and a sponsor of the Monte Vista elementary school in nearby Santa Ana. Its attorneys engage themselves in public commitment, serving as board members of the Legal Aid Foundation of Los Angeles as well as Public Counsel, the public interest law firm cosponsored by the Los Angeles County Bar Association.

While Sheppard Mullin serves its diverse community in a multitude of ways, it keeps its eye firmly affixed to the reason for its success—the service it provides to its clients. The new California Gold Rush, which has attracted top law firms from throughout the country, has made attorney attentiveness more important than ever. To focus the firm's mission, it adopted a 20-point client service credo in 1988 reminding its attorneys: "Never forget that there are competing providers of legal services available to our clients if our legal services do not measure up in every respect."

In the bustling Los Angeles community, Sheppard Mullin is firmly committed to continue anticipating and serving its clients' needs.

Skadden, Arps, Slate, Meagher & Flom

Skadden, Arps' Los Angeles senior partners are (seated left to right) Frank Rothman and Richard S. Volpert; (standing left to right) John A. Donovan, managing partner Michael H. Diamond, and Jerome L. Coben.

S kadden, Arps, Slate, Meagher & Flom—whose cornerstone is a preeminent merger and acquisition practice—today is among the largest, most respected and successful full-service law firms in the world.

Founded in New York City in 1948, Skadden, Arps grew through the 1970s as merger and acquisition transactions proliferated. Since then, under a controlled plan of growth, the firm has considerably expanded the scope of its practice, encompassing more than 1,000 attorneys in seven U.S. and eight foreign cities. Along the way, Skadden, Arps carved out an international reputation for the innovative style and quality of its legal work.

Currently Skadden, Arps represents about one-half of the *Fortune 500* industrial companies,

all 10 of the largest banks in the world, and virtually every major U.S. investment bank. Its broad range of legal services spans more than 35 areas—from Antitrust to Trusts and Estates.

The firm's Los Angeles office opened in the spring of 1983 with 12 attorneys. Although spurred by the need to service the firm's growing list of Southern California-based clients, most requiring merger and acquisition work, Skadden, Arps was equally motivated to have a permanent office here by the potential for continuing growth of the Los Angeles Basin. Firm management recognized that the region was quickly emerging as a key international business and financial marketplace, fueled by a vibrant, diverse local economy, and an increasingly strong link to the Pacific Rim.

"The power of nature can only be equalled by our own unlimited abilities, vision, and spirit."

–Michael H. Diamond managing partner Los Angeles office

In just a few years, the Los Angeles office blossomed into a significant full-service Los Angeles law firm. The Los Angeles practice has grown to more than 125 attorneys, while building an impressive list of blue chip Southern California-headquartered clients, and attracting some of Los Angeles' most talented, well-known and influential lawyers.

Now the Los Angeles office of Skadden, Arps is highly regarded for its broad range of legal services—including litigation, real estate, and corporate finance—as well as its merger and acquisition practice.

Skadden, Arps also places great importance on what it gives back to the community. Through extensive, ongoing <u>pro</u> <u>bono</u> and civic activities, such as funding outstanding law school graduates to work in local public interest organizations, and by handling many matters for indigent litigants, Skadden, Arps has become a major contributor to the Los Angeles community.

Jones, Day, Reavis & Pogue

Jones, Day, Reavis & Pogue is an international law firm that has had a major office in Los Angeles since 1973. It also has offices in major cities across the United States, including Atlanta, Austin, Chicago, Cleveland, Columbus, Dallas, New York, Pittsburgh, and Washington, D.C., and in key cities abroad, including Brussels, Frankfurt, Geneva, Hong Kong, London, Paris, Riyadh, Taipei, and Tokyo. With approximately 1,200 lawyers, it is one of the largest law firms in the world, a tribute to its historical emphasis on quality of product and service.

The firm acts as principal outside counsel or provides significant legal representation for approximately 200 *Fortune* 500 corporations that are industry leaders in a variety of fields.

The firm also represents a wide variety of other entities, including publicly held corporations, financial institutions, privately held companies, real estate developers, investment firms, international entities, major health care providers, retail chains, foundations, partnerships, educational institutions and other public service organizations, foreign governments and agencies, and individuals, estates, and trusts.

the other in Irvine, with a total of about 140 lawyers in California.

Unlike a typical law firm, Jones Day operates more as a corporation than a partnership, with a management structure rather than a voting structure. Its managing partner is the chief executive officer, with the authority to make virtually all major decisions. Managers throughout the firm are given both authority and responsibility, relieving the partners from having to get involved in every decision, freeing them to do what they do best—practice law.

Jones Day is organized into five major practice groups: corporate, government regulation, litigation, real estate, and tax. The corporate group is active in matters involving corporate finance, mergers and acquisitions, lending, project finance, financial securitization products, public offerings and securities compliance, bankruptcy and commercial law, public finance, health care, investment banking, leveraged buyouts, and international practice.

In the government regulation group, the attorneys in the Los Angeles office provide legal services for industries in which government involvement is significant and that require compliance to strict regulations, such as health care, government contracts, as well as general administrative and antitrust practice.

The litigation group, the largest in the Los Angeles office, provides the firm's clients with the highest level of litigation skills on matters ranging from contests for corporate control to complex business disputes. Recent matters include intellectual property, oil and gas, antitrust, contract and commercial, product liability, environmental, health and safety, labor and employment, securities, real property, government contracts, and corporate criminal investigations.

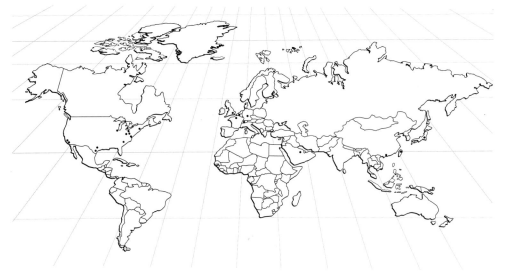

Atlanta, Austin, Brussels, Chicago, Cleveland, Columbus, Dallas, Frankfurt, Geneva, Hong Kong, Irvine, London, Los Angeles, New York, Paris, Pittsburgh, Riyadh, Taipei, Tokyo, Washington, D.C.

Jones Day is an integrated, international partnership managed by a single managing partner and is organized in a manner that promotes staffing of projects with the clients' needs in mind—bringing the best, most appropriate talent to bear on a problem regardless of their physical location. As such, no attorney or office has his, her, or its clients—all are Jones Day clients.

Founded in 1893, the firm's tradition of growth and expansion dates back to its first merger, in 1913. It first ventured outside Cleveland in 1946, when a Washington, D.C., office was opened. When its office was opened in Los Angeles in 1973, it made Jones Day one of the first out-of-state firms in California. Today the firm has two area offices, one in downtown Los Angeles and

The real estate group represents major lenders, developers, landlords, tenants, and investors in a wide variety of transactions covering every aspect of real estate law, including such relatively new ones as environmental and land use, hazardous waste issues, and regulatory and zoning problems.

The tax group provides a full range of services covering general tax, deferred compensation, and private capital.

The Los Angeles office of Jones, Day, Reavis & Pogue will continue to grow in all practice areas in tandem with the growth of the area as a manufacturing, world trade, and financial center located at the strategic hub of the rapidly growing Pacific Rim.

SCS ENGINEERS

The year 1970 is widely recognized as the beginning of the modern environmental movement. The first Earth Day, focusing the world's attention on what humanity was doing to its environment, was held on April 26 of that year. A new U.S. government organization, the Environmental Protection Agency, was formed to control pollution. And on April 1, 1970, SCS Engineers was founded.

SCS is an employee-owned environmental engineering firm specializing in solid and hazardous waste management service. Headquartered in Los Angeles County, SCS has grown from a three-person consulting firm into a firm employing 300 in 10 regional offices in North America.

Through the years SCS has earned a reputation for its technical expertise, practicality, and dedication to a profession committed to cleaning up the environment. Cofounder,

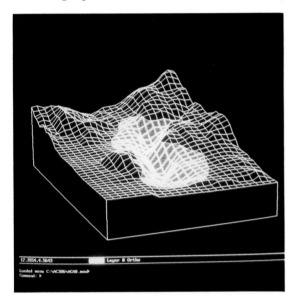

president, and chief executive officer Robert P. Stearns, and David E. Ross and Kenneth V. LaConde, who are, respectively, executive senior vice president and vice president in charge of the Los Angeles area office of the firm, attribute its success to the quality and technical expertise of their fellow staff members, many of whom have been with SCS almost from the beginning.

SCS's earliest work was in landfill gas control and sanitary landfill site location and design. Landfill gas recovery, refuse collection and transfer, and resource recovery and recycling soon followed. Looking ahead, the firm is now working to locate and design new sites for disposal of municipal solid waste from urban centers and to reduce the volume of waste that requires disposal, and to design proper closure for existing landfills.

SCS is working for a host of clients ranging from large corporations and cities to small towns and businesses, seeking cost-effective solutions to solid waste collection, waste reduction, recycling, and disposal needs. One such solution was the landmark Industry Hills Recreation and Convention Center Complex in the City of Industry, California. Constructed atop a former landfill, which includes recovery of landfill gas to heat laundry and pool water, the project earned the 1981 Outstanding Civil Engineering Achievement Award given by the American Society of Civil Engineers.

A more recent major project involves the conversion of the former Eagle Mountain Iron Mine in a remote area of Riverside County to a regional waste disposal site. Nonrecoverable waste from the Greater Los Angeles area is to be shipped by rail for disposal at this state-of-the-art landfill.

One viable alternative to landfilling is recycling, mandated for all California municipalities under legislation enacted in 1989. Critical deadlines have been issued and SCS has applied its experience to assist many clients in meeting the required goals.

As the need for improved hazardous waste management emerged in the 1980s, SCS responded by expanding its staff and resources. The firm now provides a broad range of hazardous waste management services, including environmental assessments of real estate, asbestos management, underground storage tank investigations and remediations, and services to manage uncontrolled hazardous waste (Superfund) sites. SCS has provided hazardous waste management services to control more than a dozen Superfund sites across the country, including several large sites in California. The firm also operates a state-certified laboratory for the analysis of gas, soil, water, and waste samples. An engineering contractor subsidiary firm, SCS Field Services, was established to allow SCS's development of turnkey design/build environmental services in the solid and hazardous waste management field.

SCS Engineers today is, as it has been throughout its history, a leader in helping government and industry to assure a safer environment for future generations of Americans.

Above: Robert P. Stearns, president

Far left: A conceptual design of the proposed Eagle Mountain Landfill.

Below: Industry Hills Golf Course in Industry Hills, California.

HUFSTEDLER, KAUS & ETTINGER

Hufstedler, Kaus & Ettinger prides itself on the quality of its lawyers and the product of their efforts. The firm emphasizes litigation. In civil and criminal cases, at the preparation, motion, trial, and appellate levels, the lawyers at Hufstedler, Kaus & Ettinger strive for service.

The firm represents plaintiffs, defendants, and third parties in matters that include business disputes, securities, claims, fiduciary obligations, shareholders rights, entertainment contracts, trust, estate, probate and tax matters, constitutional rights, insurance coverage, bankruptcy ad-

minstration, family law, environmental, and geotechnical matters. Hufstedler, Kaus & Ettinger lawyers appear in federal and state courts as well as before administrative and regulatory agencies.

Hufstedler, Kaus & Ettinger is one of the few downtown civil firms to have an active criminal law practice in both state and federal courts. The firm represents individuals and companies. The criminal cases range from white collar matters, to environmental prosecutions, to a variety of penal code violations. Warren Ettinger heads the criminal law department.

Left to right: Otto M. Kaus, Warren L. Ettinger, Shirley M. Hufstedler, and Seth M. Hufstedler.

The firm's partners also offer a unique appellate practice group providing expertise in state and federal courts. This experience petitions for extraordinary relief, as well as appeals. Hufstedler, Kaus & Ettinger has been the prevailing counsel in many precedent-setting appellate decisions.

In addition to the firm's litigation practice, three partners provide expertise in counseling and implementing business transactions and related matters. Each has extensively lectured and written in their respective fields. Joseph Wyatt advises clients on fiduciary matters of all types, including advice to large pension trusts. He also has an extensive estate planning practice. Fred Leydorf is nationally known in the area of estate planning and related tax, trust, and probate matters, while Dudley Lang specializes in advising clients on federal, state, and local tax matters, as well as on other areas of business law.

Several members of the firm have had judicial experience. Shirley Hufstedler is a former justice at the California Court of Appeals and a former judge of the U.S. Court of

Appeals. She left the federal court when President Jimmy Carter appointed her as the first Secretary of Education. Otto M. Kaus is a former associate justice of the California Supreme Court. Warren Ettinger served as a trial judge in Pasadena.

A deep sense of public duty and distinguished leadership in professional activities have been hallmarks of Hufstedler, Kaus & Ettinger. Charles E. Beardsley, a founding partner, Seth M. Hufstedler, and Samuel L. Williams each served as president of the California State Bar. Patricia Phillips was the first woman to serve as president of the Los Angeles County Bar Association.

Hufstedler, Kaus & Ettinger is the only Los Angeles firm with five members who have been honored with the Shattuck-Price Award, given by the Los Angeles County Bar Association for "outstanding dedication to the improvement of the legal profession and the administration of justice."

Above: (left to right) Dudley M. Lang, Fred L. Leydorf, Burton J. Gindler, and Patricia Phillips.

Far left: (left to right) Dennis M. Perluss, Thomas J. Ready, Laurie D. Zelon, Jerome H. Craig, and Leonard L. Gumport.

ROBINSON, DIAMANT, BRILL & KLAUSNER

The law firm of Robinson, Diamant, Brill & Klausner has specialized in the areas of insolvency, bankruptcy, and corporate reorganization since its founding in 1962. Originally based in downtown Los Angeles, the firm, which is a professional corporation, relocated to its present offices at 1888 Century Park East in 1973.

The firm's practice encompasses all aspects of an insolvency practice. The firm represents debtors and secured and unsecured creditors, creditors' committees, trustees in bankruptcy, and other interested parties in all facets of bankruptcy and reorganization cases. The firm also regularly represents debtors and creditors' committees in out-of-court proceedings. Members of the firm regularly serve as federal court trustees and state court receivers.

Most of its work is business related. While it has handled cases of multimillion-dollar proportions, its primary focus is mid-size businesses and it is recognized for its expertise in the reorganization of small public companies. Recently, representatives of the firm were featured on a local network television program, explaining how a virtually destitute business reorganized itself, repaid its creditors in full, and achieved financial success. The key was debt restructuring, an area in which the firm specializes.

California, because of its rapidly expanding economy and the entrepreneurial spirit that prevails in the state, has the dubious distinction of leading the nation in bankruptcy filings. Bankruptcy filings have also increased as the stigma attached to bankruptcy has greatly diminished and it has become a much more accepted business strategy. Among all U.S. District Court districts, the Central District of California, which runs from Santa Barbara to Orange County and east to San Bernardino, has the highest number of bankruptcy filings. Throughout its almost 30 years the firm has emphasized the importance of its practice in the Central District.

This branch of the law has also become much more sophisticated and complex than in former years. There has been an increased formality in the procedure and a much greater trend toward jury trials in bankruptcy cases. Accordingly, the costs of reorganization have gotten much higher, making it increasingly difficult for small companies to seek protection via a bankruptcy proceeding. Because of the time and expense involved in lengthy court proceedings, the firm uses informal as well as formal out-of-court settlement procedures whenever the circumstances warrant. The firm also has expanded by adding litigation support to help it deal with the sophisticated and complex issues which routinely arise in bankruptcy cases.

With the proliferation, especially in California, of insolvencies, bankruptcies, and corporate reorganizations, the practice of this specialty of the law has also increased substantially. But while many of the major firms have added it to their other practice areas, Robinson, Diamant, Brill & Klausner remains one of the few firms, and one of the oldest, that limits its practice to this highly specialized field.

The growth of the firm itself has kept pace with the increased number of insolvency filings. Nearly 20 attorneys and a total staff of about 60 people handle the several hundred cases that are in process at any one time. Typical cases take between

one and two years to resolve, but the most difficult ones can run for four years or more. The firm has handled more than 15,000 cases since its inception.

Often its work has been innovative and unusual. Not long ago, for example, on behalf of a trustee in bankruptcy, it accomplished the rare feat of obtaining court certification of a class of creditors in a class action law suit. The suit ultimately resulted in a recovery of several million dollars for creditors.

Nearly all bankruptcies are filed under either Chapter 7 or Chapter 11 of the U.S. Bankruptcy Code. With Chapter 7 bankruptcies, which involve liquidation proceedings, a trustee is always appointed. With Chapter 11 bankruptcies, where debtors seek protection from creditors during reorganization, the bankruptcy court may appoint a trustee or allow the company's management to continue running the company as debtor in possession under court supervision. A trustee, once appointed, has the full responsibility of managing the company.

As trustees in many Chapter 7 and Chapter 11 cases, Robinson, Diamant, Brill & Klausner lawyers have functioned as the chief executive officers of a wide variety of businesses. They include hotels, hospitals, thoroughbred breeding and racing ventures, real estate firms, boating operations, and restaurants. Often they find themselves having to face indignant creditors and to deal with situations not normally associated with the practice of law and not included in law school curriculum.

In one such case, the trustee, on his first day of operating a restaurant, found himself face-to-face with an angry "loan shark" who, in lieu of the payment he was expecting, absconded with a side of beef. In another case, the trustee took over an animal farm and was immediately faced with the complex and expensive problem of providing food for a variety of livestock, including horses, sheep, and even alligators.

Many of the firm's principals and associates actively participate in a broad range of professional activities, with particular emphasis on those that involve their areas of specialization. These activities include service as president of the California Bankruptcy Forum, as members of the board of governors and officers of the Financial Lawyers Conference, as chairman of the Executive Committee of the Commercial Law and Bankruptcy section of the Los Angeles County Bar Association, and as reporter for the Ethics Subcommittee of the Business Banking section of the American Bar Association. Firm members are also frequent lecturers and have published many articles on their specialty. In addition to their professional activities, most are also personally involved in numerous civic and charitable organizations.

Robinson, Diamant, Brill & Klausner is a relatively young firm, yet its principals have more than 135 years of combined experience in insolvency, bankruptcy, and corporate reorganization, giving it a level of expertise in this challenging and difficult field that few other firms can match.

Above: (left to right) Irv M. Gross, Martin J. Brill, and Elliott Lisnek. Photo by Ed Honowitz

Far left: (left to right) Douglas D. Kappler, Irv M. Gross, and Edward M. Wolkowitz in the library. Photo by Ed Honowitz

KNAPP, PETERSEN & CLARKE

In 1990 the law firm of Knapp, Petersen & Clarke moved to Glendale after outgrowing its original facilities in Universal City. It currently occupies the top five floors of a new 22-story office building.

The law firm of Knapp, Petersen & Clarke was formed in February 1981 by Ryan C. Knapp, Donald C. Petersen, and Laurence R. Clarke, all of whom had previously been senior partners in a Los Angeles firm specializing in litigation. Originally based in Universal City, the firm outgrew its facilities and in 1990 moved to Glendale, California, where it occupies the top five floors of a 22-story office building at 500 North Brand Boulevard.

The firm has expanded steadily over the years and in 1991 has approximately 70 lawyers and a total staff of more than 160. Most of its growth has been from within and, although there have been lateral hires, no mergers or acquisitions of other firms have occurred. The firm has an active summer associate program and recruits primarily from California law schools. Plans for the future include continued growth by some 10 attorneys per year during the 1990s.

The opportunity for long-term growth played a major role in the firm's decision to select Glendale for its headquarters. According to the Glendale Chamber of Commerce, Glendale has become the third-largest financial center in California. Recognizing the rapid growth of the Inland Empire, the firm has also established an office in Palm Springs.

Knapp, Petersen & Clarke is a general practice firm and offers a full complement of litigation and transactional legal services in a variety of fields. Its attorneys have varied educational backgrounds including economics, the social sciences, biological sciences, physical sciences, business administration, tax, accounting, and engineering.

Given the backgrounds of the founding partners, civil litigation represents a substantial portion of the practice. Collectively, the firm's attorneys have tried well over 1,500 cases before juries and have successfully represented clients in a variety of complex disputes.

The firm's major practice areas consist of: general civil litigation; financial institution and lender liability; corporate insurance matters including administrative, regulatory, and reinsurance; insurance coverage and declaratory relief; appellate advocacy; environmental, health, and safety law; labor and employment; vehicular and products liability litigation; business and real estate transactions; tax, probate, and estate planning; and construction litigation.

Knapp, Petersen & Clarke has broad experience in all facets of land subsidence and construction litigation. The firm has successfully represented first- and third-party insurers in earth movement cases such as the Big Rock Mesa and Palos Verdes Estates litigation in California. The firm has also defended selling and adjoining

The law firm's boardroom.

homeowners, architects, developers, and contractors from liability claims involving land subsidence and alleged defective design and construction.

The firm is particularly well known for its work in the insurance field, and its clients include a number of major domestic and foreign insurance and reinsurance companies. With the passage of Proposition 103 in California in 1988, the firm became actively involved in the numerous hearings and related litigation arising from its implementation. Attorneys specializing in the interpretation of insurance contracts regularly provide evaluations of coverages under all types of primary and excess insurance and assist insurers in the policy-drafting process. The firm's attorneys prosecute declaratory relief actions and defend insurers against charges of bad faith and unfair claims practices.

Environmental, health, and safety law is a growing part of Knapp, Petersen & Clarke's practice. The firm has been involved in litigating a number of significant cases in California. Some of these mass exposure cases involved groundwater pollution, exposure to fumes from dump sites, chemicals in the workplace, exposure to toxics in building materials, and a spontaneous natural gas explosion. The firm has also handled matters involving hazardous waste site clean-up and property damage caused by re-

moval of toxic building materials.

The members of the firm are strongly committed to the support of Glendale community and charitable activities, and have become active in numerous civic organizations. In addition, firm members also participate in a variety of local, county, and state bar activities.

In its relatively brief history, the firm of Knapp, Petersen & Clarke is proud of the reputation it has earned and has positioned itself well for continued growth.

The conference center.

The reception area.

FRESHMAN, MARANTZ, ORLANSKI, COOPER & KLEIN

A LAW CORPORATION

The law firm that is now Freshman, Marantz, Orlanski, Cooper & Klein was organized in Los Angeles in 1959 by Samuel K. Freshman and Philip F. Marantz. Freshman subsequently retired from the firm and Marantz is currently the senior member. The other nameplate members, all active in the firm, are Richard H. Cooper, Leib Orlanski, and Mark A. Klein.

By design, Freshman, Marantz is a local, mid-sized firm of about 20 attorneys, with offices on the Westside of Los Angeles. Many are natives of Southern California and most have earned bachelor and/or law degrees at local universities, primarily the University of California, Los Angeles,

Left to right: Attorneys Leib Orlanski, Philip F. Marantz, and Richard H. Cooper.

and the University of Southern California. They maintain close ties to the community and feel proud and privileged to serve a broad base of local clients and participate in a wide range of volunteer causes.

A general practice business law firm, Freshman, Marantz is composed of experienced and dynamic attorneys who represent clients operating in emerging as well as established industries. Well known in the community for high-quality work on complex matters, they have several areas of particular expertise and the capability to handle a variety of legal matters.

The firm has several practice areas, the principal ones being financial institutions, real estate and corporate law, securities, and litigation. Others include environmental law and bankruptcy law. Although not specialists in the sports field, the firm does represent one well-known organi-

zation that is neither local nor typical of its business and professional client base.

In the early 1970s the National Basketball Association awarded a franchise to a group organizing a team in New Orleans. A client of Phil Marantz was considering the purchase of a minor share in the team and asked him to examine the documents. Impressed with the work he had done, the New Orleans Jazz promptly retained Marantz as its general counsel.

Since that time, the team has been moved to Salt Lake City, renamed the Utah Jazz, and undergone four changes of ownership. Through it all, the one constant has been Freshman, Marantz, Orlanski, Cooper & Klein, still general counsel to the team, which is one of only three in the league to be represented by a single firm throughout their history. The firm is responsible for all player contract negotiations.

The real estate and business practice, under the leadship of Phil Marantz, provides a full complement of general corporate and business law services to its clients, including corporate formations, acquisitions, divestitures and dissolutions, shareholder agreements, employment agreements, and stock option and other employee benefit plans. It has a broad range of experience in real estate work, including purchases, sales and exchanges, construction and permanent financing, debt restructure, major leases, development joint ventures, syndications, receiverships, and foreclosures.

In its corporate securities practice, headed by Leib Orlanski and Mark Klein, the firm represents emerging high-technology companies and businesses in other growth industries, as well as investment bankers who provide venture capital, research and development financing, and underwriting services for companies making initial and follow-on public offerings. In the last-named area the firm, despite its modest size, has handled more public offerings than any other law

Attorney Tom Poletti carefully studies his notes.

firm in California for its size, demonstrating its reputation and expertise in this field.

The firm maintains a complete business litigation department, directed by Dick Cooper, who had practiced in the office of the attorney general before joining the firm. The department concentrates on large, complex types of litigation, often involving multimillion-dollar actions. They typically involve such areas as financial institutions, real estate, unlawful termination, unfair competition, and other corporate and commercial transactions. The cases are litigated in federal and state courts, both trial and appellate, as well as before arbitration tribunals and administrative agencies.

In its work with the financial industry, the firm is one of very few in California to have been approved as counsel to the U.S. Resolution Trust Corporation, the agency charged with the responsibility of taking over and operating insolvent financial institutions. The firm has also had substantial experience representing financial institutions in connection with the enforcement of secured claims in bankruptcy proceedings.

In an area of particularly high priority in California, Freshman, Marantz advises and represents clients with respect to environmental and hazardous waste issues as they relate to real estate and commercial transactions, corporate acquisitions, regulatory compliance, and potential liability for toxic waste cleanup.

In addition to practicing law, members of the firm have con-

sistently demonstrated their commitment to community service, with all the members involved in a variety of causes, including civic, charitable, educational, and religious activities. Dick Cooper, for example, has served as both chairman and president of Temple Ramat Zion and as a vice president of the Jewish National Fund.

The members also give generously of their time to bar association and other professional activities. Several teach law courses at local universities and articles written by them appear regularly in professional journals.

Looking toward the future, the members of Freshman, Marantz, Orlanski, Cooper & Klein plan to strike a balance between what they see as the advantages of a firm of their size and the growing need for the specialized services and expertise they offer. As Phil Marantz explains: "We like being a mid-sized firm. Everyone is familiar with all our cases, which not only helps us but our clients as well. We do expect to grow, while maintaining the operating style that's made us successful."

BLAKELY, SOKOLOFF, TAYLOR & ZAFMAN

Blakely, Sokoloff, Taylor & Zafman is one of relatively few firms in Southern California specializing in intellectual property law, which includes patents, trademarks, and copyrights.

The firm was formed in June 1975 by Roger W. Blakely, Jr., Stanley W. Sokoloff, Edwin H. Taylor, and Norman Zafman. Prior to launching their partnership, the four men had practiced law together at another Los Angeles firm that did intellectual property work. All four remain active in the partnership.

The organization has grown steadily since its inception and now has about 10 partners and 20 associates in four offices. All its growth has been internal, without benefit of merger or acquisition.

The firm's main office is located in Los Angeles. However, its clients include many major Silicon Valley companies, some of which it has represented since the founding of those companies. To enhance its services to those clients, several years ago the firm opened an office in Sunnyvale and another more recently in San Francisco. It also has an office in Costa Mesa to better serve its Orange County clients.

The firm has extensive legal and technical experience, representing clients engaged in a broad range of technologies and business activities. In addition to their qualifications as lawyers, the members of the firm hold engineering or science degrees, and many were employed in industry before starting their law careers. Several have master's degrees in patent law, engineering, computer science, or business administration. In addition, members of the firm include former trademark examiners from the

United States Patent and Trademark Office.

The firm prepares and prosecutes applications for United States and foreign patent protection for its clients' inventions, ranging from sophisticated high-technology products and processes to everyday consumer items. The firm also obtains copyrights for computer software, the "look and feel" of computer screens, publications, and works of art, to name a few. Obtaining domestic and foreign registrations of trademarks is another part of the firm's practice.

In addition, the firm provides intellectual property support for corporate and general practice law firms, including high-technology litigation, due diligence investigations and opinions of counsel, and preparation of high-technology agreements.

The firm represents clients in litigation involving infringement of patent rights, trademarks, trade secrets, and copyrights, as well as unfair competition and United States Customs enforcement matters. It has been in the forefront in copyright litigation, particularly in the computer area. It has also been a leader in the protection of clients against counterfeit goods, including conducting anti-counterfeit seizures and providing liaison with the United States government attorneys for prosecution of criminal trademark and copyright cases. In addition, the firm has experience in bringing actions before the International Trade Commission and in working cooperatively with United States Customs to stop the importation of infringing and counterfeit goods.

Intellectual property law today is much more international in scope than ever before, as evidenced by the growth of reciprocity and cooperation treaties among the nations of the world. The United States, for example, recently rewrote its copyright laws to bring them more into conformity with those of other countries. Such factors as the formation of the European Economic Community and emergence of the Pacific Rim as a major economic force have changed the way

Partners of the firm in the main conference room of the Los Angeles office. (Standing, from left) Eric S. Hyman, Jeffrey J. Blatt, Edwin H. Taylor, Norman Zafman, Ronald W. Reagin, and Ira M. Siegel; (Seated, from left) James C. Scheller, Jr., Stephen D. Gross, Stanley W. Sokoloff, and Roger W. Blakely, Jr.

the world does business, requiring much more of a global perspective than ever before.

In view of this rapidly changing environment, Blakely, Sokoloff, Taylor & Zafman's practice has become increasingly international in scope. Many of its clients are now multinational corporations, and the firm represents them as well as foreign-based companies in most countries of the world, using a network of local associate counsel where needed.

Because of its reputation in its areas of specialty, many of the firm's new clients are referrals from other attorneys in general practice (and, sometimes, from attorneys who had been on the opposing side in litigation).

Members of the firm participate actively in a variety of professional associations at local, county, state, and national levels and have held leadership positions in many of them. Articles written by them on various intellectual property subjects have appeared in professional journals. They also give generously of their time and talents to civic, cultural, and charitable organizations.

From its inception the firm of Blakely, Sokoloff, Taylor & Zafman has played a major role in this age of technology. "It's a very exciting area in which to practice," says one partner. "We've been instrumental in helping our clients develop new ideas and bring them to market,

and in the process we've watched them grow from tiny entrepreneurial ventures to huge corporations with worldwide impact. It's very rewarding for us to be able to say that we help make things—meaningful things—happen."

Some associates of the firm discuss a case in the hallway of the Los Angeles office.

DAMES & MOORE

Dames & Moore engineers review plans during placement of the canal lining for the Freeman Diversion structure in Ventura County. The firm prepared preliminary and final designs and managed construction of the diversion system, which diverts water from the Santa Clara River to recharge groundwater levels. The system ultimately will control a seawater intrusion problem and supply water to the 40,000-acre Oxnard Plain.

Back in 1934, when Trent R. Dames and William W. Moore received their master's degrees in civil engineering from the California Institute of Technology, their field of soil mechanics and foundation engineering was on the very frontier of development. As classmates they had discovered a shared fascination for this new field and, four years after graduation, decided to form their own firm. Thus, in 1938, the partnership of Dames & Moore, consulting engineers, was launched.

At first there was little to suggest the heights to which the firm would rise. Moore kept his job with the U.S. Army Corps of Engineers, working for the new firm on weekends and evenings. Dames worked out of his home in Pasadena. Soon, however, a major technological breakthrough in soil investigation got the firm moving. It was the direct result of the high priority the two men, true pioneers in the field of soil mechanics, placed on developing new methods for sampling and testing soils.

The growing firm opened its first branch office in San Francisco in 1941. With the onset of U.S. involvement in World War II later that year, Dames & Moore began working on many projects involving U.S. Navy and Army facilities. In 1943 the firm tackled its first international project, in Saudi Arabia. After the war the firm continued to expand, admitting additional partners in 1947 and, one year later, entering the European market for the first time.

By 1950 the firm had offices in eight cities and employed nearly 100 people, still offering just one service: soils and foundation engineering. Then, beginning in 1952, the service base was broadened to include engineering geology, groundwater development, mineral exploration, and other areas in the applied earth sciences. By the 1960s the firm had added environmental engineering, earthquake engineering, and marine services.

The emergence of nuclear power as a viable energy source gave rise to concerns about the environmental effects of proposed nuclear power plants. In 1963 the firm undertook one of its first major environmental projects, evaluating a nuclear plant site in New York State.

The enactment of the National Environmental Policy Act in 1969 heralded the rapid growth of the firm's environmental practice and, by 1975, more than one-third of its professional staff were environmental specialists.

The 1980s brought a significant expansion of Dames & Moore's waste management practice, particularly in the areas of hazardous substances and toxic waste. As has been the case in every area, the growth of this specialization was in response to client needs, the driving force behind the firm since its founding. In waste management, client needs include planning, engineering, design, and construction management services for all types of waste management facilities; industrial health and safety programs; and the remediation of contaminated sites.

The dawn of the 1990s brought renewed commitment and vision on the part of the firm's leaders, as they redefined its mission statement: "Dames & Moore will provide superior environmental, engineering, and management consulting services to a worldwide clientele that will employ these services to enhance their competitive, financial, regulatory, and technological decisions."

Key strategic goals for the 1990s were approved by the board of directors, dealing with both external and internal issues. First and foremost was a renewed commitment to developing and maintaining strong, enduring client relationships by maintaining technical excellence, emphasizing client service, communicating

Dames & Moore personnel sample vapors from a waste drum as part of a hazardous waste management project.

effectively, and working together as a team. Other goals include the provision of integrated services and environmentally sound recommendations to clients.

The client base Dames & Moore is committed to serve is composed of businesses and industries in the private sector, public and private utilities, financial institutions, developers, architect/engineers, constructors, and all levels of government. Since its founding it has completed more than 80,000 projects for about 20,000 clients in more than 125 countries. Truly worldwide in scope, it employs more than 3,500 people, working in more than 110 offices located in a majority of the states in the United States and in some 20 nations overseas.

The firm's professional disciplines are engineering and design, earth sciences, planning services, construction management, environmental sciences, and waste management, with the latter two comprising about 40 percent of the overall practice. Each of the six encompasses a broad range of disciplines and includes such diverse fields as water resources management, transportation planning, earthquake engineering, integrated manufacturing engineering, and industrial health.

Many of the projects with which the firm has been involved are well known worldwide. One, in the 1950s, was the development of Dodger Stadium in Los Angeles. Dames & Moore provided soil and foundation recommendations for the project, which required the excavation of nearly 8 million cubic yards of earth. In the 1960s the firm participated in the development of the Bay Area Rapid Transit system in San Francisco and also conducted the geotechnical investigation for the 606-foot-high Seattle Space Needle.

The firm also undertook one of its most complex projects during the 1960s—the investigation of subsurface conditions and recommendation of foundation specifications for the enormous area of wetlands in Orlando, Florida, that was to become Walt Disney World. Thanks in large measure to the four-year-long efforts of the Dames & Moore team, the Magic Kingdom became reality, built on land long considered unusable.

Although no longer active in the management of the firm they launched more than a half-century ago, Trent Dames and Bill Moore remain very much involved. The former maintains contact with the Los Angeles headquarters while the latter, based in the San Francisco of-

fice, continues his travels as a distinguished emissary for the firm.

Part of the firm's vision for the 1990s has been to encourage its employees to "think globally" as never before, in order to allow it to serve its clients even more effectively in the increasingly interdependent economies of North America, the European Economic Community, and the Pacific Rim. Dames & Moore is committed, as well, to remain on the leading edge of technology, as it continues to provide advanced technological services.

In the 1990s Dames & Moore continues to be the client-oriented firm that William Moore and Trent Dames envisioned in 1938 and remains true to the theme chosen a few years ago to express the essence of its practice: "Engineering Excellence, Environmental Responsibility."

Dames & Moore provided foundation recommendations for Dodger Stadium when it was constructed in the 1950s.

Dames & Moore uses a computer-aided drafting and design system (CADD) to facilitate earth structure design projects. Construction drawings are assembled on the CADD system by skilled designers.

MacNeal-Schwendler

The annual report of The MacNeal-Schwendler Corporation (MSC) states that it "designs, produces, and markets proprietary computer software products for use in computer-aided engineering." It is a modest description of an organization that, since its founding in 1963, has had a global impact on the field of computer-aided engineering (CAE) and includes among its clients most of the major aerospace and automotive companies in the world.

MSC was founded on February 1, 1963, by Dr. Richard MacNeal and Robert Schwendler. They had worked together at Computer Engineering Associates (CEA), a manufacturer of passive analog computers and a consulting group for stress analysis problems. The initial capital of the new company was $18,000, which would provide "engineering consulting and analysis by computational means to be decided later."

The company leased small offices at 2556 Mission Road in San Marino and completed its first project later in 1963. It was a digital computer program to simulate the analog analysis techniques used at CEA. Called SADSAM, for Structural Analysis by Digital Simulation of Analog Methods, the product remained in use until 1976 and was a forerunner of MSC's mainstay program, MSC/NASTRAN.

By 1967 MSC had outgrown its San Marino facilities and moved to 7442 North Figueroa Street in Eagle Rock. By then the development of NASTRAN was in full swing. The company, as part of a team that included Computer Sciences Corporation and the Martin Corporation, had been awarded a contract from NASA which in 1964 had decided to sponsor the development of its own finite element analysis (FEA) program, of which the passive analog computer and SADSAM were primitive examples. The development of NASTRAN was a hallmark event because it repre-

sented one of the first efforts to unify and combine structural mechanics into a single computer program.

The finite element method uses applied mathematics to create a theoretical representation of an actual structure. The strength and performance characteristics of the structure can then be analyzed by solving thousands of simultaneous equations. Finite element analysis can reliably solve a broad range of problems and can reduce the cost of building and testing prototypes. For example, a major Japanese automobile company reported that by using MSC/NASTRAN it was able to reduce the time needed to bring a new car to market from 50 to 40 months, a significant savings in time and money.

Delivered to NASA in 1967, NASTRAN revolutionized the field of structural analysis. In 1971 MSC's own proprietary version of the program, called MSC/NASTRAN, was released for public use. That marked the start of MSC's rapid rise in revenues and profits and in reputation, both domestically and internationally. In 1973 the company opened a European office in Munich, West Germany, and signed an agreement with C. Itoh to represent MSC in Japan.

Not willing to rest on its laurels, MSC continually upgraded MSC/NASTRAN. There were frequent new releases of the program, and by 1975 more than 75 percent of the original 1,408 subroutines had been upgraded. Today the company still allots a high percentage of its revenues to the development and maintenance of MSC/NAS-TRAN, making significant upgrades every year.

From its inception, MSC was determined to become a global force. In 1982, before many U.S. companies were lining up representatives in Japan, MSC established its own subsidiary in Tokyo. For the remainder of the 1980s, thanks to the huge worldwide popularity of MSC/NASTRAN, the company experienced an average annual growth rate of 26 percent in sales, 29 percent in net after-tax earnings, and 14 percent in working capital.

In the past, about 60 percent of corporate revenues have been derived from North America with the balance divided equally between Europe and the Far East. In the long run MSC expects overseas sources to provide up to 50 percent of total revenues, while at the same time the domestic sales and marketing staff is being challenged to maintain the company's dominant position.

The Beechcraft "Starship"; MSC/NASTRAN was used extensively in the design and analysis of this revolutionary aircraft.

By the close of the decade, MSC had facilities all across the United States and in several other parts of the world. In Europe it had direct offices in Great Britain, Germany, The Netherlands, and Italy. Its Asian facilities were in Japan and Hong Kong. It also had representative offices in France, Norway, Spain, Taiwan, Singapore, Korea, Argentina, Israel, and Australia.

A tragic event occurred in December 1978 that necessitated some changes in the company's management. Co-founder Robert Schwendler suddenly took ill and died the following January. Shortly thereafter, Dr. Joseph Gloudeman, who had joined MSC in 1978, was named vice president of marketing, reporting to MacNeal, president.

In May 1983 MSC became a public corporation with stock traded over the counter. In 1984 MSC's stock was listed on the American Stock Exchange, with a ticker symbol of MNS. In early 1985 Gloudeman was named president of the company and MacNeal became chairman of the board.

As the 1990s got under way, MSC had already taken major steps to broaden its base. Until then it had basically been a single-product company, although that term is misleading given the amaz-

ing applicability and versatility of MSC/NASTRAN. By January 1990 MSC/NASTRAN had been installed at more than 1,000 commercial sites and was capable of performing structural analysis prior to the development of virtually any type of product in the world, ranging in size from a contact lens to a giant space vehicle.

As explained by Gloudeman, "MSC/NASTRAN is a software package that enables designers and engineering analysts to very carefully study, in as much detail as they care to, how their products will perform under various road, flight, or usage conditions; they can simulate many more

Far left: A deep-sea submersible oil drilling platform. This structure is the largest man-made movable object ever built and was analyzed extensively with MSC/NASTRAN.

Left: An advanced prototype automobile designed by Mazda with the help of MSC's products. Almost every automotive company in the world uses MSC/NASTRAN to help design and engineer the structural integrity, handling characteristics, and safety of the cars we drive.

An advanced 5 1/4-inch hard disk storage device. Disk drive manufacturers use MSC products to analyze many components of their devices including the rotating mechanism, the read arm, and the thin-film recording/playback heads.

MSC/XL is MSC's advanced interactive graphics pre- and post-processor for use in conjunction with MSC's analysis products. Engineers use MSC/XL to develop models for analysis and to review the results of analysis. Shown here are results from an analysis of a component of the Space Shuttle solid rocket booster.

MSC/EMAS is MSC's key product in the area of electromagnetic analysis. MSC/EMAS is used in the analysis of a wide range of electrical and electronic devices, including electric motors, generators, alternators, microwave antennas, radar, and communication equipment. Shown here is an analysis of the electromagnetic flux density in an electric generator.

different types of these environments than can be done in a test program."

MSC/NASTRAN can help the engineer analyze products of almost any conceivable geometric or topological shape, thick or thin, distorted into any possible shape. The program is applicable to any product that can be designed, engineered, or manufactured.

Having virtually "fleshed out the library of finite element analysis objects," the company began looking for other types of problems to solve. An early step in the diversification process was the 1987 acquisition of a division of A.O. Smith Corporation, called CADCOMP, and since renamed E/EAD, for Engineering Electromagnetics Applications Department. The acquisition vastly broadened MSC's capabilities of analyzing electromagnetic devices and led to the introduction of several new software products.

MSC has also become heavily involved in im-

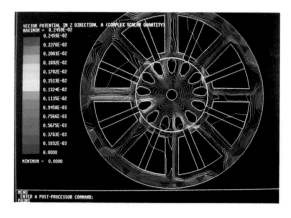

pact studies, particularly automobile and aircraft crash analysis. The program that helps engineers simulate the effects of crashes is called MSC/DYNA. "We can analyze an endless variety of impacts. Examples include an automobile collision at 65 miles per hour or bird strikes on the canopy or windshield of an aircraft. We can even simulate and analyze what would happen if a Boeing 747 crashed into a nuclear power plant," said Gloudeman.

In 1989 the company entered the high-energy physics field with the acquisition of PISCES International B.V. of Gouda, The Netherlands, further enhancing its ability to analyze high-speed impacts. The PISCES acquisition not only gave MSC a stronger marketing base in Europe but also established it as a true European company, meeting all of the requirements of the 1992 United States of Europe regulations and fully protecting its rights. Once again, as it had in Japan, the company demonstrated its ability to anticipate and stay well ahead of long-term trends.

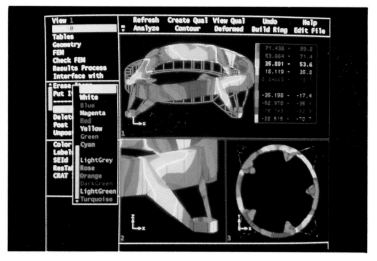

Also in 1989 MSC purchased the St. Louis-based Noetic Technologies. The Missouri company had developed a structural analysis computer program called PROBE, which complements MSC/NASTRAN.

While such wide-scale diversification signals a new corporate strategic thrust, it is all designed to complement the company's mission statement, which is "the business of providing quality engineering analysis software and related support services on a global basis, for the long term."

These support services include regular meetings with top managers of major clients, annual users conferences around the world, and the development of lower-price alternatives to MSC's comprehensive and sophisticated software programs. Most of MSC's products are flexible enough to be run on a wide range of computer hardware, including engineering workstations, minicomputers, mainframes, minisupercomputers,

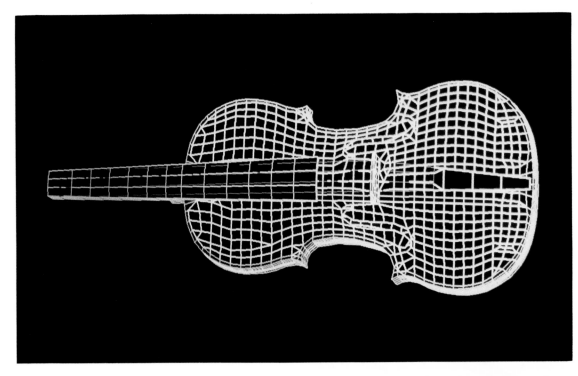

Left: MSC's products were used to analyze the vibrational and acoustic characteristics of a Stradivarius violin.

and supercomputers.

Technical support and consulting services are also provided as part of MSC's philosophy of "client as partner." More than 200 training classes are taught by MSC professionals and are available to clients. The company takes seriously its commitment to unwavering excellence in client service, support, and training.

Today The MacNeal-Schwendler Corporation conducts its worldwide operations from its headquarters at 815 Colorado Boulevard in Los Angeles, where it has been located since 1982. The original team of four employees has grown to a staff of more than 300 people, who are readily acknowledged by MacNeal and Gloudeman as the company's most important resource. "That's probably an area that gives us our best competitive posture," says Gloudeman. "We've been extremely fortunate in assimilating highly qualified technical people whose longevity is unparalleled, and that's not by accident. We focus on being a 'family' operation, and at the same time we offer a real challenge to highly capable individuals and

provide more computer resources per person than any other company I know."

As it plans to continue its pattern of growth and diversification, MSC has taken steps to assure a consistent influx of highly qualified people. In addition to a summer intern program for college students, MSC maintains ongoing relationships with leading engineering schools, funding a variety of research projects and attracting top graduates.

The MacNeal-Schwendler Corporation has come a long way from the little company formed in 1963. In a relatively short span of years, MSC has become an international corporation whose products can help engineers analyze and solve the most demanding product-development problems and challenges of companies throughout the world.

Above: The Ford Taurus was designed and engineered using MSC/NASTRAN. Use of MSC's products has enabled Ford to bring safer, more reliable automotive products to market in a shorter span of time.

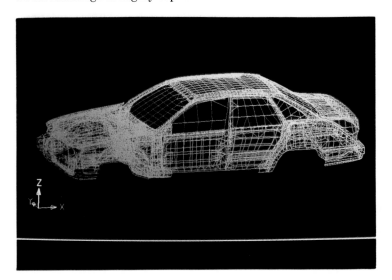

Left: Shown here is a mathematical, or Finite Element Analysis (FEA), model of a Ford Taurus body.

PAUL, HASTINGS, JANOFSKY & WALKER

On November 1, 1951, Lee G. Paul, Robert P. Hastings and Leonard S. Janofsky launched the Los Angeles-based firm of Paul, Hastings & Janofsky. In 1962 they were joined by Charles M. Walker and the firm became Paul, Hastings, Janofsky & Walker, the name it has retained to the present. The four original principals have all retired from the partnership but continue in active roles as counsel to the firm.

The firm was one of many that sprang up in Los Angeles during the 1950s and 1960s but one of just a few to survive intact. From the start, the partners focused on building an institutional law firm that would have a major role in Los Angeles. The firm's growth over the years reflects this goal. In 1974 an office was opened in the Orange County community of Costa Mesa, and another was opened in Santa Monica in 1983.

The late 1970s brought the start of a trend among law firms to establish nationwide practices; the focus of Paul, Hastings, Janofsky & Walker was adjusted accordingly. Its goal was now to continue to grow and to be perceived as one of the preeminent law firms in America. In 1980 offices were opened in Atlanta, Georgia, and Washington, D.C. In 1981 the firm was retained by a major client in New York, requiring frequent cross-country travel by many of its attorneys. That led to the opening of a Stamford, Connecticut, office in 1983 and a growing awareness of the desirability of a New York City presence. The 1986 opening of an office in mid-Manhattan solidified the firm's presence in the Northeast.

While this national growth was taking place during the early 1980s, the firm also seized the opportunity to develop an international practice. Paul, Hastings, Janofsky & Walker was fortunate to find a Japanese national who had an outstanding background in the community and an excellent law school education to be in charge of its office in Japan. The firm's eighth office was opened in Tokyo in 1988. The international practice has become a major portion of the firm's business, involving, among other things, a considerable amount of Japanese merger and acquisition work and the representation of Japanese investors in real estate in the United States.

The firm has more than 400 lawyers, placing it among the four largest in Los Angeles County and the 35 largest in the United States. In a recent publication it was listed as one of the law firms viewed as likely to be among the dominant 20 firms in the United States in the year 2000. Of those firms, Paul, Hastings, Janofsky & Walker is one of only two formed after 1945. Firm attorneys come from nearly every state, more than a dozen foreign countries, and some 60 different law schools.

Much of the firm's success is the result of the foresightedness of the name partners, who began passing the mantle of leadership to younger partners at an early stage. By demonstrating their faith in the judgment of their younger colleagues, the founding partners assured the continuity and growth of the firm, and introduced the entrepreneurial flavor and youthful spirit that has become its hallmark.

That tradition of giving younger partners leadership roles has continued. Among the more than 100 partners, only three are over the age of 60, a few are more than 50, and some have not yet reached 40. Regardless of age, all share the vision that has brought the firm to its preeminent position in a relatively short time.

The remarkable record of growth at Paul, Hastings, Janofsky & Walker has been achieved without a single merger with, or acquisition of, another firm. Even those attorneys who have joined the firm as partners have almost always come in one at a time and there have never been more than three from another firm. The firm is structured as a single partnership, in which all partners have an equal voice in the decision-making process.

Paul, Hastings, Janofsky & Walker has five major areas of specialization: litigation; business law; labor and employment law; tax and probate; and real estate. These practice areas reflect the diverse backgrounds of the founding partners. Lee Paul specializes in litigation, Robert Hastings in business law, Leonard Janofsky in employment law, and Charles Walker in taxation.

The firm's Litigation Department, the largest of the five, engages in a diverse federal and state trial practice as well as appellate litigation in all areas of commercial and business law. Litigation teams handle cases involving securities fraud, environmental requirements and toxic torts, products liability, insurance coverage issues and related aspects of bad faith claims, First Amendment, entertainment, antitrust, white-collar crime, energy, government contracts, general commercial, and real estate matters.

The firm's Business Law Department mirrors the ever changing business and financial spheres, both domestically and internationally. Its practice includes mergers and acquisitions, corporate finance, public and private offerings of securities, investment company regulations, electric energy power, creditors' rights and insolvency, financial institution law and lending transactions, intellectual property, franchising, and product distribution.

The firm has one of the largest employment practices in the United States, carrying on a tradition begun by founding partner Leonard Janofsky many years ago. The Employment Law Department represents management in all aspects of this dynamic and growing field, including

tive bargaining, arbitrations, employment discrimination litigation, equal employment opportunity counseling and training, wrongful termination litigation, employee benefits, and public sector employment matters.

The firm's tax practice began with Charles M. Walker, who had served as assistant secretary of the treasury (tax policy). Since then the tax practice has grown to provide tax planning for corporations, partnerships, individuals, and specialized tax entities (S-corporations, RICs, REMICs, REITs, cooperatives); tax structuring of real estate and commercial transactions including mergers and acquisitions, workouts, bankruptcy, leveraged leasing, and project financing; cross border tax advice to multinational clients; civil tax litigation and controversies; criminal tax; California unitary, sales, and property taxes; estate planning; and executive tax planning.

The firm's real estate department consists of more than 40 lawyers who have expertise in every aspect of real estate law. These attorneys represent international, national, and local financial institutions, landowners, developers, tenants, pensions, and investment funds. With its size, composition, and experience levels, the department is particularly adept at handling large, multi-property, multi-state/location real estate and corporate transactions. Specializations include office and industrial developments and leasing, real estate debt restructuring and workouts, lending, joint venture and equity participations, and land use.

Paul, Hastings, Janofsky & Walker has experi-

enced consistent growth in all five practice areas, with a broad client base in each, allowing it to remain free of dependency on any one practice area, industry, or client for its continued success.

From the day they joined the firm, the attorneys at Paul, Hastings, Janofsky & Walker are taught certain traditions that have characterized it since its inception. They include high moral and ethical standards, excellence in the practice of law, and commitment to the community.

Community involvement includes pro bono service and professional activities. A significant portion of its resources are commited to pro bono work and it has pledged to provide an average of 35 hours per attorney per year to pro bono matters.

From a modest beginning, Paul, Hastings, Janofsky & Walker has become one of the most rapidly growing major law firms in the United States. Its practice includes the representation of large, established *Fortune* 500 companies and smaller, emerging business enterprises. Much of the reason for its success is its focus on recruiting and retaining the best legal talent available, at both the associate and partner level. It operates as "one firm with many offices," maintaining close personal and professional links among its attorneys, whatever their location.

With strategic locations across the United States, a flourishing practice in Japan, and with European clients, Paul, Hastings, Janofsky & Walker is poised to help lead the way as the legal profession becomes even more international in the coming years.

Conferences with colleagues and with clients are a constant activity in all the firm's offices.

BALLARD, ROSENBERG & GOLPER

T he law firm of Ballard, Rosenberg & Golper hasn't wasted any time in making a name for itself in its chosen field of practice. That field is labor and employment law on behalf of manage-ment. Formed in 1986, the firm already has one of the largest labor law practices in the Los An-geles area and is among the fastest growing in that specialty. Within five years after being formed, it has grown to 20 attorneys, with two to four more being added annually.

The nameplate partners, Kenneth R. Ballard, Richard S. Rosenberg, and John B. Golper, all graduated from law school in the mid-1970s. Be-fore launching their own firm, they had been partners at other area firms, specializing in em-ployment and labor law.

The founders attribute much of their rapid growth and success to the intense focus they, along with their other partners and associates, bring to bear on their single specialty. Weekly meetings, at which one member of the firm pro-vides all the others with a detailed written and oral report on new developments in the field, keep that focus sharp.

The firm's approach is extremely practical, rather than theoretical. Ballard, Rosenberg & Golper provides its unionized and nonunionized clients with aggressive representation and coun-sel in formulating, implementing, and defending labor and employee relations policies and proce-dures. Instead of telling clients how to proceed,

they explain the full range of options and risks, allowing the client to make the choices.

Unlike many other labor law firms where liti-gation is the order of the day, Ballard, Rosenberg & Golper places as high a priority on prevention as it does on litigation. Clients are advised on formulating and implementing policies so that desired goals may be achieved without resorting to adversarial proceedings. The firm regularly conducts in-house seminars tailored to the indi-vidual needs of its clients. The seminars teach supervisory personnel how to manage effectively while maintaining compliance with federal, state, and local labor laws and regulations.

As advocates, the attorneys at Ballard, Rosen-berg & Golper regularly litigate the full range of labor and employment law cases before federal and state courts and administrative agencies. The firm is quick to respond to crises, with an approach that is efficient, enthusiastic, and ag-gressive, allowing it to achieve excellent results for clients. Its winning tradition has already been well established, earning the firm an excel-lent national reputation.

The majority of the firm's clients are located in the western United States and are engaged in a wide range of industries. Ballard, Rosenberg & Golper has established itself as one of the na-tion's leading firms representing major hotel chains throughout the nation. Other industries include aerospace, health care, home furnish-ings, beverage, music, trucking, and restaurants.

The firm looks forward to growth in the future, pointing out that the employer-employee relationship is highly regulated, with new regulations and restrictions being imposed continually.

Aggressive, efficient, responsive, knowledge-able, practical, enthusiastic, and focused—these are the attributes which have been the basis for the success of Ballard, Rosenberg & Golper.

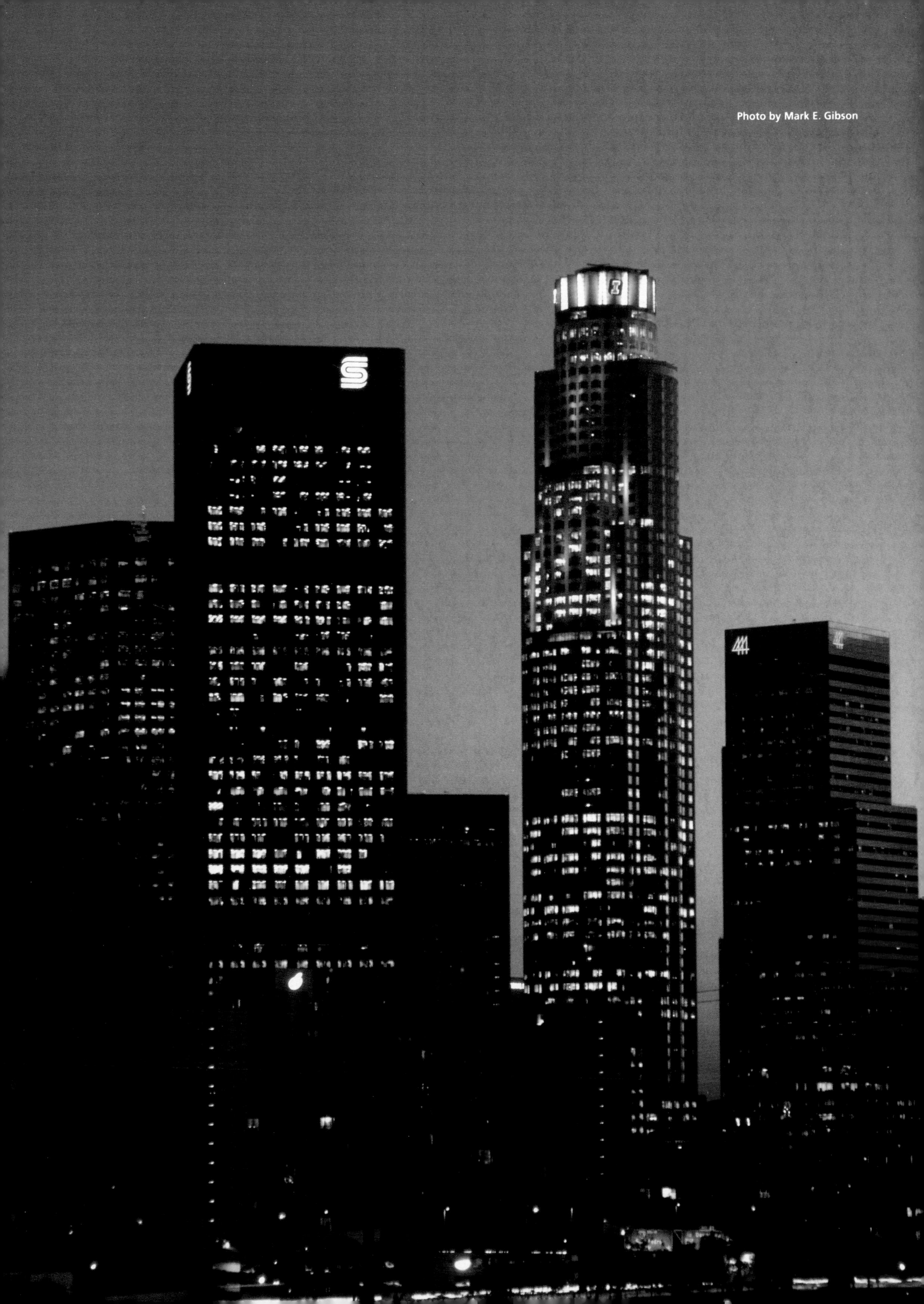

Photo by Mark E. Gibson

FROM THE GROUND UP

Building Metro L.A.

As a metropolitian leader, Los Angeles is constantly redefining its horizons with a look to the future. With this vision in mind, architects, developers, and realtors work together to enrich the city's skyline and preserve its integrity.

As a flourishing metropolis, Los Angeles is famous for many things including its distinctive buildings. These steel workers are an important part of the city's architectural backbone. Photo by Mark E. Gibson

ROCHLIN BARAN & BALBONA INC.

Hospital of the Good Samaritan Medical Office Building, Los Angeles.

ochlin Baran & Balbona Inc. (RBB), an architectural firm specializing in health care facilities, was founded in Van Nuys in 1952 by Fred Rochlin and Ephraim Baran. The firm is now headed by Joseph A. Balbona, Joel A. Jaffe, and Deneys Purcell.

RBB is the 13th-largest architectural firm in Southern California and is the largest firm in the state specializing in health care architecture. For more than a dozen years it has been among *Engineering News-Record*'s top 500 design firms. Since its founding the firm has completed more than 3,000 hospitals, clinics, medical office buildings, laboratories, skilled nursing facilities, psychiatric and rehabilitation centers, and research facilities.

RBB's entry into the health care field was based on Rochlin's and Baran's interest in and commitment to social concerns, especially those regarding health care in America. The commitment was manifested in their decision to specialize in the architectural planning and design of health care facilities. The first project assigned to the firm was a group clinic located in Van Nuys. This team of doctors was represented by an insurance company that assembled physician groups for clinics throughout the United States. The insurance company recommended the services of RBB to its clients, and this began RBB's reputation for designing and building clinics throughout the country. This led to a variety of future assignments for the firm in the health care facility design field.

Among its major clients are Cedars-Sinai Medical Center, Kaiser Permanente, Saint Francis Medical Center West in Hawaii, Saint John's Hospital and Health Center, Hospital of the Good Samaritan, the Veterans Administration, Children's Hospital of Los Angeles, the County and City of Los Angeles hospitals, and the University of California, Los Angeles, Medical Center.

The firm's work is by no means limited to the medical field. Its commercial projects include the Directors Guild of America headquarters in Hollywood; the Louis Factor Building on the UCLA campus, and Redken Laboratories. The combined value of the projects in which the firm is annually involved is about $200 million, measured by total construction costs.

RBB, which moved to its present facilities at 10980 Wilshire Boulevard in 1970, has grown steadily over the years. Its staff, which numbers about 100 people, includes architects, draftspeople, interior designers, health care planners, CAD operators, and administrative personnel.

RBB has completed projects in about two dozen states, but 90 percent of its work is concentrated in California. The firm has recently completed some assignments in Hawaii and, with the emergence of the Pacific Rim as an economic force, is looking to expand westward.

RBB has long been in the forefront of medical planning. Because hospitals present very complex design problems, the firm must keep abreast of the latest advances in medical technology and incorporate them in its work. It also places major emphasis on the most advanced technology available in its own profession, using, for example, state-of-the-art CAD (computer aided design) systems.

The changes in health care delivery systems that have been taking place in recent years call for long-range planning of medical facilities, as well as for flexibility. The twenty-first century hospital will bear little resemblance to the twentieth century version. For example, as hospitals have become increasingly competitive, an important new design theme is a noninstitutional campuslike appearance, for ease of access, comfort of the patient, and a pleasing environment, and to aid administrators in their marketing efforts.

Saint John's Medical Plaza, Santa Monica.

Another important area of consideration is maximizing available assets. With health care costs continuing to rise and greater emphasis being placed on outpatient care, better use of land and facilities, expansion capabilities, and alternative uses for surplus bed spaces are just some of the areas addressed by RBB as it designs the hospitals of the future.

Significant changes are also taking place in medical office buildings, making traditionally designed ones obsolete. Many individual practitioners who occupied smaller suites are either sharing space with other professionals or have become part of the growing trend toward group practices. RBB is now designing these facilities with enough flexibility to meet the needs of both groups.

In addition to its flourishing health care practice, the firm has established ambitious diversifi-

cation goals. Drawing on its extensive experience, it plans to focus more on commercial ventures, including office buildings, hotels, and research facilities. In its new projects, RBB will be guided by the same philosophy that has guided it successfully in the medical field since 1952.

That philosophy incorporates several key concepts. One is that the client's input is at the core of a successful design. Thus RBB consistently stimulates communication with clients as the most effective way to see that specific functional, aesthetic, financial, and scheduling requirements are met.

A second guiding principle is that buildings must be open to future change, as technology advances and markets shift. With this in mind, RBB

stresses design that will accommodate alteration and expansion.

Another important principle is that buildings are for people. Nowhere is this more evident than in health care. A building should provide the patient with an environment conducive to the healing process and the staff with one that fosters efficiency and heightens morale. For the visitor it should offer a comfortable and encouraging atmosphere.

Since its founding, Rochlin Baran & Balbona has placed heavy emphasis on both quality design and client satisfaction. Accordingly, the comprehensive services it provides extend well beyond architectural design. They include master planning, programming, feasibility studies, site and facility planning, interior design, post-occupancy evaluation, and a dozen other services. All are provided with the client's full range of needs in mind. The fact that 75 percent of the firm's new business comes from existing clients demonstrates clearly how well it has met its goals.

Above: Directors Guild of America, Hollywood.

Far left: Northridge Hospital Medical Center, Northridge.

East Canyon Health Center, Anaheim.

PROVIDENT TITLE COMPANY

Quality and service are the foundations on which Provident Title Company opened its doors in 1986. With a commitment to become one of the leading service-oriented title companies in Los Angeles County, Provident has shown outstanding growth—from 9 original employees to more than 90 employees today in the Beverly Hills, San Pedro, and Sunland offices.

In a strongly competitive market (there were 23 title companies in Los Angeles County at the time of its founding) Provident has found its nitch. "We are unique in that we do not choose or attempt to be 'all things to all people,'" says Vice President/Sales Manager Larry Edwards. "We

Ralph Khelil. This policy setting team, along with legal counsel Leonard Smith, possesses a unique and rare blend of quality experience learned from entry level positions up through the ranks to current ownership status.

Supporting the premise that the title business is a people business, Provident has dedicated a great deal of time and effort into building a team that blends both marketing and technical expertise. With a staff representing one of the most experienced and knowledgeable in the industry, Provident's formula for success is assured—quality service combined with quality customers creates a quality organization.

aggressively market to a particular segment of the real estate industry and service that market. We don't just talk about or claim that we give service—we give it!" Company statistics prove Edwards' statement—standard turnaround time on preliminary title reports is an average of less than three days.

Provident's founding partners, all of whom are still active in the company, have more than 130 years of combined title experience. The number of years is significant as it represents the commitment of just five individuals to the title field: Sam Patterson, chairman of the board and chief executive officer; Jerry Millsaps, president; and vice presidents Larry Edwards, Jack Boss, and

Remaining profitable through the early boom years of its existence, as well as during the current market climate, Provident is confident about its future.

"We will continue to grow and expand, but it will be controlled growth," says Edwards. "We believe that future expansion will be outside of Los Angeles County. However, that depends on the marketplace and the quality of people available. When we find those people who have historically done a good job and they are well known in their community, then we will consider opening additional offices. People and knowledge is what sets our company apart from the others."

McCormick Construction Company

McCormick Construction Company is truly a family business. A phone call to Mr. Mc-Cormick could be for any one of six men. The president is Jack D. McCormick, whose grandfather, George, founded the company in Arkansas in 1914. When George's son, W.R., succeeded him in 1921, W.R. moved the company to Joplin, Missouri, where it thrived. By the 1950s McCormick Construction owned its own equipment and employed 200 people. Under W.R.'s leadership the company's focus shifted from residential to commercial construction, where it remains today.

When W.R. died in 1959, his sons, Joe and Jack, took the helm, focusing their activities in Southern California. Joe served as president until his death in 1975, when he was succeeded by Jack. Joe's son, Robert, a fourth generation in the family business, joined the company in 1971 and became vice president and chief estimator in 1975.

The company grew and expanded, moving its headquarters to Burbank in 1977. By 1980 three more McCormicks had joined the company and now serve as part of the management team. They are: Jack's sons, Steve and Mike, who are controller and purchasing manager, respectively, and Jack's brother Pete, who is chief financial officer. Another brother of Jack's, Gary, signed on in 1981 and is executive vice president.

McCormick is a general contracting firm specializing in mid- to high-rise commercial and institutional buildings, industrial projects, retail and medical facilities, and interiors. Ranked among California's top 25 general contractors, with annual volume in excess of $150 million, the company has been a leader in adopting progressive construction techniques and procedures while maintaining a hands-on management style.

One division of the company handles major projects of $5 million and above, with about a dozen projects in production at a given time. Smaller projects, of which 25 or more are usually in production, are handled by the special-projects division. Regardless of the project size, every client receives the same level of attention.

Among the projects completed by the firm are the expansion of West Covina Fashion Plaza, the new Armand Hammer Museum in Westwood, the Warner Center in Woodland Hills, a 300,000-square-foot Electro-Optical Data Systems Group facility for Hughes Aircraft Company in Manhattan Beach, and the Courtyard by Marriott Hotels in Buena Park and Hacienda Heights.

Several of the McCormicks play active roles in community and professional organizations. Jack is a board member of the Burbank YMCA, St. Joseph Medical Center, and the Burbank Chamber of Commerce. He is also president of the Construction Industry Research Board, a past president of the Los Angeles Chapter of the Building Industry Association, and a former national director of the National Association of Home Builders.

Gary McCormick serves as president of the USC Architectural Guild and as a trustee of Burbank Community Hospital and member of its Health Care Foundation board. Bob McCormick is a member of the Planning Commission for the City of Glendale and also has numerous involvements including membership in the Architectural Guild of the University of Southern California. Pete McCormick is a member of the executive board of the Los Angeles Area Chamber of Commerce Construction Industry Committee. Members of the McCormick management team also teach construction management courses at Cal Poly University.

George McCormick, a preacher and school teacher by trade when he began constructing barns and farm buildings at the turn of the century, would be proud of the way his third- and fourth-generation descendants have carried on his legacy.

Far left: McCormick's corporate officers. Standing left to right: Mike McCormick, purchasing manager; Bob McCormick, vice president and director of estimating; and Steve McCormick, controller. Seated left to right: Pete McCormick, secretary/treasurer; Jack McCormick, president; and Gary McCormick, executive vice president.

Above: The Lake-Corson office building in Pasadena. This 11-story facility has approximately 220,000 square feet of office tower and four levels of subterranean parking with a granite and glass facade.

Left: The Warner Corporate Center in Woodland Hills, a 12-story, 250,000-square-foot office tower with an 11-story, cast-in-place concrete parking structure.

CHARLES PANKOW BUILDERS, LTD.

Founded in 1963, Charles Pankow Builders, Ltd., is headquartered in Altadena and has regional offices in Honolulu, San Francisco, and San Diego. Today Charles Pankow Builders, Ltd., is one of the largest design/build firms in the United States and has completed projects nationwide, from Hawaii to Massachusetts. It specializes in office buildings, hotels, high-rise condominiums, shopping malls, and department stores, operating exclusively in the private sector.

The success of the firm has been achieved by heavy emphasis upon management innovation, engineering, creativity, strict cost and quality controls, and state-of-the-art construction techniques. By stressing in-house construction engineering expertise, the company is able to guarantee, in advance, the scope, quality, cost, and timeliness of its projects. Long a leader in the field of construction technology, Pankow has consistently been highlighted in construction industry news media for innovative, rapid, and cost-saving methods.

One such method is the use of on-site casting beds to cast precast columns, beams, and precast concrete architectural building cladding. This allows for a very efficient erection and shortened construction schedules. Depending on project requirements and available working area, prestressed beams can be manufactured on or off site with Pankow's relocatable casting bed.

Another of the firm's advanced concepts involves the use of cast-in-place concrete cores in high-rise construction projects. Jump formed at a

rapid rate, these concrete cores provide enough rigidity to allow for lightweight structural steel frames instead of heavyweight steel, thus reducing erection time and structural steel costs. In addition, the early core completion allows for work to start on elevators, stairwells, restrooms, and mechanical shafts much sooner than under more traditional construction processes.

The Pankow approach of combining high technology with innovative construction techniques speeds the entire process and yields tightly compressed construction schedules. In fact, structural construction cycles as rapid as two days per floor have resulted in the completion of such projects as the 43-story, 596-unit Hobron Hotel Condominium in Honolulu in less than 11 months.

In addition to technology and innovation, the company places major emphasis on quality at every phase of its projects. Key to its success is a melding of two proven concepts: active participation in the design process and thorough quality control. Pankow, unlike some other firms that specialize in design/build, does not have its own in-house design staff, preferring instead to work with the owner to select architects and designers who have the experience best suited to a particular project.

Under the design/build concept, Pankow works with architects and structural, mechanical, and electrical engineers as well as other outside consultants from a project's preconstruction phases through its completion. The team creates a design which must be cost-disciplined, coordinated, and complete. It must also satisfy the owner's functional, aesthetic, and

The Ten Five Sixty
Wilshire condominium, a
22-story, 108-unit luxury
building with four levels
of parking in Los Angeles.

quality requirements, while precluding expensive change orders and optimizing the cost and speed of construction.

This approach allows the construction process to begin quite early. Once the contract, which includes a guaranteed bonded price and completion date, is signed, earthwork and foundation work can be well under way before working drawings for the rest of the project are completed.

At every phase, from concept to completion, quality control is given the highest priority. This combination of high-quality projects and rapid construction has brought the company a great deal of repeat business from satisfied owners and is one of the major reasons for Pankow's growth.

Among Pankow's many projects nationwide are those in the Greater Los Angeles area. They include Chase Plaza, a 22-story, 760,000-square-foot office building in downtown Los Angeles; a 22-story, 108-unit luxury condominium structure on Wilshire Boulevard near Beverly Hills; Walnut Center, the 350,000-square-foot regional headquarters of Kaiser Permanente in Pasadena; the South Coast Executive Centre office building complex and the 980,000-square-foot South Coast Plaza II parking structure, both in Costa Mesa; a General Telephone Company headquarters in Thousand Oaks; and the Montebello Town Center Regional Mall. Pankow has also performed ex-

pansions and renovations of regional malls in Brea, Westminster, and Riverside.

In Long Beach, Pankow has built Catalina Landing, a four-structure office complex on the waterfront; Crocker Plaza, a 12-story office building and bank; and Shoreline Square, a 1.1-million-square-foot, mixed-use development which includes a 21-story office tower and the 500-room Sheraton Long Beach Hotel.

Pankow projects have been the recipients of many industry awards from a broad variety of organizations, including the Precast Concrete Institute's Harry H. Edwards Industry Advancement Award, the Concrete Industry Award for Engineering Excellence from the Portland Cement Association, the Juror's Grand Award from the California Council Society of American Registered Architects, the Associated General Contractors of America's National Build America Award, and the Blue Ribbon Award given by the American Registered Architects.

Pankow's focus on technology and innovation has positioned it well for the future. The design/build process, in which the company has excelled for many years, is growing in popularity, spurred by the developers' need to control costs and maintain construction schedules. Pankow's track record of delivering quality projects on time and at a guaranteed price gives it a strong competitive advantage.

The fact that Charles Pankow Builders, Ltd., is a limited partnership, in which many of its employees have an equity interest, provides added incentive to maintain the pattern of growth that has taken the company to the forefront of its industry and has made its name synonymous with construction innovation, creativity, and technological leadership.

"Pankow City," a composite of buildings constructed by Charles Pankow Builders and subsidiaries from 1963 to 1990.

NATIONWIDE CONSTRUCTION CO., INC.

Nina S. Tate in front of a
completed section of the
Flower Street subway
project.

There have been relatively few female executives in the construction industry, even fewer with more than 25 years of experience in the field, and a mere handful owning their own construction companies.

Nina S. Tate, founder and chief executive officer of Nationwide Construction Co., Inc., has done all of the above. When she formed Nationwide in 1983, she had already accumulated 20 years of management experience in construction and, most recently, had been vice president and chief financial officer of a multimillion-dollar national general contracting firm.

At first, Nationwide focused on general contracting projects, including the relocation and rehabilitation of about 30 houses that were in the path of the new Century Freeway. Tate had obtained her general contractor's license in 1984 and, one year later, took a major step in the fulfillment of a longtime dream. That dream had been to form her own rebar company and, in May 1985, she earned her C-50 Reinforcing Steel (Rebar) Contractor's License. She may well be the only woman in California to pass the C-50 exam.

Consulting with her close friend and business associate Dorothy Erickson, who established and now runs the firm's San Francisco office, Tate launched a rebar division in her company. Adding a team of key executives with a combined total of more than 100 years in the construction industry, the division has flourished and Nationwide is now one of the largest reinforcing steel placers in the state.

About 60 percent of the company's business is now in reinforcing steel, split about evenly between government work and the private sector. The general division accounts for the other 40 percent and has been involved in projects ranging in size from $100,000 to $4.5 million, including remodeling and new construction. Projects are di-

From left: Krista Wilkie-
Boswell, vice president;
Nina S. Tate, president;
and Donald Morrison,
rebar manager, at the
Wilshire/Alvarado sta-
tion of the Metro Rail
project.

vided about equally between Northern and Southern California.

Nationwide Construction Co., Inc., which was launched with a handful of people, now has a work force of nearly 200. It has done public works projects for numerous cities in Los Angeles County and for both the Metro Rail and Light Rail transit systems. It has been involved in a wide variety of projects, including seismic upgrading, water treatment plants, restaurants, airports, harbors, and parking structures.

In addition to building a successful company, Nina Tate has achieved a distinguished record in the construction industry. A founder of Women Construction Owners and Executives, USA, she served as its chartering national president. She is active in the National Association of Women in Construction, the National Association of Women Business Owners, and the Associated General Contractors of California (AGC). In 1983 she was appointed by Governor George Deukmejian to the California Advisory Committee for Women in Apprenticeship and by Los Angeles Mayor Tom Bradley to the Los Angeles City Private Industry Council.

She is the recipient of numerous awards, including the Arthur Young/*Venture* magazine 1988 Construction Entrepreneur of the Year Award and the Governor's 1988 Outstanding Business Woman Award.

Nina Tate attributes much of her success to hard work, long hours, and the support of an excellent management team. "I was always accepted anywhere I went in the construction field as upper level management of a large construction firm but, when I went out on my own, especially in the reinforcing steel business, I really had to prove myself before I got to first base. Knowing my field so well before starting out on my own is definitely something that has helped immensely, and I enjoy what I do."

MIKE BROWN GRANDSTANDS

Mike Brown's introduction to the grandstand business came when he was 11 years old. A native Pasadenan, the youngster had a newspaper route along Colorado Boulevard. In those days Rose Parade seat sales were handled by individuals stationed at each location. One fateful December morning Mike found a box of tickets on the street and turned them in.

His honest deed earned him six choice seats for the upcoming Rose Parade which, in turn, marked the start of a lifelong infatuation with that event. It also developed within him an awareness of temporary grandstand seating. Little did he dream, however, that one day he would be providing seats for many millions of people.

After graduating from high school, Brown went to work for a man named Jack Milne who owned a motorcycle shop and was also a pioneer in the use of portable grandstands. A former world's

ing event, and the experience gained and the pressures involved in that annual project stood the company in good stead when the 1984 Olympic Games were held in Los Angeles. Through an affiliate, United Production Services, Inc., the company did all the staging for the opening and closing ceremonies. For the latter event everything had to be done within a 15-hour span. As competition ended, 46 trucks were standing by in the parking lot of the Los Angeles Coliseum to begin the massive job. Earlier, rehearsals for the project had been held at nearby Aviation High School, the very same school for which Mike Brown had provided seats a quarter of a century earlier.

Mike Brown Grandstands itself was the official supplier for the 1984 Olympic Games, providing seating at every venue.

At Santa Anita Race Track in Arcadia, where the equestrian events were held, 35,000 seats were in-

Mike Brown Grandstands has been responsible for staging several major events, including Pope John Paul's pastoral visit.

speedway champion, he frequently provided temporary seating for racing events, as well as for the Rose Parade.

In 1958 a Los Angeles high school, which needed temporary seats for an upcoming football game, called to ask if Milne's company ever rented its portable stands to other groups. Brown, who took the call, asked Milne, who replied that if Brown wanted to handle it himself, he could use the stands and they would split the profits.

A year later Brown bought the company, and in 1964 incorporated it as Mike Brown Grandstands, Inc. In its early days the firm had only 800 seats available, but that figure quickly grew to 4,000, and today exceeds 100,000. Events for which it provides seating include football games, boxing matches, golf tournaments, auto races, concerts, circuses, rodeos, and, of course, parades.

The Rose Parade is the company's major ongo-

stalled. For the modern pentathlon and shooting events, 250 seats were provided—causing a few logistics problems for Olympic organizers when 15,000 fans arrived.

Other major events for which the company provides seating include the Hollywood Christmas Parade, the Long Beach Grand Prix, and many world championship boxing events in Las Vegas.

Mike Brown has long since lost count of the number of events in which his company has been involved or the number of seats it has provided, but there is one very important statistic he watches very closely and of which he is very proud. Now in its fourth decade of operation, the company has maintained an unbeatable safety record, one that has been completely accident free. That speaks louder than anything else of the high standards that have made Mike Brown Grandstands, Inc., the dominant company in its industry.

METROPOLITAN STRUCTURES

As the nineteenth century drew to a close, Bunker Hill was the center of the young and rapidly growing city of Los Angeles. In 1867 developer Prudent Beaudry purchased the property for $55 at a sheriff's sale and proceeded to build the city's first hillside subdivision. Soon thereafter Bunker Hill became home to many prominent Los Angeles families. In the 1890s a funicular railway called Angel's Flight was built to carry passengers up the steep eastern slope of Bunker Hill from Hill Street, a distance of only 335 feet.

Angel's Flight carried passengers up the steep eastern slope of Bunker Hill from the 1890s until 1969. A re-creation of the famous attraction is being planned. Courtesy, California Historical Society

Angel's Flight became one of the city's most famous attractions, remaining in service until 1969. By then Bunker Hill had long since lost all traces of its former glory. Many of the former mansions had been converted to shabby boarding houses, with rooms available for about $15 per month.

In 1959 the Los Angeles City Council passed an ordinance calling for the revitalization of the area. The recently formed Community Redevelopment Agency cleared the area and subdivided it for development into complexes of office buildings, hotels, and retail, residential, and cultural facilities. Many more years passed, however, before the vision began to take shape.

Meanwhile, in 1969, Chicago-based developer Metropolitan Structures, whose projects today in Chicago, Los Angeles, and Dallas are the largest privately financed downtown projects in each respective city, began work on an 83-acre lakefront project in Chicago called Illinois Center, which has become the nation's largest and most successful mixed-use development. The firm had previously transformed a portion of a decaying downtown Baltimore into a 33-acre complex of commercial and retail space, residential and hotel facilities, a theater, and recreational areas. The completed project, called Charles Center, has been nationally recognized as the birthplace for many of the concepts essential to successful mixed-use development and private/public partnerships.

In 1981 Metropolitan Structures entered into a partnership with Metropolitan Life Insurance Co. and subsequently, in 1983, became managing general partner of Bunker Hill Associates, the partnership chosen by the Los Angeles Community Redevelopment Agency to develop the mixed-use California Plaza project on Bunker Hill. California Plaza encompasses more than 11 contiguous acres and is designed to be the focal point for the entire downtown community by integrating commercial, cultural, and residential uses in a single, urban setting. At a projected cost of $1.2 billion, the completed California Plaza will be one of the largest revitalization undertakings in the country. The overall master plan for California Plaza includes 3.5 million square feet of office space, the Museum of Contemporary Art (MOCA), a 469-room Inter-Continental Hotel, 750 residential units, 160,000 square feet of restaurant and other retail space, The Dance Gallery, and 5.5 acres of open public space consisting of plazas, gardens, terraces, and water features. The centerpiece of the project is The Watercourt, a 1.5-acre urban garden featuring year-round arts and entertainment programming, and much to the delight of the community and nostalgia buffs, Angel's Flight will be re-created.

The 100,000-square-foot Museum of Contemporary Art was completed in 1985 as part of California Plaza's first phase. The museum, which was built by Bunker Hill Associates to satisfy the Community Redevelopment Agency's requirement that 1.5 percent of the total cost of California Plaza be devoted to the arts, is the focus of worldwide attention and has served as a catalyst to position California Plaza as the centerpiece of downtown Los Angeles.

Los Angeles Mayor Tom Bradley has called California Plaza "the crown jewel of Bunker Hill," adding that "it was Metropolitan Structures' experience and financial resources that made California Plaza a reality. This project is giving a focus to the City of Los Angeles as the financial, business and cultural center of the west."

BENTALL DEVELOPMENT CO.

When Bentall Development Co. was incorporated in California in 1985, it marked the culmination of a two-year-long search by its Canadian parent company for the right place to begin operations in the United States. For nearly three-quarters of a century the company had operated exclusively in Western Canada before deciding that Southern California offered the growth potential and stability it sought to meet its expansion goals.

The company was founded in Vancouver, British Columbia, in 1911 as Dominion Construction Company Limited and, since 1920, has been controlled by members of the Bentall family. The founder and longtime leader was Charles Bentall, whose son, Robert G. Bentall, is now the chief executive officer. Specializing in an integrated design/build approach, the company initially concentrated on creating offices, warehouses, and other industrial facilities.

During the 1950s the organization, which had become The Bentall Group, had developed into several companies engaged in construction and engineering, electrical and mechanical contracting, architecture, manufacturing, real estate development, and property management. To facilitate its development activities, it formed a joint venture in 1963 with a major insurance company with the objective of developing investment-grade real estate projects in Western Canada. For the next quarter-century it devel-

oped a number of large office, retail, and industrial projects in the Vancouver area, virtually all in concert with institutional partners.

In 1988 a decision was made to focus exclusively on the ownership, development, and management of income-producing property. The construction, design, and other unrelated businesses were sold. Today the Bentall companies own, develop, and manage office, retail, and industrial properties in Western Canada and Southern California. A large organization, it manages approximately 5 million square feet of space and typically has more than $500 million in projects, including joint ventures, under way at a time.

The U.S. company is headquartered in a 60,000-square-foot office facility that it built, owns, and manages at 3111 North Tustin Avenue in Orange. Activities in the United States are under the direction of Bentall Development Co. President James J. Warshawski, who came from the company's Vancouver headquarters in 1985 to set up this operation. Today that includes a staff of more than 30 and a branch office in San Diego.

The company's primary Southern California focus is on development and acquisition of commercial office space and industrial parks. In the former category, its projects include a 330,000-square-foot, two-phase office project in Santa Ana. Adjacent to the Newport/Costa Mesa Freeway on Tustin Avenue, this project includes two office towers, a free-standing restaurant, retail space, and parking for more than 1,100 cars. A second major project, called One Pacific Plaza, is a 300,000-square-foot office development at the Beach Boulevard exit from the San Diego Freeway in Huntington Beach. It includes two office buildings and on-site banking, restaurant, and hotel facilities. A high-rise office project in downtown San Diego is planned. Bentall's industrial projects are located in Chino, City of Industry, and Paramount, ranging in size from 100,000 to 160,000 square feet.

Bentall Development Co. has ambitious plans for its operations in the United States. By the early part of the twenty-first century, its goal is to have its operations evenly divided between Canada and California, while continuing to maintain the growth pattern, financial strength, and reputation for quality that have been synonymous with the Bentall name for nearly a century.

Bentall Development Co.'s primary focus in Southern California is on the development of commercial office space and industrial parks.

The company's branch office in San Diego.

PRUDENTIAL PROPERTY

The Prudential Property Company is one of the nation's leading owner/developers of commercial real estate, responsible for a portfolio of more than 160 million square feet of office, industrial, retail, hotel, and residential properties.

The Prudential has made significant contributions to skylines throughout America. In the past two decades, it has developed 400 properties totaling more than 100 million square feet.

Its $21.5-billion portfolio includes more than 500 office, industrial, and retail properties (totaling nearly 150 million square feet), 64 hotels (27,000 rooms), and 50 residential properties (17,000 units).

The Prudential Property Company is headquartered in Newark, New Jersey, and has offices throughout the United States. The Los Angeles office is one of the company's largest—with responsibility for $4.5 billion worth of real estate throughout Southern California, Arizona, and Hawaii—and is ranked among the largest commercial real estate asset managers and developers in Los Angeles County.

Among its most significant local projects are the Century Plaza Towers in Century City; Citicorp Plaza in downtown Los Angeles; the Sherman Oaks Galleria mall and offices in Sherman Oaks; Grand Central Business Centre in Glendale; Cedarpointe industrial facilities at the California Commerce Center in Ontario; the Ritz-Carlton Hotel, overlooking the Pacific Ocean in Laguna Niguel; First Federal Square office project in Santa Monica; and Bunker Hill Towers Apartments, also in downtown Los Angeles.

The Century Plaza Towers, the twin 44-story office buildings that rise above a seven-acre landscaped plaza in Century City, are owned by a

joint venture of The Prudential and an affiliate of JMB Realty. The landmark three-sided buildings encompass 2.3 million square feet of premier office space.

Having undergone an enhancement program in 1990 and 1991, the Century Plaza Towers continue to be one of the most sought-after business addresses in Southern California. The Concourse level boasts the addition of a 16-foot diameter skylight above the elevator landing which helps illuminate the imported travertine marble walls and floors. These enhancements work together to create a light and pleasant place to shop, eat, and browse in the Concourse level of the complex.

Citicorp Plaza covers a full city block in downtown Los Angeles in one of the most prestigious business districts on the West Coast. Its retail courtyard, Seventh Market Place, features a 350,000-square-foot mall with two anchor tenants, Bullocks and May Company, a dozen different restaurants, and more than 50 specialty shops. Besides the daily piano playing and unique public art work found within the 2.5-acre landscaped plaza, seasonal attractions, such as the summer "Music Makers Concert Series" and Shakespeare Festival and the holiday Tree Lighting Ceremony, along with charity functions such as the United Way Drive and the food drive for "LIFE" (Love is Feeding Everyone), make Seventh Market Place a vital center in the downtown community.

Joining Citicorp Center, the 42-story office tower, is the second office building of Citicorp Plaza, the new one-million-square-foot, 55-story 777 Tower. Renowned architect Cesar Pelli designed 777 Tower's sleek aluminum "skin" to have interesting contrasts of curved and angular

faces, made to reflect the Southern California sun and create a colorful and dramatic play of light on this critically acclaimed Los Angeles building.

The Sherman Oaks Galleria combines more than 375,000 square feet of office space with a 510,000-square-foot shopping mall anchored by two national tenants, Robinson's and May Company. The complex, which draws shoppers from all over the Los Angeles Basin, is conveniently located adjacent to the San Diego and Ventura freeways.

Grand Central Business Centre has more than 2 million square feet of business and industrial space in about 80 buildings spread out over 100 acres. Its tenants include many nationally known companies, including Disney, Bekins, and Security Pacific Bank. The land was once the site of Grand Central Airport which, during the early days of flight, was the hub of the Los Angeles area's aviation empire and was used by some of the nation's most notable aviators including Wiley Post, Howard Hughes, Charles Lindberg, and Amelia Earhart. The airport's original Grand Central Terminal Building, which has become part of the new complex, was once used for filming one of the most famous episodes in motion picture history—the scene in which Humphrey Bogart bids farewell to Ingrid Bergman in *Casablanca*.

Both locally and throughout the nation, The Prudential Property Company has won numerous awards. In 1988 it was named Developer of the Year by the *Chicago Sun Times* and received an Award of Honor for Corporate Citizenship from The Denver Partnership. A number of its projects have been named Building of the Year by the

GRAND CENTRAL BUILDING

Building Owners and Managers Association (BOMA). Locally, they include Two Town Center in Costa Mesa, First Federal Square in Santa Monica, and Citicorp Plaza in Los Angeles (which has also been the recipient of the Governor of California's Certificate of Merit for Emergency Preparedness, as well as the Urban Design Award given by the American Society of Landscape Architects).

Its awards cover virtually every phase of property development and asset management. In addition to those named above, they include excellence in design and lighting, energy management, fire safety, environmental improvement, large scale development, renovation, economic development and maintenance, and beautification.

A staff of nearly 40 real estate professionals handle the $4.5-billion portfolio of the Los Angeles office. In addition, many staff members participate in a wide range of community and charitable endeavors, including the United Way, the Boy Scouts of America, and YMCA, and Drug Abuse Resistance Education (D.A.R.E.). The company is a sponsor of the Nissan Los Angeles Open, the annual PGA Tour event hosted by the Los Angeles Junior Chamber of Commerce.

In addition, The Prudential Property Company is also active in the Los Angeles Area Chamber of Commerce and various professional organizations, including BOMA and the National Association of Industrial and Office parks (NAIOP), and the Institute of Real Estate Managers (IREM).

As Los Angeles becomes an increasingly important center of the world's economy, the people of The Prudential Property Company are proud of their role in the growth and development of Southern California and are enthusiastic about the opportunities that lie ahead.

Grand Central Business Centre in Glendale was once the site of an airport that was used by such aviation luminaries as Charles Lindberg and Amelia Earhart. In addition, the airport's original central terminal building was featured in the farewell scene of *Casablanca*.

The Los Angeles office of Prudential Property Company, located in the Century Plaza Towers, is one of the company's largest and has had a significant impact on the Southern California area.

THE NEWHALL LAND & FARMING COMPANY

Henry Mayo Newhall, founder of the company.

A rendering of Valencia Town Center, Valencia's regional shopping center that is scheduled to open in 1992.

Among the thousands who hurried west after gold was discovered at Sutter's Mill in 1848 was a young Massachusetts native named Henry Mayo Newhall. At age 24, he was already a successful auctioneer, experience that proved very useful when his prospecting efforts failed. He soon became head of San Francisco's largest auction house and, a decade later, invested some of his earnings in that city's first railroad company.

When Southern Pacific bought the railroad, Newhall received more than one million dollars and decided to buy land, which was selling at distressed prices. During the 1870s he purchased six ranches totaling 143,000 acres at an average price of two dollars per acre. The most promising was the 48,000-acre Rancho San Francisco, now known as the Newhall Ranch, located 30 miles north of Los Angeles, on which he raised cattle, fruit, and wheat.

Newhall also sold a right of way to the Southern Pacific to build the tracks that would connect Los Angeles and San Francisco. Part of the ranch land along the tracks became the site of the town of Newhall.

When Henry Newhall died in 1882, his property was inherited by his wife and five sons, who had been urged by Henry not to sell the land. Following his advice, they incorporated their inheritance in 1883 as The Newhall Land & Farming Company.

A variety of problems plagued the company during the first half-century of its existence. Its cattle operations lost money and, with debts mounting, some of the more remote ranches were sold. In 1928 a dam burst just north of the Newhall Ranch, killing 420 people and causing widespread destruction. Another calamity, the 1929 stock market crash, wiped out the livelihood of some Newhall family members and threatened the company with bankruptcy.

At that point William Mayo, Henry Newhall's sole surviving son, made a move that was to stem the tide of misfortune. His son-in-law, Atholl McBean, was called in to take over the operation. A successful businessman, McBean instituted strict controls and soon had the company on solid footing. By 1934 the company was profitable and, two years later, was able to resume dividend payments, which have continued without interruption to this day. Late in 1936, oil was discovered under the Newhall Ranch. The field yielded 44 producing wells, adding substantially to the company's earnings and financial stability.

With a population explosion taking place in the West after World War II, the company began to de-emphasize its cattle operations and to buy additional land to expand its farming activities around the state. When, in 1964, the state acquired a strip of land through the ranch for construction of the Golden State Freeway, the Newhall area was soon to be within a half-hour drive of downtown Los Angeles. The time for urban development had arrived.

In 1965 the company embarked on its most ambitious project to date, the development of the planned community of Valencia, located adjacent to the town of Newhall on the Newhall Ranch. The ranch was large, more than twice the size of New York's Manhattan, and the land was contiguous presenting planning opportunities found in few other metropolitan areas.

The Old Orchard Shopping Center, Newhall

Land's first major commercial development, and the Valencia Golf Course were among the first projects opened, along with the formation of Valencia Water Company. In 1967 the first residents moved in, a second golf course opened, and development of Valencia Industrial Center began.

The company went public in 1969, and its stock was listed on the New York Stock Exchange in 1970. In 1971 Magic Mountain amusement park opened in Valencia, with the company as a partner with Sea World. In 1972 the company became sole owner and operator before selling the park to Six Flags, Inc., in 1979. By the end of the 1970s Valencia's population exceeded 12,000, and the community had schools, parks, a hospital and two medical centers, the County administration center for the area, several shopping centers and churches, and two colleges.

The 1980s brought continued expansion, with about 4,000 of the ranch's 41,000 acres developed. By the end of the decade, Valencia Industrial Center had become the fourth-largest industrial park in Los Angeles County, with more than 8.5 million square feet of completed space, 500 companies, and more than 11,000 employees.

As the 1990s began, the community's newest business/industrial park, Valencia Commerce Center, was opened. The new decade also saw the beginning of a major regional shopping center, the first in the Santa Clarita Valley. Numerous celebrations in 1990 marked the 25th anniversary of the Valencia Master Plan.

New arrivals to the area can choose from a broad spectrum of single-family homes, condominiums, or rental apartments in well-maintained neighborhoods, surrounded by plenty of open space. Neighborhoods, shopping areas, recreation centers, and schools are linked by a network of paseos—landscaped walkways complete with tunnels and bridges—allowing pedestrians, joggers, and cyclists to travel throughout Valencia comfortably, including children going safely to and from school. There are eight spacious parks, several golf courses and tennis courts, lakes, forests, and numerous other facilities, providing a wide variety of recreational, athletic, and leisure activities.

Valencia also provides excellent educational facilities. Elementary, junior high, and senior high school students are served by three respected school systems and several private schools. At higher levels, there is the College of the Canyons community college and the world-renowned California Institute of the Arts, a fully accredited visual and performing arts college endowed by Walt Disney. Houses of worship, retail centers, and a wide variety of restaurants help make Valencia a community that has something to offer everyone.

Henry Newhall would be proud of what his descendants have done in their various endeavors. Besides its primary activity of developing Valencia, The Newhall Land & Farming Company has become one of the 10 largest farming operations in California and among the 100 largest in the nation. In 1985, the company converted from a corporation to a California limited partnership. Its partnership units are traded on the New York and Pacific stock exchanges.

Under the leadership of Chairman Thomas L. Lee and President Gary M. Cusumano, the company has posted record levels in revenues and net income. The appraised value of its land holdings in Valencia has appreciated at an annual compound rate of nearly 20 percent and represents one of the premier real estate opportunities available in California to investors.

The people of The Newhall Land & Farming Company have every reason to be proud of what has been accomplished. Under their leadership, Valencia has become one of the finest master-planned communities in the nation, creating an environment ideal for living, working, playing, and enjoying the best that California has to offer.

Valencia Summit, one of the community's premier neighborhoods.

The paseo system, one of the master plan's trademarks, is the landscaped walkway system that extends through 10 miles of the community.

CENTURY WEST

In its corporate brochure, Century West Development, Inc., describes itself as "a fully integrated real estate development firm offering a unique ability to minimize risks, obtain excellent financing, and provide reasonable profits through the development of premier projects in prime locations." Its clients can be found throughout the United States and within the Pacific Rim region.

The company, headquartered in Santa Monica, was founded in March 1979, but the involvement of its principals in Los Angeles-area development projects began much earlier. One of its founders, William E. Cook, is a Southern California native who previously operated William Cook Development, Inc., specializing in building multifamily residential units.

In 1976 two aerospace engineers from the Rand Corporation, John Dudzinsky and Harry Mow, became involved in Cook projects, primarily as investors. With a third engineer, John H. Yueh, Mow and Dudzinsky formed MYD and Associates and, with Cook, were developing six or seven projects a year by 1978 on a joint-venture basis.

The early success of these ventures caused Mow, who had been program director of Advanced Technology at Rand, to resign in January 1978 in order to run the MYD partnership interests. A year later Cook and the MYD team decided to formally join forces, and Century West Development, Inc., was formed.

Yueh retired from the firm in 1985. Today it is managed by Mow as chief executive officer; Dudzinsky, who is president; Cook, chief operating officer; and Kenneth G. Walker, executive vice

Pacific Gardens is the premier Westside luxury retirement hotel for active adults. It features 88 luxurious guestrooms and suites, gourmet dining, and a full social and recreational program.

Portofino Plaza is the corporate headquarters of Century West Development. The office is situated on the bluffs of Santa Monica and has a beautiful view of the Pacific Ocean.

president. Their diversified backgrounds in development, engineering, construction, and banking, combined with years of hands-on management expertise, have been the foundation on which Century West has been built.

The firm enjoyed early success and by 1980 its staff numbered 45. A year later it launched its first commercial project, a 72,000-square-foot Santa Monica office building. The company cut back its operations during the recession that hit the real estate industry in the early 1980s but has grown steadily since that time.

Century West now employs more than 70 people on a full-time basis and builds between 25 and 30 projects a year. The company is extremely versatile and its projects include office buildings, medical facilities, apartments, condominiums, motels, retirement homes, and single-family houses. While most of its projects are in Southern California, including Orange County, Long Beach, and San Diego, some extend across the country, to as far away as Alabama and Florida.

The company is closely held, with the principals owning most of the stock. The balance is held by senior staff members who have brought to the firm considerable experience with other major construction/development companies, as well as strong educational backgrounds in architecture, civil engineering, and business administration.

Before coming to California in 1963 to join Rand, Mow had spent most of his life in New York. Born in China, he came to the United States with his family when his father was appointed to represent the Republic of China at the United Nations. He received his doctoral degree in mechanical engineering from Rensselear Polytechnic Institute in New York.

Dudzinsky, who was with Rand from 1965 to 1979, most recently as program director of Technology Applications, received his doctoral degree in electrical engineering from Carnegie-Mellon University in Pittsburgh. Cook, who studied business and architectural design at California State

University, Northridge, had formed his own development and construction company in 1968. The fourth member of the management team, Ken Walker, has a strong background in finance; before joining Century West, he was vice president of a major savings and loan association.

During its first decade in business, many of the company's projects were done on a joint venture basis with savings and loan associations. More recently, however, it has diversified both its equity partners and its product lines. Fewer apartment units and more condominiums and affordable houses are being built, with much of the equity funding coming from companies and other investors located in various Pacific Rim countries.

Despite the wide variety of Century West projects, everyone is approached with the same philosophy: careful research prior to implementation, followed by hands-on attention to even the smallest detail, every step of the way. A full-service company, Century West handles the most complex construction programs, from land acquisition to complete turnkey projects, including conceptual development, master planning, architectural and interior design, financing, construction supervision, and property management.

This philosophy, coupled with the ability to consistently maintain high returns, has enabled Century West to rapidly broaden its base and has created a history of long-standing client relation-

ships. Since its founding, the company has developed nearly 4,000 apartments and more than one million square feet of office space. It has grown steadily and, with Los Angeles strategically located in the rapidly expanding Pacific Rim, expects that trend to continue.

"We're proud and happy to have had a part in the recent development of Southern California," says Harry Mow. "We build projects that meet the needs of the communities we serve, that blend in well, that enhance the general quality of life here, and that foster creative and productive long-term working environments. We look forward to even greater contributions in the future."

A 16-unit Santa Fe-style luxury apartment building.

Palisades Promenade is a 106,000-square-foot office building that spans an entire city block. Its ground floor tenants include a gourmet Italian restaurant and an art gallery.

TOOLEY & COMPANY

It was the desire to reflect "tenant needs" in commercial real estate development that led to the "inside out" approach adopted by the owners of Tooley & Company, Bill Tooley and Craig Ruth. "We begin with the marketing," says Ruth, "asking prospective tenants what they want and then designing a building to suit their needs—it makes more sense than designing a project that suits ownership needs and trying to find tenants to occupy it."

It's a concept that works, evidenced by the fact that for many years Tooley & Company projects have been 90 percent preleased and have enjoyed an occupancy rate of 99 percent. A privately owned, full-service real estate firm specializing in development, leasing, and management of high-quality office, retail, and industrial space in the western United States, Tooley & Company has participated in projects totaling more than 7 million square feet.

Before starting their company in 1975, Tooley and Ruth were with Ketchum, Peck & Tooley, an investment building firm established in Los Angeles in 1968. They were involved in a number of prestigious projects, including the 1,500-room Westin Bonaventure Hotel and the 55-story Security Pacific National Bank world headquarters building, both in downtown Los Angeles.

Since forming their own company, Tooley and Ruth have employed the strategy of undertaking a limited number of high-quality development projects, which are usually held as investments by the firm's principals. Occasionally, projects are developed on behalf of individuals or major institutions for their investment portfolios. The firm has offices in Los Angeles, La Jolla, Santa Monica, Irvine, and San Francisco.

Major Los Angeles involvements include: Westwood Gateway, 817,000 square feet of office space in three towers in West Los Angeles; Two Rodeo Drive, a high-fashion retail center in Beverly Hills; Wilshire Palisades, an 11-story office building along the Santa Monica coastline; First Federal Square, a 12-story office tower in Santa Monica; Airport Marina Center, a seven-building project in Marina del Rey; and 800 Wilshire, a 16-story building in downtown Los Angeles.

Both of the Santa Monica developments, along with other Tooley projects, have been award winners. Wilshire Palisades, developed in a joint venture with Lawrence Welk's The Welk Group, was recognized by the Urban Land Institute in 1988 as the outstanding office building in its category throughout the United States and Canada. The building also received the California Building Officials Design Award for High-Rise Development Excellence. First Federal Square was chosen as Building of the Year in 1987 by the Building Owners and Managers Association.

In Orange County, Tooley works with The Irvine Company, owned by Don Bren, in the development, leasing, and management of the 2-million-square-foot Jamboree Center, a master-planned, 46-acre business center located at Jamboree Boulevard and the San Diego Freeway. The project includes five mid- to high-rise office towers and the 550-room Irvine Hyatt Hotel and Towers.

The same level of excellence that goes into the development of Tooley projects is emphasized in the properties it manages. For its tenants, service is paramount and includes amenities found in few other office buildings. To maintain the highest level of service, the firm

Craig Ruth

William L. Tooley

places great significance on the selection, training, and retention of its people.

"We make the hiring process a top priority," says Ruth, "and give people room to grow with major responsibilities. Pride and mutual respect sharply reduce turnover. We provide a positive, changing, and stimulating environment in an entrepreneurial setting."

Reflecting his background as an athlete and coach, Ruth adds that "to win you need teamwork. Teamwork has helped us earn the reputation we enjoy today."

As is true in many successful partnerships, Bill Tooley and Craig Ruth come from vastly different backgrounds. The former is a native of El Paso, Texas, who came to Southern California as a boy. He is a graduate of Stanford University and Harvard Business School, and served in the U.S. Naval Reserve. Tooley is on the board of directors of the Federal Reserve Bank of San Francisco, the

Central City Association, The Welk Group, and the National Realty Committee.

Ruth, who grew up in Syracuse, New York, was a star athlete in high school and later at Muskingum College in Ohio. After serving in the U.S. Marine Corps, from which he was honorably discharged as a captain, he was a high school and college coach until a visit to a former comrade-in-arms in Southern California led him to relocate and embark on a real estate career.

Both Tooley and Ruth give generously of their time to a variety of community and professional organizations. Tooley is on the advisory board for the Mission Inn Foundation in River-

side and a regent associate and former trustee of Loyola Marymount University. Ruth's activities include the Urban Land Institute, the Japan-American Cultural and Community Council, and the Los Angeles International Business Center (LAX-IBC).

Summing up the success of their partnership, Bill Tooley and Craig Ruth say: "Our philosophy of business brought us together initially, and we find the same philosophy guiding us today when temptation might invite us to do otherwise. Do fewer things, but do them well! Listen to what the market is saying, and create a plan that reflects those needs, keeping in mind the end result: value at a competitive price."

It is a philosophy that has served them well.

SIKAND ENGINEERING

Since 1959 Sikand has been committed to a tradition of excellence, innovation, and technological improvement. Backed by the extensive professional experience gained through more than three decades of service, Sikand continues to provide the highest quality of civil engineering, surveying, and land planning services to private developers, public agencies, and municipalities. To date, Sikand has provided services for improvements valued in excess of one billion dollars. To find a high quality civil engineering firm which has successfully shaped much of Los Angeles County and its environs, a Southern California developer or home-builder need look no farther than Sikand Engineering Associates of Van Nuys, California.

Besides being one of the largest construction surveyors in the Los Angeles area, Sikand is adept in all phases of residential, commercial, and industrial development. The firm is noted for its expertise in hillside design, but its capabilities range from computer-aided design of tract maps to creating whole new infrastructures for communities responding to the fast-paced growth of the area.

This enterprising and dynamic firm had its auspicious beginnings in India, where its founder and president, Gunjit Sikand, earned a bachelor's degree from the University of East Punjab. From there Sikand ventured to the United States, where in 1950 he earned a bachelor of civil engineering degree from Auburn and a master's degree in civil engineering from the University of Colorado in 1953. Five years later he settled in Los Angeles, and it was here that the foundations for Sikand Engineering Associates were laid.

Sikand began teaching at California State University, Los Angeles, and a year later, with a partner, formed his own consulting firm. In 1964 Sikand bought out his partner and changed the name of the company to Sikand Engineering Asso-

ciates. Nine years later Sikand's home office settled at 15230 Burbank Boulevard in Van Nuys, the company's current address. Satellite offices are located in Orange County, the Antelope Valley, and the Inland Empire.

Gunjit Sikand's professional affiliations are impressive. A member of the Urban Land Institute, he also serves on the board of the California Council of Civil Engineers and Land Surveyors (CCCE&LS) and is past president of its Los Angeles Chapter. He stays connected to the education community as Professor Emeritus at California State University, Los Angeles, as a member of the advisory board of its School of Engineering, and as a member of the board of counselors of the School of Urban and Regional Planning at the University of Southern California. The central theme of these organizations is a commitment to design excellence and professionalism within the engineering community, a theme that is readily apparent at Sikand.

Sikand's executive vice president and head of planning, Ronald R. Horn, is equally well qualified. Also a registered civil engineer, he earned a bachelor's degree in civil engineering in 1962. Horn serves as Chairman of Community Planning & Environmental Affairs for CCCE&LS (1990), as vice president in 1990 and president in 1991 of the Board of Directors for the Los Angeles County Chapter of CCCE&LS, and as a member of the Land Development Advisory Group for Los Angeles County's Department of Public Works (1985-1990). He has also been past chairman (in behalf of CCCE&LS) for the Los Angeles County Flood Control Design and Maintenance Standards Criteria Committee. He is often engaged to speak at the various governmental planning seminars in Southern California.

Other key members of Sikand's talented staff include Kurt Rheinfurth, a licensed architect and director of planning, and vice presidents Gerald R. Price and Mark R. Sikand, both of whom had extensive experience with Los Angeles County's Flood Control District before joining the firm.

But it is Sikand's award-winning and ongoing projects that give the best testimony to the company's talents and capabilities as a whole. From its inception, this innovative company has received the praise and recognition of its peers and clients which continues today. In the early 1960s the Palos Verdes Chamber of Commerce bestowed its Award of Excellence on Sikand for engineering 388 custom lots from 183 acres of precipitous terrain. In 1966 the CCCE&LS presented Sikand with its annual award of merit for the design of La Canada Country Club Estates and Golf Course, which included 670 housing units on 224 acres of land in the San Gabriel Mountains that had long been considered too steep to develop. The project included the design of a wastewater treatment that provides effluent for irrigation.

Working hand-in-hand with the Santa Clarita Valley's largest and most respected developer, the Newhall Land and Farming Company, Sikand has garnered esteem while assisting the home builder in developing an entire valley. The relationship between the two companies began with the design of a network of major highways that opened the 44,000-acre Newhall Ranch and resulted in, among many other ongoing ventures, two residential communities which received 1989 "Project of the Year" awards from the CCCE&LS. Valencia Northbridge, the winner in the engineering/surveying category, posed the challenge of designing a community of 1,800 hillside homes while preserving the privacy and views for homes already adjacent to the project. Other problems were achieving compatibility with existing water lines and relocating electrical transmission lines.

Valencia Westridge was acclaimed in the planning category for its recreation-oriented community of 1,900 homes designed around a championship golf course. Preservation of the oak trees in the area was the major challenge and re-

quired a modification of street standards and an innovative cluster design of the homes. In addition, a water reclamation system was incorporated for purposes of irrigation to help solve drought-related problems in the Santa Clarita Valley.

Commercial and industrial design is another area in which Sikand excels. The Valencia Commerce Center is 820 acres designed to accommodate a broad range of businesses, but will include such recreational amenities as jogging and equestrian trails. The expansion of the Valencia Industrial Center is another project, the primary objective of which is to provide a high school site with a capacity of 2,000 students in an area that in the 1980s saw overcrowded schools develop into one of its chief concerns. As part of the Valencia Master Planned Community, the Industrial Center expansion also includes retail commercial and light industrial space and is designed to serve the growing business and educational needs of the surrounding communities. Other developments, such as East Copperhill in San Francisquito Canyon, will integrate several elements of design. Comprising 1,766 housing units, 35.8 acres of commercial use, an elementary school and park site, and related open space, the development is a prime example of the master planning to which Sikand commits itself.

Now a firm of more than 150 employees, Sikand is indeed an engineering/planning firm whose technology keeps up with the time to meet the needs of its clients, while simultaneously maintaining a strong sense of integrity. The 1990s will be even more revealing of that commitment to integrity as Sikand continues to play a major role in reshaping our long-neglected infrastructure. "We want to have an active part in the reconstruction process," says Gunjit Sikand, "and help close the gap." With his firm's penchant for tackling and solving major problems, Southern California will soon see few gaps in need of closing.

RAY WILSON COMPANY

Fergus Falls, Minnesota, seems an unlikely birthplace for a construction company that has become a major force in Southern California. Yet it was there that C.W. Wilson launched his two-man venture in 1885 for the purpose of building houses. In 1901 the firm moved to Los Angeles and began branching out into industrial and commercial construction. By the mid-1950s a third generation of Wilsons, Ray's sons, C. Ray and Brooks, had taken over the leadership and in 1955 the Ray Wilson Company was incorporated.

In 1981 the Wilsons sold their interest to a major Swedish construction company, ABV. However, the Wilson family has continued its more than a century of involvement and is currently represented by Project Manager Gregg Wilson, great-grandson of the founder.

In January 1987 ABV began negotiating with another prominent organization, Tokyu Group, based in Tokyo, Japan, and a year later the Ray Wilson Company was acquired by Tokyu. It was an unusual transaction in that the Japanese rarely acquire an existing entity intact. The Ray Wilson Company was the first construction company so acquired by a Japanese firm.

The more than 350 companies that comprise the Tokyu Group are divided into the following five subgroups: development, transportation, retailing, recreation and leisure, and cultural foundations. As one of the larger companies in the development group, Tokyu Construction Co., Ltd., has an annual volume of more than $3 billion of construction in Japan and other Pacific Rim countries. Tetsu Gotoh, president of Tokyu Construction, serves as the chairman of the board for Ray

Wilson, and Nobuo Saito is the CEO and principal liaison with the parent company.

The Ray Wilson Company is an operating segment of Tokyu Construction and is organized as a subsidiary of Pan Pacific Development, a Tokyu holding company. Wilson is a broad-spectrum general contractor, with project experiences that run the gamut from correctional facilities to elegant hotels. Its, projects, which are primarily in Southern California, range in size from $500,000 to $50 million.

The firm has built large office complexes, parking structures, multistory condominiums, hotels, and a variety of municipal facilities. Among its completed projects in the latter category are the new Los Angeles International Airport headquarters, the Santa Ana Transportation Center, the dockside and visitor-handling facilities for the famed Queen Mary in Long Beach Harbor, and a new Rose Bowl press box that was the finest in the country in the early 1960s.

The Los Angeles County Museum of Natural History has been a client for many years. A recent project has been Adventure Island, the new $8.6-million children's zoo at the Greater Los Angeles Zoo. Taking advantage of existing resources, the company enlisted the resident elephants to aid in the demolition and clearing process!

India-born K.C. Gopal, who has been president of the firm since 1985, is a strong advocate of the team concept, a philosophy that permeates the organization. Thus the Ray Wilson Company works closely with developers, planners, and architects to complete projects in which everyone takes pride. "We seek to be a constructive ally," says Gopal, "rather than passively document another party's lack of performance." Ray Wilson Company's record of success in helping to build Southern California is clear evidence of the effectiveness of that philosophy.

NATIONAL PROPERTIES GROUP

"**W**e don't sell real estate; we educate our clients so they can make informed decisions." This is the philosophy of National Properties Group (NPG) as expressed by its president, Jack Karp. Founded by Karp in 1974, NPG is a full-service brokerage company specializing in industrial, office, and commercial real estate.

Karp began his career in the industrial real estate brokerage field in 1962, launching his company 12 years later. It began as National Industrial Properties (NIP), but the name did not reflect the firm's activities as it expanded into office and commercial real estate. Therefore the names National Office Properties (NOP) and National Commercial Properties (NCP) were created. Later a new corporation, National Properties Group, was formed, bringing the other three entities together under one umbrella.

NPG has been located in the South Bay area of Los Angeles since its founding, including its recent move to 108 West Walnut Street, Suite 200, Carson (Gardena zip code 90278). Over the years it has marketed millions of square feet of properties, much of it outside the Greater Los Angeles area.

NPG has been involved in a wide variety of real estate transactions all across the United States, including sale/leasebacks in Illinois; location study and acquisition in New Jersey; facility acquisitions in Maryland, in Orange and San Diego counties and in the San Francisco Bay area; golf course acquisitions in Arizona; and the development and marketing of an industrial park in Texas. "If you understand real estate," says Karp, "you understand it anywhere." The firm has set its sights on international business.

Personal service and integrity are the foundation stones on which Karp has built his business. "We don't merely show property," he says, "we function as our clients' real estate department, helping them to design and meet needs, to take the long-range view, and to eliminate potential problems before they occur.

"It's an educational process," he notes. "Sometimes what the clients think they want may not, however, be in their best interests. We therefore offer the client alternatives that allow them to make an informed decision."

Karp has received a number of awards for his achievements in real estate and for his participation in various professional organizations. In 1976 and 1977 he served as president of the American Industrial Real Estate Association (AIR) and received that organization's coveted Outstanding Service Award. An active member of the Society of Industrial and Office Realtors (SIOR), a national real estate organization, he earned its Inter-City Transaction Award for the Largest Dollar Transaction (industrial) in 1987.

A former Los Angeles County Fire Commissioner, he serves as technical advisor to the Los Angeles County Fire Department. His knowledge of fire protection and its related fields has proven beneficial to his clients. He has completed graduate and undergraduate work at the University of Southern California and is a former president of its School of Commerce (now School of Business).

Karp has held key positions in many other organizations, including the Los Angeles Area Chamber of Commerce, the Economic Development Corporation of Los Angeles County (a group he helped form), and the board of directors for the Los Angeles Headquarters City Association.

Karp has written numerous articles in publications and served as guest lecturer at various seminars and universities. He is a coauthor of the AIR's "Standard Offer, Agreement, and Escrow Instructions For Purchase of Real Estate" as well as the Standard Industrial/Commercial Lease forms.

"We never tell prospective clients what we can do for them, we merely show them what we've done," says Karp. Based on his record and that of National Properties Group, that has to be a very convincing argument.

Jack Karp, president of National Properties Group.

CB Commercial

The CB Commercial Real Estate Group, Inc., has had a distinguished past, dating back to its founding in San Francisco in 1906. And the company, now owned by its employees and a small group of outside investors, holds the promise of an even more distinguished future.

Colbert Coldwell was just 23 years old, with two years of real estate experience, when he started the business as a partnership in 1906. The company opened its first office in Southern California in 1924, and its first out-of-state office (in Arizona) in 1950. By mid-century the company had become the dominant commercial real estate broker in California, with a dozen offices in its system. In 1962 the company was restructed from a partnership to a corporation, and in 1968 public trading of Coldwell Banker stock began.

By the late 1960s the company was expanding into new territories and new types of business including, for a time, residential property. During the 1970s and early 1980s the company became a nationwide organization, with two autonomous divisions devoted to commercial and residential real estate, respectively.

Late in 1981 Sears, Roebuck and Company and Coldwell Banker announced an agreement in principle for Sears to acquire Coldwell Banker. Final agreement and completion of the acquisition was effective January 1, 1982. In October 1988 Sears announced its intention to sell the Coldwell Banker Commercial Group and retain ownership of the Coldwell Banker name and the Coldwell Banker Residential Group as part of a business restructuring. Commercial Group employees and outside investors formed a company, CB Commercial Holdings, Inc., to negotiate with Sears for the purchase of the Commercial Group. The successful purchase was completed on April 19, 1989.

Commercial Group employees responded with enthusiasm to the opportunity to become owners of their own company through the purchase of stock. In February 1991 the company announced that its new name would be CB Commercial Real Estate Group, Inc., and the new identity is presently being introduced across the nation.

Today the activities of CB Commercial cover the full spectrum of commercial real estate, including brokerage and management, mortgage banking, real estate investment banking, appraisal and consultation, realty advisory services, real estate research, and national corporate services. It has approximately 4,500 employees in almost 90 locations in the United States and Canada. Close to 23,000 transactions are completed annually, with aggregate property values of $17.4 billion in 1990.

CB Commercial is headquartered in Los Angeles, where since 1922 it has played a major role in the evolution of the city into one of the world's leading and strategically located economic centers. For many years the company has ranked first among Los Angeles County commercial real estate organizations, according to independent surveys, and is more than double the size of its nearest competitor.

The chairman of the board and chief executive officer of CB Commercial is James J. Didion, who has been with the company since 1962. President of broker-

Jerry Asher, senior vice president. Photo courtesy of David J. Lans Photography

age and management is Gary J. Beban, who joined the company in 1970.

Geographically, the business is divided into Eastern, Central, and Western divisions, the latter under the direction of Executive Vice President Peter L. Marr. The Western Division comprises nine western and southwestern states.

The Southern California region, headed by Executive Vice President Jerry Asher, is composed of offices in Beverly Hills, Glendale, Los Angeles, the San Fernando Valley, South Bay, and Wilshire. Asher states that "our most valuable asset is our people. It is through the power of our people that we excel in serving our clients and our community." The regional offices are in the same location as corporate headquarters, at 533 South Fremont Avenue in downtown Los Angeles.

While they are proud to be part of one of the largest commercial real estate service firms in the world, the people of CB Commercial have never forgotten that real estate is a local business. Throughout most of the twentieth century and for 70 years in Los Angeles, the business has been built by emphasizing strong, in-depth knowledge of each market, and by honoring the individual relationships between each client and the people of CB Commercial who serve them.

From its earliest days CB Commercial has taken seriously its responsibility to join in the work that must be done to keep the communities it serves vital, not only as places to do business, but as places to live, raise families, and provide for the future. Various units of the company provide financial support to hundreds of organizations working in the fields of health, youth, social services, education, collegiate and community athletics, civic and economic activities, arts and science, culture, and environmental causes.

Community service, client loyalty, thorough knowledge of the marketplace, and experience are among the foundation blocks laid in 1906 by Colbert Coldwell. He was a man of integrity and he instilled that spirit in those who followed him.

Those qualities served the company well and continue to do so as it plans for continued strong growth into the new century. In the words of Chairman Jim Didion, "We share a long-standing, unshakable commitment to the absolutes of ethics and integrity. As a supplier of service and information, we are guided by one primary standard: the best interests of our clients."

Moonrise over the Los Angeles skyline. Photo courtesy of Joe Sohm/Chromosohm

RE/MAX OF CALIFORNIA

The name RE/MAX stands for "Real Estate Maximums." And it befits a company that, in less than 20 years, has gone from inception to the second-largest real estate franchise firm in all of North America. The remarkable story began in 1973, when a Denver real estate agent opened his own office based on a concept of paying agents 100 percent of the standard commission.

The RE/MAX concept is similar to that of a co-operative. Sales agents retain all of the standard commission on properties they sell, paying the broker/owner a monthly fee to cover the agent's proportionate share of the expenses. The 100 percent of the commission concept, compared to the 50/50 or 60/40 split in the traditional real estate offices, has attracted thousands of top producers in the industry.

The result is that RE/MAX agents have an average of 9.5 years of experience, compared with an industry average of 4 years, and earn 3.5 times as much as the average agent. They also handle about 60 percent more transactions annually than their counterparts in traditional offices.

Nowhere has the growth of RE/MAX been more dramatic than in California, due to the efforts of two men who had already built an extremely successful real estate sales organization of their own. By 1982 Spring Realty, under the leadership of Sid Syvertson and Steve Haselton, had grown with quality, dignity, and pride to become one of the 10 largest privately held real estate firms in the United States, with some 30 offices and 1,000 sales agents in Southern California. The firm was founded in 1962 by Syvertson, and Haselton became his partner in 1968.

As successful as they had grown, both men realized they were a long way from their common goal of becoming a significant factor in California real estate. While considering various traditional ways to expand their operation, they were convinced that, whatever their decision was to be, it required an idea that was revolutionary, not evolutionary. They studied the RE/MAX concept carefully and decided it met their requirements by offering the best opportunity for achieving their long-term objectives.

On August 30, 1982, RE/MAX of California was launched, with all Spring Realty offices shifting to the new operation in a transition that was to be the largest conversion in the history of RE/MAX. Managers of the old offices became owners and franchisees under the California master franchise owned by Syvertson and Haselton.

In the hands of the two men, the RE/MAX concept has given a new dimension to real estate in California. RE/MAX of California had grown to more than 200 offices and 3,000 agents by the end of the 1980s. In 1989 alone its agents closed 41,000 transactions representing nearly $10 billion in sales, making it the largest RE/MAX region in the United States. It reached that lofty position after just seven years within the RE/MAX network.

RE/MAX of California's more than 3,000 agents are always "top of mind" for Syvertson and Haselton. Since these agents form the basis of the region's remarkable success, the two men view their main task as seeing that the agents have the support they need.

The support mechanism the pair have devised

RE/MAX's annual awards ceremonies are very special occasions. Care is taken to make them exciting events, such as this sit-down dinner for 1,600 recipients and guests under the wing of the world-famous *Spruce Goose* in Long Beach.

The RE/MAX of California outdoor campaign features billboards such as this one on a major thoroughfare to the opulent Century City, adjacent to Beverly Hills.

during their seven-year RE/MAX alliance ranges from choosing broker/owners who can recruit the best agents in the first place to aiding these brokers in creating work environments attractive to California's best real estate sales agents. Office design, advertising, communications, and awards ceremonies also play major parts in the regional programs. In every area function takes precedence over cosmetic concerns.

Syvertson and Haselton's philosophy for success is practical rather than theoretical: Find out what agents and owners want and make it easy for them to get it. One of the first factors in keeping agents productive and happy, the two men believe, lies in selecting broker/owners who understand the RE/MAX concept and its potential. Great care and emphasis is placed on the selection of new franchisees to assure the people selected can recruit the caliber of professionals needed to build an office of top producers. People who can build their dreams as well as those of RE/MAX of California.

Syvertson and Haselton feel the region's success can also be attributed to support programs like communications and advertising as exemplified by the award-winning *RE/MAX in California* bimonthly regional magazine, the advertising program, and the annual awards banquet.

Both men stress it is important to remind agents of the revolutionary nature of the RE/MAX organization, and the magazine is designed to convey this message. The regional advertising program is also multipurpose. In the mediums of television, billboards, and print, the current slogan "RE/MAX—100 Percent Maximum Real Estate Service" is used.

In the outdoor campaign, billboards are rotated throughout the state on a monthly basis in targeted communities. Exposure on some freeway locations is as high as 14 million people per month.

RE/MAX of California agents like to celebrate their success together. To provide a gala occasion for the celebration, Haselton and Syvertson produce an annual awards weekend which is a production of staging, lighting, sound, and big-screen videos.

Sid Syvertson and Steve Haselton are justifiably proud of their success but, in typical fashion, have set much higher goals for themselves and their company. Determined to be the largest real estate firm in a state where the population increases by 600,000 annually, they plan to have 550 offices and 13,000 agents throughout California by the mid-1990s.

Never failing to recognize and seize opportunities to build their organization, the two men decided a few years ago to expand from a strictly residential operation into commercial real estate sales as well. Several offices in the Greater Los Angeles area, using the same 100 percent concept, have been opened and now account for about 20 percent of the firm's business.

The story of RE/MAX of California is a classic example of the principle of synergism, elements that combine to produce a total effect that is greater than the sum of the individual elements. The combining of an already very successful real estate firm with the "revolutionary" RE/MAX network system is an excellent example of synergism. An even better example is the combination of Sid Syvertson and Steve Haselton, two very successful but very different men who, in joining forces, have produced a total effect that not only is greater than the sum of their individual accomplishments but at the same time has made real estate history in California.

OVERTON, MOORE & ASSOCIATES, INC.

"Building for Business in Southern California" are the six words printed on the cover of Overton, Moore & Associates, Inc. (OMA), corporate brochure, which summarize the OMA philosophy and explain the company's effort to provide value and problem-free tenancy for its clients and customers.

Founded in 1973, OMA today is a leading Southern California real estate development company specializing in the building of office, industrial, and mixed-use projects. It is a fully integrated organization featuring in-house capabilities for land planning, general contracting, construction of off-site improvements and on-site product, marketing, and asset management.

The company was founded by Jon Overton and Stanley Moore. Overton retired in 1977, and Moore is now president and chief executive officer. Born and raised in Cleveland, Ohio, and following a tour of duty with the U.S. Navy, Moore attended Villanova University in Pennsylvania, earning his liberal arts degree in 1962. Following graduation, a desire to roam led him to Southern California where he met his future partner, planting the seed that would become OMA.

During the early years the company faced much adversity due to a severe real estate and economic recession. But from a base of less than 100,000 square feet of warehouse space, the company currently has more than 2 million square feet in design and construction stages of development.

In the mid-1980s, needing more space for a staff that had grown from 15 to more than 50 people, OMA purchased land at the intersection of the Harbor and San Diego freeways. In March 1988 the firm moved into new headquarters on the second floor of the 28,000-square-foot building it owns at 1125 West 190th Street in Los Angeles.

During its relatively brief history, Overton, Moore & Associates has constructed more than 20 million square feet of office, industrial, and mixed-use space and has developed more than 1,000 acres of raw land throughout the Southern California basin.

The company normally develops projects on a joint-venture basis with major pension funds, insurance companies, and other investors. The organization owns and manages more than 7 million square feet of office and industrial space. OMA does the construction for its own as well as other projects, on either a bid or a negotiated basis, as a general contractor.

The firm focuses exclusively on the 60-mile circle around Los Angeles, an area of dynamic growth tempered by strong competition. Location, quality, and service are the cornerstones of projects selected for development, and a partial list of projects conveys a clear picture of the company's development expertise and capacity:

• SOUTH BAY INDUSTRIAL/BUSINESS PARKS. Five separate parks located between the 91 Freeway and Long Beach where OMA and its partners acquired some 300 raw acres, producing and marketing more than 5 million square feet of industrial, office, and R&D space for such clients as Xerox, Toyota, Pacific Telesis, Konica Business Machines, Sony, and Digital Equipment, to name a few.

• PACIFIC CONCOURSE. In 1987, in what was reportedly the largest public/private venture of its kind in Los Angeles County history, OMA was selected by the county's Economic Development Corporation (EDC) to develop its first large-scale real estate project, on a 30-acre site at the intersection of the San Diego and Century freeways. In a joint venture with Copley Realty Advisors, OMA began development of the more than one million square feet of office, hotel, and commercial space in the $200-million project. At the dedication ceremony, U.S. Senator Pete Wilson called it "a model for others to emulate," and Los Angeles County Supervisor Kenneth Hahn described it as "the finest office park anywhere in America."

Pictured here are OMA management (from left) Douglas Carlton, Tom J. Anderson, Donald W. Koch, Gaye Tomita, S.A. Moore, Kathe Rodgers, Malcolm O'Donnell, and Dwight L. Merriman.

• SAN FERNANDO BUSINESS CENTER. A 30-acre business park located at the northern end of the San Fernando Valley at the 210 and 118 freeways near the 5 junction. DataLok, Otsuka Pharmaceutical, All American Products, and General Connectors occupy the majority of the 650,000 square feet built at this premier San Fernando Valley location.

• CYPRESSPOINTE. A 48-acre site in the City of Cypress in North Orange County. The park features hotels, shopping, office, and headquarters space for JVC America, PacifiCare, Proton, and others in the more than one-half million square feet produced in the park at this time.

• REDONDO BEACH BUSINESS COURT/TECH II. Developments in the City of Redondo Beach comprising more than 30 acres and now fully occupied by a "company called TRW." Built in three phases over several years, the buildings total 635,000 square feet: two-story complexes requiring extensive and sensitive community negotiations with the city, its constituents, and school board, which resulted in the city council's award for Project of the Year when completed in 1988.

• LA MIRADA BUSINESS CENTER. A 25-acre business park located in this namesake locale at the Santa Ana Freeway. The site is being developed with Cox Broadcasting and its radio subsidiary KFI. Phase One of the ultimate 500,000 square feet to be produced here is now just completed, and space is being prepared for its first occupants which include VIP Computers.

• WEST CORONA INDUSTRIAL PARK. A 50-acre site in northern Riverside County being developed to meet the emerging demand for quality distribution space in that part of the Inland Empire. Phase One is currently under construction and marketing is now under way.

• EL SEGUNDO RESEARCH CENTER. 400,000 square feet of two-and three-story office space in a campus setting on Sepulveda just south of Los Angeles International Airport. The site is completely leased to such firms as Hughes Aircraft, Inference Corp., Caltrans, Great Western Bank, and LifePLUS-Vista, Inc. A Marriott Courtyard Hotel is an integral amenity of the center.

• UNIVERSITY PARK. A 15-acre development in Placentia on the 57 Freeway just north of the 91 junction in Orange County. Seven buildings comprise development featuring two hotels and more than 100,000 square feet of office and business space, and the park was selected by State Farm Insurance for their Claims headquarters in Orange County.

• CHRYSLER DISTRIBUTION CENTER. A build-to-suit, 315,000-square-foot Regional Parts Facility built for the Detroit-based automotive giant on 18 acres in Ontario purchased from the Southern Pacific Railroad Company.

Praise and recognition are nothing new to OMA or Stan Moore. The firm, which is ranked among the top 10 real estate developers and property management companies in Los Angeles, has received numerous awards and citations, and Moore has been frequently honored for his professional and community leadership. A past president of the Los Angeles chapter of the National Association of Industrial and Office Parks and a founder of the LAX International Business Council, he serves on the board of the Economic Resources Corporation of South-Central Los Angeles, which helps meets the need for employment in that area.

Moore has also held various leadership posts with the National Conference of Christians and Jews and received the National Jewish Humanitarian Award from the National Jewish Center for Immunology and Respiratory Medicine. In 1989 the Women in Commercial Real Estate presented him with their Crystal Award.

Moore is quick to credit his partners and employees for the company's success. "I have outstanding partners and great people," he says, "who work with my style, which I call random management." He sees his role as that of a "supply sergeant." The success of Overton, Moore & Associates, Inc., is ample evidence of the good job he has done in keeping his people supplied with everything they need to keep on "Building for Business in Southern California."

A CLIMATE FOR BUSINESS

L.A.'s Marketplace

Los Angeles area residents and visitors alike can partake of a variety of services within this cultural mecca. Retail establishments and hotels offer unique and quality experiences.

As a cultural trendsetter, L.A. has an eclectic group of establishments such as Via Rodeo in Beverly Hills, where visitors are greeted with exceptional service. Photo by Mark E. Gibson

BUGLE BOY INDUSTRIES

By any measure, Dr. William C.W. Mow, chairman, chief executive officer, and founder of Bugle Boy Industries, is far from the image of the typical garment merchant. The first clue is in the title that precedes his name. Rarely, if ever, has a garment industry leader emerged from an education in electrical engineering that includes a doctoral degree.

When Bill Mow founded Bugle Boy in May 1977, he had absolutely no experience in the clothing industry. One of six sons of a Chinese diplomat, he came to the United States at age 13, when his father was assigned to a post with the United Nations in New York. After graduating from high school, he worked his way through college, earning his electrical engineering degree at New York's Rensselaer Polytechnic Institute. He then went on to Purdue University in Indiana, where he received his Ph.D. degree.

After working briefly on the East Coast, he decided to follow an older brother, Harry, to Southern California. In 1969 he launched an electronics company called Macrodata, which grew rapidly and which he sold during the mid-1970s. Unjustly accused by the firm's buyer of misstating certain financial data—charges of which he was later completely exonerated—he was forced to resign as president of Macrodata. Out of work and with his reputation in his chosen field under a cloud, Mow had to take quick action to support his family and to raise the substantial legal fees needed to defend himself.

Thus was launched what is today a major international clothing company with 11 divisions, approximately 1,000 employees, and more than 10,000 accounts. It produces and markets casual slacks and dress slacks, and jeanswear and sportswear for men, women, and children under the Bugle Boy and Vincente by Bugle Boy labels.

Originally called Buckaroo International, the company was anything but an instant success, losing $300,000 in its first season. In 1981 it posted losses of $750,000, and three years later a disastrous commitment to the short-lived "parachute pants" boom brought it to the brink of collapse, with a negative $5 million net worth.

Bill Mow, however, would not give up. As he had so clearly demonstrated in his legal battles, he is a tenacious fighter. Within months of the 1984 fiasco, his company designed and introduced a new line of clothing that proved very successful and launched Bugle Boy on the road to success.

Originally conceived as a collection of better young men's merchandise, Bugle Boy was redirected toward the moderately priced fashion-sportswear market in 1981, following the appointment of Vincente Nesi as president. Nesi had joined the company shortly after it was founded and today owns 10 percent of the stock, with the other 90 percent owned by Mow. Nesi, who works out of Bugle Boy's New York office, is in charge of sales and merchandising.

After becoming established in the early 1980s as a major resource of fashion casual slacks for young men, the company launched marketing ventures in other categories that have made it an important supplier in virtually every apparel classification.

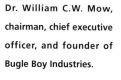

Dr. William C.W. Mow, chairman, chief executive officer, and founder of Bugle Boy Industries.

Bugle Boy's modern corporate headquarters, located in Simi Valley.

Young men's slacks were introduced under the Vincente Nesi label in 1983, and the Bugle Boy and junior divisions were formed in 1984.

Menswear and girlswear debuted in 1987, followed a year later by the introduction of the jeans and missy divisions and the entry of Bugle Boy into Canada. A licensing agreement covering eastern Asia was signed in 1989. In the United States, Bugle Boy products, including tops, hosiery, underwear, swimwear, children's activewear, infant and toddler apparel, neckwear, and footwear, are distributed through licensees with product expertise in those fields and are sold in major department stores, chain stores, and specialty shops.

To enable the firm to maintain its commitment to affordably priced clothing, most manufacturing is done in various countries overseas, including Taiwan, Hong Kong, China, and the Philippines. The company does, however, utilize American production sources for some of its jeanswear. Since 1989 it has been based in Simi Valley, California, where it owns and occupies a modern glass-and-steel facility encompassing 215,000 square feet in two buildings linked together by a glass-enclosed bridge.

In addition to its sales and merchandising operation in New York, the corporation also maintains sales offices in major American cities, including Atlanta, Boston, Chicago, Dallas, and Seattle. Bugle Boy Industries is among the largest privately held apparel companies in the United States and is considered the leader in casual slacks for young men and boys. Its young men's division (ages 12 to 17) is its largest, followed by its men's and boys' divisions. Women's apparel is also playing a growing part in the company's product mix.

With an annual budget of $25 million, Bugle Boy advertises on television, in newspapers and magazines, and through various outdoor media. Under the direction of Mow's daughter Genevieve Mow Squires, Bugle Boy advertising has demonstrated a distinctive and creative flair. Recently, for example, the firm signed an agreement with the National Football League to sponsor its well-known "helmet" cars, with the Bugle Boy name emblazoned on them.

Bill Mow's daughter is just one of several family members who play key roles in the company. His wife, Rosa, is executive vice president, and a nephew, Barney Mow, is senior vice president, operations. Kathy Mow works with her sister, Genevieve, as art director in the Advertising Department.

Bugle Boy is a major supporter of various charitable causes in the Los Angeles area and works closely with such organizations as the City of Hope, Juvenile Diabetes Foundation, and the National Council of Christians and Jews. Each year, it helps make the spirit of Christmas real to hundreds of homeless and poor children by donating generous amounts of clothing.

Dr. William Mow and the people of Bugle Boy Industries have learned their lessons well and look to the future with confidence. Much of the firm's success is due to the disciplines brought to it by its founder from a seemingly unrelated background. But it was exactly that background that gave Bugle Boy a new and different approach to the garment industry, one that is less trendy and volatile and more businesslike.

Electrical engineering may not be the traditional doorway to the garment industry but, for Dr. William C.W. Mow, it appears to have been the key to success.

THRIFTY CORPORATION

I n the early 1900s Los Angeles was becoming a boomtown, fueled by the prospects of inexpensive land and bottomless oil wells. Responding to the opportunity, two brothers, Harry and Robert Borun, and their brother-in-law Norman Levin, opened a wholesale drug warehouse in Los Angeles. For the next 10 years the family-run business reaped the rewards of a juggernaut economy, while planning for even bigger and better things.

Then came 1929, and a depression that plunged many businesses into bankruptcy, including some of the retailers the Boruns had depended upon. A decision had to be made, and the wholesale warehouse became Thrifty Cut-Rate Drug Store.

It was a wise choice; within five years there were 17 stores in operation. In 1935 the company incorporated as Thrifty Drug Stores Co., Inc., and seven years later opened one of the first self-service drug stores in the United States. By the end of 1942 there were 58 stores, with combined sales of $17 million.

In the mid-1940s the aircraft industry, driven by World War II, turned Los Angeles into one of the major employment centers in the nation. With it rose the fortunes of local retailers, including Thrifty. The full-service pharmacies in every store put Thrifty on the flight path to success.

The postwar boom brought a huge influx of people—nearly 280,000 per year—causing a severe housing shortage. Soon, houses sprouted like weeds and freeways snaked their way to all ends of the basin. New and suddenly accessible neighborhoods represented a prime opportunity for Thrifty, and the "neighborhood Thrifty" soon became a valuable community member.

The quick, one-stop convenience of each store lent itself well to the Southern California lifestyle, and in the early 1950s Thrifty renovated its entire operation to keep pace with the times. The new "Super Drug Store" concept was born, with much larger stores and an enormous selection of merchandise.

Dramatic changes followed, with broadened merchandise lines, an emphasis on promotional items, and an aggressive expansion program.

The 14 years between 1952 and 1966 were

golden ones for Thrifty, as a 20 percent compound growth rate in net income spurred expansion from 96 to 272 stores, and the company earned itself a place on the New York Stock Exchange.

Thrifty expanded its interest in specialty retailing in 1971, acquiring Los Angeles-based United Merchandising Corp. (Big 5 Sporting Goods) and the Newman Importing Company. The city itself continued attracting major corporations and industrial interests, leading to a virtual renaissance for Thrifty Drug. Pharmacy prices were restructured; grocery items returned to the shelves for the first time since the 1950s; and a massive store renovation program was launched.

In 1977 Thrifty Drug Stores Co., Inc., became Thrifty Corporation, reflecting the broadened scope of the organization.

Recognizing a new market niche—high-density communities—the company formed a second chain known as Thrifty Jr. Smaller, more compact versions of the larger stores, they provide a complete pharmacy and large selection of goods. Public response was favorable and new stores continue to open at key locations.

The 1980s were dynamic times for Thrifty. Headquarters were shifted to a towering mid-Wilshire location in 1984. New acquisitions (Pay 'n Save Drug Stores, Gart Bros. Sporting Goods, and a number of smaller sporting goods chains) made Thrifty the largest drug store chain on the West Coast, fourth-largest in the nation, and America's second-largest sporting goods chain.

In 1986 Thrifty Corporation merged with Pacific Lighting Corporation (now Pacific Enterprises), which counts Southern California Gas Co. among its subsidiaries. The move provided extra punch and opened new vistas for a company with a tradition of setting and attaining high goals. Sales in 1990 topped $3 billion, and the company was operating 1,055 stores.

Thrifty's tremendous growth has paralleled that of Los Angeles. Neither has reached its highest potential and the closing years of the twentieth century bring the promise of great things from both.

Big 5 Sporting Goods

There have been a lot of changes at Big 5 Sporting Goods since the company was founded in 1955. In the beginning, it had a slightly different trade name, didn't sell sporting goods, and operated only five stores.

Officially, the company is still United Merchandising Corp., the name chosen by Maurie I. Liff, Harry A. Liff, and Robert W. Miller when they joined forces to start the business in September 1955. Since there were five retail locations, they felt "Big 5 Stores" was as good a name as any.

At that time, they were not concerned with the number of stores the name reflected, or how it would sound as new stores were added. Rather, their focus was to make the name synonymous with good value, service, and integrity, whether there were 5 or 500 locations. Those principles continue to guide the company today.

The five original stores were located in downtown Los Angeles, Burbank, Inglewood, Glendale, and San Jose. The product lines included World War II surplus items, tents, sleeping bags, air mattresses (manufactured in the company's own plant), housewares, hand tools, and other merchandise. Sound buying practices, good values, and friendly service, coupled with integrity and high principles, helped the new company to grow.

Sporting goods gradually found its way into the product mix, and over a period of time, the popularity and demand for this merchandise made it apparent that the future success of the business lay in the sporting goods field. Thus, on December 7, 1963, the trade name was changed to "Big 5 Sporting Goods." The decision proved to be a wise one, and Big 5 continued to flourish.

By 1971 the company had 19 Big 5 locations, and in March of that year, it merged with Thrifty Corporation, who operated a major retail drug store chain. For the next 15 years, with encouragement from Thrifty, Big 5 Sporting Goods opened, on the average, five new stores per year. Up until 1984, most of the stores were in California, with a few in Nevada. In November of that year, the company expanded into the Northwest, opening 10 new stores in the Seattle, Washington, area.

In September 1986, Thrifty Corporation merged with Pacific Lighting Corporation (now Pacific Enterprises) and an even more aggressive expansion program for Big 5 was adopted. By the start of the nineties, Big 5 had more than 110 stores in operation, and was continuing to open new ones at an accelerated rate. Big 5's explosive growth necessitated new technology to meet the demands of the business. To meet these challenges, Big 5 converted all of its stores to a computerized, point-of-sale system, a milestone in the sporting goods industry. Additionally, an interactive, video training program called InfoWindow was developed to teach its employees

how to use the point-of-sale system.

In February 1990 the company replaced its Hawthorne warehouse with a near 500,000-square-foot distribution center in Fontana. A few months later, the corporate headquarters was relocated to El Segundo, where its flagship Big 5 Store opened next door in September 1990.

Bob Miller, president, credits much of the company's prosperity to being located on the West Coast, where recreation, sports, and outdoor activities are a way of life. Other key factors include strong and consistent advertising and the philosophy that the customer is the number-one priority. However, it's the people that have made Big 5 so successful. The longevity and low turnover rate attest to the loyalty of its more than 2,000 employees and is undoubtedly a contributing factor to why Big 5 Sporting Goods is one of the leading sporting goods retailers in the nation.

From its modest five-store beginnings, Big 5 Sporting Goods has grown to 132 stores with more on the way.

In order to better serve the customer's needs, the Big 5 chain, with its huge array of merchandise, has converted to a state-of-the-art, computerized, point-of-sale system.

LANZ

It wasn't a covered wagon that brought the Scharff brothers, Werner and Kurt, across America to California in 1938. Rather, it was a Ford convertible into which they had piled their worldly possessions for the journey from New York to Los Angeles.

In 1936 the Scharffs had come to the United States from their native Germany. Former food merchants in Munich, they brought with them little more than their dreams and ambitions, and a penchant for hard work.

In New York they met an Austrian named Sepp Lanz, who had come from his native Salzburg in 1937 and opened a women's apparel store and a small factory where he manufactured peasant-type blouses, embroidered garments, and other traditional Austrian clothing. At the Scharffs' invitation, he joined their California trek to help them launch a new business, a retail store selling Lanz creations.

That first store, at 6150 Wilshire Boulevard, opened on November 2, 1938, and served as the company's headquarters until 1978, and continues as a Lanz store to this day. At first the store sold only merchandise manufactured by Sepp Lanz in New York, and it became so successful that it led to the opening of stores in Pasadena, Hawaii, Palm Springs, and San Francisco.

It wasn't as easy as it may sound, however. Co-founder and chairman of the board Werner Scharff recalls those early days, when he functioned as janitor, salesman, and bookkeeper. At

day's end, he became the delivery man, using a borrowed car, and then returned to stock the shelves. Money was so scarce that only one of the four employees could cash his paycheck each week.

Ironically, it was the company's scarcity of funds that led directly to the introduction of its best-selling and most famous product, the perennial Granny Gown, which Werner Scharff himself designed. Intending it to be a dress, Scharff was unable to afford the necessary material and used an inexpensive flannel instead. When a customer observed, "Oh, what a cute nightgown," a legend was born.

Today, more than 3,000 of the granny gowns are produced daily under the Lanz of Salzburg label, and are worn and treasured by women of all ages. In all, more than 15 million of the gowns, which retain their classic styling but are updated regularly through signature prints, have been produced.

The start of World War II brought a number of changes to the young company. Shipping restrictions forced the closing of the Hawaii store, and with raw materials hard to obtain, Lanz began a West Coast manufacturing facility to supplement the merchandise made by Sepp Lanz in New York. In 1946 the Scharffs bought out their partner's interest, closed the New York factory, and consolidated all manufacturing and wholesale operations on the West Coast.

The postwar era began with the opening of stores in such areas as Carmel. In the early 1950s the firm began to sell its products to other specialty retail and department stores, in addition to supplying the needs of its own outlets. Today Lanz, Inc., sells to more than 3,000 retail outlets nationwide, including such famous stores as Lord and Taylor, Bloomingdales, and Neiman Marcus.

Lanz also merchandises more than 150 in-store shops in better department stores across the United States. Its own retail network has grown to 30 stores, all in California, and, during the 1980s, it began a highly selective franchise program, which now includes nearly a dozen franchisees in California and around the nation. One of those franchises, in Santa Monica, is owned and operated by Werner Scharff's daughter, Alexis.

Throughout its history Lanz has been very much a family operation. Co-founder Kurt Scharff passed away in 1984, but the second generation, represented by Werner's two sons, is now guiding the company's destiny. The older son, Peter, has been president since the late 1970s and his brother, Christopher, is director of franchise marketing and licensing.

Though not blood relatives, the employees of Lanz are also very much a part of the family and many of them represent the second and third generations of company workers. One long-term member of the staff, Elizabeth Lahn, who is vice president/design, is given much of the credit for the corporation's growth and success over the past two decades.

"At Lanz," says Lahn, "we don't rush out to catch the momentum of the latest fashion trends from Europe, and we don't imitate the styles of our competitors. We emphasize a simple, under-stated, traditional look which is what our customers have come to expect from us. In Lanz of Salzburg sleepwear, we strive for a classic look that is soft, feminine, and pretty."

The Lanz line has expanded considerably from its original dresses, peasant blouses, and night-gowns. Today "Lanz Originals" dresses and sportswear are designed by an in-house team of designers. The exclusive Lanz signature prints used for "Lanz of Salzburg" sleepwear are spe-cially created by designers in both Europe and the United States. Licensees of Lanz, Inc., manu-facture girls' sleepwear, slippers, dolls, daywear, dresses and sportswear, and—for adults—scented soaps, slippers, and flannel bedding. The company also recently introduced a line of dresses and sleepwear for the large-size market, called Lanz II, and has begun exporting both its own products and those of its licensees to Europe, where its traditional designs originated.

In an industry where the average successful apparel manufacturer stays in business for only 10 years, Werner Scharff is proud of the uncom-promising commitment to design and to the high-est quality that has kept his company flourishing for more than a half-century. Still very much in-volved in its affairs, he now spends much of his time pursuing other ventures close to his heart. Honored by Governor George Deukmejian and the City of Hope for his philanthropic activities, he has also devoted more than 25 years of time and effort to the development and restoration of the famous Venice section of Los Angeles and is an active supporter of the Venice Family Clinic.

Werner Scharff chose wisely in coming to Cali-fornia so many years ago and launching a busi-ness in the Los Angeles area.

The commitment to quality that characterized the company then has never wavered. "Today, as in the past," says Scharff, "we are dedicated to bringing our customers quality apparel that is classic in styling and contemporary in design—a combination we call 'Tradition in Touch with Today.'"

In addition to the 30 Lanz company-owned shops, there are a dozen newly franchised locations.

Mother/daughter looks and complementary li-censed products are helping the Lanz of Salzburg flannel sleep-wear division set impres-sive sales records.

HITACHI, LTD.

H itachi, Ltd., based in Tokyo, Japan, is one of the world's industrial giants. Its global work force of about 310,000 men and women produces more than 20,000 products, generating annual sales revenues in the $50 billion range. The company is divided into five product divisions: power systems and equipment; consumer products; information and communication systems and electronic devices; industrial machinery and plants; and wire, cable, metals, chemicals, and other products.

The venture was founded in Japan in 1910 by Namihei Odaira, the first products being small five-horsepower electric motors, produced in the repair shop of a mining company. Odaira was supervisor of one of the firm's work crews. It was he who chose the new company's name, based on two Chinese characters.

The first is "hi," meaning "sun." The second, "tachi," meaning "rise," depicts a man with his feet firmly planted on the ground. For Odaira, the combination of the two characters expressed his vision of a better life for man himself and a brighter future for mankind.

Odaira built his enterprise on two basic principles that remain Hitachi's core philosophy: the integration of production capabilities so that each resource can contribute to the development of technology, and an extraordinary commitment of the firm's human and financial resources to research and development and training.

As Japan's economy expanded so did Hitachi, becoming a leading supplier of electrical power generators, turbines, electric machinery, construction equipment, locomotive and railway equipment, and an expanding spectrum of production equipment and instrumentation indispensable in building an industrial economy.

Along with that growth came a rise in the Japanese standard of living, with demand for consumer products soaring. Hitachi responded by becoming a leading manufacturer of home and personal appliances, from refrigerators and washing machines to television sets and air conditioners.

Although approximately two-thirds of its sales are domestic, Hitachi is truly a global corporation. More than 184 manufacturing subsidiaries and sales and service facilities are located abroad, with operations in North and South America, Europe, Australia, Asia, Africa, and the Middle East. The organization employs more than 33,000 people in these overseas facilities.

Although Hitachi's U.S. operations are a rela-

tively small part of the overall picture, the figures are nonetheless impressive. There are more than 60 companies, most of which maintain an office in California. They have a combined total of approximately 9,000 U.S. employees, with more than one-third of them in California. Sales for Hitachi America, Ltd., which was founded in 1959, first reached the billion-dollar level in 1985.

Hitachi has more than a dozen manufacturing firms in the United States, the largest of these firms, Hitachi Consumer Products of America, Inc., located in Anaheim, merged with Compton based Hitachi Sales Corporation of America to form Hitachi Home Electronics (America), Inc., combining both manufacturing and sales.

Located in Compton, this new company manufactures projection televisions and VCRs. The sales force is responsible for the sales of consumable products, including TV sets, VCRs, other home appliances, and a variety of leading edge, highly technological and innovative products. The company employs more than 1,000 people.

Other California-based manufacturing affiliates include Hitachi Instruments, Inc., in San Jose and HMT-Technology in Fremont.

Another 1990 development was the opening of the Hitachi Chemical Research Center on the campus of the University of California, Irvine. Named Plumwood House, the $16.5-million research facility was established by Hitachi Chemical Company, Ltd., which became the first

Japanese corporation to set up a research facility on an American campus. The center will conduct basic research in four different areas focusing on the development of pharmaceuticals, including those which could treat Alzheimer's and other diseases related to aging; diagnostic systems; industrial bioreactors; and medical electronics.

In 1989 Hitachi Data Systems Corporation (HDS) was formed, based in Santa Clara, California. A joint venture between Hitachi Ltd. and Electronic Data Systems, the company acquired 100 percent of the shares of National Advanced Systems (NAS) from National Semiconductor Corporation. HDS markets and services industry-standard mainframe computers and peripheral subsystems, with more than 20,000 installed worldwide.

Other major U.S. facilities include: Hitachi Computer Products (America), Inc., in Norman, Oklahoma; Hitachi Automotive Products (USA), Inc., in Harrodsburg, Kentucky; and Hitachi Telecom (USA), Inc., in Norcross, Georgia.

In Los Angeles Hitachi maintains a public affairs office which was opened in 1986. It is unique among the hundreds of Hitachi facilities around the world in that it is not part of any business unit or business operation and not involved in the manufacture, research, sales, or service of any of the more than 20,000 company products.

The office was established to manage Hitachi community relations, public relations, and public affairs activities in California and the western United States. California was chosen as the site of the office because of the company's numerous major facilities in the state and because the state in general, and Los Angeles in particular, represents a major link in the Pacific Rim trading connection.

Hitachi's American contributions extend well beyond the commercial and industrial realm. One illustration is The Hitachi Foundation, established in 1985 with an endowment of $20 million and headquartered in Washington, D.C.

Its role is to help develop the human resources, skills, and understanding necessary to enrich the lives of individuals in an increasingly technological world. It awards grants in two program areas: education and community development.

In recent years, Hitachi, Ltd., has joined forces with the California Chamber of Commerce in sponsoring top-level forums on topics of critical importance to the state. These forums, held in San Francisco and Los Angeles, have focused on such issues as transportation, the environment, growth, and housing. Attendance at these forums has included many business and government leaders.

Hitachi, Ltd., has come a long way since it produced those three small electric motors in 1910. Today it stands at the forefront of the revolution in various high-tech areas, from semiconductors to computers, and from robots to total factory automation systems. Yet each of its shifts in product lines represents not a transformation but an evolution. The company continues to manufacture new generations of many of the same products and systems that carried the Hitachi name 80 years ago.

Despite its enormous growth, Hitachi has never wavered from the vision and philosophy of its founder, Namihei Odaira, expressed not only in the name he chose but in this stanza from an ancient Chinese poem: "Though we cannot live 100 years, we should be concerned with 1,000 years hence."

ALPINE ELECTRONICS OF AMERICA, INC.

Performance is the name of the game in Alpine's specialty car-audio equipment. Imagine having up to 12 hours of continuous high-quality stereo music in your car—thanks to a revolutionary compact disc remote changer installed in the car trunk. The unit—so sophisticated it would impress James Bond—changes CDs in response to signals from a dashboard control.

The 7618 FM/AM cassette player sports Alpine's upgraded T-10 II SP tuner and a host of exclusive tuner features such as music category presets, intelligent preset scan, and intelligent auto memory to simplify operation or enhance the listening experience.

The unit is but one example of sonic excellence designed and produced by Alpine Electronics of America, Inc., whose equipment has been called the "Lamborghini of stereos." The company's products won numerous awards to back up acclaim in the marketplace. In a recent Car Audio Nationals competition, where the sound of the nation's best car audio systems was judged, the entry that won the top division of the pro class had an Alpine 7907 CD tuner in the dash. Several other winners—who had beaten some 700 others in regional contests—used the same tuner or other Alpine components to make their marks with the judges.

Alpine Electronics of America, Inc., headquartered in Torrance, produces completely finished merchandise: primarily auto stereos—tape players, radios, and CD players—as well as mobile security systems, cellular phones, and home audio equipment.

In Japan, the Alps Group embraces three companies: Alps Electric, Tohoku Alps Co., Ltd., and Alpine Electronics. Together their technologies rank their products among the finest in terms of quality and production volume. The parent is a Japanese public company, with major worldwide interests and annual sales of $3 billion.

Alps Electric manufactures a diverse line of products ranging from individual and integrated components to complete systems. As the core elements in numerous fields—audiovisual and other consumer equipment, computer terminals enabling office and home automation, car electronics, satellite broadcasting equipment, and more—the products are geared to meet constantly changing demands.

While Alps exports from Japan, it also participates as a multinational corporation involved in production and sales at more than 30 locations in 11 countries. Alps established its first overseas office in New York in 1963 and its Torrance presence through Alpine in 1978.

Alpine actually started making electronic parts for car audio equipment in 1967 as a joint venture between Alps and Motorola, Inc. When Alps bought out Motorola's interest in 1978, the venture became Alpine. The following year the company began selling complete car audio systems.

Alpine achieved $16 million in net sales for the first year of operation. By 1989 net sales had climbed to $250 million, including the sales of car audio products manufactured at its Indianapolis factory. Meanwhile Alpine Electronics of Japan opened its stock ownership to the public in March 1988. Today its shares are traded on the Tokyo Stock Exchange.

Alpine products are targeted to the high end of auto stereo systems, for discriminating audiophiles who believe that climbing into a car should not mean compromising their listening standards—regardless of driving, weather, or geographical intrusions. The products, known by

Alpine's introduction of the improved half-DIN sized 3331 graphic EQ/pre-amp and Active Dividing Network is a marked improvement over its predecessor because it allows car enthusiasts to fine-tune their vehicles with greater flexibility and control than ever before.

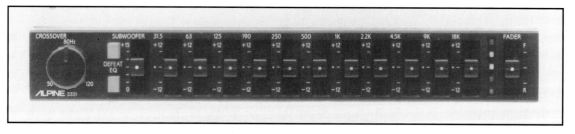

Alpine is part of the globally prominent Alps Group, whose parent, Alps Electric Co., Ltd., is headquartered in Tokyo. The company was founded in 1948, initially to manufacture rotary switches. It soon grew into the independent specialty supplier it is today and one of the world's leading general manufacturers of a multitude of electronic components.

their Alpine green glow—a special technology using green liquid crystal illumination—are becoming more and more sophisticated as upgrades are even more in demand. Among the Alpine components are compact disc players, tape players, tuners, amplifiers, graphic equalizers, and speakers. Alpine has helped lead the industry revolution of components and circuitry crucial to

The new, high-powered 6963 2-way 6-by-9-inch speaker design incorporates a soft silk dome tweeter, the same type used in automotive speaker separates and finer home systems.

consumer and industrial electronics.

With such success in its primary business, Alpine has gone on to develop other product lines: since 1984 Alpine has introduced cellular telephones and automotive security systems with a highly innovative feature that calls the user anywhere, anytime.

Alpine diversified into home audio equipment in the early 1980s, when it acquired the Luxman line, already known for its high-end products. Today Luxman receivers are consistently rated the best in the industry through test results, independent dealer surveys, and audio magazine competitions.

Alpine's Torrance plant, at 19145 Gramercy Place, is a 105,000-square-foot facility that houses the company's United States headquarters, research and development, marketing, and distribution divisions. The firm completed and opened this building in 1983; four years later it began production in an Indiana plant as well, which was incorporated as Alpine Electronics Manufacturing of America, Inc.

Alpine started out as a marketing company in the United States; it now has 400 employees in Torrance and the Indianapolis facility. "My constant motivation is to find ways our business can thrive here in the U.S. market," says Tsuyoshi "Tom" Ohki, Alpine Electronics of America president and the force behind current marketing and production procedures in the operation. "We have an almost obsessive commitment to testing and retesting, to continue as a leading-edge company in the industry, and to better meet our customers' demands."

Advanced technology is an Alpine commitment from development and design through testing and production. One important criterion is to test equipment under continuously changing conditions, such as in mountains, rain, and electrical interference. "Performance and sonic excellence are synonymous with Alpine," says David Black, senior vice-president, Marketing/Car Audio Division. "We serve customers who insist on perfor-

mance and sonic excellence, and are willing to pay for what they value very highly. With that in mind, we have structured what we think is the most sophisticated product portfolio in the car audio industry."

What makes Alpine equipment special? According to its developers it is a combination of craftsmanship and imaginative features in tape player mechanisms, tape heads, tuner circuitry, and digital operation. More specifically, tape player mechanisms manifest special materials, machining, and quality control—the GZ mechanisms introduced in 1985 incorporate advanced technologies that restrain "wow and flutter" on the road to a low level of less than 0.06 percent. Magnetic heads use amorphous materials that yield faithful reproduction of sound, another determinant of tape player performance. Tuners are noted for circuit modules that assure optimum clarity. Digital operation of single-unit tuner-CD player assemblies is an Alpine feature using optical data transfer in system control.

All company technologies undergo stringent

The 3566 is Alpine's first six-channel amplifier. Consumers can use it to build a high quality biamplified sound system with up to two subwoofers—but without the inconvenience of installing a separate crossover and two or more amplifiers.

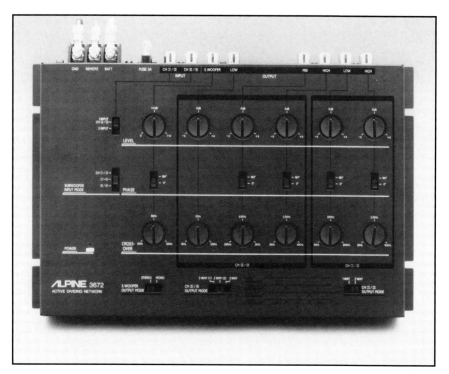

With the new 3672 active crossover network, audiophiles can create a 12-channel quad-amplified sound system with dedicated amplifiers for powering tweeters, midranges, midbass drivers, and subwoofers.

Ohki feels so strongly about personnel involvement, he has a credo framed and hung in his office. It reads, in part: "Business is people. People make the business work, not materials, equipment, or money. Human relations are the most important . . . to feel satisfaction in a job well done."

Apparently Alpine employees agree. In a recent enterprise special edition of a local newspaper, one spokesperson was quoted as saying, "Here, even my company president listens to my ideas."

The credo on Ohki's wall also spells out ways to deal with customers: "Build customer confidence through quality. We care about the quality of our product and the integrity of our company, and cherish the spirit of challenge." Alpine has a two-pronged marketing strategy—supplying automakers with factory equipment, the legacy of its early years when all output was geared to established makers for sale under their brand names, and for individuals through dealers in the retail market.

"Auto manufacturers are very much interested in having our product in their cars," says James O'Neill, senior vice-president, Marketing/Original Equipment Manufacturing Division. "We have focused our merchandising strategy on the world's top automakers as well as the high end of the retail market." The selected automakers include Honda, BMW, Jaguar, Volvo, Saab, Peugeot, General Motors, and Chrysler.

The underlying—and ongoing—theme in the company is one of determination to supply the newest and most advanced electronic technologies and products to markets worldwide, according to its executives. To do that, Alpine provides comprehensive services to augment its product line—in other words, selling sound, installation, and continuing service through its dealers.

For instance, correct installation technology is a prerequisite for deriving the full promise of

quality control. It begins in the development and design phases, is emphasized in the manufacturing phase through a flexible system that includes detailed product inspections and analyses, and continues through product movements and distribution.

Alpine's business philosophy is based on the traditional Japanese belief that it takes time to nurture an endeavor to maturity. Says Ohki, "It takes something like three years to lay a foundation, 10 years to build a business—to put down roots and bring one product to fruition. Patience and hard work are the conditions for being successful." But he quickly adds, "There is no business without a good reputation, and a reputation is the people who work with a good product, who give good service, and who in the end result make the consumer happy. We are very fortunate here to have expert, capable people on our team."

The 7915 FM/AM CD player features improvements such as new flexibility in using tuner controls and in programming presets and a new Hybrid-I digital-to-analog converter (DAC) technology to enhance the performance of the CD section.

Alpine sound systems, so the company provides in-depth training and a constant flow of information for its dealers. There are seminars, frequent visits from Alpine sales engineers, conferences in Japan, open forums, and other technical support to maintain customer service as a major competitive strength for Alpine. Products are promoted to the consumer through dealers who basically encourage potential buyers ". . . to listen and hear the difference between Alpine and competing systems," Black explains. "That's the way we compete successfully with far larger and more visible manufacturers in the consumer market."

Distribution gets much attention at Alpine, which describes itself as ". . . a small company that has cultivated a position of global leadership in a prestigious market." As the largest overseas subsidiary for its parent, and in its largest market, Alpine protects its market position through a well-managed system. (Alps' global network also includes a highly successful Canadian subsidiary—the oldest overseas subsidiary—and other units in Europe, Australia, Asia, Africa, and South America.)

As part of the mix for Alpine's continued success, Ohki points to another part of his credo: "Good timing and bold decision making are essential for top management." Says Ohki, who has been in Torrance for 18 of his 20 years in the United States, "The business atmosphere in this community is remarkable, and a great help to our growth. You can single out many positive elements: The presence of many major industries

here. Room to grow. Good organization and balance in the city, which gives us excellent conveniences and a fine labor pool from which to draw."

Because of Alpine's successes in Torrance, it has an extensive corporate policy that helps fund worthy civic projects. Among its contributions is a major grant to the city's education system.

The future growth of Alpine Electronics of America, Inc., is tied to upcoming products that are expected to break new ground, in keeping with its tradition. Says Ohki, "Our mission is to continue producing the audio equipment of choice—and we'll do so with the tenacity of an English bulldog with a toy between its teeth. We just won't let go."

A significant number of vehicles utilize 4-by-6-inch speakers which provide mediocre factory sound. With the new Alpine 6045CX 4-by-6 plate system, customers can now have Alpine sound quality utilizing the factory hole.

On its flagship Shuttle, the 5959, Alpine goes back to using pure mulltibit DACs, but with a twist: These 20-bit DACs use a sign-magnitude configuration (two DAC per channel) to eliminate zero-cross distortion and to improve THD, separation, and dynamic-range specifications beyond that offered by its sister Shuttles.

Sparkletts Drinking Water Corporation

Sparkletts Drinking Water Corporation opened in 1925 and by 1929 it expanded to occupy two city blocks in Eagle Rock.

Bow ties, knickers, and kneehigh boots were part of Sparkletts Drinking Water Corporation's traditional uniform in the 1920s. Today, Sparkletts delivers more than 70 million gallons of bottled water to Southland residents every year in its trademark sparkling green trucks that have become a California tradition.

The date was July 4, 1925. As Americans everywhere celebrated the 149th anniversary of the nation's independence, several hundred gathered in the Eagle Rock section of Los Angeles. They came, not with picnic baskets, but with empty buckets, not for parades or fireworks, but for water—sparkling-clear well water being distributed free of charge by the new owners of the "old Glassell well."

The giveaway was part of the preopening publicity for a brand-new business called the Sparkling Artesian Water Company. The founders/owners were Burton N. Arnds, Sr., Glen Bollinger, and Arthur Washburne. Arnds, who had recently arrived from Toledo, Ohio, with his wife and three young sons, envisioned the need for a bottled-water company and joined forces with Bollinger and Washburne to launch the business. Among them, they scraped together $34,000 as their initial investment.

The free distribution went on longer than the founders had planned. When heavy storms and a broken aqueduct turned city water muddy, the company came to the rescue, with radio announcements offering free water to everyone. The program continued for several weeks. Thus, even before earning its first dollar, the firm had demonstrated the community spirit that characterizes it to this day.

Finally, in August 1925, the newly completed plant was opened and the first two trucks of the Sparkling Artesian Water Company began delivering water to thirsty customers. The cost was 50 cents per five-gallon glass bottle. Arnds' vision proved to be accurate and the young company

grew rapidly. By 1928 more than one million bottles were sold, delivered by a fleet of 52 trucks.

In that same year the name of the company was changed to Sparkletts Bottled Water Corporation. The new name was suggested by Arnds' wife, who chose the name from a popular song called "Sparklets." She is also credited with selecting the now-familiar green color for the firm's trucks, a color she said signified growth.

Sparkletts expanded its original facility and, in 1929, completed a huge new plant on two city blocks in Eagle Rock. Located at 4500 York Boulevard, it remains the company's headquarters. More than 1,300 employees work for the firm at its seven bottling plants (four in Southern California) and 23 distribution centers (18 in Southern California).

The company's fleet of more than 600 trucks delivers billions of gallons of water to more than 500 communities, from Santa Barbara to the Mexican border and as far east as Dallas, Texas. Its distinctive green trucks, with the name "Sparkletts" surrounded by shimmering mylar disks, are familiar sights throughout the southwestern United States.

Every drop of water Sparkletts delivers is purified artesian well water, taken from the company's own deep, protected wells under natural pressure. The company sells three types of water: Purified Water (made mineral-free) for all distilled water purposes; Crystal-fresh Drinking Water, containing selected natural food-grade minerals for flavor; and Fluoridated Water, drinking water to which fluoride has been added to help prevent tooth decay. In the past Sparkletts experimented with other products, including soft drinks, but abandoned them during the 1950s in order to focus exclusively on producing clean, fresh, quality drinking water.

Arthur Washburne died in 1930 and his interests were acquired by his cofounders. Ownership of the company remained in the hands of the Arnds and Bollinger families and some 300 shareholders until 1964, when it was sold to Foremost

Crates of bottled water are loaded onto a delivery truck.

Dairies. In 1967 Foremost was acquired by McKesson-Robbins, now McKesson Corp., based in San Francisco. Sparkletts is the largest company in the McKesson Water Division. Other California bottled water companies in the division include Alhambra, Union City; Sparkletts Grocery Products, Monrovia; and Aqua-Vend, Los Angeles.

The sale of the firm did not, however, signal the end of the founding families' involvement. From the time of the Foremost acquisition in 1964 until 1978, the president of Sparkletts was Burton N. Arnds, Jr., known as Jim. He was one of the founder's seven sons, all of whom worked for the company at one time or another.

Sparkletts, with its focus on quality, service, and innovation, is today the largest American-owned and -operated bottled water company in the nation.

For Sparkletts, innovation has been a company hallmark throughout its history. Its fully equipped laboratory, where water samples undergo constant analysis, was the first to be approved by the State of California's Department of Health. Other "firsts" include bottled fluoridated water, hydro coolers, and electric water coolers designed for home use. The firm also originated half-gallon water containers and water vending machines, and was the first to switch from glass to plastic five-gallon containers.

In 1990 Sparkletts was the first bottled water company to introduce a home-delivered three-gallon water container in the history of the industry, the first major innovation in the water business since the switch from glass to plastic 20 years earlier. Square in shape for more compact storage, it has a built-in handle and weighs 15 pounds less than the five-gallon container, making it especially convenient for women, older consumers, and single-person households.

The future for Sparkletts Drinking Water Corporation is bright. Bottled water consumption in the United States has grown sharply in recent years, and the trend is continuing. California, where one of every three residents drinks bottled

water, accounts for half of the nationwide consumption. According to a company official, "It's popular here because of the high health and environmental awareness in the state."

Sparkletts today remains true to the traditions of community service established by its founders. The firm was the official sponsor of the track and field trials during the 1984 Olympics in Los Angeles. It also participates in fund-raising events for local hospitals, the March of Dimes, the American Heart Association, and other charitable organizations. Sparkletts has distributed hundreds of University of Southern California football tickets to children's organizations and senior groups.

The company is also quick to provide free water for the victims of earthquakes, fires, and other disasters, responding in the same way it did when the people of Los Angeles needed pure water back in 1925. Many years and countless billions of gallons later, Sparkletts Drinking Water Corporation proudly carries on the traditions and principles of its founders.

From the very beginning Sparkletts prided itself on delivering only the purest drinking water to its customers.

SUNRIDER

The story of Sunrider International, headquartered in Torrance, California, is truly a remarkable one. Founded late in 1982 in Orem, Utah, the company began distributing its products in January 1983. By the time it completed its fifth year, 1987, annual sales were $50 million. By the end of 1988 sales had doubled and, midway through 1989, doubled again, reaching $200 mil-

was a weak child, unable to participate in the physical activities of other children his age. Health rather than wealth was his dream and he promised himself he would find the way to a healthy, productive, and meaningful life.

As he grew up, he dedicated himself to the study of Chinese herbalism, realizing early on that his quest for health and vigor would be suc-

Sunrider's ambitious herb-processing facility on Sixth Avenue in the City of Industry, California.

cessful if he could find a way to apply the Philosophy of Regeneration to the mental, spiritual, and physical aspects of life. That philosophy, that life replenishes life, expresses a 5,000-year-old tradition that better health is the result of harmony, balance, and good nourishment in the body.

By the time he entered the Pharmacy School at Taiwan's Kaoshiung Medical College, Tei Fu's personal studies were focused almost exclusively on herbalism. But he now saw the tremendous opportunity to expand his horizons with the

lion. By the end of 1990, the then-eight-year-old company passed the $300 million sales mark and had operations in 10 countries.

But the real beginning of this story took place long before 1982, based on a philosophy that has its roots in ancient China. It began in April 1948 in Taiwan, with the birth of a son to a family named Chen. Given the name Tei Fu Chen, he

study of modern pharmacology and the other sciences. Gradually his dream of good health became reality. Before graduating from college, he earned black belts in several styles of martial arts, thanks to the diet and exercise program he carefully followed.

During his last semester Tei Fu married Oi Lin Chen, a medical student at the same college. After

Sunrider's herb-storage facility on Salt Lake Avenue, City of Industry.

earning his degree in pharmacy, he served two years as a medical officer in the Taiwanese Air Force. In 1974 Oi Lin moved to the United States and Tei Fu arrived later that year after the birth of their first child.

Their first few years in a new country were not easy for the Chen family. Tei Fu continued his studies at Brigham Young University in Utah, while his wife completed her residency requirements in a Pennsylvania hospital before returning to Utah to open her medical practice. He also was a teaching assistant in chemistry and physical education at BYU and, by 1979, had joined an herb company as research and development director, following the vision of his childhood to even greater discoveries about herbalism and health.

Feeling a need to communicate to the world both the teachings and the herbal formulations born of the Philosophy of Regeneration, Tei Fu Chen launched Sunrider International in 1982 in Orem, Utah. With a staff of about six people, the company's first year sales amounted to some $350,000.

Chen became chairman of the board and chief visionary of the company. Due to his persistence and drive, plus the undeniably high quality of his herbal products, Sunrider International began the amazing growth that has continued into the 1990s. In 1984 the firm opened its first foreign office, in Canada.

As the business grew during those early years, Chen saw the advantages of moving its headquarters to a larger, more strategically located area. Firmly convinced that Los Angeles was destined

Tei Fu Chen, Sunrider's president and chairman of the board.

to become the economic capital of the world, he decided a move to Southern California made sense. In 1987 the company opened its new offices in Torrance.

That year also saw Sunrider expand into Taiwan and Hong Kong. Since then it has begun operations in Thailand, Australia, Japan, and New Zealand, and has developed an ambitious European expansion plan.

Sunrider has extensive manufacturing facilities both in the United States and abroad. Two of these plants, located in the City of Industry, California, measure 188,000 and 110,000 square feet, respectively, and house state-of-the-art customized herb-processing equipment. The former

The world headquarters of Sunrider International, located in Torrance, California.

A view inside the Sunrider warehouse, Torrance, California.

is perhaps the largest and finest such facility in the world.

Overseas, Sunrider has major production facilities in Taiwan, where it has also enjoyed phenomenal growth. Within three years after starting operations in that country, it had become the largest of the hundreds of herbal companies based there.

It seems entirely appropriate that Sunrider is the dominant firm in the land where its founder was born and raised, and where the seeds that were to blossom into this amazingly successful company were planted and cultivated.

In addition to an array of more than 100 high-quality products, there is another key factor in the growth of Sunrider International, also conceived in the fertile mind of Tei Fu Chen. Because of his deep desire to help people with their financial as well as their physical lives, he developed the company's unique network-marketing plan. Thus, with a single program, he was able to offer people health and balance, through his products, as well as a chance for financial freedom, via the marketing system.

Under the network-marketing program, independent distributors earn commissions and bonuses, supplemented by outstanding awards and incentives. The network today includes more than 100,000 distributors.

Sunrider products fall into three general categories. The first, called Sunergy, is a concentrated herb-food program, based on the Philosophy of Regeneration, and formulated to supplement a healthy diet. The Sunergy products created by Tei Fu Chen are a result of the marriage of the wisdom of the ancients to the technology of the modern world.

The second product line, Vitalite, is a weight-management program. It combines herb food nutrition with a life-style of whole food nutrition to create and maintain harmony in the body so it reaches internal balance and functions the way nature intended. As Tei Fu Chen explains, "You hear a lot of talk about individual vitamins and minerals in health care. For instance, Vitamin C is often singled out. Our whole food approach is

Another typically busy day for Sunrider's phone order department.

based on our belief that the body, given its proper nourishment, adjusts automatically, reaching its own harmony."

As with all Sunrider products, the third major line, called Kandesn, is rooted deep in Chinese history. In ancient times, the wives of Chinese emperors often numbered in the thousands. To attract the emperor's attention, each wife sought to discover herbal formulas that would enhance her beauty and preserve her youthful glow. Formulas based on these ancient discoveries have been tested and improved through technology by Tei Fu Chen and became Kandesn, Sunrider's revolutionary skin-care program.

The Kandesn line, designed for total body care, includes a wide variety of high-quality skin and hair care and cosmetic products. Available for both men and women, are all formulated to nurture and pamper skin and hair and to enhance natural beauty.

Each year, millions of dollars are spent to improve current formulas and develop new, stable products. Such a commitment is clearly in keeping with Tei Fu Chen's belief that a healthy company is best prepared for the future only when it is willing to invest money in itself, for research and development as well as manufacturing and quality control.

That last category, quality control, is also an integral part of the firm's process, ensuring consistency through standardized methods. Sunrider has invested millions of dollars in state-of-the-art manufacturing, processing, and packaging equip-

ment, and closely monitors every step to see that all its products meet its very high quality standards.

Continuous refinement, ongoing improvement, and never-ending progress—these are the hallmarks of Sunrider International, and of its founder, Tei Fu Chen, whose accomplishments have brought him considerable acclaim. A special resolution passed by the California State Senate honored him as a businessman and entrepreneur. In 1990 he received an honorary doctor of agriculture degree from Chinese Culture University, one of the largest universities in Taiwan. Tei Fu Chen thus became only the sixth person so honored by that institution in its history.

Having experienced so much success and recognition, Tei Fu Chen could retire easily and live worry-free for the rest of his life with his wife and five children. Instead, with Oi Lin, who runs the company's day-to-day operations, at his side, he continues pursuing his vision. Sunrider, for all its staggering growth, is still in its infancy. Already a large multinational company, it still has clearcut potential for phenomenal growth well into the twenty-first century.

Tei Fu Chen honored the vision of his youth with the creation of a company that carries that vision still, a company with one foot planted firmly in a time-honored tradition and the other planted firmly in the future. Tei Fu Chen and Sunrider—a man and his company, a man and his vision—have proven that the dreams of one small child can truly change the world.

THE BEVERLY HILLS HOTEL

A bean field "out in the middle of nowhere," as some characterized it, seems an unlikely place for a legend to be born, especially a legend that has come to be linked with such terms as "elegance," "glamour," "tradition," "quality," "service," and "luxury." Yet it was on exactly such a site that the now world-famous—and legendary—Beverly Hills Hotel was built.

The year was 1912. Pioneer settler Burton E. Green, president of the Rodeo Land and Water Company, was determined to attract people to what he envisioned as an ideal residential community and decided that a luxurious hotel would be the magnet to draw them. So The Beverly Hills Hotel was built, for the then-staggering cost of $500,000. It was the first major building constructed in an area that, two years later, would become the City of Beverly Hills.

Margaret J. Anderson, then manager of the highly successful Hollywood Hotel, was hired to run the new resort hotel. She did so against the advice of friends and associates, who saw little chance of success for a fledgling venture "out in the middle of nowhere." An attractive offer that included an option to buy the hotel persuaded her to take the risk, and the hotel, under her leadership, became an almost instant success.

Within a few years The Beverly Hills Hotel had developed an international reputation. Guests came from near and far to enjoy its picturesque bungalows, lush lawns, beautiful gardens, and exquisite hospitality. The hotel also became the gathering place for many of the most illustrious names in the still-young motion picture industry. The legend was born.

In 1920 two significant events took place. Anderson bought the hotel, and Douglas Fairbanks and Mary Pickford established residence at

nearby Pickfair. Other film stars, including Charles Chaplin, Gloria Swanson, Buster Keaton, John Barrymore, Harold Lloyd, Rudolph Valentino, Tom Mix, and Will Rogers soon followed, transforming the bean fields surrounding the hotel into one of the world's most exclusive neighborhoods.

As the movie industry flourished, so did The Beverly Hills Hotel. In the early days it was the focal point of the community, with formal dances and weddings in the ballroom and worship services on Sundays. In 1926 Will Rogers was inaugurated as honorary mayor of Beverly Hills on the hotel grounds.

Anderson sold the hotel in 1928, and in 1930 the financial pressures brought on by the Great Depression caused it to close its doors. Two years later the trustee of the property, the Bank of America, reopened it and in 1935 assigned one of its vice presidents, Hernando Courtright, to operate it. It was to prove an excellent choice.

In 1941 Courtright and some friends, including movie luminaries Loretta Young, Irene Dunne, and Harry Warner, formed a new company and bought the hotel, which prospered under his leadership. It was Courtright who changed the name of the hotel's restaurant from El Jardin to the Polo Lounge, in honor of cowboy Will Rogers and his rough-riding friends, Darryl Zanuck and Tommy Hitchcock. The three played polo on the grounds behind the hotel and regularly stopped by for refreshments after a match.

Today the Polo Lounge, birthplace of the "power breakfast," "power lunch," and "power dinner," is world-famous and still a favorite haunt of the movers and shakers of the entertainment, financial, and fashion worlds.

The enigmatic and elusive Howard Hughes also played a major role in building the legend. In 1942 he took up residence in four of the hotel's 21 bungalows: one for himself; a second for his actress wife, Jean Peters; and two for use as decoys. Periodically, over the next 30 years, the billionaire recluse lived at the hotel in privacy.

Others who took advantage of the hotel's legendary privacy included Clark Gable and Carol Lombard, Marilyn Monroe and Yves Montand, and Elizabeth Taylor, who spent seven of her eight honeymoons there. The emphasis on privacy extends to a ban on cameras, so that even the most famous celebrities can relax and enjoy themselves, without bulbs flashing and shutters clicking.

The Beverly Hills Hotel has also been a favorite of royalty throughout its history. Its guest list has included Prince Philip, the Duke and Duchess of Windsor, Princess Margaret and Lord Snowden, King Albert of Belgium, the Crown Prince of Monaco, and many other heads of state.

In 1954 the hotel was acquired by Ben L. Silberstein who, with his daughters, Muriel Slatkin and Seema Boesky, continued the traditions of elegance, comfort, and service that had come to be recognized the world over as the hotel's landmarks. Silberstein died in 1979 and in 1985 control passed to Ivan Boesky and his wife, who sold it a year later to oilman Marvin Davis. Today the legend of The Beverly Hills Hotel lives on, under the ownership of the Brunei Investment Agency, which purchased it in 1987.

Kerman Beriker currently serves as general manager and chief executive officer of The Beverly Hills Hotel and brings more than 30 years of expertise to his post. Beriker has managed some of the world's most luxurious hotels, all of which were named "The World's Best Hotels" by *Institutional Investor* magazine, including the Hotel Bel-Air, in Bel Air, and the King Edward in Toronto, Canada. It is through Beriker's vision and knowledge of how to run a world-class property that has enabled The Beverly Hills Hotel to continue to provide the same high-quality level of service that its guests have grown to expect.

Proud of its illustrious past, The Beverly Hills Hotel is nevertheless very much focused on the present and the future, with a commitment to preserve and enhance the outstanding traditions of this world-class facility. A place of service and style, it treats each guest, whether a first-timer or a regular, as a member of the family. A large percentage of the staff have been at the hotel for many years and greet returning guests as old friends.

Few, if any, hotels in the world can match the amenities found at The Beverly Hills Hotel. For example, on warm summer days, guests at poolside are provided with chilled towels and served refreshing afternoon sorbet. Many of the 268 rooms, suites, and bungalows feature private pools or Jacuzzis, fireplaces, balconies, private patios, and mini/full kitchens, and a hand car washing and refueling service is available for the convenience of the guests. For the fitness-conscious, an exercise room was recently added to supplement the popular swimming and tennis facilities. Even a Wimbledon pro is provided for private tennis instruction.

Food and beverage service is available 24 hours a day, and staff members have been known to go to extraordinary lengths to satisfy the request of a guest or customer. A Polo Lounge patron called one evening and requested 20 pounds of Dungeness crab for a party he was hosting the next day. Within hours, a waiter with crabs in hand was dispatched to the party's location—in upstate New York—nearly 3,000 miles away.

The Beverly Hills Hotel also has a strong tradition of community involvement. It is the hotel of choice for many social and charitable functions and was the only major local sponsor of the Diamond Jubilee of the City of Beverly Hills in 1989. The hotel supports many local charities, particularly those which focus on education, health concerns, and the needs of children.

Whether extending a hand to help children's causes or to welcome arriving royalty, the attitude of the staff of the hotel is always the same—warm, friendly, and caring. It's part of the tradition of this magnificent urban oasis, which combines the finest in traditional service with the relaxed and comfortable atmosphere of Southern California. The Beverly Hills Hotel is indeed legendary—and the legend continues.

Several of the 268 rooms, suites, and bungalows feature private pools or Jacuzzis as well as fireplaces, balconies, and private patios.

The tradition of providing guests with picturesque accommodations, quality service, and distinctive amenities, continues today.

HOTELS OF L'ERMITAGE INTERNATIONAL

L'Ermitage Suite makes it "hard for guests to leave and easy for them to return."

"A collection of originals." That is the term chosen by the brothers Ashkenazy, Arnold and Severyn, to describe the luxury hotels conceived, designed, built, owned, and operated by them—it is an apt one. The original in this "collection of originals" is L'Ermitage Hotel de Grande Classe, which opened at 9291 Burton Way in Beverly Hills on October 6, 1976.

Today this "collection" includes nine all-suite luxury hotels located in Beverly Hills and West Hollywood. Operating as "Hotels of L'Ermitage International," they include West Hollywood's BelAge Hotel de Grande Classe, Mondrian Hotel de Grand Luxe, Valadon Resort de Ville, Le Parc Hotel de Luxe, Le Dufy Hotel de Luxe, Le Reve Hotel de Ville, and Cezanne Hotel. The ninth is Le Petit Ermitage, a luxurious postoperative retreat located adjacent to L'Ermitage in Beverly Hills.

It was during the mid-1970s that Severyn Ashkenazy decided to build a hotel that met his standards of luxury and service. A very successful real estate developer, he traveled extensively and began formulating ideas of what would most appeal to him in hotel accommodations and of the conveniences, amenities, and services he would make available were he to build one. "I knew that if I built a hotel that satisfied me, it would please others who expected more of a hotel than uniformity, cleanliness, and a very small measure of comfort," he explains.

L'Ermitage, the first all-suite luxury hotel in North America, established the philosophy and set the standards for the company's future ventures. Each of the nine hotels has a distinctive ambience but all provide luxurious all-suite accommodations, caring and personal service, a restful atmosphere, and individual personalities.

It is the service and an abundance of amenities that set the Hotels of L'Ermitage International apart. These amenities include free chauffeured limousine service to and from nearby business or social engagements, private balconies, fireplaces, three multi-line telephones with conference capabilities in every suite, 24-hour-a-day suite service, a variety of appliances, and an abundance of personal care items.

The suites are luxurious, with living and sleeping areas separated so they can be used for business or social meetings. Dining areas adjoin a kitchenette with wet bar, refrigerator, and private liquor cabinet that can be stocked at the guest's request. Bathrooms feature large tubs, whirlpools, steam baths, TV sets, telephones, and four different lighting systems.

No expense is spared to assure the comfort of guests. The beds, for example, are made in Sweden, and retail for $3,000 each, more than what many other hotels spend to furnish an entire room. "Our goal," says Severyn Ashkenazy, who serves as president of Hotels of L'Ermitage International and president and chief executive officer of L'Ermitage International, "is to make it hard for our guests to leave and easy for them to return."

The fact that guests stay an average of seven days and that as many as 80 percent are repeat guests clearly indicate how well Ashkenazy has met his goal.

Despite his success in the hotel business and the establishment of a standard against which luxury facilities are measured, Severyn Ashkenazy is neither satisfied nor content to rest on his laurels. Not long ago, he commissioned a study by the University of Southern California Graduate School of Business to determine what people would expect in luxurious hotel accommodations in the year 2010. Architects, futurists, affluent men and women, and many others were interviewed at length and their responses were carefully tabulated.

Among the desired features most often mentioned were security; quiet, comfortable, and romantic surroundings; clean air; pure water; and state-of-the-art communications facilities. These and all recommendations in the study have been or are being installed in the L'Ermitage Hotels.

Says Severyn Ashkenazy, "We have long set the standards for the luxury hotel industry. No hotel in the world offers half the amenities we do. When we've finished implementing the USC recommendations, we'll be 20 years ahead of anyone else."

The pool at the Mondrian Hotel de Grand Luxe.

HILL, HOLLIDAY, CONNORS, COSMOPULOS, INC.

It was back in 1968 that Jay Hill, Alan Holliday, Jack Connors, and Steve Cosmopulos decided to leave the major advertising agencies where they worked and launch their own firm. Based in Boston, they started Hill, Holliday, Connors, Cosmopulos, Inc., without a single account and with very little capital.

From that inauspicious beginning, the agency, under the direction of Jay Hill and Jack Connors, has blossomed, enjoying a growth rarely if ever seen in the advertising business. In less than 20 years it became New England's largest agency, with annual billings nearly double those of its closest rival and more business than all other Boston-based agencies combined. In 1988 the firm opened offices in New York and Los Angeles, and total billings are now around $400 million.

Nationally, the firm is ranked among the top 30 agencies and, despite its fairly recent arrival in Los Angeles, it is one of the 10 highest-ranking agencies in this market. All of its growth has been without benefit of either merger or acquisition.

Opening a Los Angeles office was part of the agreement between Hill, Holliday and Nissan Motors when the agency landed the prized Infiniti account. About 150 people staff the local office in Marina del Rey.

There are a number of factors that have contributed to the rapid growth and success of Hill, Holliday. Perhaps of greatest significance is the continuing leadership of first-generation management. Two of the founders, Jay Hill and Jack Connors, remain vitally involved on a full-time basis, the former as chairman of the board and worldwide creative director and the latter as chief executive officer.

Key members of their team include Jack Sansolo, president/USA, chief marketing strategist and general manager of the Los Angeles office (the agency also has offices in London and Hong Kong), and, in the Los Angeles office, executive Vice President/Creative Director Dan Mountain and Senior Vice President/Director of Research and Planning Marshall Rogers. Under the leadership of Hill and Connors, Hill, Holliday has built an enviable client roster, including such well-known companies as John Hancock Financial Services, Hyatt Hotels & Resorts, Wang, L.L. Bean, Spaulding Top Flight Golf Balls, Labatt's, Heinz, Marshall's, Staples, and many others. Because of the priority placed on client service, the agency's retention rate is significantly higher than the industry average.

A key element in that service is the use of a "core team" approach rather than the typical account service team approach. At Hill, Holliday, representatives from each communications discipline are part of the core team. That approach works well, largely because, in Sansolo's words, the company only hires people who are "nice, smart, and flexible."

Another key to Hill, Holliday's success is the extremely high priority placed on community service.

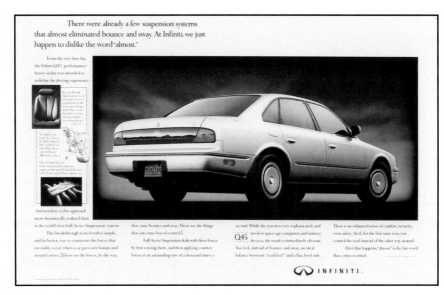

Every employee is expected to become involved in some form of volunteer activity and senior managers are evaluated, in part, on that basis. All employees with five years or more at the company can take a four-month sabbatical at full pay to do any kind of public service work they choose—with their jobs waiting for them when they return.

Together, these factors and others add up to the remarkable success story that is Hill, Holliday, Connors, Cosmopulos, Inc. Not content to rest on its laurels, however, the agency is clearly focused on the future. That philosophy is perhaps best expressed by Jay Hill: "If you talk in yesterday's words, use yesterday's picture, target yesterday's market, and aim for yesterday's psyche, you'll wind up being yesterday's agency."

The "nice, smart, flexible" —and highly creative—people at Hill, Holliday have no intention of letting that happen.

Can a magazine ad be chockful of technical information, describe the workings of a highly complicated mechanism (in this case, Infiniti's breakthrough Full- Active Suspension™ System), be elegant and inviting to read, yet remain visually uncluttered, impactful, and tasteful? Hill, Holliday proves it can.

The stunning engine power of the Q45™, Infiniti's elegant flagship sedan, takes center stage in this ad produced for major national magazines. Hill, Holliday, however, adds a verbal twist by using a well known analogy–"a wolf in sheep's clothing"–to contrast the performance with its understated, functional styling.

THE PICTURE OF HEALTH

Educating and Caring for Angelenos

Hospitals, universities, and health care organizations serve as the guardians for Los Angeles area residents by furnishing timely and essential assistance.

Institutions and organizations that are expressly dedicated to meeting the educational and medical needs of residents continue to expand their services as the city's population grows. Like this museum art, each of these components is inextricably connected to the other. Photo by Mark E. Gibson

CENTINELA HOSPITAL MEDICAL CENTER

I ts slogan, "World-Class, Community Close," is brief, yet it describes exactly what Centinela Hospital Medical Center is all about. A full-service, multifaceted, nonprofit medical facility, Centinela has earned the respect of the medical community throughout the world, with renowned physicians, state-of-the-art diagnostic and therapeutic treatment, and sports medicine facilities that are second to none.

At the same time, Centinela's reputation in the world community has not obscured an enduring commitment to its many surrounding communities. From the Inglewood-based Centinela Hospital Medical Center and eight satellite facilities that stretch throughout the South Bay area, the Centinela network provides affordable, world-class health care for thousands of people, close to home.

It all began on a very small scale, back in 1924, when the 12-bed Milton Hospital opened on the Inglewood site. Three years later it was purchased by Letha C. Dunn, who operated it for 20 years, during which time it grew to 62 beds and became known as Centinela Hospital. When she retired in 1947 the medical staff raised the money to buy the facility, formed a nonprofit corporation, and began operating as Centinela

Valley Community Hospital.

A series of major building programs got under way in 1950 and, by 1962, the hospital had 150 beds. The completion of two eight-story towers, the first in 1968 and the second 10 years later, increased patient bed capacity to the current level of 403. The hospital serves more than 12,000 inpatients a year, with nearly 5,500 inpatient surgeries. Its staff includes approximately 700 physicians, 2,000 employees, and 250 volunteers.

The fully accredited, acute-care medical complex at Centinela offers complete medical and surgical facilities in a wide array of specialized services. They include such innovative services as the Pain Relief Center, Eye Care Laboratory, Gastroenterology Department, Long-Term Rehabilitation Program, Cardiac Noninvasive Laboratory, Oncology Program, Alternative Birth Center, and Day Surgery Center.

As a major-medical treatment, research, and training center, Centinela provides quality health care for many surrounding communities. Its eight satellite facilities include medical centers in El Segundo, Lawndale, and Manhattan Beach; the Centinela Medical Center-Fox Hills in Culver City; the Centinela Hospital

Centinela Hospital Medical Center in Inglewood.

Airport Medical Clinic, adjacent to Los Angeles International Airport; and the Centinela Women's Health Center. In addition to the broad range of traditional medical-care services available at these facilities, each offers different specialized programs such as family planning, occupational health, women's services, male potency, and diabetes.

Two other satellites, Centinela Hospital's Fitness Institute in Culver City and the Centinela Sports Medicine Center/Kerlan-Jobe Orthopaedic Clinic in Santa Monica, underscore the hospital's long-standing commitment to health and fitness testing and enhancement, and to the diagnosis, treatment, and rehabilitation of sports injuries. Its leadership in these fields is recognized around the world.

At the Fitness Institute the principal function is fitness testing. Institute professionals have developed a sophisticated battery of tests to evaluate the health and fitness levels of both athletes and private citizens. The Centinela Sports Medicine Center specializes in the diagnosis and treatment of orthopedic and sports injuries and illnesses, as well as research and education in the field of orthopedics and sports medicine.

Centinela has long been a favorite choice of professional and amateur athletes for treatment, surgery, and rehabilitation. Many professional teams in the Los Angeles area, including the Dodgers, Kings, Lakers, Rams, and Angels, have chosen Centinela as their hospital of choice. It is also the hospital of choice for the PGA TOUR, Senior PGA TOUR, Lewitzky Dance Company, and the Great Western Forum (home of the Kings and Lakers). It was also selected as an Official Hospital for the 1984 Olympics.

No program better demonstrates Centinela's leadership in sports medicine than the pioneering research done in the world-famous Biomechanics Laboratory, formed in 1979 as part of the hospital's Orthopedics Department. Here ortho-

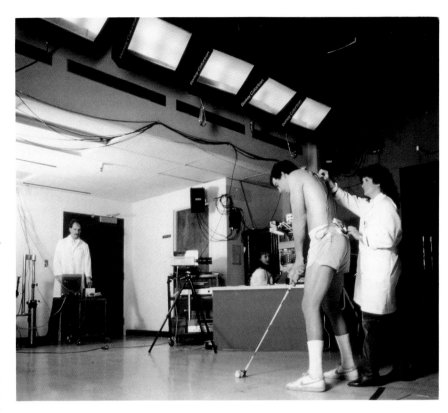

Centinela Hospital's Biomechanics Laboratory.

pedists, biomechanical engineers, and other specialists use advanced technology and engineering to study the body mechanics of both athletes and nonathletes.

Researchers in the Biomechanics Laboratory have analyzed walking, running, pitching, swinging, and other moves important to athletes by photographing them with ultra-high-speed cameras. At the same time, a force plate set in the floor measures ground pressures (downward, forward-to-back, and side-to-side) exerted by each foot. Instrumented inner soles in the subject's shoes provide information about the speed, rhythm, and symmetry of movement patterns. Extremely fine wire electrodes implanted in the muscles record electrical impulses.

This information and other technical data is analyzed to form a clear picture of what happens in the body when the athlete performs specific movements. Researchers can then explain to the athlete exactly how to move in order to function near full potential. Work performed in the Biomechanics Laboratory has also resulted in exercises to prevent tears of the rotator cuff musculature, an injury that can end a baseball, football, or golf career. The lab also maintains computerized national records of professional baseball and football injuries, which are tabulated to

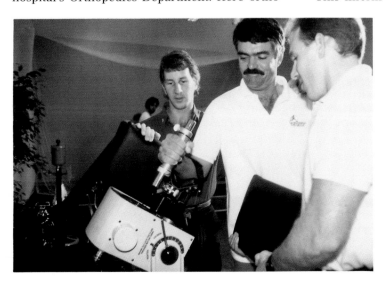

The Golf Performance Evaluation at Centinela Hospital's Fitness Institute.

prevent or reduce the frequency of similar injuries in the athletes of the future.

These findings not only help athletes perform better and reduce the risk of injury but are of great value in the development of new surgical procedures and rehabilitation programs for everyone. In fact, no other center in the nation has taken the development and research of joint replacement for the treatment of arthritis as far as Centinela Hospital. The research currently being done includes bone research, development of implants, and patient care research.

"Our goal," says a spokesman for the Biomechanics Laboratory, "is to help a greater number of people fulfill their maximum physical potential. Our research is helping athletes compete and orthopedic patients receive the best that rehabilitation and medicine can offer."

Much of the research done at the laboratory has been implemented at the Fitness Institute, the hospital's nonprofit medical and fitness affiliate in Culver City. Founded in 1973 by internationally renowned orthopedic surgeons and sports medicine specialists Robert Kerlan, M.D., and Frank Jobe, M.D., the institute's clientele not only includes most of the Los Angeles-area professional sports teams but also the Los Angeles City Firefighters, the Los Angeles Police Department, major corporations, other municipalities, and leaders in business and industry.

The institute's medically supervised programs include: comprehensive health and fitness evaluations, supervised exercise programs

for achieving and maintaining fitness, a variety of health programs, and a Golf Performance Evaluation that is the most comprehensive in the world.

The institute's expertise in the physical aspects of golf testing began several years ago with a research program conducted by the Biomechanics Laboratory that examined the swings of a number of professional golfers. The results led to the development of an exercise program designed specifically to improve a golfer's performance and help prevent injury.

The findings have been published by Dr. Jobe, who is medical director of the PGA TOUR, in his book, *30 Exercises For Better Golf,* and are also available on videotape.

These products, along with other books, including *The Shoulder and Arm Exercises for Athletes,* are published by Champion Press, another entity sponsored by Centinela Hospital Medical Center.

The Golf Performance Evaluation, available to professionals and amateurs alike, is divided into four components: the medical history and physical exam, the golf-specific physical assessment, the golf swing analysis, and the follow-up testing. Endorsed by the PGA TOUR, the program has been immensely popular with golfers from all over the world.

The hospital has developed expandable, mobile gyms in vans that follow the PGA TOUR and Senior PGA TOUR. Called the Centinela Hospital Player Fitness Centers, these vans are 45 feet in length and can expand from 8 feet to 24 feet wide in 10 minutes. They contain a variety of exercise equipment, including weight machines, free weights, and exercise bikes. Each center is staffed with professional physical therapists and athletic trainers. Their use has resulted in sharp declines in both the incidence and degree of injury on both professional tours.

Centinela Hospital Medical Center is also

widely known and respected for its work in chemical dependency treatment, cardiac care, oncology, radiology, obstetrics/gynecology, pediatrics, rehabilitative medicine, occupational health programs, and home health care. Its chemical dependency program, called Life Starts, has won the Alcoholism Information Center Award for excellence. The highly successful program offers the most comprehensive treatment available for people with drug and alcohol problems.

LifeStarts treats both the disease and the individual, helping people learn to live drug-free, sober lives. Patients, referred to as guests on the unit, receive professional evaluation and treatment from an experienced staff of chemical-dependency experts, under the direction of a physician with years of success in the field. All inpatients take advantage of the hospital's sports medicine expertise by incorporating physical therapy into their daily regimen. Guests are monitored by therapists and tested weekly as they use a variety of vehicles to work out, including a full-service gymnasium, pool, and outdoor track.

Private rooms and baths are featured, which no other treatment facility in the city can claim.

LifeStarts also has special programs to involve family members in the recovery process and to treat the trauma of codependency, which often leads to substance abuse and other forms of compulsive behavior.

Intensive aftercare, providing six months of follow-up for adults and their families, is a major part of the LifeStarts program. Speakers are also provided for business and community events, as part of LifeStarts' commitment to prevent alcohol and drug problems, as well as to treat them.

Community outreach at Centinela Hospital Medical Center is by no means limited to alcohol and drug prevention programs, but is a well-established tradition that is expressed in a variety of ways, primarily through the Centinela Hospi-

tal Foundation. Funded by the generous support of grateful patients and special friends, the foundation contributes to the hospital's operating expenses and supports a number of essential charitable programs throughout the hospital and the community.

The most active of the foundation's programs is the Children's Charity Fund, which provides medical care to sick and injured children whose families lack adequate financial resources and have nowhere else to turn. In cooperation with health officials and local churches, the foundation hosts immunization clinics for schoolchildren and has developed programs to help improve the health care of students in the Inglewood School District. Many of the hospital's departments have also been recipients of foundation donations.

For the newborn infant, injured child or professional athlete, drug-addicted professional or disabled worker, heart patient or cancer victim—whatever the needs—Centinela Hospital Medical Center has been there to meet them. Over the years, it has demonstrated again and again that it is indeed "World-Class, Community Close."

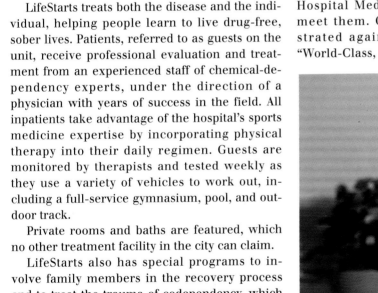

KENNETH NORRIS JR. CANCER HOSPITAL

The Kenneth Norris Jr. Cancer Hospital was built exclusively for cancer research and patient care.

The Kenneth Norris Jr. Cancer Hospital and Research Institute opened in April 1983 on the Health Sciences Campus of the University of Southern California. A wholly owned subsidiary of the university, it is the only facility in the Pacific Southwest built exclusively for cancer research and patient care.

The Norris Cancer Hospital is a referral facility for patients who can best benefit from the special knowledge and skill of USC oncologists in a setting devoted entirely to cancer treatment and research. The Norris is home to more than 200 specialists in laboratory and clinical sciences.

Its medical staff of specialists from many fields define the best possible treatment for a given cancer—treatments not commonly available except at one of the nation's 24 comprehensive cancer centers. Norris Hospital physicians all hold teaching positions in the USC School of Medicine. They treat all cancers except those of children, and are particularly expert in cancers of the genitourinary system, central nervous system, female reproductive system, breast, lung, and gastrointestinal tract, and in melanoma, leukemia, lymphoma, and AIDS. Pediatric cancers are treated at Childrens Hospital of Los Angeles, which is also affiliated with the USC School of Medicine.

The Norris Cancer Hospital provides complete care for both in-and outpatients, including

surgery, radiation therapy, and chemotherapy, plus newer approaches to cancer management, such as immunotherapy and biologic response modification. There are two 30-bed nursing units, including a six-bed bone marrow transplantation unit and a seven-bed intensive care unit.

Other patient facilities include a surgery suite, with four operating rooms and a recovery room, and a division of diagnostic radiology and nuclear medicine. The latter offers the most modern imaging technology available, including the three-dimensional Pixar system, CAT scanning, ultrasound, digital angiography, and nuclear medicine imaging.

Outpatient care is provided by the Parsons Outpatient Clinic and Day Hospital, which records more than 2,300 visits a month. Pain management services for cancer patients are available in the clinic. The radiation oncology department is equipped with two powerful linear accelerators for the delivery of radiation therapy and a hyperthermia unit for experimental work in combination with radiation therapy to treat both superficial and deep-seated tumors.

In addition to cancer patient care, the Norris Cancer Hospital has strong and vigorous research programs directed at a more complete understanding of the basic aspects of cancer. These programs cover four general areas: basic research, clinical investigations, cancer cause

The outpatient clinic records more than 2,300 visits a month.

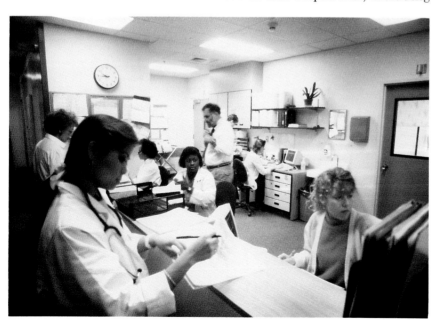

and prevention, and education.

Three entire floors of the hospital are used for research, where laboratory scientists are working on a broad range of projects, including studies of the biology of cancer and the immunologic aspects of cancer cells. They are also attempting to gain a better understanding of anticancer drugs.

The long-term goal of these integrated programs is to improve the knowledge and treatment of the many diseases, more than 100, that are known as cancer.

Extensive research is also conducted at the Norris Hospital on the cause and prevention of cancer. An outstanding group of physicians, epidemiologists, statisticians, and other health professionals have established a system for detailing information on all new cancer cases registered in Los Angeles County—more than 30,000 a year. By studying these cases, and looking for differences between cancer patients and the general population, they have obtained clues to factors that increase the risk of certain cancers.

Education is another weapon used actively and effectively by the hospital in its fight to eradicate cancer. Programs are conducted for students from the USC Schools of Medicine, Dentistry, Pharmacy, and Public Administration and the USC Department of Nursing. They include oncology grand rounds, tumor boards, and research conferences; continuing education conferences; education programs for physicians and other professionals in community hospitals; participation in various professional cancer-oriented health associations; and the student-directed St. George Society, which presents a series of dinner seminars related to cancer research and patient care.

Supporting the professional staff in its four-pronged mission of cancer diagnosis, treatment, research, and education is a large and loyal band of volunteers who serve in a wide variety of ways and are key members of the comprehensive healthcare team. Realizing cancer patients are

going through the most challenging moments of their lives, the men and women volunteers help make each day nicer for these very special individuals. In every way the volunteers, along with members of the Norris Auxiliary, represent the quality and spirit of the Norris Hospital. To further increase its effectiveness and enlarge its capabilities, the Norris is undergoing a multimillion-dollar expansion that is scheduled for completion in 1994. Examination, treatment, clinical laboratory, and waiting areas for outpatients are being enlarged to accommodate the increasing volume of visits; space has been designated for physicians' offices, new research laboratories, and epidemiological research into cancer cause and prevention. A conference center, meditation room, meditation garden, and coffee shop are also planned.

The expansion project is being funded primarily by contributions from friends of the Norris Hospital, many of whom have been faithful supporters since its founding. The hospital's donors, led by the Cancer Research Associates and numbering in the thousands, have given generously to ensure that the dream shared by the entire Norris staff—"that we shall conquer cancer in our lifetimes"—will come true.

For everyone at the Kenneth Norris, Jr., Cancer Hospital and Research Institute, the primary goal is to work themselves out of a job and to close the doors of the facility that since April 1983 has been meeting the needs of thousands of cancer patients with "extraordinary quality, efficiency, and compassion."

The nursing station is the center of patient-related activity.

Patients register to benefit from the special knowledge and skill of USC oncologists.

ST. VINCENT MEDICAL CENTER

In October 1855, when Franklin Pierce was in the White House and California celebrated its fifth year of statehood, six Daughters of Charity of St. Vincent de Paul began a lengthy journey from Maryland to California. What today would be only a few hours by air took them three months.

From their base in Emmitsburg, Maryland, the sisters traveled to New York, where a ship took them to Panama. The canal was still more than 50 years in the future, so they crossed the isthmus by mule to meet another ship to take them as far as San Pedro. Finally, a 10-hour stagecoach ride over bumpy, dusty roads brought them to their destination—El Pueblo de Nuestra Señora la Reina de Los Angeles. The date was January 8, 1856.

The sisters had come in response to a call from the bishop of the young city to care for its poor and nurse its sick. Just one month after arriving, the pioneer sisters had established an orphanage and dispensary—the first hospital in the city of 6,000 people. In 1858, with the help of more sisters from Maryland, they opened County Hospital in the Aguilar adobe on Eternity Street, now North Broadway. Patients paid $2.50 a day for a private room and $1.50 for the ward.

Then as now, the Daughters of Charity were guided by the philosophy of their founders: "We are committed to the ideal that a health care delivery system should promote Christian community and enhance the dignity of all human beings."

The new hospital grew rapidly, and in 1860 moved to a two-story brick building between North Main and San Fernando streets. In 1869 the sisters named the hospital The Los Angeles Infirmary. Its patients included sheepherders, stagecoach drivers, livery stable operators, and sea captains.

In 1883, needing still more space, the sisters purchased six-and-a-half acres of land at Beaudry and Sunset for $10,000 and built a larger hospital that opened in 1885. It was during this period that a severe smallpox epidemic broke out and the Daughters of Charity were among the few who volunteered their services to aid the victims. Two of the sisters died as a result.

In 1913 the Los Angeles Infirmary became the first hospital in California to be accredited by the American College of Surgeons. Five years later, as the sisters marked their 60th year of service to the people of Los Angeles, the name was officially changed to St. Vincent's Hospital, in honor of St. Vincent de Paul, founder of the Daughters of Charity.

Again the demand for the sisters' services outgrew the facilities. In 1923 a new site was purchased at Third and Alvarado streets, where the fourth St. Vincent's Hospital opened its doors in 1927. A new building for the education of nurses was built in 1952, and in 1956 a new wing was added to the hospital and named in honor of its benefactor, Estelle Doheny. Also in 1956 the Department of Nuclear Medicine, the first in Los Angeles, was established.

"We are committed to the ideal that a health care delivery system should promote Christian community and enhance the dignity of all human beings."

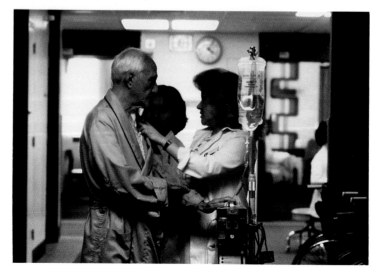

The first open heart surgery in the western United States was performed at St. Vincent's Hospital in 1957, launching a tradition of cardiac care that continues to this day. The hospital has also pioneered kidney treatment, initiating dialysis in Los Angeles in 1964 and kidney transplantation in 1970.

Continued advances in medical technology created a need for a more modern facility. In May 1971 St. Vincent broke ground for a new 386-bed hospital; construction began the following year. In 1974, in order to more

accurately reflect what the hospital had become, its name was changed to St. Vincent Medical Center. A year later the new facility received its first patients.

Today St. Vincent Medical Center has a staff of more than 600 physicians, more than 1,300 employees, and 100 volunteers. It is especially renowned for its specialties in adult and pediatric cardiac care, ear and hearing problems, cancer, kidney treatment, and organ transplantation. St. Vincent also offers a wide scope of services, among them physician referral, weight control, wound care, orthopedics, ophthalmology, neurosurgery, and urology, as well as the latest medical technology, including magnetic resonance imaging (MRI) and lasers.

One of the most innovative modalities in the fight against cancer, bone marrow transplantation, also is offered at St. Vincent Medical Center. In fact, when the Los Angeles Oncologic Institute and St. Vincent Medical Center established a bone marrow transplant unit in 1990, St. Vincent was the only community-based hospital in Southern California offering such a program. The five-bed unit allows for both allogeneic (donor other than patient) and autologous (patient donor) transplants. In addition, the medical center houses a specialized laboratory for storing and processing bone marrow, as well as a specialized pharmacy to meet the unique demands of bone marrow transplantation.

The range of diagnostic equipment available at St. Vincent includes X-ray, CAT scan, ultrasound, mammography, surgical, needle and stereotactic brain biopsies, and magnetic resonance imaging (MRI). Additionally, St. Vincent is one of a handful of hospitals on the West Coast with magnetic resonance capabilities that include spectroscopy—the examination of individual cells—which can be used to study the behavior of cancers and their response to various therapeutic agents.

Since its pioneering efforts in open heart

A nurse comforts a patient on kidney dialysis.

This statue of St. Vincent
de Paul stands outside of
the hospital.

surgery in 1957, St. Vincent heart teams have treated more than 50,000 heart patients. The number of heart catheterizations and surgeries performed at St. Vincent Medical Center ranks it among the foremost cardiac centers in the world, year after year. A regional referral center for heart disease, it offers a full spectrum of services, including every invasive and noninvasive diagnostic technique, and a scope of treatment options including angioplasty, bypass surgery, and heart transplantation.

Every known cardiac diagnostic and treatment capability is available, including four state-of-the-art catheterization laboratories, one dedicated to electrophysiology. Much of the work of the cardiac program is made possible through the support of the Los Angeles Heart Institute, which was established as a nonprofit organization at St. Vincent in 1974.

The institute, true to the tradition of the Daughters of Charity, has a great involvement in the charitable care effort at St. Vincent. Its "Miracles Across Miles" program has brought children from around the world to St. Vincent, where all physician and hospital care is donated, while host families provide a place to recuperate.

Another specialty in which the medical center is preeminent is otology, the treatment of hearing,

This statue of St. Vincent de Paul stands outside of the hospital.

The original hospital established by the Daughters of Charity.

ear, and balance disorders. The House Ear Institute located at St. Vincent developed the cochlear implant, a tiny device that provides the sensation of sound to the totally deaf. The first cochlear implant surgery and more than 75 percent of the procedures worldwide have been performed at St. Vincent.

The medical center has also long been a leader in the fight against cancer. In 1956 it was one of the first cancer programs in California approved by the American College of Surgeons.

Today its approach to cancer care has become a widely emulated model. Patients at St. Vincent are treated by a multidisciplinary team in a special unit with the finest and latest technology available for their care and comfort. Depending upon the particular case being treated, the team may include dietitians, social workers, physicians, nurses, pharmacists, hospice and home health service representatives, and physical, respiratory, speech, and occupational therapists.

The Los Angeles Oncologic Institute (LAOI) at St. Vincent is an acknowledged leader in cancer care, conducting the kind of research usually found only at major educational centers. St. Vincent is among an exclusive group of U.S. hospitals to be awarded a Community Clinical Oncology

St. Vincent Medical Center is also well versed in a variety of other surgical specialties. Among them are neurosurgery, ophthalmology, urology, orthopedics, and many techniques to save recuperation time, such as laser surgery. The center has also made great strides in the areas of physical therapy, occupational therapy, speech therapy, and respiratory care.

The St. Vincent Senior Citizen Nutrition Program, also known as Meals on Wheels, delivers more than 1,100 hot, nutritious, low-cost meals each day to area seniors, making it the largest such program in Los Angeles County. The program also offers sit-down meals to mobile seniors each day at a nearby Catholic church.

Program (CCOP) grant from the National Cancer Institute that qualifies LAOI to offer innovative protocols nearly two years before most hospitals.

At least 14 different cancers, including breast, leukemia, and Hodgkins disease, are considered curable at LAOI. Even lung cancer is no longer a hopeless diagnosis. Every known conventional therapy is available, along with virtually all of the experimental methods available anywhere in the country.

Since initiating dialysis in Los Angeles in 1964 and kidney transplantation in 1970, St. Vincent has remained in the forefront of advances that hold out new hope to sufferers of kidney disease. In 1977 the medical center, home of the National Institute of Transplantation, established the Southern California Organ Procurement and Preservation Center, where donor kidneys can be maintained on machines for as long as 60 hours to allow time for recipient selection and testing.

Throughout its existence as a major kidney transplantation center, St. Vincent has innovated and incorporated medical breakthroughs. One example was the early adaption of a new technique to reduce rejection, which builds up the recipient's tolerance to the donor kidney and widens the scope of potential donors. In 1989 a major breakthrough was made when a St. Vincent physician successfully performed a kidney transplant between individuals of incompatible blood groups, which had been virtually impossible until then. That procedure was particularly significant for individuals with rare blood types, who often have to wait years before a compatible donor kidney becomes available.

In caring for the poor and the sick, the activities of the Daughters of Charity have by no means been limited to Los Angeles. St. Vincent Medical Center is but one of 51 facilities run by the sisters, giving them the distinction of operating the largest not-for-profit network of hospitals in the country.

Much has changed since the first Daughters of Charity arrived in Los Angeles in 1856 to establish the community's first hospital. One thing, however, has remained constant for more than 135 years—the tradition of compassion, care, and respect for the sanctity of life that has always guided the Daughters of Charity of St. Vincent de Paul in their mission based on service to the sick and the poor.

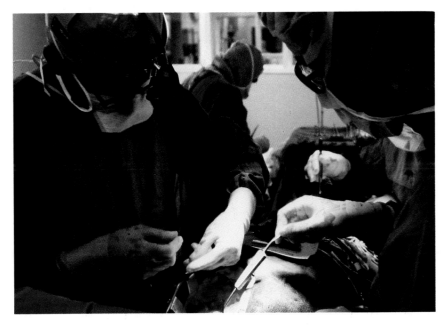

DANIEL FREEMAN HOSPITAL

Daniel Freeman Memorial Hospital has earned a reputation in the health-care community as an outstanding medical facility.

Daniel Freeman Marina Hospital provides high quality medical care to the coastal communities.

Daniel Freeman Hospitals have experienced dynamic growth since their doors opened in 1954. Daniel Freeman Memorial Hospital in Inglewood and Daniel Freeman Marina Hospital in Marina del Rey are nonprofit Catholic medical facilities owned and sponsored by the Sisters of St. Joseph of Carondelet.

Part of the hospitals' strength is the staff's emphasis on the total human being, embracing the physical, spiritual, and emotional needs of each patient.

Totaling 606 beds, the hospitals are capable of providing an extremely wide range of top quality services to patients and their families. Although patients come from all over the world to benefit from the hospitals' programs, services, physicians, staff, and equipment, Daniel Freeman Hospitals' primary service is to their communities. In addition to offering such sophisticated care as open-heart surgery, the hospitals also fill the everyday health care needs of their communities.

Thousands of local residents benefit from the hospitals' many community programs throughout the year, including health fairs, cancer support groups, community seminars, and the speakers bureau.

Two of 14 not-for-profit medical facilities owned and sponsored by the Sisters of St. Joseph of Carondelet across the United States, the Daniel Freeman Hospitals were named after a Canadian lawyer who settled in Southern California in the 1870s and later founded the city of Inglewood. Daniel Freeman Memorial Hospital admitted its first patients in Inglewood on May 24, 1954. The Sisters purchased the former Marina Mercy Hospital in Marina del Rey in 1980. The hospital's named was changed to Daniel Freeman Marina Hospital in 1982.

Today, Freeman's combined medical staff includes more than 1,000 physicians representing every major medical specialty and holding key positions in medical professional associations. The hospitals' nursing staff continually win awards of commitment to professional nursing care.

Community support has been a hallmark of Daniel Freeman Hospitals since the beginning. Community and philanthropic donations built many of the hospitals' facilities and purchased much of their state-of-the-art medical technology, and a dedicated group of community volunteers

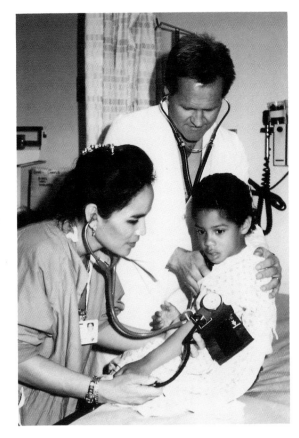

donate thousands of hours of volunteer service each year.

The following specialized programs are just a few of many featured by the Daniel Freeman Hospitals:

• The Breast Center at Marina Hospital offers centralized services for the prevention, diagnosis, and treatment of breast diseases. A team of Daniel Freeman specialists assure the comprehensive and efficient evaluation of breast diseases.

• Special oncology units at both hospitals offer a wide range of treatments for patients with cancer. Special cancer support programs for patients and family members are also offered.

• State-of-the-art medical technology is available at the hospitals' orthopedic units for an assortment of orthopedic needs, including sports and traumatic injuries. Daniel Freeman Memorial was named Official Hospital of the 1984 Summer Olympics in Los Angeles, providing emergency care for spectators, athletes, and officials at the games. Daniel Freeman Hospitals also provided the medical care for the Olympic Festival '91 in Los Angeles.

• Behavioral Health Services at Daniel Freeman Marina Hospital encompasses programs for mental health services and chemical dependency recovery. The warm, family atmosphere is conducive to treatment, recovery, and an open interaction between patients, staff, and families. The ultimate goal is to help the patient return to productive living. Treatment is designed to help meet the immediate needs of the individual and help him or her develop long-term coping strategies.

• The Wound Care Center—the first one of its kind in Los Angeles—opened at Daniel Freeman Memorial Hospital in September 1990. Specializ-

ing in the treatment of chronic wounds, such as those caused by a weakened immune system or poor circulation, the center serves primarily as an outpatient facility. Experts estimate that the center will eventually save thousands of limbs that would have been lost to amputation as a result of chronic wounds.

• For more than 35 years, the Daniel Freeman Heart Center has been considered one of the finest cardiac care programs in California. From crisis through rehabilitation, patients have the benefit of top-flight equipment, services, procedures, and personnel, including cardiologists, surgeons, and specially trained cardiac care nurses, technicians, and therapists.

• Among doctors and others in the professional medical community, Daniel Freeman Hospitals may be most renowned for the Center for Diagnostic and Rehabilitation. Since it opened in 1978, the rehabilitation center has been visited by rehabilitation professionals from all over the world. The center is the only institution to be twice named the outstanding rehabilitation center in the world by the National Association of Rehabilitation Facilities.

Emphasizing the health of the total human being, including the physical, emotional, and spiritual needs of each patient, the Daniel Freeman Hospitals will continue to serve the health care needs of its communities for decades to come.

The hospital prides itself on providing quality care and attention to all its patients.

Caretakers such as Sister Margaret Walsh offer comfort and support to patients during their recovery.

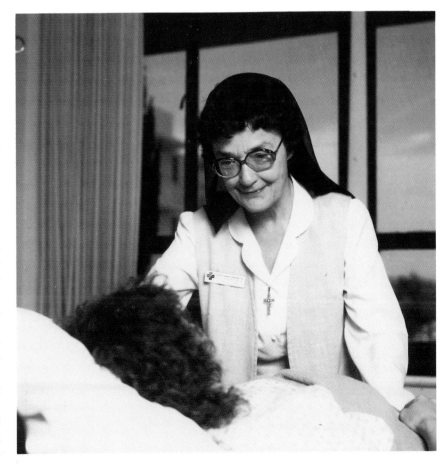

CITY OF HOPE

In 1912 a small band of working men and women gathered in Los Angeles to "do something" about the deadly disease of tuberculosis that was striking down their loved ones and coworkers. Many of the sick had come westward with the hope that the mild and dry Southern California climate would bring relief from the terrible disease, only to find death instead.

At that first meeting, plans were made to start a small hospital where tuberculosis patients could be treated. Fund-raising efforts over the next few months brought in about $2,500, enough for a down payment on 10 acres of land in Duarte, some 25 miles northeast of downtown Los Angeles, in what was then arid wilderness.

On January 11, 1913, the pioneering group pitched two tents to house the hospital's first patients and staff, made up entirely of two tuberculosis victims and one nurse to care for them. At first, fear of the disease brought some resistance from neighbors, and a few months after the tiny hospital opened a flash flood washed away the tents. At that point, there was little to suggest that one day the seed planted by a few working men and women, motivated by compassion for the less fortunate among them, would one day become the City of Hope, a beacon of light and hope for suffering people from all over the world.

Gradually, those first tents were replaced by

wooden and then stucco buildings, constructed primarily by volunteers and financed by donations from various parts of the country. It was the beginning of a tradition that continues to this day, an organization run by volunteers and supported by a far-flung network of generous and committed donors. Nonsectarian from the start, City of Hope nevertheless retains a strong spiritual flavor, as reflected in the motto wrought into the Golter Gate in its rose garden: "There is no profit in curing the body if, in the process, we destroy the soul."

The gate is named in honor of Samuel H. Golter, the first of only three men to serve as executive director of the City of Hope throughout its history. A Russian immigrant and successful businessman, he agreed in 1926 to serve for three months to help the young institution get better organized. Soon gripped by what he described as "a spirit of kindness and goodwill which was manifested towards the patients to a degree that was unprecedented in my experience," he stayed on not for three months but for three decades.

It was Golter's leadership that transformed City of Hope from a small, local tuberculosis sanitorium to a world-renowned medical center dedicated to stamping out a variety of life-threatening

diseases, while caring for their victims with love and compassion. With tuberculosis all but eliminated through the advances of medical science, Golter recognized the need to refocus on such catastrophic diseases as cancer, respiratory disease, and heart ailments. Thus, in 1946 City of Hope became a national medical center.

Golter himself was afflicted with cancer in 1951. Believing his death was near, he drafted a document for presentation at the institution's biennial convention in 1951. Known as the "Thirteen Articles of Faith," it set forth his premises for the City of Hope, eloquently expressing the principles that guide it to this day.

Happily, Golter's disease was successfully treated at City of Hope and he remained closely affiliated with it until his death in 1971. In 1953, having reached the age of 65, he turned over the executive director's reigns to Ben Horowitz, whom he had personally recruited in 1945.

The Brooklyn-born Horowitz brought a new perspective to the hospital. Until then, its primary focus had been just on treating those patients who came through its doors. But Horowitz had a burden—and a vision. "We can't make any pretense," he often said, "that our bed facilities for catastrophic diseases can adequately take care of the problem. Victims of these diseases are numbered in tens of millions, but specialized beds for them can be counted only in the thousands."

The concept of City of Hope as a pilot medical center, dedicated not only to patient care but to research, began to form in his mind. He envisioned the medical center as a place where great discoveries in the treatment and cure of catastrophic diseases would be made and then freely shared with the rest of the world. After years of study, the plan was presented at the 1959 convention, where it was unanimously approved.

Horowitz retired as executive director in 1986

and was succeeded by Sanford M. Shapero, D.D., D.H.L., who had joined City of Hope as associate executive director in 1979 and is now president and chief executive officer. An ordained rabbi and former U.S. Navy chaplain, Shapero had also had a successful business career, serving as vice president of two public companies, one in gerontology and the other in basic pharmaceutical production.

Shapero, who founded the Institute for Creative Development—a national gerontology training center—in 1973, is a prolific author and nationally known speaker on human development, aging, and health care subjects. Recently he received an appointment to the National Advisory Council on Aging of the National Institutes of Health. Today Shapero guides an organization nationally recognized as a leader in giving care and treatment to thousands and acclaimed around the world for its medical and research achievements. Officially named the City of Hope National Medical Center and Beckman Research Institute, it has a staff of more than 2,000 and occupies a 102-acre campus in the city of Duarte, on the exact location where those first two tents were erected in 1913. Over 100 buildings now stand in their place, housing hospital, research, administrative, and service facilities.

The "hospital" part of the City of Hope includes extensive outpatient facilities and 212 beds for inpatients. About 100,000 patient visits are recorded annually. The medical center provides innovative health care to men, women, and children with a variety of illnesses, including leukemia and other cancers, diabetes, and cardiopulmonary and neurological disorders.

Patient care facilities are all at ground level, with windows which look out on prize-winning landscaped gardens. Special areas, decorated with cartoon characters, are provided for the

This gate, located in City of Hope's rose garden, states the institution's philosophy, "THERE IS NO PROFIT IN CURING THE BODY IF, IN THE PROCESS, WE DESTROY THE SOUL."

Sanford M. Shapero, D.H.L., D.D. (left), president and chief executive officer of City of Hope, with Richard S. Ziman, chairman of the board of directors.

According to Kazuo Ikeda, Ph.D., the City of Hope is in the process of exploring the connection between the genetic code and the nervous system. This research may one day make it possible to correct the genetic codes of people afflicted with nervous system disorders such as Parkinson's, Huntington's, and Alzheimer's diseases.

youngest inhabitants, children who are being treated for leukemia, juvenile diabetes, solid tumors, and other malignant or viral conditions.

Designated as one of only 14 Clinical Cancer Research Centers nationwide by the National Cancer Center, City of Hope has gained prominence especially for its compassionate treatment of leukemia and other cancer patients. Its familial Bone Marrow Transplant Center is the largest such non-university connected facility in the United States.

The medical staff includes some 100 full-time medical doctors, nearly all of whom are engaged in research as well as patient care. More than 120 Ph.D.s in the Beckman Research Institute direct their efforts to discovering new treatments for cancer and other diseases. Other investigations are conducted in genetics, biology, immunology, and brain and nerve function.

The Beckman Research Institute has produced many scientific breakthroughs, including laboratory synthesis of human insulin and growth hormone, investigations into the origins of Alzheimer's disease, and development of a new test for AIDS which detects the virus just days after infection. Consistent with the vision of Ben Horowitz, City of Hope provides the results of its research to anyone in the world who wants them.

Unquestionably the most remarkable facet of this remarkable institution is its people. The same altruistic and humanitarian motives that led to its founding remain clearly in evidence today. For instance, recognizing that when a family member is ill the entire family needs help, City of Hope established itself early on as a home away from home. The Duarte campus includes Hope Village and Parsons Village, 40 units of motel-like housing where patients' families can stay close to their loved ones who are undergoing treatment. Family members are also included in counseling and education programs so that recovery can continue at home.

The people who make City of Hope work are not only in Duarte, California, but all across America. They are the volunteers and donors, hundreds of thousands of them, who have made the organization's achievements in science and medicine possible. Each year nearly 500 support groups, or auxiliaries, located in more than 200 cities in 30 states engage in a broad range of fund-raising activities that bring in millions of dollars, or about one-third of the annual budget.

Because of that kind of whole-hearted commitment by its volunteers, City of Hope can meet the needs of patients unable to pay for their care and give them and their families the quality care, compassion, and dignity they deserve.

The auxiliary groups are served by 15 regional offices in major cities across the country, which provide administrative support for the volunteer activities in their areas.

Until the late 1960s, when the organization began accepting reimbursement from third-party payers for health care costs, virtually all its income was provided by the efforts of volunteers and donors. Today, with less than half of its revenues coming directly from patient services, City of Hope continues

Medical needs are not the only aspect of care which is treated with unsurpassed quality. City of Hope offers compassionate care for the whole person, encompassing physical, emotional, psychological, and social needs.

Tommy Mottola, president of CBS Records, seen here with singer Gloria Estefan, is a 1990 recipient of the Spirit of Life award from the music industry support group of the City of Hope.

to rely heavily on the generosity of its donors. These efforts will become even more critical in the future as City of Hope seeks to maintain its leadership position in the world of science and medicine.

Volunteers have also played a major role in allowing City of Hope to keep administrative and fund-raising costs among the lowest of charitable organizations in the United States. A national magazine recently ranked City of Hope as one of the 10 most cost-effective health and medical charities in the country, with fund-raising and administrative costs of only 3.3 percent and 2.6 percent, respectively.

Volunteers conduct tours of the Duarte campus for 25,000 visitors annually. Members of the Special Services Department, they are well-trained and take obvious pride in all that City of Hope has accomplished. Many of them have served for years and clearly display the loving concern for people that characterizes everyone connected with the organization.

The nonprofit City of Hope is governed by volunteers. The Board of Directors, several of whom represent the second and third generations of their families to serve in that volunteer capacity, report in turn to a plenary of volunteers from all across the United States. Once every two years a national convention is held, at which delegates learn firsthand of progress and new outlooks in research and medicine. The conventions also acknowledge volunteers for their fund-raising efforts and provide opportunities to honor individuals and auxiliaries for outstanding achievements.

One who is quick and proud to identify himself as a volunteer is City of Hope Board Chair-

man Richard S. Ziman. Paying tribute to his fellow volunteers, while at the same time challenging them, he recently commented: "It gives me pleasure to applaud you for your past volunteer efforts, which have helped our unique institution gain its outstanding position in today's world of medical science. I am convinced that, with your help, the 1990s will bring even greater progress toward achieving our objectives at the City of Hope."

Those objectives remain the same as they were in 1913 and are perhaps best summed up in these words of Louis Pasteur: "We do not ask of an unfortunate, what country do you come from or what is your religion? We say to him: You suffer, that is enough. You belong to us, we shall make you well."

Pat Riley, formerly head coach of the Los Angeles Lakers, currently head coach of the New York Knicks, was honored with the Spirit of Life award in 1990 by the City of Hope's Orange County chapter.

KAISER PERMANENTE

In 1943 Kaiser Permanente's first Southern California hospital was built in Fontana.

I n 1933 a young Los Angeles surgeon, Sidney R. Garfield, saw an opportunity to provide medical care for workers building an aqueduct across the Mojave desert. He conceived a plan in which workers would agree to have five cents a day deducted from their pay to cover the cost of future medical care. Garfield's success and workers' praise for the plan attracted industrialists Henry and Edgar Kaiser, who asked him to set up a similar prepaid group health care plan for workers building the Grand Coulee Dam during the 1930s.

During World War II Dr. Garfield established prepaid plans at Kaiser shipyards in San Francisco Bay Area and the Pacific Northwest and at the Kaiser steel mill in Fontana, California. Toward the end of the war, former shipyard workers eager to continue receiving prepaid medical care urged Dr. Garfield and the Kaisers to continue their program and open enrollment to the community.

The Permanente Foundation—named after Permanente Creek, where one of Kaiser's early ventures was located—was formed to raise the funds needed for existing and future medical care facilities. Henry Kaiser retained his strong interest and involvement and agreed to allow his name to be used in connection with the program. From this evolved the name Kaiser Permanente Medical Care Program, by which the widely spread and complex organization is generally known today.

Kaiser Permanente is a group practice prepayment plan providing comprehensive medical and hospital services to approximately 6 million volun-

Combining state-of-the-art technology with a complete health curriculum, the Health Pavilion in Orange is devoted to promoting members' health.

tarily enrolled members in 12 regions across the United States. Each of the regions is a federally qualified health maintenance organization or HMO.

The Southern California region, begun in Fontana in 1943, has grown steadily over the years. The second-largest of the 12 regions, its enrollment exceeds 2 million members. The program consists of three entities: the Kaiser Foundation Health Plan, which enrolls members and arranges for their care; the Southern California Permanente Medical Group, an independent partnership which provides professional medical services; and Kaiser Foundation Hospitals, a not-for-profit charitable organization which operates 10 community hospitals and a mental health center to provide inpatient services.

The Health Plan contracts with both the hospitals and the medical group to provide medical care exclusively to its members. Although corporately separate, the three entities operate jointly. The medical group numbers some 2,500 partners, making it the largest partnership of any kind in the world.

Each of the 12 regions operates autonomously and has, in effect, two chief executive officers representing the business and medical operations, respectively. In the Southern California region they are Hugh A. Jones, senior vice president and regional manager, and Frank E. Murray, M.D., medical director. Based at the regional headquarters in Pasadena, they oversee an organization that reaches from Bakersfield to San Diego, and from Santa Monica to San Bernardino.

The people of Kaiser Permanente are proud of the pioneering role the organization has played in the development of the HMO concept. They are equally proud of its reputation for excellence in providing medical care to millions for nearly 50 years. Its theme and its operating strategy is "good people/good medicine"—a philosophy that has clearly been successful. For example, in a recent study of heart bypass surgeries performed by California hospitals, Kaiser Foundation Hospital in San Francisco had the lowest mortality rate,

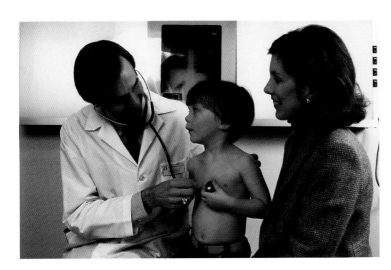

one percent, followed closely by Kaiser Foundation Hospital in Los Angeles, at 1.3 percent. Both were substantially below the statewide average of 5.3 percent.

Looking to the future, the more than 34,000 members of the health care team of the Southern California region of Kaiser Permanente have developed a vision statement to guide them through the remainder of this century and into the next. It includes two primary goals. The first is to clearly demonstrate the value of its services, defined as the optimum balance of the quality of its medical care, the quality of its overall service, and a controlled and reasonable cost structure.

The second goal is to maintain a superb work force, by attracting, developing, and retaining the most highly skilled and qualified professionals. With the eligible pool shrinking and the need for and intensity of medical care growing, Kaiser Permanente is building a multicultural work force and creating an atmosphere in which people of all ethnic backgrounds can succeed.

Part of the strategy to develop a highly skilled health care team involves a recently launched program called "Make Nursing Your Future." The program provides stipends for high school students who are considering nursing careers and who serve as nurses' aides while they go on for further training.

Another major emphasis is on community service. Kaiser Permanente has long recognized its interdependence with the communities it serves and is committed to the success of those communities. For example, its Summer Youth Program, begun in Los Angeles in 1968, is aimed mostly at disadvantaged high school students, providing them with short-term jobs and exposing them to careers in the health care industry.

Another program launched in 1968 is the Watts Counseling and Learning Center. It offers educational development programs, preschool education, and individual, family, and group counseling. Kaiser Permanente was also an early supporter of

L.A.'s Best, an after-school program operated by the L.A. Unified Schools with funding from the City of Los Angeles.

The organization contributes to the community in many other ways as well. Kaiser Permanente provides grants and donates equipment to local nonprofit agencies to help support health-related community service programs. The Kaiser Permanente medical centers are active in their communities through participation in Adopt-A-School programs, chambers of commerce, and local special events.

One unique program, "Professor Bodywise's Traveling Menagerie," is a live theater production that uses puppets and full-body costumed characters to teach basic health education to elementary schoolchildren. Another production, "Secrets," helps school students understand the behaviors that lead to AIDS. The award-winning production has been seen by thousands of Southern California students.

Proud of their organization's long and distinguished record of leadership, innovation, and quality, the physicians, employees, nurses, managers, and volunteers who comprise the health care team of the Kaiser Permanente Southern California Region are determined to reach the goals expressed in their vision statement. Speaking for all of them, Hugh Jones and Frank Murray expressed it this way: "We are committed to evaluating every action our region undertakes to be sure it is consistent with our vision. We will not achieve our vision overnight, perhaps not even by the year 2000. What is important is that we work together to try to make our vision a reality."

USC UNIVERSITY HOSPITAL

USC University Hospital, the newest hospital facility in the Los Angeles area, opened its doors May 20, 1991. A collaboration between the University of Southern California (USC) and National Medical Enterprises, Inc. (NME) the 275-bed, 330,000-square-foot facility offers advanced diagnostic and treatment services and care that are beyond the capabilities of most community hospitals. The joint effort has combined the strength of private enterprise with one of the nation's leading universities.

The USC School of Medicine had long recognized the need for a private teaching hospital on its Health Sciences Campus and explored a wide range of options. For more than a century, USC medical faculty and students had conducted the majority of their clinical practice at Los Angeles County facilities, including the School of Medicine's primary teaching facility, the Los Angeles County USC Medical Center. None of the various options proved financially feasible, however, until NME offered to finance and operate a $150-million complex to be staffed by the USC School of Medicine faculty. USC University Hospital is the cornerstone of the Richard K. Eamer Medical Plaza, named in honor of NME's founder, chairman, and chief executive officer. The facilities of the Eamer Medical Plaza complement the Doheny Eye Hospital, the Doheny Eye Institute, and the Kenneth Norris, Jr., Cancer Hospital and Research Institute on the USC Health Sciences Campus, as well as the adjacent Los Angeles County USC Medical Center.

In addition to USC University Hospital, the Richard K. Eamer Medical Plaza includes the USC Healthcare Consultation Center, an ambulatory care center housing physician offices and private practice suites; and a multilevel parking structure. A guest facility for patients' families, outpatients, and visiting physicians is planned. The ambulatory care center is designed for the twenty-first century, geared to make outpatient care accessible, pleasant, and convenient.

The unique collaboration between NME and USC includes a 25-year pact, renewable for an additional 25 years. The University of Southern California administers medical policy and procedures, staffs the complex with faculty physicians, governs medical education programs, and manages clinical research activities. NME, which financed the construction and owns and operates the hospital, also equipped the facilities with its diagnostic and treatment technology.

USC University Hospital helps fill a critical need in the community. While Greater Los Angeles ranks first in population among the nation's 10 largest metropolitan areas, it is last in the number of private teaching hospital beds available. With only 3.7 beds for every 10,000 residents, Los Angeles falls well below the average of 11 beds for every 10,000 people in the country's 10 largest cities.

That shortage of university-based beds leaves unfortunate gaps in the quality of medical care available. Teaching hospitals provide medical services otherwise unavailable or limited in the region; they also enhance the opportunities for instruction and clinical practice available to a medical school. For these reasons, each of the major medical schools in the country operates its own teaching hospital.

USC University Hospital's private teaching beds enhance the community's access to specialized medical care. Without a private teaching hospital, residents of Southern California have not been able to take full advantage of the skills and expertise of the USC School of Medicine faculty, many of whom are internationally recognized leaders in their respective fields. This situation will improve markedly as an increasing number of faculty physicians develop private practices centered around the hospital's specialized programs.

The opportunity for USC School of Medicine faculty members to establish private practices while continuing their involvement in specialized research programs greatly enhances the School of Medicine's ability to retain the many respected clinical specialists on its faculty and to recruit others. This is vital to maintaining the standards of excellence for which the school is known. The opening of the hospital also improves USC's opportunities to receive grants and endowments essential to the support of faculty research, which can lead to an improved understanding of disease prevention, treatment, and ultimately, cures.

As faculty members develop their private practices at USC University Hospital, portions of the income generated will be returned to the School of Medicine, expanding the support from the private sector. This "practice plan" is not unusual among medical schools; the key to its success is providing faculty with a complex where they can establish their private practices and develop innovative applications of the most advanced technology. USC University Hospital fills this need.

The new hospital facility provides high-tech/high-touch care: high technology resources in an atmosphere grounded in the caring traditions of medicine and nursing. USC University Hospital provides a full range of special diagnostic and treatment services, including cardiac catheterization, open heart surgery, kidney stone lithotripsy, magnetic resonance imaging (MRI), positron emission tomography (PET), and organ transplantation.

There are 10 operating suites, two cystoscopy rooms, a nine-bed surgical intensive care unit, an

eight-bed medical intensive care unit, a coronary care unit, and a step-down unit. The hospital also has 30 psychiatric care beds and 32 comprehensive medical rehabilitation beds.

The high priority on the personal touch for its patients extends to the private physicians who refer patients to USC University Hospital. Studies have shown that difficult access and poor communication with faculty are the biggest complaints that referring community physicians have about academic medical centers. To preclude such complaints and to promote community physician access and communication, the hospital has installed a program called PACE: USC Physician Access and Communication Exchange.

The PACE program is a toll-free telephone service that assists physicians in getting medical consultations or other information, discussing patient care techniques, arranging referrals, exploring the latest research findings, or registering for continuing education, ordering books, or seeking the latest data on a topic. The hospital also has an Office of Referral Services that ensures that referring physicians receive notice of their patients' admission and discharge, and appropriate communication throughout the course of treatment.

Together, National Medical Enterprises, Inc., one of the largest health care services companies in the United States, and the University of Southern California, with an illustrious history of medical care that spans more than a century, have brought to the people of the Los Angeles area a new and technologically advanced medical care facility designed to meet their needs well into the twenty-first century—USC University Hospital.

PEPPERDINE UNIVERSITY

At the focal point of Pepperdine University is Seaver College, a liberal arts, undergraduate, four-year residential program. Along with the School of Law, it is housed on the 830-acre campus, which offers a magnificent view of the Pacific Ocean.

"I am endowing this institution to help young men and women to prepare themselves for a life of usefulness in this competitive world and help them build a foundation of Christian character and faith which will survive the storms of life."

It was with those words, spoken on September 21, 1937, at the founding of the college bearing his name, that George Pepperdine launched what is now Pepperdine University. The school opened with 167 students on a 34-acre site at 79th Street and Vermont Avenue in South-Central Los Angeles. Today the enrollment exceeds 6,500 students in the four schools that comprise the private, nondenominational Christian university. It is accredited by the Western Association of Schools and Colleges and earned that accreditation in its very first year of operation—a remarkable achievement.

Two of the schools, Seaver College, for undergraduate students, and the School of Law, are housed on a magnificent 830-acre campus overlooking the Pacific Ocean at Malibu. The others, the School of Business and Management and the Graduate School of Education and Psychology, are headquartered at Pepperdine Plaza in the Corporate Pointe complex in Culver City.

It was the huge success of his new company, Western Auto Supply, that brought George Pepperdine his fortune and enabled him, a deeply committed Christian, to become heavily involved in philanthropic work.

When he finally decided, in February 1937, to build his school, he set about the project with the same energy and determination that had animated him throughout his life. Within eight months the new college opened, to the amazement of everyone but George Pepperdine.

Pepperdine's dream has been joined by many others over the years. Blanche Seaver, the widow of Frank R. Seaver, contributed more than any single donor in Pepperdine's history. It was she who founded Pepperdine's Frank R. Seaver College, echoing the words of her late husband: "If you want to do something for the future of your country, do something for the youth, for they are the future of the country."

The university not only has been "something for the youth," but for adults as well. The two schools headquartered at Pepperdine Plaza are geared primarily to meet the needs of working adults. In addition to conducting classes at the West Los Angeles Pepperdine Plaza, there are programs at the Orange County Center in Irvine and the San Fernando Valley Center in Encino. The Graduate School of Education and Psychology, as the name indicates, is focused on the "helping professions," teaching and counseling. It offers several master's degree programs and the doctor of education and the doctor of psychology degree programs. It has grown steadily in recent years, with an average annual increase of 10 percent in student enrollment.

The School of Business and Management, founded in 1969, is the largest of the four Pepperdine schools and the largest business school west of the Mississippi River. Recognized as one of the premier business schools in the nation, it offers a bachelor's and several MBA degree programs at Pepperdine Plaza and the other educational centers, including a center for technology management in Long Beach. It also

In addition to receiving quality education, students can enjoy the lush, beautiful surroundings of the campus.

offers a traditional daytime graduate program on the Malibu campus.

The School of Law was acquired in 1969 and was located in Orange County until a new facility was completed on the Malibu campus in 1978. It offers a three-year, full-time program leading to the Juris Doctor degree. In its relatively short history, the school has established an excellent reputation and now has one of the highest California Bar examination passing rates in the state.

The flagship of Pepperdine, Seaver College of Letters, Arts, and Sciences is a liberal arts, undergraduate, four-year residential program with a student enrollment of about 2,600. Each year it receives nearly 3,000 applications for the approximately 700 positions in the freshman class. Students come from all 50 states and 65 countries. California students represent about 40 percent of the student body. As with the graduate schools, the heartbeat of Seaver College is the learning process. An impressive 98 percent of all faculty hold earned doctoral degrees, and the student/faculty ratio for the undergraduate program is 14 to 1.

In addition to the Malibu campus, Pepperdine Plaza, and the education centers, Pepperdine maintains three permanent programs and facilities in Europe—in London, England; Heidelberg, Germany; and Florence, Italy. Also, there are several other opportunities to study abroad at both the undergraduate and graduate levels in France, Spain, Japan, and other locations.

As it entered the final decade of the twentieth century, Pepperdine had emerged as a world-class university, with academic quality that at times rivaled the best and with a spirit-captivating mission that exceeded the best. It had also emerged as a "world-minded" university with an expanded vision of the global village called earth. Looking into and beyond the 1990s, Pepperdine is determined to build on its strengths, personal-izing, broadening, and deepening education.

From its founding, Pepperdine has always placed the highest priority on people. True to the vision of George Pepperdine, the university constantly affirms that priority in this statement, which appears in many of its publications: " . . . the student, as a person of infinite dignity, is the heart of the educational enterprise." It is the love of people, in the context of God's love, that carries the university into tomorrow.

In this era of specialization and technology, Pepperdine remains convinced that there will always be a demand for truly educated people—who have a knowledge of the broad sweep of history; who are familiar with the lasting beauty of art and literature; who understand something of the workings of such diverse areas as government, natural science, and the human mind; who have learned to think clearly, logically, critically, and strategically; and who can communicate ideas and concepts in concise intelligible ways.

Lastly, Pepperdine remains committed to deepening education, firmly convinced that ethics, morality, and faith cannot be separated from the other pursuits of education. Whatever the events that transpire in the future, Pepperdine University will hold to its mission of presenting the gentle words of Christ alongside the works of Plato, Shakespeare, Jefferson, Lincoln, and other great minds of the past and present.

CHILDRENS HOSPITAL LOS ANGELES

T he twentieth century, now rapidly drawing to a close, had barely dawned when a women's group called Kings Daughters converted a small, two-story house into a four-bed hospital for children. The forerunner of Childrens Hospital Los Angeles (CHLA), it was the first medical facility in California to care for sick children regardless of their ability to pay.

Kings Daughters, the first philanthropic organization in Los Angeles, opened the facility in 1901. The original furniture and equipment were donated and the founders paid a nominal rent for the building. The first physician who treated patients volunteered his services, and during its first year Childrens Hospital cared for 46 young patients.

It wasn't long before the hospital outgrew its tiny quarters. In 1914 it moved to its present location at Sunset and Vermont, and expanded its facilities to accommodate 100 beds. Some of the founding women were concerned about filling that many beds in what was still a largely undeveloped part of the city. The fears proved groundless, however, and in 1926 another 100 beds were added.

Later, outpatient clinics, a rehabilitation center, and research facilities were added. By the late 1950s the hospital's original 3.5-acre site had been expanded to nine acres. In the 1960s and 1970s new buildings replaced some of the original structures.

A Ronald McDonald House was completed in 1978 to help house the families of patients with cancer and other catastrophic diseases who traveled long distances for treatment. In 1988 the hospital opened its nine-story H. Russell and Jeanne R. Smith Research Tower, the only facility west of Philadelphia dedicated specifically to comprehensive pediatric research.

Today CHLA still sits on the same nine-acre campus. The location now lies in the heart of Los Angeles and the hospital has become a multi-complex treatment, research, and educational center that includes a 331-bed hospital, ambulatory patient and pediatric trauma center, research building, and a soon to be completed six-story outpatient tower.

Through nearly a century of change and growth, CHLA has never wavered from its commitment to children. A private nonprofit hospital, it has become

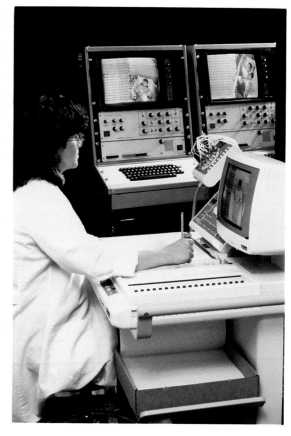

widely recognized as an international leader in pediatric research, the preeminent pediatric healthcare facility in the western United States and a major referral center for young patients from around the world. More than 200,000 children visit the hospital and its outpatient practices each year.

That lone volunteer physician of 1901 has given way to a medical staff of more than 600 physicians. They are assisted by a staff of nearly 700 nurses, plus occupational and physical therapists, pharmacists, respiratory therapists, medical social workers, laboratory technicians, and others, all skilled in pediatrics and sensitive to the needs of children. These professional men and women, assisted by hundreds of dedicated volunteers, work as a team to ensure that each child receives the best and most compassionate care available.

The hospital is also a leading pediatric teaching center that has been affiliated with the University of Southern California School of Medicine since 1932. Its training program in pediatric surgery is the only one in California and one of two in the entire western half of the United States.

More than 150 of the physicians on the CHLA staff are full-time faculty members at the medical school, training medical students, interns, resident physicians, and post doctoral fellows in clinical care and research. Training in the hospital's outpatient and inpatient services provides these young physicians with a breadth of experience in pediatric medicine they might never encounter elsewhere.

In addition to training USC School of Medicine

students and physicians, the hospital is affiliated with allied health teaching programs at several schools and universities, providing training for nurses, physical and occupational therapists, and other healthcare personnel. By providing quality education, CHLA assures that the kind of superior care it provides will continue as these young professionals take leadership roles, wherever they are.

Superior care is what Childrens Hospital Los Angeles has been known for throughout its long and distinguished history. Far different than the pediatric department of a community hospital and even most other children's hospitals, CHLA is fully capable of handling the most serious injuries and the rarest and most complicated forms of illness in children, from newborn infants to adolescents. In a comprehensive survey of America's best hospitals conducted by *U.S. News & World Report*, the magazine reported in its April 30, 1990, issue that CHLA was ranked as one of the top pediatric facilities in the country, and the best pediatric hospital on the West Coast.

The hospital has been at the forefront in the evolution of pediatric medical and surgical care. In its early years many of the physicians on staff were primarily in general practice, devoting part of their time to the care of children. Today the medical staff is comprised of physicians and surgeons whose only specialty is pediatrics. CHLA is capable of handling any procedure at any hour of the day or night, every day of the year.

Surgery on children differs from adult surgery

because the physiology, growth, nutritional requirements, and disease entities are different from those found in adults. At CHLA more than 8,000 surgeries requiring general anesthesia are performed on children every year. Many are not done anywhere else in the West because only CHLA has the experience and the equipment to perform them.

Many of these surgical procedures involve children born with defective hearts, who have been referred to CHLA because of its international renown in this field. Its thoracic surgery division, where the first pediatric cardiac surgery in the western United States was performed in 1939, is the oldest on the West Coast. Operations today are performed on even the most delicate infants, whose hearts may be no larger than a walnut.

CHLA operates the largest pediatric dialysis program in the United States, and since 1967 has performed approximately 600 kidney transplants. Its Craniofacial and Cleft Center, staffed by the largest single group of pediatric plastic surgeons in the country, treats approximately 1,000 patients with cleft lips and/or palates. Many referred to CHLA have had treatment elsewhere that failed to fully correct the defect.

Other surgical disciplines at CHLA include orthopedics and neurosurgery, with thousands of young patients treated each year for a broad range of disorders of the musculoskeletal or nervous systems, including muscular dystrophy, which involves a cooperative effort of the two divisions.

One of the hospital's busiest services and one of the largest in the United States is the hematology/oncology division, which cares for children with leukemia, lymphoma, and bone or soft tissue tumors, as well as children with hemophilia, sickle cell anemia, and other blood disorders. Young patients are referred from throughout the United States and foreign countries.

Staffed by nationally recognized physicians, the division treats children who suffer the most debilitating and life-threatening diseases. Innovative treatments pioneered at CHLA are saving more than 60 percent of children diagnosed with cancers

Toni Velasco, a childlife specialist, prepares patients for an upcoming procedure. Photo by Michael Chiabaudo

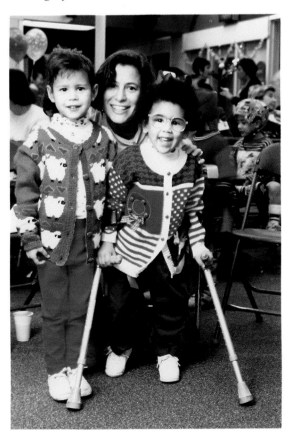

Patients at Childrens Hospital Los Angeles can participate in a variety of activities. Brittany (left), her sister, and her physical therapist enjoy a party in the rehabilitation area. Photo by Michael Chiabaudo

The H. Russell and Jeanne R. Smith Research Tower. Photo by Michael Chiabaudo

today—children who previously faced certain death.

Other units at the hospital specialize in rheumatology, epilepsy, dermatology, neurology, endocrinology/metabolism, gastroenterology/nutrition, cystic fibrosis, allergy and clinical immunology, ophthalmology, otolaryngology, and psychiatry. CHLA maintains 25 beds for patients with infectious diseases, the largest pediatric service of its kind in the area. The pediatric dentistry division offers complete dental care, including

orthodontics.

CHLA also has one of the most active medical genetics programs in the nation. State funded and approved for children with genetic diseases, the division treats some 3,000 patients a year. The hearing and speech division is considered one of the two best in the nation, and works with children from infancy through adolescence, including youngsters with multiple challenges.

Adolescent medicine is another important specialty at CHLA that has been widely recognized for its innovative contributions to the field. Its High Risk Youth Program, established in 1982, has won numerous honors and awards for meeting the needs of teens and for training physicians and allied health professionals to work with them. Other outreach programs include Project Pace, an intervention project for child victims of juvenile prostitution, and Project NATEEN, which assists pregnant and parenting teens.

Located on the top floor of the hospital is the Pediatric Rehabilitation Center, which wraps around a cheerful, skylighted playroom, kitchen, and eating area. Here children can interact with one another, their families, and friends. Opened in 1960, it is the only pediatric rehabilitation facility in Los Angeles.

At CHLA, treating children goes well beyond medical and surgical care. The patient and family services department works with patients and their families in a variety of ways, including individual, family, and group counseling, crisis intervention, and information and referral services. Interpreters are provided for those who do not speak English.

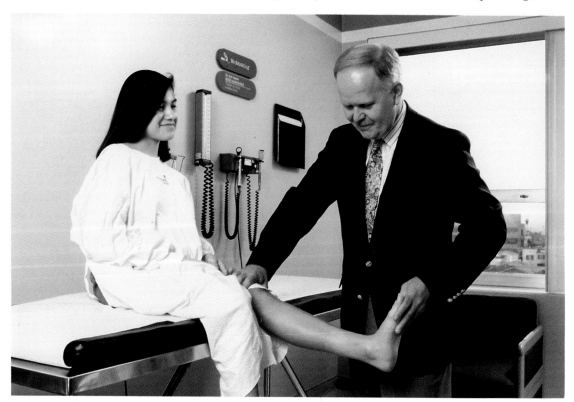

Recognized internationally for his work in orthopedics, Vernon Tolo, M.D., performs a preliminary examination. Photo by Michael Chiabaudo

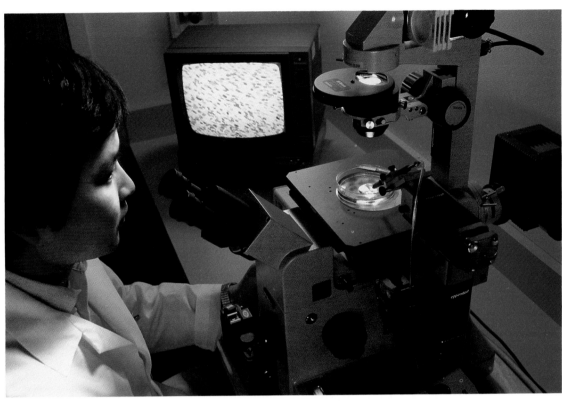

Much of the success gained by CHLA in pediatric medicine is the result of a deep, ongoing commitment to research. Scientists have been conducting research at the hospital since the 1920s. Over the last three decades Childrens has recruited researchers of international stature to focus their talents on five major areas of pediatric research: cancer; genetics; immunology as it relates to organ and bone marrow transplantation; neuroscience; and cell biology.

Working alone and in conjunction with other children's hospitals, CHLA researchers have made dramatic and lifesaving breakthroughs in all these areas. For example, thanks to pioneering efforts with a new treatment called autologous bone marrow transplantation (BMT), many young leukemia patients who otherwise would have had no hope now have a chance to lead healthy, happy lives. And that's the primary focus to CHLA research, which is always geared toward understanding disease at the bedside.

None of the accomplishments of Childrens Hospital Los Angeles during its near-century of service to children would have been possible without the unflagging dedication and generous support of people like Mary Duque and the hospital's 32 associate and affiliate groups. Over a span of many years, she alone has been responsible for helping CHLA raise more than $100 million. And recently the Associates donated $5 million to endow a faculty chair in surgery.

As it nears its second century of service, the leadership at Childrens Hospital Los Angeles is determined to maintain its position as one of the premier pediatric institutions in the world. Its mission is to integrate the highest quality clinical services, teaching, and research programs, and to provide them in an atmosphere of love and compassion for children, who represent the future of the nation and of the world.

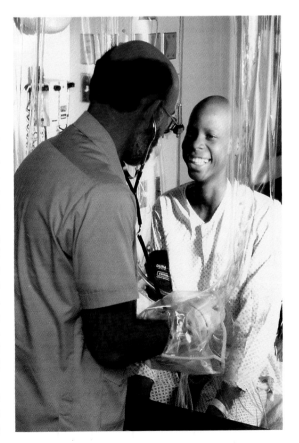

TARZANA REGIONAL MEDICAL CENTER

The Tarzana Regional Medical Center was established in 1974 by a group of community-minded physicians who saw a need for a high-quality medical facility in the rapidly growing San Fernando Valley area around Tarzana. The 212-bed general acute care hospital is located at 18321 Clark Street, adjacent to the heavily traveled Ventura Freeway and close to other major thoroughfares.

The land on which much of the community and the hospital itself sits was once owned by Edgar Rice Burroughs, who named Tarzana after his world-famous comic strip creation, Tarzan of the Apes. When the founding physicians acquired the hospital site, they decided to design the main building itself as a hotel. They were concerned about leaving the community with a vacant, single-purpose facility, should their hospital venture prove unsuccessful.

Those concerns, albeit worthy, proved groundless. Welcomed and well-supported by the communities it serves, including Encino, Woodland Hills, and Reseda, as well as Tarzana, the Medical Center has been a pioneer in innovative, high-quality health care in California throughout its history.

In the early 1980s the hospital was sold by the founding group to American Medical International and it became the AMI Tarzana Regional Medical Center. The transaction resulted in a substantial infusion of capital, allowing the medical center to continue providing the finest, most advanced technologies to the community.

The medical center enjoys considerable autonomy and its affairs are supervised by a board of directors comprised entirely of local physicians, business executives, and professionals. Its medical staff numbers about 1,000. Ninety percent of its active staff is board certified and many are certified in two or three specialties. Overall, the

medical center is the largest employer in Tarzana.

In addition to traditional medical and surgical facilities, the Tarzana Regional Medical Center has provided a unique approach to the community's needs in numerous ways, including its Surgicenter. Treating thousands of patients annually, the center offers a wide variety of treatment without the necessity and expense of overnight admission.

Much of the success of this program is the result of the medical center's pioneering work in noninvasive and low-invasive surgical technology. It was among the first health care facilities in the United States to offer lithotripsy, the noninvasive alternative to kidney stone surgery. It also specializes in what is popularly known as "keyhole" surgery, a far less invasive technique than traditional ones for gallbladder surgery.

Previously, gallbladder removal meant major surgery, a week or more in the hospital, and several weeks of recuperation and lost time. Now, thanks to a type of "keyhole" surgery called laparoscopic cholecystectomy, the gallbladder is removed via a technique requiring incisions only half an inch long. The hospital stay is reduced to one day and full recuperation takes about a week.

The medical center's success in these and other forms of noninvasive and low-invasive surgical procedures is the primary reason that some 80 percent of the thousands of surgeries performed each year are on an outpatient basis. Additionally, its Cardiopulmonary Services, Clinical Laboratory, Imaging Services (Radiology, CAT Scan, and MRI), and Rehabilitation Department provide single-day services with convenient hours and rapid, competent, personalized care.

The hospital also enjoys an outstanding reputation for its leadership in the development and delivery of maternal and child health services. While most of the approximately 2,000 babies born there each year are healthy, the Tarzana Regional Medical Center provides highly specialized care for those who are not and because of their expertise, the hospital receives and cares for criti-

cally-ill newborns transferred from other area hospitals. It offers both a Department of Maternal-Fetal Medicine, which specializes in the care of high-risk mothers, and an Intensive Care Newborn Nursery, providing the best in both highly trained personnel and state-of-the-art equipment. Among its features is a monitoring system, allowing the parents of these at-risk infants to take them home, where they can be monitored around the clock and are as close as the telephone when a need arises.

Heading up the latter is Louis Gluck, M.D., the founder of this specialized practice and generally known as "the father of neonatology" and his associates, Doctors James Banks and Jeffery Martin. The skill of the neonatologists and the NICU team including nurses, respiratory therapists, and others is evidenced by the fact that the medical center consistently has the lowest mortality and morbidity rates in this field of specialty.

To complete the range of care for women and children, in 1990 the hospital opened a Pediatric Intensive Care unit to provide continuing care for critically sick children one month to 21 years of age.

That same level of commitment is maintained in all the medical center's areas of specialization. For example, it was the first hospital in the San Fernando Valley to establish a Diabetes Treatment Center for children and adults. It also places a major emphasis on geriatrics in order to meet the needs of its older patients. A recent major expansion of its emergency room facilities includes facilities where doctors can schedule appointments with their patients, outside of their normal office hours.

Tarzana Regional Medical Center has also distinguished itself in the field of medical education. Its Continuing Medical Education (CME) program is rated as one of the finest in the United States. The program is under the direction of Norman Lavin, M.D.

In addition to providing the finest available medical care to its patients and the highest level of medical education to its professional team, the medical center has a strong commitment to keep-

ing the people of the communities it serves healthy. Since its founding, it has been in the forefront of promoting preventive health measures. Among the programs it offers are classes in cardiopulmonary resuscitation, smoking cessation, child safety, childbirth education, and successful parenting.

Founded by a group of local physicians with a vision of providing the community with the finest in health care, Tarzana Regional Medical Center stands today as the fulfillment of that vision.

GOOD SAMARITAN

Robert McKenna, Jr., M.D. (pictured), and other members of The Lung Center team offer a multidisciplinary approach to treating lung cancer and other lung disorders.

Joseph Mirra, M.D., pathologist, assists other members of Good Samaritan's bone oncology team with expert diagnosis of bone and soft tissue tumors.

Located downtown at Wilshire Boulevard and Witmer Street, The Hospital of the Good Samaritan applies the latest technology and research to provide the best, most individualized treatment for its patients.

The hospital houses many regional centers of excellence that draw patients from Southern California, the western states, and other countries. The centers include a comprehensive heart care program; an orthopedics service; a neurosciences program with new treatments for brain cancer and other brain disorders; high-technology reproductive medicine; and centers for men's health, perinatal care, microsurgery, lung diseases, pancreatic-biliary disorders, neuromuscular diseases, and pain management.

Good Samaritan has met the health care needs of the Los Angeles community for more than a century. While the 411-bed, not-for-profit facility is affiliated with the Episcopal Church, patients and staff represent a diverse community. With 1,800 employees, Good Samaritan has approximately 550 nurses and more than 600 physicians on staff. Charles T. Munger heads the Board of Trustees, and John H. Westerman serves as president and chief executive officer.

Sister Mary Wood of the Episcopal Church founded what began as a nine-bed facility in 1885. The following year, St. Paul's Episcopal Church entered into an agreement with the California Diocese to assume control of the facility, then known as the Los Angeles Home for Invalids. The hospital soon moved to larger quarters, reflecting a period of growth for the city.

Following another move in 1896, Good Samaritan received its name in honor of Annie Severance, who donated the funds needed to purchase the new property. In 1898 the hospital became a training school for nurses—a commitment mirrored today by Good Samaritan's on-site training programs and continued emphasis on nurse-patient education.

The move to Good Samaritan's current location took place in 1911, when it merged with Columbia Hospital. New facilities were completed in 1927, with an addition in 1953 to enable care for more than 400 patients. Finally, Good Samaritan opened its new hospital building in 1976. More recent

additions include the medical office building in 1981 and spacious, new cardiothoracic surgery and intensive care wings in 1990.

Good Samaritan is especially well known for heart care. Physicians performed more open heart operations at Good Samaritan than at any other center in the state in 1987, 1988, and 1989, and more cardiac catheterization procedures than at any other center in the state in 1988. This program's growth is due largely to the arrival of David Cannom, M.D., in 1985 to head the Cardiology Division, and the relocation of the surgical practice of Jerome and Gregory Kay to Good Samaritan in 1986. These physicians and many others joined a distinguished and successful cardiovascular services program.

The high volume of heart procedures contributes to a complete familiarity with all aspects of heart care and, therefore, increased safety for patients. Each patient benefits from an individualized approach that includes safe emergency transport, the latest in diagnostic services, specialized nursing, patient education, and rehabilitation. Very ill heart patients are brought to Good Samaritan from hospitals throughout Southern California.

Established in 1986, The Heart Institute combines expert clinical and laboratory research with medical education in its mission to improve treatment and knowledge of cardiovascular disorders.

The Orthopedic Institute, established in 1990, reflects Good Samaritan's long tradition of providing excellent orthopedic care, most notably during the tenure of orthopedic surgeon and past president John Wilson, Jr., M.D., who led the hospital in the 1970s and early 1980s. Among the many orthopedic services offered are a pelvic reconstruction program under the direction of Joel Matta, M.D., and a hip and knee joint replacement service. The comprehensive bone oncology program, under the direction of Lawrence Menendez and Joseph Mirra, is one of only two such programs in Southern California.

At a time when knowledge and skills in the field of reproductive medicine are still in their infancy, the patient may suffer if the new technology remains unregulated. Richard Marrs, M.D.,

director of The Institute for Reproductive Research, has been working feverishly on developing new methods to enable his patients to conceive. An avid researcher and eminent leader in the development of safe and effective techniques, he is also at the forefront of the effort to regulate reproductive medicine.

Skip Jacques, M.D., a specialist in the field of brain tumor immunotherapy, directs the hospital's Neurosciences Institute. He joined Good Samaritan in 1989, bringing with him the clinical department portion of a program he originated in 1985 at Huntington Medical Research Institutes and Memorial Hospital in Pasadena. In addition to offering new protocols in brain tumor immunotherapy, physicians at The Neurosciences Institute conduct research into the treatment of Parkinson's disease.

In 1991 Good Samaritan became the seventh hospital in the nation to offer "bloodless brain surgery" with the Gamma Knife. Not a knife at all, the device causes 201 beams of gamma radiation to intersect at an exact point within the skull—treating brain tumors, vascular malformations, and other brain disorders with the precision of surgery and without a single incision.

Officially designated a Jerry Lewis ALS Clinical and Research Center in 1988, Good Samaritan's Neuromuscular Center is one of five Muscular Dystrophy Association-sponsored centers in the country for the study of amyotrophic lateral sclerosis (Lou Gehrig's disease) and related disorders. Under the direction of W. King Engel, M.D., the center has earned national and

international attention for its research and treatment of neuromuscular diseases.

The Pancreatic-Biliary Center was established in 1990, when gastroenterologist Ian Renner, M.D., joined the staff to treat diseases of the biliary tract, common duct, and pancreas. Renowned for his mastery of endoscopic procedures, Renner is one of a few physicians in the United States using laser lithotripsy to obliterate pancreatic and giant common bile duct stones. Major surgery was previously the only option for these patients. With Renner's help and these latest, minimally invasive procedures, patients are now experiencing far less pain and are recovering far more quickly.

The reopening of Good Samaritan's Perinatal Center in 1989 marked its return to obstetrical care after a 17-year hiatus. The new obstetrical unit was one of the first in Los Angeles equipped with single labor-delivery-recovery-postpartum rooms (LDRPs), where the patient may go through the entire birth experience in the same room. The center's state-of-the-art neonatal intensive care unit, staffed around the

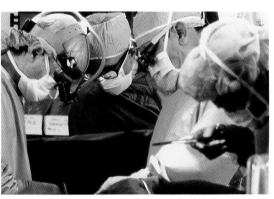

clock by specialists in the field, offers the highest level of care recognized by the American Academy of Pediatrics and the American College of Obstetrics and Gynecology.

Recently established facilities include The Lung Center, directed by cardiothoracic surgeons Robert McKenna, Jr., and Richard Hughes, offering a multidisciplinary approach to treating lung cancer and other lung disorders, and the Center for Functional Rehabilitation and Pain Management, directed by anesthesiologist Clayton Varga, M.D. The Men's Health Center, headed by urologists Carol Bennett and Harin Padma-Nathan, offers treatment for male infertility and impotence.

These are but a few of the services offered at The Hospital of the Good Samaritan, where for more than a century, skilled and dedicated professionals have combined research, advanced technology, and a pioneering spirit to develop, maintain, and expand health care programs that are second to none. Further expansion of facilities and services is in the planning stages—part of Good Samaritan's continuing mission to provide the best and most compassionate care to Southern California and beyond.

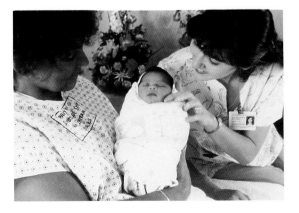

CareAmerica

With more than 150,000 members and more than 2,500 employer groups offering its HMO and PPO health and life benefit options, CareAmerica Health Plans has become one of Southern California's most rapidly growing health plans. CareAmerica is currently licensed in Los Angeles, Orange, Riverside, Ventura, and San Bernardino counties.

Founded in 1986, CareAmerica is part of UniHealth America, one of the nation's 10 largest nonprofit health care systems. Based in Burbank, UniHealth also owns a network of 10 acute care hospitals, the LifePLUS behavioral medicine network, the ElderMed senior membership program, and CliniShare's pre- and post-hospital technologies and services.

It is CareAmerica, however, that is one of the most critical members in the UniHealth family. This is because CareAmerica provides a customized response to the growing needs of employers and their employees by providing quality, customized, and accessible health care in a cost-effective and service-oriented manner.

CareAmerica Health Plans consists of two companies. The first is CareAmerica Southern California, a health maintenance organization (HMO) fully licensed by the California Depart-

ment of Corporations. The second is CareAmerica Life Insurance Company, which encompasses both an indemnity company and a preferred provider organization (PPO) and is licensed by the California Department of Insurance.

Unlike the staff model HMO, where physicians are employees of the HMO, CareAmerica is structured in an IPA model, whereby independent groups of physicians (independent practice associations) contract with the HMO to provide medical services. CareAmerica Southern California presently has contracts with about 50 (or approximately one-third) of the IPAs in its five-county region. This large base of physician participation—more than 6,500 physicians in total—is one of the reasons CareAmerica is able to offer its members a wide freedom of choice. Another reason is the more than 50 premier hospitals which contract with CareAmerica.

Once an employee chooses CareAmerica, every member of his or her family is free to choose their hospital as well as their own personal primary-care physician affiliated with one of the IPAs. This is particularly significant in Southern California, where the mobile life-style often means that people live, work, or go to school in different parts of the city. Once a physician is chosen, he or she works in

CareAmerica's corporate offices in Chatsworth.

partnership with the member to coordinate all of that patient's health care needs.

Under the leadership of President Larry D. Gray and Chief Operating Officer Arthur Southam, M.D., CareAmerica's HMO has grown rapidly. The company had just 16 employees when Gray joined three years ago; that figure now exceeds 300 and the company's corporate offices in Chatsworth have spread to an impressive three-building campus. Southam has been with the HMO since its "pre-launch" days, and has played a key role in CareAmerica installing state-of-the-art office technology systems that are expected to provide faster service and lower administrative costs, resulting in lower premiums.

For maximum flexibility, some employers and employees turn to the CareAmerica Preferred Plan (PPO). Administered by the CareAmerica Life Insurance Company, the plan combines the advantages of an HMO with the total freedom of physician choice found in a traditional insurance plan. In the PPO, members are given the option of using the organization's preferred provider network of physicians and hospitals for maximum benefit coverage or, if they prefer, selecting their own.

But whether it is the HMO or the PPO that is selected, the goal of CareAmerica extends well beyond providing comprehensive care and a reasonable cost. Central to its structure is CareAmerica's dedication to enhancing the well-being of its members at every stage of their lives, from prenatal to senior years.

One innovative example of this is CareAmerica's infant car seat program, where the company purchases car seats in large quantities and resells them to new parents at cost. Better still, parents who attend CareAmerica's early pregnancy classes receive a free infant car seat and a baby care book.

A variety of other wellness programs are aimed at adults of all ages. Health promotion classes on topics such as nutrition, weight loss, and smoking cessation are offered at work sites and other locations. Workers' compensation is another area to which CareAmerica is paying close attention. Never before integrated into overall health care plans, it often creates a conflict be-

CareAmerica's health promotion programs enhance healthy life-styles.

tween the two programs that leaves the affected employee in the middle. The company is studying ways to integrate workers' compensation coverage with medical insurance coverage.

One major segment of the California work force that has been largely neglected is farm workers. Traditionally viewed as a migrant population, the image has slowly been changing. With more steady work becoming available in agribusiness, CareAmerica is seeking ways to provide this huge group with adequate medical coverage, while recognizing the unique challenges presented by such factors as larger-than-average families and increased exposure to pesticides.

The aging of America presents still another series of challenges that CareAmerica is preparing to meet. Demographic studies make it clear that Americans are living longer than ever before.

Programs to meet the needs of this enormous senior population are essential. One such program, providing supplemental benefits to Medicare, was introduced by CareAmerica in 1990. For millions of current and future retirees, the gap between basic Medicare coverage and major medical plans has been a cause of great concern. The CareAmerica plan is designed to meet that need at a reasonable and affordable cost.

NATIONAL MEDICAL ENTERPRISES, INC.

John E. Meeks, M.D. (left), medical director at a Psychiatric Institutes of America hospital and a nationally recognized specialist in adolescent medicine, counsels patients using varied expressive therapies as creative tools for communication and recovery.

An astute man with vision, Richard Eamer first approached fellow attorney and USC Law School classmate John C. Bedrosian in 1962 with the revolutionary idea of creating a multi-facility health services organization. This innovative concept—ahead of its time—took several years to come to fruition. During that period Eamer, also a certified public accountant, continued his work as a hospital attorney and financial consultant.

In pursuing his concept, Eamer turned to Leonard Cohen, one of the partners in his former law firm, for tax, securities, and legal advice. In 1968 the timing and circumstances seemed perfect. With Cohen and Bedrosian as cofounders, Eamer launched National Medical Enterprises, Inc. (NME). The new company's initial public stock offering occurred one year later, in May 1969. As a result of the founders' diligence and patience, the corporation began its road to success on very firm footing. With the $23 million raised from selling stock, NME emerged as the owner of four general hospitals, three convalescent hospitals, a medical office building, and three potential hospital building sites, all in California. The company employed 1,400 persons, and 750 physicians served its seven hospitals that contained 816 beds.

Strong threads running through NME's history include loyalty to its work force and a willingness by top management to encourage employees to grow into larger roles. This decentralization allowed NME's entrepreneurial founders to explore new horizons, diversify, and tackle new business challenges—driving the company's growth both internally and externally.

This growth came rapidly. By 1972, NME had tripled in size, operating 18 hospitals with 2,400 beds. In 1973, it acquired its first medical facility outside California and, one year later, created an international division to assist in developing and managing hospitals overseas.

By 1979, only 10 years after its founding, NME owned or managed 59 acute care hospitals and skilled nursing facilities containing 6,500 beds. The company employed nearly 10,000 persons, with more than 5,000 attending staff physicians at its hospitals and medical facilities—seven times as many as at its origin.

Today, well into its third decade, the Santa Monica-based company constitutes one of the nation's largest health care services providers, with more than 48,000 employees dedicated to efficiently delivering high-quality health care services. NME maintains operations in 29 states, the District of Columbia, and abroad.

The company's 150 hospitals include the acute care facilities of its Hospital Group and those of its Specialty Hospital Group.

NME's Specialty Hospital Group includes more than 70 freestanding psychiatric hospitals, 30 physical rehabilitation facilities, and 12 substance abuse treatment centers. The group also manages more than 50 psychiatric, physical rehabilitation, and substance abuse units in other acute care hospitals.

The company's stock is listed on the New York, Pacific, and London stock exchanges, with a ticker symbol of NME. National Medical Enterprises ranks among the top 30 California companies by both the *Los Angeles Times* and *California Business*, and occupies a similar position on *Fortune*'s list of the nation's 500 largest service companies.

The same management team that launched the company continues to guide its future. Eamer serves as chairman of the board and chief executive officer, Leonard Cohen serves as president,

At a National Medical Enterprises acute care hospital, a nurse and a physician observe a 30-minute-old infant.

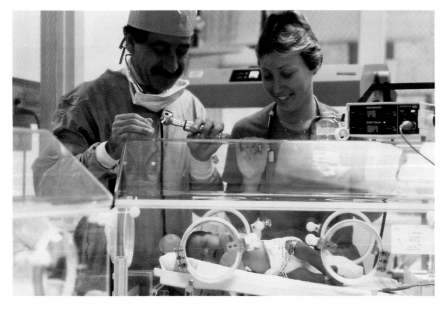

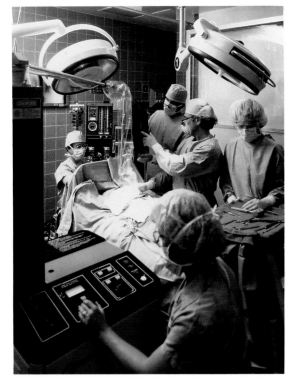

chief operating officer, and vice chairman of the board, and Bedrosian is senior executive vice president and a director.

A key to NME's success, especially during its early years, lay in its astute recognition that physicians serve as the backbone of the hospital business. The company listened carefully to them and focused on satisfying their needs. NME established a unique concept of hospital governing boards, with local boards of trustees and administrators running the hospitals and making the day-to-day decisions. Physicians represent the majority of members on these boards.

Another major factor in NME's success has been its attention to specialized health care delivery systems. In 1982, foreseeing a growing national trend toward psychiatric and other specialty hospitals, it completed a milestone acquisition with the purchase of Psychiatric Institutes of America (PIA), which became the nucleus of its Specialty Hospital Group. A year later, they formed Recovery Centers of America (RCA) and in 1985, acquired Rehab Hospital Services Corporation (RHSC).

The plan proved to be brilliant. As the number of admissions to acute care hospitals dropped during the 1980s, the trend toward specialty hospitals continued. Consequently, all three of these companies achieved financial success. By the close of the decade, these Specialty Hospital Group facilities accounted for more than 50 percent of net operating profits and played a major role of importance in the parent corporation's overall strength.

In 1987, NME broke ground on the University of Southern California's Health Science's campus for construction of a new $150-million teaching hospital. And in May 1991, Eamer, Cohen, and Bedrosian joined Governor Pete Wilson, university officials, and more than 2,000 people for the dedication of the 275-bed hospital.

Financed and operated by the company, and staffed by faculty from USC's School of Medicine, USC University Hospital serves as the cornerstone of the Richard K. Eamer Medical Plaza, named in honor of NME's founder.

Eamer, a native of Southern California, earned both his bachelor of science and bachelor of laws degrees at USC. He serves as director of Unocal Corporation and Imperial Bank; a member of The Conference Board and a member of the board of The French Foundation for Alzheimer Research; board of trustees of The UCLA Foundation; and chairman of the board of trustees of the Hugh O'Brien Youth Foundation. He also serves on the Pepperdine University board of regents, the boards of trustees of the Hope for Hearing Foundation and the National Commission Against Drunk Driving, and is a USC Associate. He is the recipient of a USC Merit Award, as well as Pepperdine University's Private Enterprise Award and its honorary doctor of laws degree.

Following the example of its founder, NME has earned a reputation for promoting corporate social responsibility. Eamer professes that corporate America holds one of the keys to helping solve the nation's ills. He maintains that corporate America has the ingenuity and the clout to accomplish great things.

NME's Overcoming Challenges initiative represents one such program in which the company is committed to filling numerous jobs with qualified persons with disabilities. The NME commitment has also been demonstrated through a recent pledge of $2.5 million on behalf of the UCLA School of Medicine to establish the Victor Goodhill Ear Center.

For these and for its many other contributions to both local and national charitable concerns, NME received honors in 1990 as the "Outstanding Corporation in Philanthropy" at the Los Angeles celebration of National Philanthropy Day, for its exceptional civic responsibility, concern, and leadership through financial and other support of charitable projects.

Looking to the future, Eamer believes National Medical Enterprises will remain in the vanguard of America's health care providers by carefully adhering to a tradition established at its founding: providing the highest-quality care in a cost-efficient manner. This tradition will continue through the establishment, modernization, and management of hospitals and other health care institutions—creating an environment that fosters a responsive, effective system to care for those in need of myriad health care services.

Doctors prepare a patient in a National Medical Enterprises hospital for a laser excision of a tumor in the abdominal wall.

A Rehab Hospital Services Corporation therapist guides a patient in relearning to walk at the parallel bars.

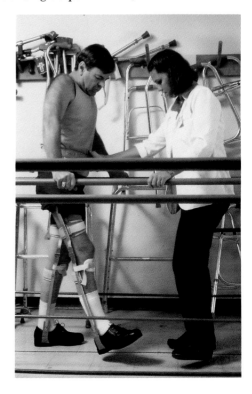

ALPHA THERAPEUTIC CORPORATION

Alpha Therapeutic Corporation, headquartered in Los Angeles, is the world's largest private blood-plasma collection organization and among the world's three largest plasma fractionators. Based in Southern California since the 1940s, it was acquired by Abbott Laboratories during the 1960s. The company, which became a subsidiary of The Green Cross Corporation, in August 1978, is a self-supporting operation, doing business as an independent U.S. corporation. Its cooperative ventures with Green Cross have generated a series of new products and resulted in a compounded growth rate of 30 percent per year since 1978.

Alpha is presently structured with two operating divisions: A biological division for sourcing, manufacturing, and marketing the finest life-saving plasma and plasma products and a pharmaceutical division to focus on the development of new pharmaceutical products.

Alpha, with annual sales in excess of $220 million, has approximately 2,000 employees. In addition to its headquarters facility and adjoining plant at 5555 Valley Boulevard in Los Angeles, it operates a plant in Compton, and a warehouse, a research laboratory, and a subsidiary, Alpha

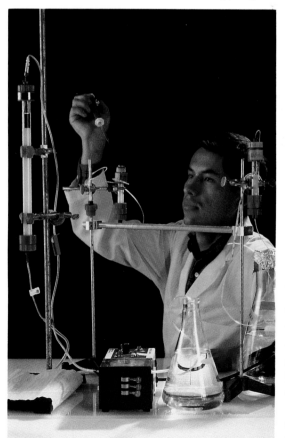

A scientist at the Alpha R&D facility prepares a chromatographic column which is used in protein separation during Alpha-Nine® production.

Therapeutic Services, Inc., all located in City of Industry.

Internationally, the firm has wholly owned subsidiaries: Alpha Therapeutic, GmbH, in Germany, and Alpha Therapeutic, U.K., Ltd., in England. It also operates an affiliate office in Sweden. Alpha owns 50 percent interest in the Grupo Grifols companies of Barcelona, Spain, whose activities center around plasma products, hospital solutions, and diagnostic reagents.

In the past, international markets accounted for as much as 80 percent of Alpha's sales. While sales have continued to climb, domestic sales have increased at a faster pace and now account for about 50 percent of revenues.

Alpha owns and operates approximately 50 plasma centers nationwide, with an additional 100 centers under contract. More than 3 million donations, equaling 2 million liters of plasma, are sourced at these centers each year. The company also operates a plasma screening center in Memphis, Tennessee, where it conducts millions of tests annually on its own behalf, as well as for other manufacturers, hospitals, and laboratories.

The use of plasma, which is the liquid part of blood, first came into prominence during World War II. Able to be stored for much longer periods than fragile whole blood, it saved the lives of countless American troops wounded in action on the battlefields. Today the plasma fractionation process has produced a wide array of plasma products, with many applications in the medical care field. These products include albumin, which is used to treat shock, burns, and other traumatic conditions; coagulation factors for the effective management of hemophilia; and gamma globulins to supply a broad spectrum of antibodies for the treatment of primary immunodeficiencies caused by bacterial and viral infections.

The plasma donation process is a relatively simple one that takes about one hour. The company, in addition to complying with all U.S. Food

and Drug Administration regulations, has established a rigid set of procedures to ensure both donor safety and product reliability.

Alpha has developed a reputation as a highly reliable source of quality plasma products. Innovation and creativity ignite the company's continuous efforts to improve present products and to also develop new proteins from the present supply of plasma. Pharmaceutical division activities represent another major focus of the business and have helped transform its product line from plasma products into a diverse range of new pharmaceutical products. One such product, Fluosol, an intravascular oxygen-carrying fluid, was approved by the Food and Drug Administration in December 1989.

Fluosol, which is utilized during coronary "balloon" angioplasty, is the first drug of its type to be approved in the world. The procedure, first developed in 1979, uses a balloon-tipped catheter that helps relieve the obstruction of arteriosclerosis or plaque buildup within a coronary artery. During the time the balloon is inflated, the delivery of oxygen to the heart is interrupted and may lead to a loss of cardiac function and pumping action. These critical changes may be avoided when oxygen delivery is maintained with Fluosol during balloon inflation.

With the number of balloon angioplasty procedures performed annually in the United States now exceeding 250,000 and climbing rapidly, Fluosol is proving to be of significant value. The product is also being studied to evaluate the use of Fluosol to reduce heart muscle damage from myocardial infarction, or "heart attack," and as an addition to radiation therapy and with chemotherapeutic agents in the treatment of cancer.

Another important aspect of the firm's commitment to quality health care is provided by its subsidiary, Alpha Therapeutic Services, Inc., which provides home infusion service for people with hemophilia and immune deficiencies. Not long

ago patients with these conditions spent many hours in the hospital receiving treatment. Today the alternatives offered by Alpha Therapeutic Services, Inc., mean better care and a more normal life for these people.

Alpha Therapeutic Services, Inc., maintains an inventory of all major brands. Its pharmacists are on call 24 hours a day, seven days a week, with deliveries within 48 to 72 hours. The company provides the prescribing doctors with complete documentation, handles insurance claims, and bills the responsible parties.

As Alpha Therapeutic Corporation looks to the future, it plans to continue its significant participation in the plasma industry through expansion of its current plasma base and the introduction of new plasma-derived products. In addition to Fluosol, the company also plans to pursue other new, non-plasma products as part of an overall strategy to become a major U.S. pharmaceutical corporation.

The people of Alpha Therapeutic Corporation are justifiably proud of the reputation they have earned as "the reliable source" for state-of-the-art health care products in the United States and around the world.

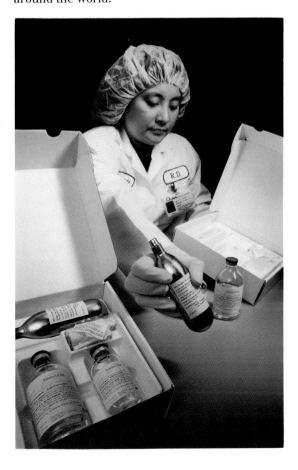

FHP

For more than 30 years FHP Health Care® has provided high quality health care at an affordable cost.

FHP, a federally qualified health maintenance organization (HMO), offers a broad range of health care services to more than 650,000 "members" in California, Utah, Arizona, New Mexico, and Guam.

The company operates several types of health care delivery systems: a staff model HMO, in which FHP-employed physicians, nurses, and other medical professionals provide health care in the company's 45 medical centers, two hospitals, and two skilled nursing facilities; individual practice associations, which provide care through physicians, hospitals, and pharmacies on contract; preferred provider organizations, which allow members to choose from a large directory of FHP-affiliated medical professionals; a prepaid dental plan through staff dentists and dentists on contract; and traditional indemnity health insurance through a subsidiary, FHP Life Insurance Co.

FHP is also one of the few HMOs to successfully serve the growing Medicare market. Through FHP Senior Plan℠, Medicare beneficiaries receive comprehensive health care services—including routine physician visits, prescription drugs, hospitalization, specialty care, and health education classes—for no additional premiums beyond that paid to Medicare. FHP was the first Medicare HMO in the West and is now the second largest in the nation, with more than 250,000 Medicare members.

FHP is an entrepreneurial success story. The company was founded in 1961 by Robert Gumbiner, M.D., the managing partner of a six-doctor medical group in Long Beach, California. He observed that his patients were often forced to pay medical bills when they were sick and least able, so he formed the nonprofit Family Health Program, providing health care services for a set prepaid monthly fee.

Dr. Gumbiner's idea proved popular. His original base of 2,000 patients grew to 10,000 in 1967,

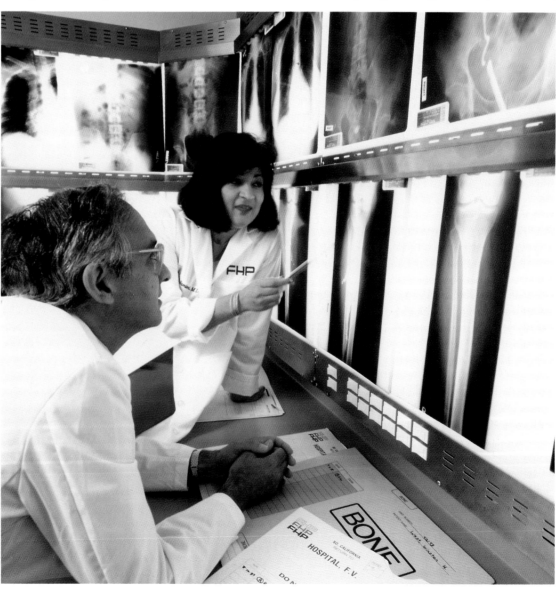

Radiologists discuss a case at FHP Hospital in Fountain Valley, California.

when he opened a second medical center in downtown Long Beach. A year later, service was expanded to Orange County with the opening of a Fountain Valley medical center. By FHP's 10th anniversary in 1971, its membership had reached 30,000 and prepaid Medicaid, prescription drug, and dental programs were established.

In the 1970s FHP expanded into Utah and the Pacific island of Guam. New medical centers opened in each region. In 1977 FHP became a federally qualified HMO and opened a public affairs office in Washington, D.C.

The company experienced exceptional growth during the 1980s. FHP Senior Plan was launched in 1983. Two years later FHP expanded into Arizona and New Mexico, and converted to the for-profit FHP International Corporation.

In 1986, its silver anniversary year, FHP became publicly held, with its stock trading on the NASDAQ over-the-counter market under the symbol FHPC. The company also opened its first hospital, a 125-bed acute care facility, in Fountain Valley, California, and began managing Charter Community Hospital in Hawaiian Gardens, California.

The dramatic growth continued, reaching 312,000 members by 1987. At the close of the decade, FHP had more than half a million members and a staff of more than 7,000 full- and part-time medical and technical professionals, managers, administrators, executives, and support personnel.

To complement this growth and advance cost-reduction efforts, FHP brought many services in-house. Today the company operates a fleet of ambulances, pharmacies stocked with FHP-brand over-the-counter pharmaceuticals, a central laboratory, an optical laboratory and lens-grinding facilities for prescription eyeglasses, and two skilled nursing facilities in Westminster and Norwalk, California, which provide an essential link between acute and home care.

As the 1990s began, Westcott W. Price III was appointed chief executive officer, while Dr. Gumbiner remained chairman of the board. New FHP hospitals were planned for Utah and Arizona, and FHP established the Ultralink[sm] national HMO network, which provided care through affiliated HMOs throughout the country.

FHP has grown from a local medical practice to a multistate corporation with more than a billion dollars in revenue, but its commitment to high quality, affordable health care remains. Though the next century may bring new health care policies and demands, FHP will continue to thrive by following its original mission: "The improvement of the physical and emotional health of our members in a cost-effective manner."

The FHP corporate and medical campus in Fountain Valley, California.

SYNCOR

Syncor International Corporation, founded in 1974, is a leading pharmacy services company primarily engaged in compounding, dispensing, and distributing radiopharmaceutical products to hospitals and clinics. Through its nationwide network of more than 90 company-owned pharmacies, Syncor compounds and delivers 15,000 radiopharmaceutical prescriptions every day to the nuclear medicine departments of approximately 5,000 hospitals and clinics.

These radiopharmaceutical products are principally used for diagnostic imaging of various physiological functions and organ systems. Time is always a critical factor, requiring delivery within one to two hours after a prescription is ordered. Accordingly, Syncor's 700 drivers travel some 100,000 miles daily, equal to four trips around the world, delivering their precious cargo 24 hours a day, 7 days a week.

In 1986 Syncor began diversifying into the infusion therapy segment of the home care market, by providing intravenous therapy products and support services to the increasing number of patients being treated outside the traditional hospital setting. Today this has become the fastest growing segment of the health care industry, a trend that is expected to continue.

Unlike the products Syncor delivers to hospitals and clinics, which are primarily used for diagnosis, the home care products are treatment oriented. They include antibiotics, chemotherapy prescriptions, pain management medication, nutritional products, and drugs used to treat AIDS and other infectious diseases.

In covering this broad spectrum of health care providers, from hospital nuclear medicine departments to physicians' offices and their patients at home, Syncor has become the only national pharmacy network of its kind to service the diagnostic, therapy, and monitoring needs of patients, wherever their treatment site.

The concept of a centralized radiopharmaceutical operation was developed during the early 1970s by Richard E. Keesee, assistant professor of pharmacy and medicine at the University of New Mexico, and three of his pharmacy students. From that small group emerged three companies that eventually became Syncor. One of those students, Monty Fu, cofounded Pharmatopes, Inc., which was acquired by Syncor in 1982. Today Fu is chairman of the board of Syncor and Keesee is a vice president.

The president and chief executive of Syncor International is Gene R. McGrevin, who joined the company in 1989. McGrevin, who holds an MBA degree from the Wharton Graduate School of Finance and Commerce at the University of Pennsylvania, has had many years of experience in the health care industry.

Syncor International Corporation is at the forefront of an industry that has achieved outstanding results in the diagnosis, treatment, and monitoring of disease. The medical profession began using nuclear medicine (radiopharmaceutical) technology in the late 1950s. Today more than 12 million procedures are conducted annually—safely, painlessly, and without side effects.

The technology allows physicians to investigate the function

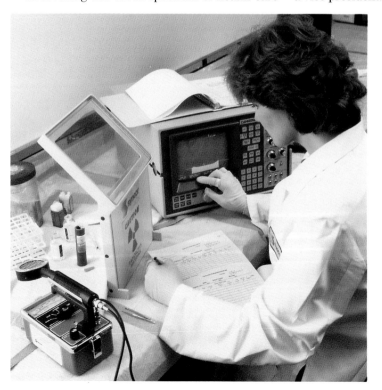

of various organs without the need or the expense of surgery. Patients are given a small amount of a radiopharmaceutical which travels through the bloodstream to the specific area or organ being studied. Harmless radioactive rays are then released and are photographed by a gamma camera, providing the examiner with a detailed picture of the organ and allowing for accurate diagnosis and treatment.

The amount of radioactive material needed for this procedure is miniscule, less than what an airplane passenger is exposed to in one hour in a jet at 30,000 feet. Within 48 hours after the procedure, virtually all traces have been eliminated from the body. Nuclear medicine technology is an excellent example of how radiation, once seen only as an agent of suffering, has become a powerful element in mankind's efforts to alleviate suffering and disease.

By its very nature, nuclear medicine is a multidisciplinary field, dependent on contributions from physics and chemistry as well as medicine. It has had a significant impact on every field of medicine, especially cardiology (heart), neurology (brain and nervous system), oncology (cancer), orthopedics (bone), endocrinology (hormonal system), gastroenterology (digestive system), hematology (blood), nephrology (kidney), and pulmonary (lung).

The rapid growth in this field has created a severe shortage of qualified personnel. Today there is a great need for nuclear medicine specialists—technologists, and nuclear pharmacists—in hospitals, clinics, universities, research laboratories, and industry. Syncor is helping to fill this need through its radiopharmacist training program and technologist recruiting program.

By the year 2000 the field is expected to grow by 65 percent or more, offering enormous opportunity for qualified technologists. Many universities and community colleges now offer courses in nuclear medicine technology, equipping their students to participate in what has every indication

of being an exciting future.

The New York-based Society of Nuclear Medicine, a nonprofit organization of more than 10,000 scientists, physicians, and technologists, anticipates major breakthroughs in both the monitoring and treatment of disease, in addition to its more traditional diagnostic applications. Research presented at one of the society's recent annual meetings "shows that nuclear medicine has a much greater potential to provide treatment for various types of cancer, and the specialty is heading toward becoming a powerful tool in therapy as well as diagnosis."

As nuclear medicine continues to explore new frontiers, the management team at Syncor International Corporation has positioned the company to play even more significant roles as it serves both hospitals and clinics, as well as its rapidly expanding home care markets through its nationwide pharmacy network. The corporate theme, "Partners in Excellence," signifies the quality and excellence Syncor recognizes as essential in its employees, in its service to customers, and in its support of its shareholders.

The stock of the Chatsworth-based company is traded in the national over-the-counter (NAS-DAQ) market under the symbol SCOR. Its approximately 2,500 shareholders include many employees who, under the company's incentive plan, will own some 20 percent of the company in the near future.

Syncor is proud of its employees—a team of health care professionals and business managers dedicated to providing quality services to hospitals, clinics, and patients in their homes.

A Syncor home care coordinator instructs a patient who is on home infusion therapy.

A customer service assistant delivers to a home care patient.

CEDARS-SINAI MEDICAL CENTER

Cedars-Sinai Medical Center is the largest voluntary, nonprofit hospital in the western United States. It is internationally renowned for its diagnostic and treatment capabilities, broad spectrum of programs and services, and breakthrough biomedical research. The Cedars-Sinai reputation for the highest standards in health care and the quality of its professional staff attract patients not only from the Los Angeles area, but from around the world. For all its present magnitude, however, the origins of CSMC were modest.

In 1902, a small house in East Los Angeles opened its doors to care for patients with tuberculosis and in doing so became the Kaspare Cohn Hospital. The Boyle Heights Los Angeles Home for Incurables, established in 1921 for victims of a national influenza epidemic, had only six beds. During a growth process that involved more than one relocation, these two hospitals moved to the west side of Los Angeles, and were renamed Cedars of Lebanon and Mount Sinai.

Then, in 1961, those who supported the hospitals agreed that the community would be better served by merging the two facilities. In 1973, following a decade of planning and preparation, the Thalians Mental Health Center opened and the first phase of construction on the CSMC complex was completed. The primary, eight-story structure of 1.6 million square feet, built at a cost of more than $100 million, was dedicated in 1976. Since that time, several other facilities have been added, including the off-campus, 11-story Mark Goodson Building for outpatient programs, the totally renovated structure housing the Steven Spielberg Pediatric Research Center, and the seven-story, state-of-the-art Barbara and Marvin Davis Research Building.

The goal of the community volunteers who serve on the Cedars-Sinai board of directors has been to make the medical center a world class facility in every respect, one committed to excellence in all endeavors. According to a recent consumer survey in which CSMC was compared to other Los Angeles-area medical centers, Cedars-Sinai has achieved the board's goal: it was selected first in all major categories.

Cedars-Sinai ranks among the top hospitals in the nation in voluntary biomedical and clinical research. Los Angeles' first coronary care unit was at CSMC, as was the first hospital-based blood bank. The medical center is a pioneer in fetal monitoring, and has made a major commitment to genetic research with more than 100 scientific investigators pursuing projects in this field. The Swan-Ganz catheter for monitoring the condition of cardiac patients was developed at CSMC and is now used throughout the world.

The medical center's cardiology division has gained worldwide stature for its research and applications of procedures that have become standard in the international community. For example, CSMC was the first medical facility in the world to develop a procedure in which clogged arteries could be opened without invasive surgery. A collaboration between scientists at NASA and the Jet Propulsion Laboratories with medical center physicians resulted in a space age event: blocked arteries were opened with beams of excimer laser light. Cedars-Sinai has also received national recognition for treatment of kidney disease and its neonatal intensive care unit.

As a tertiary care hospital, the medical center has many multi-speciality, critical care units. Treatment centers include the Comprehensive

Cedars-Sinai Medical Center has established a reputation for maintaining the highest standards in health care.

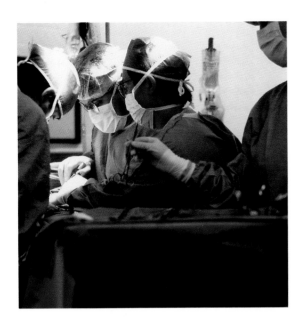

Cancer Center; DOTEC (Diabetes Outpatient Training and Education Center); the Center for Reproductive Medicine; the Medical Genetics-Birth Defects Center for genetic risk information, screening, and knowledge, as well as prenatal diagnosis, an international registry for skeletal dysplasia, and diagnosis and treatment of the many birth defects afflicting children; the Bone Disorder Center; the Sleep Disorders Center; and the Ellis Eye Center. The Department of Psychiatry offers a comprehensive program at the Thalians Mental Health Center, and elsewhere on the CSMC campus, including help for addictive behavior and substance abuse.

The Transplantation Center reflects CSMC's reputation for excellence and leadership in transplantation surgery, with capabilities in the replacement of various organs, including heart, liver, lung, kidney, and bone marrow transplants. More than 22,000 surgical procedures in 14 specialties—including cardiovascular, transplantation, neurosurgery, and plastic—are performed annually.

The medical center is also known for its AIDS research and treatment; pulmonary disease program; diabetes research; gastroenterology research and clinical care; endocrinology program, including thyroid function and reproductive medicine; rheumatology program (arthritis, lupus); and rehabilitative medicine program, including inpatient and outpatient care. All laboratory-based activities of the medical center are supported by the Department of Pathology & Laboratory Medicine and its state-of-the-art equipment.

The CSMC Department of Obstetrics & Gynecology functions as a comprehensive women's hospital. Some 8,000 babies are delivered annually, and high-risk maternity care and neonatology intensive care are provided. A full range of medical services for children include the Amie Karen Center for treating children suffering from cancer, leukemia, AIDS, and blood disorders; and the Medical Genetics-Birth Defects Center for diagnosis and treatment of children born with hereditary conditions and birth defects such as cystic fibrosis, mental retardation, sickle cell anemia, spina bifida, juvenile onset diabetes, and growth disturbances.

Cedars-Sinai is one of the finest teaching hospitals in the country. Residency training is offered in seven specialties, and as many as 300 physicians are in training at any one time. Training programs also are available in nursing, pharmacy, and medical technology. The medical center has an academic affiliation with the UCLA School of Medicine, and all of its medical department heads hold faculty status at the university.

Service to the community is part of the Cedars-Sinai mission, as is health care for the poor and indigent. Costs over and above donations provided by social services, such as the Jewish Federation Council and United Way, are absorbed by the medical center. The Ambulatory Care Center sees many patients who cannot pay, and Cedars-Sinai is one of the few Los Angeles-area hospitals still participating in the Los Angeles Trauma System as a Level I Unit. Other community services include physician referral, wellness education, support groups, senior citizen programs, an

Far left: Surgeons in the Transplantation Center perform replacement procedures of various organs including heart, lung, and bone marrow.

The medical center's Department of Obstetrics & Gynecology offers a variety of services and treatments for children.

Thousands of dedicated people work together to ensure that patients receive the finest health care available.

Staff members use the latest technology in their research.

emergency response system for the elderly and disabled, a hot line for troubled teenagers, and the Adopt-a-School program.

Delivering all of these services takes the combined efforts of thousands of dedicated people. The medical staff is comprised of more than 2,200 attending physicians and 250 full-time staff physi-cians, supported by 2,000 nurses and nearly 4,000 other employees. More than 1,400 volunteers donate about 265,000 hours annually, and 31 support groups raise funds through charitable events to benefit Cedars-Sinai.

The medical center is licensed for 1,120 beds, and all inpatients are housed in private rooms. A wide selection of fine food is available, and there are preparation kitchens on each floor supplementing the main kitchen.

For therapeutic purposes, a collection of more than 8,000 art objects, such as paintings and sculptures, are to be found throughout the medical center. Supervised by its own in-house curator, this is the largest collection of fine art to be found at any hospital in the world.

All of those who work or volunteer at Cedars-Sinai are proud of its reputation as one of the great medical centers in the world. To maintain this position at the leading edge of patient care, medical technology, and pioneering research efforts in the future, the CSMC board of directors is building a $250-million endowment fund. With this type of support, the medical center can continue to achieve its mission of providing the finest quality health care to be found anywhere.

PATRONS

The following individuals, companies, and organizations have made a valuable commitment to the quality of this publication. Windsor Publications gratefully acknowledges their participation in *Los Angeles: Realm of Possibility.*

Alpha Therapeutic Corporation*
Alpine Electronics of America, Inc.*
Alschuler, Grossman & Pines*
Argue Pearson Harbison & Myers*
Ballard, Rosenberg & Golper*
Bank of America*
Bateman Eichler, Hill Richards*
Bentall Development Co.*
The Beverly Hills Hotel*
Big 5 Sporting Goods*
Blakely, Sokoloff, Taylor & Zafman*
Mike Brown Grandstands*
Bugle Boy Industries*
The Capital Group*
CareAmerica*
CB Commercial*
Cedars-Sinai Medical Center*
Centinela Hospital Medical Center*
Century West*
Childrens Hospital Los Angeles*
City of Hope*
Dames & Moore*
Daniel Freeman Hospital*
1st Business Bank*
FHP*
First Interstate*
A. Foster Higgins & Co., Inc.*
Freshman, Marantz, Orlanski, Cooper & Klein:
      A Law Corporation*
Good Samaritan*
GTE*
GTEL*
Haight, Brown & Bonesteel*
Hill, Holliday, Connors, Cosmopulos, Inc.*
Hitachi, Ltd.*
Hotels of L'Ermitage International*
Hufstedler, Kaus & Ettinger*
Jones, Day, Reavis & Pogue*
Kaiser Permanente*
KBIG-FM*
KCET*
Kenneth Norris Jr. Cancer Hospital*
KFWB*
Knapp, Petersen & Clarke*
KNX NEWSRADIO*
Lanz*
Loeb and Loeb*
Los Angeles Business Journal*
Los Angeles Department of Water and Power*
MacNeal-Schwendler*
McCormick Construction Company*
Metropolitan Structures*
Milbank, Tweed, Hadley & McCloy*

Mission Energy Company*
National Medical Enterprises, Inc.*
National Properties Group*
Nationwide Construction Co., Inc.*
The Newhall Land & Farming Company*
Overton, Moore & Associates, Inc.*
Pacific Bell*
Charles Pankow Builders, Ltd.*
Paul, Hastings, Janofsky & Walker*
Payden & Rygel*
Pepperdine University*
Price Waterhouse*
Provident Title Company*
Prudential Property*
RE/MAX of California*
Robinson, Diamant, Brill & Klausner*
Rochlin Baran & Balbona Inc.*
Rockwell International Corporation*
Rotary Club of Los Angeles*
St. Vincent Medical Center*
Sanwa Bank California*
SCS Engineers*
Search West*
Sheppard, Mullin, Richter & Hampton*
Sikand Engineering*
Skadden, Arps, Slate, Meagher & Flom*
Southern California Edison Company*
Sparkletts Drinking Water Corporation*
Sunrider*
Syncor*
Tarzana Regional Medical Center*
Thrifty Corporation*
Times Mirror*
Tooley & Company*
Towers Perrin*
Unocal*
USC University Hospital*
U.S. Trust*
Ray Wilson Company*

*Participants in Part Two, "Los Angeles Enterprises." The stories of these companies and organizations appear in Chapters 9 through 14, beginning on page 253.

DIRECTORY OF CORPORATE SPONSORS

Alpha Therapeutic
    Corporation, 432-433
5555 Valley Boulevard
Los Angeles, CA 90032
W.P. DeHart
213/227-7526

Alpine Electronics of
    America, Inc., 382-385
19145 Gramercy Place
Torrance, CA 90501
Penny Curtis
213/326-8000

Alschuler, Grossman & Pines,
    306-307
1880 Century Park East,
    12th Floor
Los Angeles, CA 90067
Bruce Warner
213/277-1226

Argue Pearson Harbison &
    Myers, 312-313
801 South Flower Street
Los Angeles, CA 90017
Don M. Pearson
213/622-3100

Ballard, Rosenberg & Golper,
    340
10 Universal City Plaza,
    Suite 1650
Universal City, CA 91608
Kenneth R. Ballard
818/509-7100

Bank of America, 286
Corporate Communications
    #4124
555 South Flower Street
Los Angeles, CA 90071
Charles Coleman
213/228-3258

Bateman Eichler, Hill Richards,
    300-301
700 South Flower, 27th Floor
Los Angeles, CA 90017
Terry Chase
213/683-3500

Bentall Development Co., 353
3111 North Tustin Avenue,
    Suite 150
Orange, CA 92665
James Warshawski
714/974-5050

Beverly Hills Hotel, The,
    392-393
9641 Sunset Boulevard
Beverly Hills, CA 90210
Kerman Beriker
213/276-2251

Big 5 Sporting Goods
3424 Wilshire Boulevard
Los Angeles, CA 90010
Rick Hamill
213/251-6628

Blakely, Sokoloff, Taylor &
    Zafman, 330-331
12400 Wilshire Boulevard,
    Seventh Floor
Los Angeles, CA 90025-1026
Rochelle Silas
213/207-3800

Brown Grandstands, Mike, 351
Post Office Box 1700
Monrovia, CA 91017
Mike Brown
818/357-1161

Bugle Boy Industries, 374-375
2900 Madera Road
Simi Valley, CA 93065
William Mow
805/582-1010

Capital Group, The, 294-295
333 South Hope Street
Los Angeles, CA 90071
Peter Langer
213/486-9401

CareAmerica, 428-429
20520 Nordhoff Street
Chatsworth, CA 91311
Larry Gray
818-407-2206

CB Commercial, 366-367
533 Fremont Avenue
Los Angeles, CA 90071
Jerry Asher
213/613-3146

Cedars-Sinai Medical Center,
    438-440
8700 Beverly Boulevard
Los Angeles, CA 90048
Ronald L. Wise
213/855-4767

Centinela Hospital Medical
    Center, 398-401
555 East Hardy Street
Post Office Box 720
Inglewood, CA 90307
Julius D. Mason, Jr.
213/673-4660, Extension 8411

Century West, 358-359
1401 Ocean Avenue, #300
Santa Monica, CA 90401
Harry Mow
213/458-1631

Childrens Hospital
    Los Angeles, 420-423
4650 Sunset Boulevard, Box 59
Los Angeles, CA 90027
Cheryl Trinidad
213/669-2306

City of Hope, 410-413
1500 East Duarte Road
Duarte, CA 91010
Karen Warren
818/359-8111

Dames & Moore, 332-333
911 Wilshire Boulevard, Suite 700
Los Angeles, CA 90017
Harry Klehn, Jr.
213/683-1560

Daniel Freeman Hospital,
    408-409
333 North Prairie Avenue
Inglewood, CA 90301
Sister Regina Clare Salazar
213/674-7050, Extension 1613

1st Business Bank, 290-292
601 West Fifth Street
Los Angeles, CA 90071
R.W. Kummer, Jr.
213/489-1000

FHP, 434-435
9900 Talbert Avenue
Fountain Valley, CA 92708
Ria Marie Carlson
714/963-7233

First Interstate, 287
707 Wilshire Boulevard
Los Angeles, CA 90017
Simon Barker-Benfield
213/614-5791

Foster Higgins & Co., Inc., A.,
    288
2029 Century Park East,
    14th Floor
Los Angeles, CA 90067
Joseph A. Salzillo
213/551-3869

Freshman, Marantz, Orlanski,
    Cooper & Klein: A Law
    Corporation, 328-329
9100 Wilshire Boulevard,
    Eighth Floor
Beverly Hills, CA 90212
Philip F. Marantz
213/272-2155

Good Samaritan, 426-427
616 South Witmer Street
Los Angeles, CA 90017
Denise Trudeau
213/977-2340

GTE, 264-265
One GTE Place, R.C. 3130/BC 500
Thousand Oaks, CA 91362
Dan Smith
805/372-6082

GTEL, 266-267
One GTE Place, R.C. 3110/BC 500
Thousand Oaks, CA 91362
Jay Pinkert
805/372-6641

Haight, Brown & Bonesteel,
    314-315
Post Office Box 680
Santa Monica, CA 90406
Gary C. Ottoson
310/458-1000

Hill, Holliday, Connors,
    Cosmopulos, Inc., 395
4640 Admiralty Way
Marina Del Ray, CA 90292
Clifford Scott
213/822-7088

Hitachi Ltd., 380-381
2029 Century Park East,
    Suite 3940
Los Angeles, CA 90067
M. Kohama
213/286-0243

Rochlin Baran & Balbona Inc,
344-345
10980 Wilshire Boulevard
Los Angeles, CA 90024
Joseph A. Balbona
213/473-3555

Rockwell International
Corporation, 298-299
2230 East Imperial Highway
El Segundo, CA 90245
Susan K. Paul
213/647-5472

Rotary Club of Los Angeles, 270
900 Wilshire Boulevard
Los Angeles, CA 90017
John Westwater
213/624-8601
St. Vincent Medical Center,
404-407
2131 West Third Street
Los Angeles, CA 90057
Maxine Surks
213/484-5591

Sanwa Bank California, 289
601 South Figueroa Street
Los Angeles, CA 90017
Margaret Merrett
213/896-7776

SCS Engineers, 321
3711 Long Beach Boulevard,
Ninth Floor
Long Beach, CA 90807
Robert P. Stearns
310/426-9544

Search West, 293
1875 Century Park East,
Suite 1025
Los Angeles, CA 90067
Bob Cowan
213/203-9797

Sheppard, Mullin, Richter &
Hampton, 316-317
333 South Hope Street, 48th Floor
Los Angeles, CA 90071
Anne M. Bothwell
213/620-1780

Sikand Engineering, 362-363
15230 Burbank Boulevard
Van Nuys, CA 91411
Mark Sikand
818/787-8550

Skadden, Arps, Slate, Meagher
& Flom, 318-319
300 South Grand Avenue
Los Angeles, CA 90071-3144
Michael H. Diamond
213/687-5000

Southern California Edison
Company, 256-259
2244 Walnut Grove Avenue
Rosemead, CA 91770
Lewis M. Phelps
818/302-1212

Sparkletts Drinking Water
Corporation, 386-387
4500 York Boulevard
Los Angeles, CA 90041
John Stallcup
213/259-2069

Sunrider, 388-391
3111 West Lomita Boulevard
Torrance, CA 90505
Customer Service Department
213/534-4786

Syncor, 436-437
20001 Prairie Street
Chatsworth, CA 91311
Gene McGrevin
818/886-7400

Tarzana Regional Medical
Center, 424-425
18321 Clark Street
Tarzana, CA 91356
Jody Dunn
818/708-5192

Thrifty Corporation, 376-377
3424 Wilshire Boulevard
Los Angeles, CA 90010
Rick Hamill
213/251-6628

Times Mirror, 271
Times Mirror Square
Los Angeles, CA 90053
Stephen C. Meier
213/237-5000

Tooley & Company, 360-361
11150 Santa Monica Boulevard,
Suite 210
Los Angeles, CA 90025
Craig Ruth
213/473-9505

Towers Perrin, 282-283
1925 Century Park East,
Suite 1500
Los Angeles, CA 90067-2790
Cecile Hurley
213/551-5600

Unocal, 262-263
1201 West 5th Street
Post Office Box 7600
Los Angeles, CA 90051
Mike Thacher
213/977-6821

USC University Hospital,
416-417
Richard K. Eamer Medical Plaza
1500 San Pablo Street
Los Angeles, CA 90033
Sylvia K. Kelly
213/342-8500

U.S. Trust, 302-303
555 South Flower Street,
Suite 2700
Los Angeles, CA 90071
Maureen Gallogly
213/488-4000

Wilson Company, Ray, 364
199 South Los Robles, #250
Pasadena, CA 91101
K.C. Gopal
818/795-7900

INDEX